Jane Austen's *Emma*

A CASEBOOK

CASEBOOKS IN CRITICISM

RECENT TITLES

James Joyce's *A Portrait of the Artist as a Young Man*: A Casebook
Edited by Mark A. Wollaeger

Chinua Achebe's *Things Fall Apart*: A Casebook
Edited by Isidore Okpewho

Richard Wright's *Black Boy (American Hunger)*: A Casebook
Edited by William L. Andrews and Douglas Taylor

William Faulkner's *Absalom, Absalom!*: A Casebook
Edited by Fred Hobson

Edith Wharton's *The House of Mirth*: A Casebook
Edited by Carol J. Singley

James Joyce's *Ulysses*: A Casebook
Edited by Derek Attridge

Joseph Conrad's *Heart of Darkness*: A Casebook
Edited by Gene M. Moore

Ralph Ellison's *Invisible Man*: A Casebook
Edited by John F. Callahan

Orson Welles's *Citizen Kane*: A Casebook
Edited by James Naremore

Alfred Hitchcock's *Psycho*: A Casebook
Edited by Robert Kolker

D. H. Lawrence's *Sons and Lovers*: A Casebook
Edited by John Worthen and Andrew Harrison

D.H. Lawrence's *Women in Love*: A Casebook
Edited by David Ellis

Cervantes' *Don Quixote*: A Casebook
Edited by Roberto González Echevarría

Fyodor Dostoevsky's *Crime and Punishment*: A Casebook
Edited by Richard Peace

Charlotte Brontë's *Jane Eyre*: A Casebook
Edited by Elsie B. Michie

JANE AUSTEN'S

Emma

◆ ◆ ◆

A CASEBOOK

Edited by
Fiona Stafford

UNIVERSITY PRESS

2007

OXFORD

UNIVERSITY PRESS

Oxford University Press, Inc., publishes works that further
Oxford University's objective of excellence
in research, scholarship, and education.

Oxford   New York
Auckland   Cape Town   Dar es Salaam   Hong Kong   Karachi
Kuala Lumpur   Madrid   Melbourne   Mexico City   Nairobi
New Delhi   Shanghai   Taipei   Toronto

With offices in
Argentina   Austria   Brazil   Chile   Czech Republic   France   Greece
Guatemala   Hungary   Italy   Japan   Poland   Portugal   Singapore
South Korea   Switzerland   Thailand   Turkey   Ukraine   Vietnam

Copyright © 2007 by Oxford University Press

Published by Oxford University Press, Inc.
198 Madison Avenue, New York, New York, 10016
www.oup.com

Library of Congress Cataloging-in-Publication Data
Jane Austen's Emma : a casebook / edited by Fiona Stafford.
p. cm.—(Casebooks in criticism)
Includes bibliographical references and index.
ISBN-13: 978-0-19-517530-1
ISBN-10: 0-19-517530-1
ISBN-13: 978-0-19-517531-8 (pbk.)
ISBN-10: 0-19-517531-X (pbk.)
1. Austen, Jane, 1775–1817. Emma.   I. Stafford, Fiona J. II. Series.
PR4034. E53J36 2005
823'.7—dc22   2005049876

1   3   5   7   9   8   6   4   2

Printed in the United States of America on
acid-free paper

Credits

Austen, Jane. "Opinions of *Emma*." In *Minor Works*, vol. 6 of *The Novels of Jane Austen*. Edited by R. W. Chapman, Oxford: Oxford University Press, 1954. Reprinted by permission.

Booth, Wayne C. "Control of Distance in Jane Austen's *Emma*." In *The Rhetoric of Fiction* Chicago: University of Chicago Press, 1961. Reprinted by permission of the publisher and the author.

Dussinger, John. "Desire: Emma In Love." In *The Pride of the Moment: Encounters in Jane Austen's World*, Columbus: Ohio State University Press, 1990. Reprinted by kind permission of the author.

Ferguson, Frances. "Jane Austen, *Emma*, and the Impact of the Form." *Modern Language Quarterly* 61, no. 1 (March 2000): 158–80. Copyright © 2000 by the University of Washington. All rights reserved. Used by permission of the publisher and the author.

Johnson, Claudia L. "Emma: Woman, Lovely Woman, Reigns Alone." In *Jane Austen: Women, Politics, and the Novel*, Chicago: University of Chicago Press, 1988. Copyright © 1988 by the University of Chicago Press. Reprinted by permission of the publisher and the author.

Litvak, Joseph. "Reading Characters: Self, Society, and the Text in *Emma*."
   PMLA 100 (1985): 763–73. Reprinted by kind permission of the Modern
   Languages Association of America and the author.
Southam, Brian. "*Emma*: England, Peace, and Patriotism." In *Jane Austen and
   the Navy*. London and New York: Hambledon, 2000. Revised by author
   2005. Reprinted by kind permission of author.
Trilling, Lionel, ed. "*Emma* and the Legend of Jane Austen." Introduction to
   Emma, by Jane Austen. Boston: Houghton Mifflin, 1957. Copyright ©
   1957 by Houghton Mifflin Company. Used by permission.
Troost, Linda, and Sayre Greenfield. "Filming Highbury: Reducing the Com-
   munity in *Emma* to the Screen." *Persuasions On-Line*, Occasional Papers
   No. 3: Emma on Film, Fall 1999, www.jasna.org/persuasions/on-line/
   opno3/troost_sayre.html. Reprinted by kind permission of the authors
   and the editors.
Wald, Gayle. "*Clueless* in the Neo-Colonial World Order." First Published in
   Camera Obscura: A Journal of Feminism and Film Theory, 42 (September, 1999),
   51–69. Reprinted in *The Postcolonial Jane Austen*. Edited by Rajewari Sunder
   Rajan and You-me Park. London: Routledge, 2000. Reprinted by kind
   permission of the publisher and the author.
Waldron, Mary. "Men of Sense and Silly Wives: The Confusions of Mr.
   Knightley." In *Jane Austen and the Fiction of Her Time*. Cambridge University
   Press, 1999. Copyright © 1999 by Cambridge University Press. Reprinted
   by permission of the publisher and the author. First published in *Studies
   in the Novel* 28, no. 2 (1996). Copyright © 1996 by the University of
   North Texas. Reprinted by permission of the publisher and the author.
Wiltshire, John "*Emma*: The Picture of Health." In *Jane Austen and the Body*.
   Cambridge: Cambridge University Press, 1992. Copyright © 1992 by
   Cambridge University Press. Reprinted by permission of the publisher
   and the author.

Contents

Abbreviations   ix

Introduction   3
FIONA STAFFORD

Opinions of *Emma* (1816)   37
JANE AUSTEN

*Emma; a Novel. By the Author of Sense and Sensibility,
Pride and Prejudice, &c. 3 vols. 12mo. London. 1815.*   43
WALTER SCOTT

Jane Austen, ob. July 18, 1817 (1917)   57
REGINALD FARRER

Emma and the Legend of Jane Austen (1957)   83
LIONEL TRILLING

Control of Distance in Jane Austen's *Emma* (1961)   101
WAYNE C. BOOTH

Emma: "Woman, Lovely Woman, Reigns Alone" (1988)   123
CLAUDIA L. JOHNSON

Reading Characters: Self, Society, and
Text in *Emma* (1985)   149
JOSEPH LITVAK

Desire: Emma In Love (1990)   169
JOHN DUSSINGER

Emma: The Picture of Health (1992)   189
JOHN WILTSHIRE

Men of Sense and Silly Wives: The Confusions
of Mr. Knightley (1999)   215
MARY WALDRON

Filming Highbury: Reducing the Community
in *Emma* to the Screen (1999)   239
LINDA TROOST AND SAYRE GREENFIELD

Clueless in the Neo-Colonial World Order (2000)   249
GAYLE WALD

Emma: England, Peace and Patriotism (2000)   269
BRIAN SOUTHAM

Jane Austen, *Emma*, and the Impact of Form (2000)   293
FRANCES FERGUSON

Further Reading   315

Abbreviations

The authors of the essays included in this casebook originally used a variety of different editions for their quotations. For the ease of readers of the casebook, all references to Jane Austen's novels are now taken from *The Novels of Jane Austen*, ed. R. W. Chapman [1923], 3rd ed., rev. Mary Lascelles, 5 vols. (Oxford: Oxford University Press, 1965–1969). Works not published in her lifetime appeared as *The Works of Jane Austen: Volume VI: Minor Works*, ed. R. W. Chapman [1954] (Oxford: Oxford University Press, 1954), revised by B.C. Southam (Oxford: Oxford University Press, 1969).

The following abbreviations are used throughout:

E	*Emma*
MP	*Mansfield Park*
MW	*Minor Works*
NA	*Northanger Abbey*
P	*Persuasion*
PP	*Pride and Prejudice*
SS	*Sense and Sensibility*

References to Austen's correspondence have also been brought up to date and refer to *Jane Austen's Letters*, ed. Deirdre Le Faye, 3rd ed. (Oxford: Oxford University Press, 1995).

Jane Austen's *Emma*

A CASEBOOK

Introduction

FIONA STAFFORD

◆ ◆ ◆

Opinions of *Emma*

LIONEL TRILLING'S ESSAY on *Emma* begins with the startling observation that, in the case of Jane Austen, "the opinions which are held of her work are almost as interesting, and almost as important to think about, as the work itself."[1] The comment is especially surprising in view of the essay's origin as an introduction to the Riverside edition of *Emma*: rather than take readers straight into the novel, Trilling ponders the impossibility of approaching it "in simple literary innocence," because of the powerful feeling generated by the name "Jane Austen."[2] Almost half a century later, opinions of Austen have multiplied as fresh issues have arisen to divert and divide subsequent generations of readers. If the mid-twentieth century saw vigorous debate over the nature of Austen's moral vision, her artistry, personality, or domestic circumstances, by the 1990s, arguments were more likely to be focussing on her feminism, politics, historical context, or transformation to the screen. The questions raised by her work may change, but the strength of related opinion does not. No critical essay can ever match the inexhaustible interest of Austen's own novels, but the liveliness of the discussions stimulated by her words—and the very many words about her words—more than bears out Trilling's point. The essays collected in this volume have been chosen to represent some of the most intelligent and enlightening analyses of *Emma* published in the last fifty years. Together they demonstrate the immense and continuing interest of the opinions the novel provokes.

Before embarking on the essays, it is helpful to grasp the nature of the debates that influenced Trilling's observations, as well as those of more recent critics. Many of the views expounded by twentieth-century readers have developed in response not only to the novel but also to the rich and varied critical tradition. A full account of the earlier criticism would be inappropriate here, and readers seeking more detailed knowledge of Austen's reception in the nineteenth and early twentieth century should consult the *Critical Heritage* volumes edited by Brian Southam and the bibliographical work of David Gilson. To gain maximum benefit from the essays reprinted in the casebook, it is nevertheless important to have a sense of the evolution of Austen's reputation, and, in particular, of the emergence of *Emma* as a distinct literary masterpiece.

Austen's work has been a subject of dispute since its original publication. *Emma*, in particular, seems designed to stimulate amicable contention. Austen set out with the playful intention of unsettling her readers, judging by one of her rare surviving authorial comments: "I am going to take a heroine whom no one but myself will much like."[3] This remark first became public in 1870, in James Austen-Leigh's *Memoir of Jane Austen*, but readers entirely unaware of her comment could still find plenty in the novel itself to encourage discussion. It is obvious from the opening chapter that *Emma* delights in friendly disagreement, as Mr. Knightley dares to demur over the fate of "poor Miss Taylor" and doubts Emma's skills as a match-maker.[4] Subsequent scenes allow many different characters to exchange views on the appearance, feelings, behaviour, or social standing of others, and to reveal their own prejudices and values in the process. Harriet seeks Emma's opinion of Robert Martin, of riddles, of marriage, and of muslins. Mrs. Weston consults Mr. Knightley over Emma's friendship with Harriet, Emma over Mr. Knightley's admiration for Jane Fairfax, and her husband over Frank Churchill's regard for Emma. Miss Bates looks on everyone with kindness, Mrs. Elton on no one. Emma has opinions about everyone and everything, almost none of them reliable. Faced with so much discussion and speculation, readers have always been drawn to develop their own views of the action and characters: very often, opinions of *Emma* are conditioned by instinctive responses to Emma Woodhouse.

The reactions of the novel's first readers were carefully gathered by Austen herself, whose acute awareness of audience was essential to her art.

Given her own prediction about the unpopularity of her new protagonist, Austen must have been amused to hear that her niece Fanny Knight "could not bear Emma herself," while Isabella Herries, whom she had met at a dinner in London, regarded the heroine as an insult to the female sex.[5] From her first appearance, Emma divided families: Austen's niece, Anna, "preferred Emma herself to all the heroines," but her new husband, Benjamin Lefroy, confessed that he "[d]id not like the Heroine so well as any of the others."[6] The care with which Austen recorded the opinions of her family ad friends, even urging her nieces to send comments from anyone else who might have mentioned the new novel, shows that she minded very much about the responses of her readers and knew perfectly well that not everyone responded in the same way. She was clearly pleased by the opinion of Fanny's friend, Mrs. Cage, who wrote: "Miss Bates is incomparable, but I was nearly killed with those precious treasures! They are Unique, & really with more fun than I can express. I am at Highbury all day, & I can't help feeling I have just got into a new set of acquaintance."[7] Not all the original readers were quite as happily diverted by Austen's realism as Mrs. Cage, however; Mrs. Guiton thought it "too natural to be interesting."[8]

The list of "Opinions" collected by Austen is not merely a record of personal likes and dislikes but also carries signs of contemporary value judgments: Mrs. Sheen's disapproval of the clerical characters is shared by Mrs. Wroughton, who "thought the Authoress wrong, in such times as these, to draw such clergymen as Mr. Collins and Mr. Elton."[9] As she recorded such views, Austen was at once reflecting on her own work and drawing creatively on the comments and attitudes of those around her. At times, her notes seem to be turning into her characteristic free indirect style: "Mrs. Digweed—did not like it so well as the others, in fact, if she had not known the Author, could hardly have got through it."[10] Austen worked within a close-knit community which was reflected in her art as well as providing reflection on her art. By the time she wrote *Emma*, her fourth published novel, she knew exactly how her new work would strike readers and the diversity of response it would inspire. She was both an observer of society and of the observations that society made.

Austen's sense of an immediate, varied, critical audience was fostered from childhood. As the seventh child of an intelligent, literate, and energetic family, she grew up in a home where people read, wrote, and performed for each other. Her father, a well-educated Hampshire clergyman, encouraged all his children to read extensively, while his wife, Cassandra, was not only a mother of eight and manager of a large household but also wrote witty verses and encouraged her children's various talents. Austen's earliest surviving writings were addressed to her parents—a tale in seven letters for her mother, a series of little plays for her father.[11] From the beginning, writing was a matter of dialogue between Austen and her audience, and many of the early pieces were gifts for particular individuals. *Frederic and Elfrida* was written for her friend Martha Lloyd "as a small testimony of the gratitude" felt by Austen for Martha's help with finishing her "Muslin Cloak," while the miniature novel *Jack and Alice* was inscribed to her brother Frank, "Midshipman on board his Majesty's ship the Perseverance."[12]

These experiments were written to entertain specific readers; and the same desire to please those who mattered is evident in her collection of opinions. We do not know what Frank thought of *Jack and Alice*, but when he read *Emma* many years later, he "liked it extremely."[13] His brother Charles, also in the navy, was so delighted with his sister's new novel that he read it "three times" on his voyage home from active service in the Mediterranean.[14] As Brian Southam points out in the essay included in this volume, Charles's rereading was partly a result of family loyalty and affection, and partly because of *Emma*'s "evocation of village England in all its locality and parochialism, the flavour of its characters and community, things which much have meant so much to a sailor on the high seas."[15] By the time she wrote *Emma*, Austen was no longer producing little *jeu d'esprits* for particular friends and family, but her long training in amusing those closest to her helped with the gradual creation of novels that could please or provoke a wide range of people for a variety of reasons. *Emma* may be dedicated to the Prince Regent, but it was evidently written for a much larger audience, with different tastes, interests, and senses of humour.

Nineteenth-Century Opinion

For twenty-first-century readers, Austen's collection of opinions about her work helps to convey the excitement of the newly published novel. In 1816, "Jane Austen" had not acquired classic status and so the responses of friends and family have the air of a modern reading group rather than that of serious critical analysis. Her list may include one of the most influential reviewers of the day, but Francis Jeffrey's opinion, though gratifying, is afforded no more attention than anyone else's. With the publication of *Emma*, however, came the beginning of a more substantial, public assessment of Austen's work in the form of an extensive review by Walter Scott in the *Quarterly Review*.

Although there had been brief, but generally favourable, accounts of *Sense and Sensibility* and *Pride and Prejudice*, Scott's review of *Emma* was a major contribution to the establishment of Austen's critical reputation and anticipated many later views of her work. What is remarkable about Scott's reaction to *Emma* in 1816 is his sense of its importance to the English novel as an evolving kind. Although he summarises the plot with great elegance, he presents Austen's achievement in terms of her transformation of the novel from a form which revelled in romance, adventure, and idealised sentiment to one which drew on "nature as she really exists in the common walks of life."[16] He was probably the first writer to recognise Austen's crucial contribution to the development of the novel, his prescient criticism anticipating many later accounts of the shift from eighteenth-century experimental fiction to the great realist novel of the nineteenth century. Many years later, F. R. Leavis would pronounce Austen "the first modern novelist," while in his influential account of *The Rise of the Novel*, Ian Watt regarded Austen's innovative combination of subjectivity and external narrative as crucial to the novel's maturation into an established genre.[17] For Scott to recognise the larger importance of Austen as her novels were being published shows a rare union of perception and wide perspective, and reflects his own personal interest in the form and possibilities of the novel.

For Scott, Austen's "knowledge of the world, and the peculiar tact with which she presents characters that the reader cannot fail to recognize" was reminiscent of the Flemish school of painting—an analogy that anticipates George Eliot's well-known celebrations of artistic realism in *Adam Bede* or the essay, "The Natural History of German Life."[18] The careful literary painting of the world in Austen's novels continued to attract praise from readers throughout the nineteenth century, a cumulative assessment that must have influenced Virginia Woolf's admiration for her peculiar ability to fill "every inch of her canvas with observation."[19] Many decades later, in one of the more recent essays in this collection, Linda Troost and Sayre Greenfield begin their analysis of film versions of *Emma* by evoking Scott's praise of Austen's "Flemish" attention to detail and the "precision which delights the reader."[20] Troost and Greenfield develop the insight by aligning two different films of *Emma*, both released in 1996, with Vermeer and Brueghel, in an essay that brings together the earliest review of the novel with the much newer discipline of film criticism. Nineteenth-century insights are still lighting the way to fresh approaches to *Emma*, in exchanges that demonstrate the long-lasting energy generated by earlier critical opinion.

Although the publication of Scott's substantial review in one of the major journals of the day was an important affirmation of Austen's talent, its praise was not undiluted. Even as he recognised the power and originality of Austen's realism, Scott registered a note of regret at some aspects of her extraordinary artistic control. Restraint, so important to her art, could disappoint as well as delight: "[A]t Highbury, Cupid walks decorously, and with good discretion, bearing his torch under a lanthorn, instead of flourishing it around to set the house on fire."[21] Scott admired his contemporary enormously, but his own fiction, which began to appear in the very year that Austen completed *Emma*, testifies to his continuing attraction to stories in which the houses might go up in flames.[22]

Despite Scott's perceptive judgment of Austen's importance, her reputation in the nineteenth century was slow to solidify. The continuing demand for her work is evident in Richard Bentley's decision to republish the complete set of six novels in 1833. Further editions appeared sporadically in London, New York, and Boston, but after 1870 and the publication of *Memoir*, the trickle of new editions turned into a flood.[23] Evidence from diaries, memoirs, and letters shows that Austen was being read and enjoyed throughout the Victorian era, even though critical assessments are relatively sparse until the closing decades. It is obvious from an article on "Female Novelists," published in 1852, that Austen had yet to be widely recognized as a major writer, as the essayist laments her failure to reap "her rightful share of public homage."[24] This challenge seemed to be answered almost at once by George Lewes, who wrote in the *Westminster Review,* "Let Jane Austen be named, the greatest artist that has ever written," but it was not until 1859 that Lewes produced a sustained critical essay on "The Novels of Jane Austen." His essay has been described by Southam as "the great appraisal," and although it is not sufficiently *Emma*-centred to be included in this casebook, its importance for the development of the general critical understanding of Austen is considerable and therefore demands consideration here.[25]

Lewes was a long-term admirer of Austen; for him, the great test of her novels was not immediate pleasure but the more sustained enjoyment that leads to re-reading and more re-reading. He admits in his essay to having "outlived many admirations," but the passing years have taught him only "to admire Miss Austen more."[26] It is a kind of critical judgment not open to first-time readers of a new novel and, throughout his essay, Lewes adopts the tone of the retrospective judge, looking back on the opening decades of the century to assess which books had continued to attract readers and which had slipped away from public memory. At the same time, his response is deeply personal, and although he emphasises Austen's artistry, he is still alert to the effects of her skills on readers: "We never tire of her characters. They become equal to actual experiences. They live with us, and form perpetual topics of comment. We have so personal a dislike to Mrs. Elton and Mrs. Norris that it would gratify our savage feelings to hear of some calamity befalling them."[27] At moments like this, the great critic, though authoritative enough to write in abstract terms of the "art of the novelist," reveals the same kind of passionate opinion about Austen's characters as readers had felt on first publication—and which many readers continue to feel to the present day. Austen's truthful representation of life, which Lewes saw as fundamental to the novelist's art, resulted in characters sufficiently lifelike and memorable to live in the mind like real acquaintances. And though the manners of those she created now seemed part of a vanished age, the vividness and truth of her creations had a Shakespearean power to transcend its own time: "Such art as hers can never grow old, can never be superseded."[28]

For Lewes, Austen's talent was essentially dramatic rather than descriptive, but her work revealed powers of observation and selection as much as inventiveness:

> Her dramatic ventriloquism is such that, amid our tears and laughter and sympathetic exasperation at folly, we feel it almost impossible that she did not hear those very people utter those very words. In many cases this was doubtless the fact. The best invention does not consist in finding *new* language for characters, but in finding the *true* language for them.[29]

In his emphasis on dramatic brilliance, Lewes articulated a persistent element in the steadily growing nineteenth-century appreciation of Austen. Archbishop Whately, for example, had already celebrated her talent for creating witty conversation and brilliant fools, while Lord Macaulay presented her as the somewhat surprising heir to Shakespeare—"a woman of whom England is justly proud."[30] Although the language of the camera is very different, the strength of the tributes paid to Austen's dramatic genius by twentieth-century film-makers is every bit as powerful as that of her literary champions in the previous century. The essay on "Filming Highbury" by Troost and Greenfield in many ways demonstrates the longevity of critical opinions of Austen, for in its emphasis on Austen's "Flemish" realism and its focus on the dramatisation of her text, they effectively single out the qualities that most impressed Lewes.

Even the most fervent admirers of Austen in the nineteenth century were conscious of certain limitations, however. Just as Scott's laudatory review ended with a note of disappointment at Highbury's over-decorous

Cupid, so too Lewes's essay concludes with the reluctant admission that "with no power over the more stormy and energetic activities which find vent even in everyday life," Austen could not be placed very high in the ranks of great artists: "Her place is among the Immortals; but the pedestal is erected in a quiet niche of the great temple."[31] Austen's mildness had been the subject of considerable disagreement between Lewes and Charlotte Brontë, who had written to him in disbelief, "Why do you like Miss Austen so very much?"[32] After reading *Pride and Prejudice* on Lewes's recommendation, Brontë declared that she would "hardly like to live with her ladies and gentlemen, in their elegant but confined houses," and dismissed Austen's art as merely "shrewd and observant."[33] In a subsequent letter to W. S. Williams, who worked for her publisher, Smith and Elder, she expressed her views on *Emma*, beginning with the same admiration of the domestic detail that so impressed Scott: "She does her business of delineating the surface of the lives of genteel English people curiously well; there is a Chinese fidelity, a miniature delicacy in the painting."[34] What appears to be positive praise soon develops into a damning assessment, however, with the brilliant delineation of "surface" being seen as a sign of inexperience and superficiality:

> [S]he ruffles her readers by nothing vehement, disturbs him by nothing profound: the Passions are perfectly unknown to her; she rejects even a speaking acquaintance with that stormy Sisterhood; even to the Feelings she vouchsafes no more than an occasional graceful but distant recognition; too frequent converse with them would ruffle the smooth elegance of her progress.[35]

As Brontë warms to her criticism of *Emma*, her own prose pulses with what she feels to be absent or repressed in Austen's novel:

> Her business is not half so much with the human heart as with the human eyes, mouth, hands and feet; what sees keenly, speaks aptly, moves flexibly, it suits her to study, but what throbs fast and full, though hidden, what the blood rushes through, what is the unseen seat of Life and the sentient target of Death—*this* Miss Austen ignores.[36]

The passionate sentence concludes with the distinctly unsisterly observation that "Jane Austen was a complete and most sensible lady, but a very incomplete and rather insensible (*not senseless*) woman." It was an issue that would continue to divide opinion in the next century, and although the charge would be vigorously refuted, Brontë's frustration with Austen's elegant restraint anticipates comments such as that of D. H. Lawrence, who described her as "an old maid" whose novels, lacking the "old blood-warmth," demonstrated "the sharp knowing in apartness instead of the knowing in togetherness."[37]

The lack of passion lamented by Scott, acknowledged by Lewes, and castigated by Brontë, figures persistently in nineteenth-century responses to Austen. Even Richard Simpson, the Shakespearean scholar, who composed one of the most important Victorian essays on her work, still observed her "ethical dread of the poetic rapture" and her refusal to touch the "heroic passions."[38] Often Austen's very strengths—her minute depiction of the life around her and her astonishing fidelity to the everyday—seemed to fix her within a popular, but very limiting, image of the English lady working with great care and tact on a tiny work surface. Part of this idea originated with her own remark about "the little Bit of Ivory" on which she worked, which had been included by her brother Henry in the first biographical notice, published posthumously in 1818, with *Persuasion* and *Northanger Abbey*.[39] In 1870, the comment re-emerged with a vengeance in the *Memoir of Jane Austen*, published by the recipient of the original, James Austen-Leigh. Its impact on readers is registered at once in Simpson's review of the biography, which eschews the earlier critical comparison of her work with Dutch painting in favour of "her own comparison of it to miniature-painting on ivory."[40] Austen-Leigh's affectionate memoir included not only extracts from letters, however, but also a description of Aunt Jane working at home on tiny sheets of paper at her little mahogany desk in the secluded English village of Chawton. For later-nineteenth-century readers, the image of Jane Austen, the English lady, protected within the family circle and as skilled with her pen as with her needle, seemed settled.

While the publication of Austen-Leigh's *Memoir* stimulated a huge revival of interest in Austen, and encouraged the publication of attractive new editions of the novels, its legacy for her critical reputation was decidedly mixed. For although it attracted reviews such as Simpson's, which were really important reassessments of Austen's work, *Memoir* also encouraged the biographical approach and general popularity that so annoyed readers like Henry James: "[O]ur dear, everybody's dear, Jane . . . a beguiled infatuation, a sentimentalized vision, determined largely by the accidents and circumstances originally surrounding the manifestation of genius."[41] When Lionel Trilling wondered at the partisan character of Austen criticism in 1957, his remarks reflect the long-standing influence of the late-nineteenth-century biographical approach to Austen. His own perspective, as an

American, on the underlying class prejudices of the critical battle over Austen reveals much about the terms of engagement in the early twentieth century: "[N]ot to like Jane Austen is to put oneself under suspicion of a general personal inadequacy and even—let us face it—of a want of breeding."[42] His observation seems a direct response to earlier critics such as George Saintsbury, who had suggested that "a fondness for Miss Austen" might be a "patent of exemption from any possible charge of vulgarity."[43] Trilling's distaste for the social dimension of the opinions about Austen is reminiscent of Charlotte Brontë's impatience with those "ladies and gentlemen in their elegant but confined houses," or Lawrence's dislike of her Englishness "in the bad, mean, snobbish sense of the word."[44] His comments relate not to the novels, however, but to the opinions they inspired, which by 1957 had already reached voluminous proportions.

The Emergence of Austen's "Masterpiece"

The steady rise of Austen's reputation through the nineteenth century was reflected in the increasing biographical and critical interest, and in the publication of handsome new illustrated editions of her novels. By 1917, the centenary of her death seemed worthy of public recognition, and so a subscription was duly raised for the erection of a monument at Chawton. The simple stone reads, "Such art as hers will never grow old," but Lewes's words had a new poignancy in the context of the First World War. Austen's peculiar importance at such a moment was emphasised by Clarence Graff, who represented the American subscribers at the unveiling ceremony:

> It is perhaps a remarkable thing that, in these days of war, we can turn aside, even for a day, from the sterner demands of the moment to come together to pay this homage to the genius of Jane Austen, and may we not take from this thought a new hope of the civilisation that we are fighting together to save?[45]

Graff's moving tribute is evidence of the quality Trilling would later attempt to define as the special "promise" offered by her work, in contrast to the cosy nostalgia that sometimes seemed to constitute its appeal.[46]

The centenary of Austen's death gave rise to critical memorials, too, none more perceptive than that written by the botanist Reginald Farrer. A minor novelist and ardent admirer of Austen, Farrer had travelled to remote areas of Tibet and China equipped with only "the materials of washing and the novels of Jane Austen," returning to find his world convulsed in warfare.[47] Austen's work seems to have been essential to his general well-being, and so the centenary of her death gave him an opportunity to give thanks and to share his deep love of her art. In a volume packed with articles on "Sea Power," the "Munitions of War Act," and the "Russian Revolution," Farrer's essay takes pride of place, as the first article, celebrating the perennial refreshment afforded by Austen to those in "water-logged trench, in cold cave of the mountains, in sickness and in health."[48] For the purposes of this collection, his essay is especially important for its judgment of *Emma*, the novel he regarded as Austen's masterpiece.

Much of the criticism in the nineteenth century had dealt generally with Austen's perceived strengths and weaknesses, mentioning individual novels or characters only to illustrate some particular aspect of her larger achievement. With the publication of new collected editions, which included brief critical prefaces, there was more awareness of the distinct character of each novel, and a related tendency to judge them relatively. Although Farrer begins with a general discussion of Austen's circumstances and of earlier critical opinion, he then engages with each novel in turn, reaching a climax with "the Book of Books, which is the book of Emma Woodhouse."[49] It is here that his familiarity with Austen's work becomes a rhetorical tool to give weight to what might otherwise seem to be mere personal preference, as he observes:

[T]his is not an easy book to read, it should never be the beginner's primer, nor be published without a prefatory synopsis. Only when the story has been thoroughly assimilated, can the infinite delights and subtleties of its workmanship begin to be appreciated, as you realise the manifold complexity of the book's web, and find that every sentence, almost every epithet, has its definite reference to equally unemphasised points before and after in the development of the plot.[50]

The very difficulty of reading *Emma* is the key to its infinite reward. Earlier in the essay, he writes of the "minute and far-reaching felicities" of Austen's mature novels, which are only revealed through endless re-reading.[51] Farrer's essay envisages an active reader, working "in eager co-operation with a sympathetic writer."[52] And the novel which yields the most pleasure is *Emma*:

[W]hile twelve readings of *Pride and Prejudice* give you twelve periods of pleasure repeated, as many readings of *Emma* give you that pleasure, not repeated only, but squared and squared again with each perusal, till at every fresh reading you feel anew that you never understood anything like the widening sum of its delights.[53]

In an essay predating Roland Barthes by fifty years, Farrer emphasises the vital role of the reader in enjoying the pleasure of the text. Evidently frustrated by the biographical cloud that hung about his idol, Farrer also argued for the "elimination of the author" on the grounds that the true artist was impersonal, and concerned only with the work at hand.[54] With a confidence defiant of the current international upheavals, Farrer declared Art to be "outside and beyond daily life."[55] Rather than respond to Austen's novels as brilliant representations of the time in which they were written, he presents them accordingly as universally truthful—and therefore immortal. Such a reading also has the effect of freeing Austen from the image perpetuated by the *Memoir*, of the accomplished but confined spinster lady, and directs attention instead towards the novels themselves, and, in particular, *Emma*. In this way, Farrer can be seen as a bridge between the nineteenth-century readings of Austen's Shakespearean capacity to present living characters and the New Critical trends of the mid-twentieth century.

Farrer presents *Emma* as "*the* novel of character," but his analysis is emphatically literary rather than personal.[56] Emma herself is seen as the culmination of the great tradition of English high comedy because of the complexity of Austen's conception and the way in which the plot and the central character develop inseparably. Unlike many later critics who regard Emma's humiliation and recovery in moral terms, Farrer sees the novel's happy ending as an inevitable part of the great comic character, who is "saved in the very nick of time, by what seems like a happy accident, but is really the outcome of her own unsuspected good qualities."[57] For Farrer, *Emma* is the "ripest and kindliest of all Jane Austen's work" because the characters are both funny and "lovable": Emma, Harriet Smith, Miss Bates, Mr. Woodhouse are all "candidates for love as well as laughter."[58] Characterisation and structure are co-dependent, and Farrer points to the subtle use of triangular patterns ("[T]wo sympathetic figures, major and minor, set against an odious one") and the necessary subordination of male figures in the scheme.[59] Jane Austen emerges from Farrer's centenary tribute as a consummate artist, in complete control of her creation, who left a rich legacy of intricate works which future generations might learn to enjoy. Farrer's Austen is a novelist for the twentieth century: technically brilliant, elusive, and difficult.

The more serious treatment of Austen urged by Farrer was given concrete form in the 1920s. R. W. Chapman's *The Novels of Jane Austen*, complete with textual notes, commentary, and extensive appendices on contextual matters, was the first scholarly edition of an English novelist. Such a handsome set of books, issuing from Oxford University Press, made a clear statement that Austen was an author who demanded not just adulation but also serious critical attention. She could no longer be regarded as a minor female novelist, lacking in passion and limited in scope; the Oxford edition seemed to announce the canonisation of a major author. Readers of *Emma* could now choose to read a reliable text with editorial notes on the topography of Highbury, Regency wedding customs, supper, dancing, and fashionable furniture, as well as punctuation, textual variants, and the chronology of the novel.

Like Farrer, Chapman also regarded *Emma* as Austen's finest work, though the reasons he gave for his judgment were slightly different. In Chapman's authoritative opinion, the supremacy of *Emma* lay not in the characterisation, but

> in the matchless symmetry of its design, in the endless fascination of its technique, above all in the flow of the blood beneath the smooth polished skin: a flow of human charity and sympathy that beats with a steady pulse, rarely—but the more momentously—quickening to a throb that sets our own veins leaping in unison.[60]

In his advocacy of *Emma*, Chapman was countering the old charge that Austen evaded deep feeling. It was a point addressed briefly by Farrer, who had referred rather dismissively to Austen's "cruder critics," observing that she had "no taste for expressed erotics" and commenting that the "epical instants of life are not to be adequately expressed in words."[61] Chapman's answer to the complaint is much more economical and persuasive: he simply reveals his own excitement over the "flow of blood" beneath *Emma*'s polished skin. Behind his remark echoes Charlotte Brontë's objection, now widely known since the appearance of the Shakespeare Head edition of the Brontës's correspondence, that Austen ignored "what throbs fast and full, though hidden, what the blood rushes through."[62] In effect, Chapman's strategy of defence is to imply that readers such as Brontë and Scott lacked the sensitivity and imagination to enjoy the physical pleasure of Austen's great novel.

Although the Brontëan/Lawrentian view of Austen's coldness continued to find increasingly sophisticated support in the twentieth century, Chapman's enthusiastically throbbing response lies in the background of some of the best recent criticism. Discussions such as those of John Dussinger in 'Emma in Love' or John Wiltshire's "Emma: The Picture of Health," both included in this collection, are fully alert to the physicality of *Emma*. The more popular film adaptations, which have added such an important dimension to Austen's reputation in the late twentieth century, are also responding in part to the erotic potential of her book, as evident in the choice of the American superstar Gwyneth Paltrow in the 1996 Miramax film of *Emma*.

While Chapman was attracted to *Emma* by the powerful feelings the novel aroused, not all his contemporaries were similarly moved. Marvin Mudrick, for example, presented Austen's irony as "at times almost inhumanly cold and penetrating" and her general attitude to life as that of the serious, but detached, writer seeking "material for comedy."[63] In his influential but deliberately iconoclastic study, *Jane Austen: Irony as Defense and Discovery*, irony emerges as a mode of defence, designed to preserve the artist's distance from both her subject and readers. Mudrick's perception of an altogether ungentle Jane was driven largely by the sentimental tone of intimacy adopted by so many of Austen's admirers, and specifically by the virtual "consecration" of *Emma*.[64] In Mudrick's own reading of the novel, there is none of Farrer's sense of kindliness towards lovable comic characters: instead, the impetus is irony. Like Charlotte Brontë, he sees the novel playing on surfaces, but develops this insight into an exploration of the deceptiveness of charm and material fortune.

In his emphasis on Austen's art, Mudrick is influenced by Farrer, but the tone of his approach reflects the more recent psychoanalytical approach of D. W. Harding, whose exposure of Austen's "Regulated Hatred" had shocked readers of the 1940s. For Harding, Austen was far from being the dear aunt immortalised by her Victorian nephews and nieces. In contrast, his essay depicts a highly intelligent, hugely frustrated writer, doomed by her circumstances to represent and be read by the very people she most despised. It was not an argument to please R. W. Chapman, but it did open new avenues into Austen's work by drawing attention to the less kindly remarks in her letters and the more caustic observations in the novels.[65] Mudrick acknowledges his debt to Harding in his choice of epigraph—"[H]er books are, as she meant them to be, read and enjoyed by precisely the sort of people whom she disliked; she is a literary classic of the society which attitudes like hers, held widely enough, would undermine"—and the idea of "regulated hatred" runs in the background of his own analysis of her irony.[66] Although he argues that Austen's purpose is primarily artistic, Mudrick's obvious distaste for Emma's snobbery, egoism, and preference for women whom she can dominate, leads to a reading that is strongly moralistic. The blend of critical analysis and moral judgment is characteristic of its time and, while many subsequent critics would take issue with Mudrick's opinion of *Emma*, their own readings of the novel were clarified by the seriousness of his approach.

Mudrick's study of Austen's irony was an important contribution to the broader understanding of Austen's technical achievement, which had occupied the best critics of her work since the 1930s. Mary Lascelles's groundbreaking analysis, *Jane Austen and Her Art*, with its substantial chapters on "Reading and Response," "Style," and "Narrative Art," appeared in 1939, and was followed by a series of perceptive articles by Q. D. Leavis in *Scrutiny*.[67] These studies helped to establish proper grounds for assessing Austen's literary significance, by publishing evidence of Austen's reading and working practices, and offering models for analysing her prose. The Austen who emerged from the pages of Lascelles and Leavis was a meticulous writer who read intelligently, revised her novels carefully, and worked incessantly to resolve narrative problems with increasing subtlety.

Lascelles, especially, was not content to recognise Austen's greatness without going on to pursue the "exciting 'how' and 'why' of analysis."[68] The challenge of literary analysis was seized by numerous critics in the following decades, and the essay by Wayne Booth has been chosen as representative of the fine, mid-twentieth-century criticism of Austen's art. The discussion of *Emma* is a chapter of his seminal book, *The Rhetoric of Fiction*, which, as its title suggests, is a wide-ranging study of the ways in which novelists control their readers through rhetorical strategies. As the account moves from the great eighteenth-century novelists to the impersonal narration of Henry James, *Emma* is singled out as an early "triumph in the control of distance."[69]

Although Booth's discussion of Austen is part of his own ambitious analysis of narrative rhetoric, he is also responding, as all critics of *Emma* do, to both the novel itself and to earlier opinion. While Mudrick's reading is criticised as over-simplistic in its view of Austen's conscious intentions, Booth is nevertheless indebted to Mudrick in his own emphasis on authorial control and irony. As in Mudrick's work, and many others before him, the character of Emma is a major focus of the essay, but Booth's purpose is not so much character assessment as analysis of Austen's rhetorical control of the reader's reaction to her heroine. How does Austen evoke sympathy for a character whose mistakes and shortcomings are so obvious? In his emphasis on the brilliant solution—"showing most of the story through Emma's eyes"—Booth isolates (though does not name) a feature of Austen's technique that would subsequently come to be regarded as her major contribution to the English novel: free indirect speech.[70] His analysis is not confined to developing this insight, however, for he also identifies other key features of the novelist's rhetoric, including the use of dialogue and direct speech to act as correctives to the subjectivity of so much of the narration, and, above all, the creation of an implied narrator to be a "friend and guide" to the reader.[71] For Booth, the dramatic illusion of the narrator's presence is crucial to both the tone of the novel and the reader's enjoyment. It also helps to account for the warmth with which critics had responded to Austen—the partisanship so puzzling to Trilling, the sentimental intimacy so aggravating to Mudrick. The notion, shared by Katherine Mansfield, that over the course of the novel readers become "the secret friend of their author," is an astute observation.[72] As in so many of the best essays, it also anticipates much later criticism in the emphasis on "friendship" as a prevailing idea and in its openness to the curious affection displayed by the "Janeites" towards their author-heroine.[73]

Alhough Booth's careful attention to the effects of Austen's varied narrative strategies influenced numerous subsequent critics, it also provoked important disagreement. W. J. Harvey's essay on "The Plot of *Emma*," for example, was written to counter Booth's emphasis on the problematic nature of mystery in the novel. For Harvey, the idea that the novel's irony depended on solving its mysteries—specifically the secret engagement between Frank Churchill and Jane Fairfax—was rather wide of the mark, and he argued that the withheld narrative was actually necessary to maintain focus on Emma and to subdue "an otherwise oppressive and facile irony."[74] Far more interesting, according to Harvey's reading, is the binary structure of the plot, and the central narrative's "unwritten twin whose shape is known only by the shadow it casts."[75]

Harvey's own essay acts as a more substantial shadow to Booth's influential chapter, demonstrating the way in which fine criticism tends to stimulate further discussion. Such close analyses of *Emma* helped to point the way towards the detailed studies of Austen's style that were published in the 1960s and 1970s by critics attentive to the rhetorical devices, plot structure, and language of the novels. In penetrating analyses such as Howard Babb's *Jane Austen's Novels: The Fabric of Dialogue* or Barbara Hardy's *A Reading of Jane Austen*, Austen's work was examined in loving detail, the narrative skills of the successive novels revealed in increasing richness. Norman Page's study *The Language of Jane Austen* alerted readers to the range of linguistic and syntactical choices in *Emma* by considering its use of dramatic dialogue, innovative monologue, free indirect speech, and epistolarity. At the same time, Kenneth Phillipps and Stuart Tave were scrutinising particular words to illuminate the texts with their own knowledge of semantics, syntactical development, and the social and philosophical contexts of linguistic usage. The old critical concern with gentility now found a more objective focus, as Mrs. Elton's modes of address "Mr. E.,"

"Jane," "Knightley" were pronounced vulgar, and Harriet Smith's speech was found wanting by standards of the eighteenth-century grammarians.[76] Appreciation of Austen's technical excellence in the 1950s and 1960s was often accompanied by an admiration for her morality, the precision of the language being taken as a sign of unambiguous standards. In 1948, F. R. Leavis had placed Austen at the beginning of his account of the great English novelists, presenting the "formal perfection" and "moral intensity" of *Emma* as the inauguration of the modern tradition.[77] Although he then proceeded to devote his critical attention not to Austen but to Eliot, James, Conrad, and Lawrence, his emphatic endorsement of Austen's importance—and in particular of *Emma*'s importance—was enormously influential. Critical analyses from the 1950s to the 1970s often combined close reading of the texts with an emphasis on Austen's moral vision, seeing *Emma*, especially, as a narrative of the reformation necessary to redeem a flawed heroine. Edgar Shannon's essay, "*Emma*: Character and Construction," for example, saw *Emma* in terms of the heroine's enlightenment, while Mark Schorer's well-known analysis of the novel's form was based on a perception of the "social and moral scale that is the heart of the book."[78] For Walton Litz, as for most commentators of the period, *Emma* represented Austen's greatest achievement, but he also saw Austen's triumphant creation as a warning against the dangers of an overactive imagination.[79] The Leavisite conjunction of technical achievement and moral seriousness dominated readings of the mid-century, and, while *Emma* continued to be regarded as Austen's masterpiece, it was almost invariably viewed as a brilliant portrait of a rather imperfect lady.

For Leavis, Austen's originality lay in her relationship to earlier literature: she exemplified T. S. Eliot's notion of the individual talent by making "tradition for those coming after" and also "giving a meaning to the past."[80] The emphasis on her importance to the English tradition gave impetus to the investigation already begun by Chapman, Lascelles and Q. D. Leavis of Austen's reading and the relationship between her work and that of earlier writers. In the 1960s, Frank Bradbrook's detailed study of *Emma* led him to pursue a wider project exploring Austen's reading, which showed how her work "gave meaning to the past," by revealing a wide network of neglected texts that could be fruitfully read in conjunction with the novels. Bradbrook's *Jane Austen and her Predecessors* and Kenneth Moler's *Jane Austen's Art of Allusion* both traced the various ways in which Austen's novels absorbed and responded to earlier writings, and thus helped to counter the tendency to treat Austen in isolation, as a consummate artist, alone with her creations.

Frustration with the tendency of New Criticism to treat Austen independently of her context gave impetus to one of the major studies of the 1970s, Marilyn Butler's *Jane Austen and the War of Ideas*, which followed Bradbrook's lead in emphasising the importance of reading Austen in relation to other contemporary writing. Her book retains a Leavisite emphasis on Austen's moral outlook, but its method of investigation is to survey the political allegiances of other novels of the period, thus establishing a convincing intellectual context for Austen's work. The moral issues in Austen's texts are accordingly read as reflections of eighteenth-century philosophical enquiries into human nature, which had turned deeply political in their implications for readers during the French Revolution. The opposition between reason and passion, self-interest and selflessness, and individual ambition and social responsibility were endlessly explored in the fiction of the 1790s, which Butler divided into broad political camps. Radical or conservative? Austen is placed firmly in the latter camp, her manner defined as "that of the conservative Christian moralist of the 1790s."[81]

For Butler, Austen's novels divide between those with an exemplary and those with a fallible heroine, both kinds amenable to a conservative purpose. *Emma* is read, accordingly, as a story of "gentle correction," showing a heroine saved from her dangerous, private imagination by openness, reason, and good sense, until she is finally secure in a "clearly defined and permanent role in the community."[82] The plot of *Emma* can be read as an endorsement of social integration over individuality, in the light of contemporary conservative fears over the possible excesses of French revolutionary ideas. Butler's reading also draws on the stylistic analyses of the 1960s and 1970s, but although she recognises that *Emma* brilliantly develops the "subjective insights which help to make the nineteenth century novel what it is," the conservative morality of the plot keeps the novel's interior potential firmly in check.[83]

Butler's book emerged at a time when the moral and aesthetic value of literature still seemed of paramount importance, yet while her study is informed by similar assumptions, it was also steering critical attention towards more historicised readings of the novels. In its emphasis on the political significance of literary influences, Butler's book had much in common with Alistair Duckworth's important study, *The Improvement of the Estate*, published in 1971. Duckworth, like most critics of the time, emphasised Austen's moral seriousness, but anticipated Butler in associating her moral outlook with a conservative position, pointing out strong connections with the writings of Edmund Burke. In his discussion of *Emma*, he shares Butler's assumptions about Austen's suspicion of individualism, presenting the riddles, games, and wordplay as antisocial elements which threaten to undermine the social and moral structures that the novel affirms. Emma is still a heroine in need of reformation, but for critics of the 1970s, her errors were acquiring a political complexion.

Duckworth's book was intended to defend Austen against the kind of criticism that saw her as a secret subverter of the social values she seemed to promote, whose outlet for her hidden dislikes was irony. If his initial research was goaded on by the iconoclastic interpretations of Harding and Mudrick, however, Duckworth has maintained his opposition to more recent waves of "subversive" critics. In the preface to the paperback edition of his study, which was republished in 1994, he acknowledges the insights afforded by a new generation of scholars, but still objects to any denial of Austen's fundamental conservatism.[84] For Duckworth, Austen remains closer to Burke than to Wollstonecraft, despite the claims of gender that had now been urged so forcefully. His later preface is an eloquent demonstration of the continuing disputes over Austen's position in the modern critical war of ideas and a revealing indicator of the revolution in Austen scholarship that overturned so many conventional readings during the two decades following the appearance of his own book.

Emma Transformed

Duckworth's reiteration of Austen's conservatism in 1994 owes much to the opposition: the great body of feminist criticism that began to appear in the 1970s and 1980s. As feminist critics argued for a new understanding of the English novel which would give full credit to the numerous women writers working in the eighteenth century, Austen took on a new critical significance. In their seminal polemic *The Madwoman in the Attic*, Sandra Gilbert and Susan Gubar revived the late-nineteenth-century image of Austen as the spinster lady, to expose the limitations of her domestic circumstances and their regrettable effects on her work. For Gilbert and Gubar, Austen's exuberant creativity, which shines so unmanageably in the early, unpublished writing, was cut and polished to produce acceptable novels for middle class ladies, similarly conditioned by contemporary ideals of female submissiveness. In their account, Emma, though the centre of her novel, still "has to learn . . . her commonality with Jane fairfax, her vulnerability as a female."[85] The story of Emma Woodhouse is, in this reading, not a tale of moral reformation depicting the salvation of a wayward heroine, but rather a narrative of subjugation through which lively female intelligence is forced into "a secondary role of service and silence."[86] It is perhaps the most startling revision of a critical consensus in the history of the novel's reception, for it challenged the widely held assumptions about Emma's humiliation, enlightenment, and happy reinstatement in society.

Gilbert and Gubar's study was followed by further research by literary historians such as Dale Spender and Jane Spencer to establish a distinctively female tradition of English novel writing, in opposition to the standard account presented by Ian Watt in *The Rise of the Novel*.[87] By the late 1980s, Austen was being seen not as an isolated artist transforming the eighteenth-century novel into the great tradition of the nineteenth, but as an important member of a rich community of women who had struggled to make the new genre of the novel a form in which their sex could excel. Books such as Nina Auerbach's *Communities of Women* (1978) and Mary Poovey's *The Proper Lady and the Woman Writer* (1984) explored the development of women's writing within a patriarchal society and set Austen in the company of other brave writers such as Frances Burney, Mary Wollstonecraft, and Mary Shelley.

Throughout the 1980s, the new awareness of a male-dominated literary culture led to fresh forays into familiar territory. The conduct literature identified by Bradbrook as an important context for Austen's moral outlook was now revisited by Nancy Armstrong, with an eye to exposing the construction of the "domestic woman." The increase in conduct literature in the mid-eighteenth century, which reflected both the rising middle class of women readers and improvements in printing and book distribution, meant that by the time Austen began to write, a new ideal of domesticity had become firmly entrenched in British culture. Like Burney, Austen could, according to Armstrong's reading, "leave the rest of the world alone and deal only with matters of courtship and marriage," but in doing so, her writing was contributing to the regulation of social interraction between classes and sexes.[88] *Emma* is the novel identified by Armstrong as paradigmatic of Austen's special awareness of the power of language to influence human behaviour because of its preoccupation with misreading and its challenge to male definitions of social status.

Armstrong's reading of *Emma* is part of an ambitious, Foucauldian analysis of the rise of domestic fiction, rather than a study concentrating primarily on women's writing or on Austen. Many of the feminist studies of the 1980s were, however, concerned first and foremost with Austen as a female writer. The essay included in this volume as representative of this major critical development is taken from Claudia Johnson's *Jane Austen: Women, Politics and the Novel*, published in 1988 and now generally regarded as the most sophisticated and exciting feminist reading of Austen's work from the 1980s. Johnson's book devotes a chapter to each of Austen's novels, carefully examining them in relation to what seemed at the time to be a neglected tradition of feminine political writing. Throughout, intelligent analysis is sharpened by a sense of the inadequacies of earlier critical discussions, which Johnson felt had overlooked the crucial factor of Austen's gender. Lionel Trilling's amazement that Emma Woodhouse should have "a moral life as a man has a moral life" acts as a goad to the entire study, which rises to defend Austen's novels against a great tradition of lurking misogyny.[89]

Emma is, of course, the key text, since Johnson defines its subject as "female authority itself." Criticism seemed to have moved a long way from Wayne Booth's observation in 1961 that "[m]arriage to an intelligent, amiable, good, and attractive man is the best thing that can happen to this heroine."[90] For the first time in her one-hundred-and-seventy-year history, Emma Woodhouse was being seen not so much as a cautionary figure but as a possible role model for young women readers. For as soon as "female strength, activity and good judgment" are seen as positive virtues rather than as undesirable and somewhat threatening traits in a beautiful young woman, Emma ceases to be an imperfect heroine in need of humiliation and recovery, and instead becomes an emblem of unashamed female independence. It is among the most significant turns in the tide of *Emma*'s critical fortunes since the novel's publication, and one that reveals the rapidly changing attitudes and social values of its readers.

As feminist criticism encouraged new ways of reading *Emma*, many of the traditional lines of entry began to give way. In Mary Waldron's essay, which is reprinted in this collection, the corollary of Emma's transformation is evident in her analysis of Mr. Knightley. If Emma was no longer a heroine in need of correction, then the role of her mentor and guide required some reconsideration too. Like Bradbrook and Butler, Waldron recognises the importance of seeing Austen's novels in the context of contemporary didactic writing and fiction, but her own reading reveals "an ironic and richly contrapuntal" narrative style emerging from Austen's sophisticated engagement with her predecessors.[91] As she explores the representation of Knightley in the light of eighteenth-century conduct books, and didactic and burlesque novels, Waldron develops a reading of *Emma* that suggests something more complicated than straightforward literary influence. If Knightley appears initially to be cast in the role of the Grandisonian hero/guardian, gathering authority from Frances Burney's mentor figures, Austen's playful text subsequently delights in demonstrating his misjudgments and shortcomings. Waldron's reading is greatly enhanced by a familiarity with the long-established critical tradition that routinely placed Knightley at the moral centre of the novel, but it is also one that uses the radical feminist approaches to Austen to shed new light on an area as well-trodden as Austen's literary context.

The change in critical attitudes towards *Emma,* and to traditionally gendered readings, was by no means confined to feminist scholars, of course. Joseph Litvak, for example, was as sceptical as Mary Waldron of the old critical admiration of Knightley, though his method of analysis was deconstructive rather than contextual. Litvak's lively essay, included in this collection, begins by taking Gilbert and Gubar to task for not being sufficiently radical, and presents their desire to separate self from text in their approach to both Austen and her heroines as a version of traditional, character-based readings of the novels. In place of such an approach, Litvak offers a reading in which "difference" is a more helpful term than "opposition," and sets Emma against Knightley not as characters but as representatives of two distinct modes of interpretation.[92] For Litvak, the traditional Knightleyan virtues of "strength of mind," "steadiness," "openness," and above all, "reading" are modes of surveillance through which masculine power seeks to exercise control, while Emma's fluidity, fiction-making, and love of riddles are signs of her subversive escape from any fixed (i.e., controllable) identity. Instead of seeing *Emma* as the story of a flawed heroine redeemed by good sense, Litvak focusses on the novel's wordplay and evasiveness, arguing not for a straightforward linear plot and denouement but rather for a "potentially endless circuit of fiction, interpretation and desire."[93] In such a reading, "uncertainty," "polish," and "surface" are positive terms, while the acts of deciphering and clarifying, traditionally seen as the duty of the intelligent reader, are deeply suspect. Though his critical method, which is strongly influenced by the deconstructive practices of its day, seems worlds away from Reginald Farrer's approach to the great novel of character, Litvak's argument for the importance of Emma's superficiality and the related emphasis on play and endlessness is oddly reminiscent of Farrer's advice that "Emma herself . . . *is never to be taken seriously,*" and his stress on the pleasures of perpetual difficulty and perpetual re-reading.[94] Although Litvak avoids the kind of critical language that treats Austen's characters as if they were real people, he acknowledges the force of desire in the gendered dynamic central to *Emma.* The final twist in his essay turns on Knightley's desire for an "indefinite postponement of that conquest toward which he seems to aspire," an insight which is in part a retort to the many critics who had admired Knightley's moral rectitude and high-minded wish to educate Emma into more sensible behaviour.[95]

Litvak's interests are linguistic and interpretative, but other male critics have been more inclined to explore the sexuality of the text more openly, in readings that would have undoubtedly surprised Charlotte Brontë. For if Lionel Trilling had been startled to discover that Emma had a moral life just like a man, John Dussinger was able to treat the character as a subject driven by desire. The essay included in this volume presents *Emma* as a Gallic novel, propelled by desire and frustration, which turns the traditional critical interest in the mystery of the plot and the heroine's self-delusion into an analysis of narrative dynamics. In place of the Christian language of self-ishness, pride, and humiliation, Dussinger employs parallels from French literature to uncover the workings of ennui and egoism in a reading that counteracts the longstanding critical assumptions about Austen's moral purpose. Although his analysis is broadly indebted to the new readiness to admire rather than condemn the heroine's active subjectivity, Dussinger by no means adopts a feminist line. For while some contemporary critics em-phasised the importance of female friendship in *Emma*, Dussinger pointed to the sexual rivalry between Emma, Harriet, and Jane Fairfax. His reading thus contrasts with both female critics of the 1980s and a number of male critics of the 1950s, including Mudrick, whose discussion of *Emma* was strongly co-loured by unease over the heroine's apparent preference for women rather than men. In Dussinger's account, Emma emerges as a passionate character whose development is determined by the triangular structures of the plot. As such, she appeared poised to inspire the film adaptations of the 1990s, in which the romantic plot and desirability of the central character were paramount.

Dussinger's reading of *Emma* is strongly influenced by the French struc-turalist approaches that pervaded much of the literary criticism of the 1980s and early 1990s, and his focus is kept accordingly on the text. In the same critical moment, however, others were turning to reassess the idea of Emma as the flawed heroine, but adopting very different methods for their studies. John Wiltshire's important book, *Jane Austen and the Body*, is notable for its sympathetic approach to Emma; the key chapter is included in this col-lection. Like Johnson and Dussinger, Wiltshire avoids the old presentation of Emma as an opinionated young woman in need of a few lessons, em-phasising instead her quiet resistance to her valetudinarian father. Rather than abandoning the traditional idea of Austen as a moralist, however, Wiltshire argues that the novel's obsession with sickness and health has an important ethical dimension—"to think about health is necessarily to think morally."[96] Instead of dwelling on Emma's faults, Wiltshire ventures to point to her virtues—her active charity and free-flowing generosity—which often work in direct opposition to the negative, confining tendencies of her father's hypochondria. *Emma* emerges from his analysis as the "picture of health," its energetic, rhythmic prose the linguistic counterpart of its vital, life-affirming, and intensely physical heroine.

Wiltshire's obvious admiration for the strong female protagonist reflects the changing attitudes to *Emma* of the 1980s and 1990s; his critical approach is similarly characteristic of its moment, with its careful deployment of contextual information to substantiate the close reading of the text. Mr. Woodhouse's nervousness is illuminated through reference to an early-nineteenth-century medical book on the Nervous Temperament, in which Dr. Thomas Trotter described nervous ailments and suggested possible remedies. Unlike many critics of the 1950s and 1960s who tended to analyse Austen's texts in isolation, or as part of an exclusively literary tradition, Wiltshire places passages of Trotter's textbook side by side with Austen's representations of Mr. Woodhouse to encourage insight into the medical assumptions of the novel's original audience. The approach could hardly be more different from Dussinger's evocation of Girardian desire and his parallels with Flaubert, even though both critics are responding to their powerful sense of *Emma*'s physicality.

Emma in History

In his awareness of context, and in the importance of contemporary non-fictional sources, Wiltshire demonstrates the influence of one of the major critical trends of the later twentieth century: New Historicism. His book was published in 1992, at the beginning of a decade which saw renewed interest in the historical contexts of Austen's work, the material conditions of its publication, and the various manifestations of its popular appeal in the twentieth century. Books such as Roger Sales's *Jane Austen and the Representations of the Regency England* were similarly concerned with the need to understand the world in which Austen lived and worked, but approached the medical context of *Emma* in relation to the 1815 Apothecaries Act. In the same decade, critics such as Edward Copeland and Juliet Mcmaster investigated both the economic references in Austen's work and her own financial affairs, enabling readers to grasp the relative poverty of Jane Fairfax and Harriet Smith, or the fabulous wealth of Mr. Knightley.[97] Maggie Lane's *Jane Austen and Food* used Regency cookery books to explain the numerous references to drinking and dining in the novel, developing a critical reading of *Emma* that approached its physical and social dimensions through food. By the end of the twentieth century, readers could no longer approach the novel as a purely formal or linguistic structure, for the details of the text had been firmly grounded in a well-researched Regency context.

The debate over whether or not Austen should be read in the context of her time is one of the longest-running issues in the critical tradition, even though the language in which it has been argued has altered over the years. The nineteenth-century emphasis on her Shakespearean capacity to create timeless characters and express transcendent truths may sound very different from the New Critical emphasis on the words on the page, or from structuralist concerns with the organisation of the plot, but in each case, history is relegated. The case for context has an equally long life, however, and can be seen in the nineteenth-century emphasis on Austen's realistic depiction of the world she knew so well, in the later biographical readings of her novels, and in the illustrated sets that presented her characters in pretty period dresses for Edwardian readers to enjoy. Chapman's appendices to the Oxford edition of the novels helped to confirm Austen as (in the words of Marvin Mudrick) "the gentle-hearted chronicler of the Regency order," an image which provoked much of the mid-twentieth-century New Critical revisionism.[98]

Although fear of "antiquarianism" stalks the textual discussions of the 1950s and 1960s, the critical preoccupations of the following decade began to promote research into Austen's historical context. The linguistic studies of Phillipps, Page, and Tave showed readers that their understanding of particular words might be rather different from that of Austen and her contemporaries, while the emphasis on the social dimension of speech brought a renewed awareness of class issues in *Emma*. At the same time, as Romantic scholars focused increasingly on the French Revolution, the question of Austen's own background, and its influence on the political tendencies and scope of her novels, became an urgent critical matter.

During the 1970s and 1980s, Austen's politics were generally read in relation to the broader debates surrounding the French Revolution, with particular attention focused on questions of class, property, and inheritance, as well as on the place of the individual in society. With the growing interest in colonialism and in post-colonialist approaches to texts, however, new aspects of Austen's novels began to attract attention. Her allegiance to a particular class, Church, or social order no longer seemed as important to some readers as her stance on slavery and the British Empire. Edward Said's *Culture and Imperialism* startled many Austen lovers by condemning the author of *Mansfield Park* for her callous and complacent references to Antigua, while Moira Ferguson argued that the novel must be seen as a post-abolition narrative.[99] The new post-colonial readings derived some of their energy from feminist scholarship on the radical discourse of the 1790s, which was especially alert to metaphors of slavery. Margaret Kirkham's *Jane Austen: Feminism and Fiction,* which appeared in 1983, was one of the first studies to emphasise Austen's enthusiasm for the work of the prominent anti-slavery campaigner, Thomas Clarkson, and to point out the relevance to *Mansfield Park* of the Mansfield Judgment, a landmark in the history of the Abolition Movement.

As critical interest moved beyond *Mansfield Park,* a new volume of essays came out, entitled *The Postcolonial Austen,* which explored not only Austen's immediate historical moment but also the ways in which her texts have reached subsequent generations of readers in very different contexts. In the essay selected for this volume, Gayle Wald examines Amy Heckerling's film adaptation of *Emma* and the "Americanization" of Austen's novel. The conjunction of *Clueless* and *Emma* may seem wildly unhistorical, but in fact the film reveals a new approach to Austen's wealthy heroine as "the unwitting heiress of British imperial and colonial enterprises."[100] This far-reaching response to the novel may seem far removed from the painstaking research into the material conditions of England in 1815 that forms the basis of so much recent critical writing on Austen, but in its emphasis on power relations, citizenship, consumerism, private experience, and gendered agency, Wald's essay sits intriguingly beside the essays devoted exclusively to *Emma,* pointing to fresh directions and debates. The analysis of *Clueless* demonstrates the ways in which texts inspired by *Emma* can work in dialogue with the original novel, revealing aspects that might otherwise remain invisible. In this way, it reflects not only the general impact of post-colonial criticism on readings of canonical texts but also recent critical interest in Austen's vital presence in popular culture, whether through screen, sequel, society, or visitor centre. Although in the translation from printed page to screen much of Austen's art is inevitably discarded, the remaining images of her text can shed important light on the novel's essential qualities and enduring popularity.

The Americanization of *Emma* seems all the more surprising when considered in conjunction with Brian Southam's reading of the novel, published in the same year as *The Postcolonial Austen.* Southam's essay, reprinted in this collection, is part of his substantial study of *Jane Austen and the Navy,* which includes *Emma* not for some mysteriously undiscovered naval dimension, but for its unique examination of "Englishness and patriotism."[101] Southam's approach combines historical, literary, and linguistic research, to situate *Emma* at the end of the long war with France. In this context, the novel's French loanwords, national stereotyping, and above all, the praise of rural England become central features, reflecting a national mood of celebration at the end of the Napoleonic conflict. While his study reflects the late-twentieth-century emphasis on contextualisation, his argument also has strong affinities with Trilling's view of the satisfactions afforded by *Emma*: "Idyllic and pastoral, its mood of high comedy and good humour is as far from the shadows of war as could be."[102] For Trilling, of course, Austen's idyllic world, where the only battlefields were psychological, was far removed from the "actual England" in which she lived, finding its counterparts in the Forest of Arden or in Schiller's wistful definitions.[103] Southam, in contrast, is just as sensitive to the pastoral mood of *Emma*, but for him Austen's idealisation of village life is an act of patriotism entirely consistent with her own experience of England in 1815. The opinions garnered by the author herself from among the novel's first readers are witness to the special "promise" discerned by Trilling, but it is a feeling specifically deepened by an understanding of the historical Peace.

Southam's study, with its eclectic selection of evidence and insights, suggests a desire to find reconciliation between historical and formal approaches to Austen. Neither exclusive focus on the text, nor on literary sources and traditions, nor on the immediate prose context, nor on the facts of social or political history are entirely adequate to an understanding of *Emma*. As critical trends have evolved and transmuted, impelled by scholars who have reacted against or developed ideas from earlier readings, the layers of opinion concerning *Emma* have reached mountainous proportions. And while even the briefest survey of earlier criticism might lead to uncomfortable doubts as to whether there could be anything left to say about Austen's finest novel, it should be apparent from this discussion that exciting new studies continue to appear, and with them new facets of *Emma*. Among the best new contributions are in fact those which re-examine aspects of Austen's work that have already attracted detailed and brilliant analysis. Frances Ferguson's essay "Jane Austen, *Emma*, and the Impact of Form" is an excellent example, and hence its inclusion as the final essay in this casebook.

In her examination of "free indirect style," Ferguson is revisiting a rhetorical device often singled out as the defining feature of Austen's style and subject to the careful analysis of close readers in the 1960s and 1970s. Her own approach is, however, also honed by the theoretical debates of the 1980s and 1990s, so that in place of more traditional practical criticism, she considers the values and shortcomings of formalism, the usefulness of Foucauldian and post-modern readings, the newer understandings of the eighteenth-century novel, and the feminist/historicist concerns with the status of marriage in the early nineteenth century. Her central argument for the need for criticism to recognise "character" may sound like a return to nineteenth-century enthusiasm for Austen's living, breathing people, but a glance at the opening pages of her essay shows that this is hardly a nostalgic response to Austen. Ferguson's analysis of formalist criticism of *Emma* and her alignment of Foucault with formalism demonstrates the ways in which different readings of Austen's novel have themselves become the subject of critical enquiry. Ferguson's language and the terms of her debate may be remote from Trilling's essay on *Emma,* but her very approach bears out his belief in the intrinsic interest and intellectual importance of the opinions which are held of Austen's work. While *Emma* continues to be read and enjoyed by vast numbers of new readers, the rewards of the novel, as so many have asserted, are renewed and multiplied by awareness of earlier critical responses. The essays collected in this volume, though representing only a fraction of the vast secondary literature on Austen, have been chosen to encourage the kind of careful reading urged by Farrer on the centenary of Austen's death. Together they provide an emphatic testimony to Austen's continuing importance and the ever-increasing pleasure afforded by *Emma.*

Notes

1. "*Emma* and the Legend of Jane Austen," first published in 1957, is reprinted in this casebook.

2. Ibid., 83.

3. James Austen-Leigh, *A Memoir of Jane Austen* (1870), ed. R. W. Chapman (Oxford: Oxford University Press, 1926), 157.

4. All references to *Emma* are to volume 4 of *The Novels of Jane Austen,* ed. R. W. Chapman [1923], 3rd ed., rev. Mary Lascelles (Oxford: Oxford University Press, 1965–69).

5. "Opinions of *Emma,*" collected by Jane Austen, first published in *Minor Works,* ed. R. W. Chapman [1954], rev. B. C. Southam (Oxford: Oxford University Press, 1967), 436–37. Reprinted in this casebook, 37.

6. Ibid., 39.

7. Ibid.

8. Ibid., 38.

9. Ibid., 39.

10. Ibid., 38.

11. Park Honan, *Jane Austen: Her Life* (London: St Martin's Press, 1987), 52–53; Clair Tomalin, *Jane Austen: A Life* (London: Viking, 1997), 58–59. Many of Austen's surviving early writings are included in *Minor Works*, ed. R. W. Chapman (1954), rev. B. C. Southam (Oxford: Oxford University Press, 1967). See also Jane Austen, *Catharine and Other Writings*, ed. Margaret Anne Doody (Oxford: Oxford University Press, 1993).

12. *Minor Works*, ed. R. W. Chapman (1954), rev. B. C. Southam (Oxford: Oxford University Press, 1967), 3, 12.

13. "Opinions of *Emma*," collected by Jane Austen, are reprinted in this casebook, 37.

14. Ibid., 39.

15. Brian Southam, "*Emma*: England, Peace and Patriotism," from *Jane Austen and the Navy* (London: Hambledon Press, 2000). Reprinted in this casebook.

16. Walter Scott, unsigned review in the *Quarterly Review*, xiv (1815–16): 188–201. Reprinted in this casebook, 48.

17. F. R. Leavis, *The Great Tradition* (London: Chatto and Windus, 1948), 7; Ian Watt, *The Rise of the Novel* (London: Chatto and Windus, 1957), 296–99.

18. George Eliot, *Adam Bede* (1959), ed. Carol A. Martin (Oxford: Clarendon, 2001), 166–67; "The Natural History of German Life," first published in the *Westminster Review*, lxv (April 1856): 628–33.

19. Virginia Woolf, review of Sybil G. Brinton's *Life and Letters* and *Old Friends and New Faces*, in the *London Times*, 8 May 1913, included in B. C. Southam, ed., *Jane Austen: the Critical Heritage, Vol. II: 1870–1940*, (London, Routledge & Kegan Paul, 1987), 135.

20. Linda Troost and Sayre Greenfield, "Filming Highbury: Reducing the Community of *Emma* to the Screen," first published in *Persuasions On-Line*, Occasional Papers No. 3: Emma on Film (Fall 1999). Reprinted in this casebook.

21. Walter Scott, unsigned review of *Emma*, in *Quarterly Review*, xiv (1815–16): 188–201. Reprinted in this casebook, 51.

22. *Waverley* was published in 1814, inaugurating Scott's remarkable series of novels.

23. For full details of Bentley's editions and subsequent publication by Bentley and other nineteenth-century publishers, see David Gilson, *Jane Austen: A Bibliography* (Oxford: Soho Books, 1982).

24. Anonymous, "Female Novelists," *New Monthly Magazine* xcv (May 1852): 17–23, included in B. C. Southam, ed., *Jane Austen: The Critical Heritage, Vol. 1: 1811–1870* (London: Routledge & Kegan Paul, 1968), 244.

25. Lewes, "The Novels of Jane Austen," *Blackwood's Edinburgh Magazine* lxxxvi (July 1859): 99–113, included in *Critical Heritage*, I.148–66.

26. Ibid., 152.

27. Ibid., 153.

28. Ibid., 166.

29. Ibid., 157.

30. Richard Whately, unsigned review of *Northanger Abbey* and *Persuasion, Quarterly Review* xxiv (January 1821): 352–76, included in *Critical Heritage*, I. 87–105; Macaulay, unsigned review of "The Diary and Letters of Mm. D'Arblay," *Edinburgh Review* lxxvi (January 1843): 561–62, included in *Critical Heritage* I: 122–23.

31. *Critical Heritage,* I. 166.

32. "To George Henry Lewes, 12 January 1848," *The Letters of Charlotte Brontë,* ed. Margaret Smith, 3 vols. (Oxford, Clarendon, 1995–2004), II. 10.

33. Ibid.

34. "To W. S. Williams, 12 April 1850," *Letters,* II. 383. Brontë had received a copy of *Emma* in March 1850, which was probably the edition published in 1849 by Simms and M'Intyre; see *Letters,* II. 361.

35. *Letters* II: 383.

36. Ibid.

37. D. H. Lawrence, "A Propos of *Lady Chatterley's Lover,*" in *Lady Chatterley's Lover,* ed. Michael Squires, *The Cambridge Edition of the Works of D. H. Lawrence,* (Cambridge: Cambridge University Press, 1993), 303–35, 332–33.

38. Richard Simpson, unsigned review of Austen-Leigh's *A Memoir of Jane Austen,* in the *North British Review* (April 1870), included in *Critical Heritage* I: 244, 250.

39. "Biographical Notice of the Author," *Northanger Abbey* and *Persuasion,* Chapman, vol. v, 3–9, 8.

40. *Critical Heritage* I: 253.

41. Henry James, "The Lesson of Balzac" (1905), included in *Critical Heritage,* I. 230. James's view of the contemporary popularity and commercialisation of Austen made him place her "in the same lucky box as the Brontës."

42. See Trilling's essay included in this casebook, 85.

43. *Critical Heritage,* II. 215.

44. *Letters of Charlotte Brontë,* II, 10. "A Propos of *Lady Chatterley's Lover,*" 333.

45. *Jane Austen Centenary Memorial* (London and New York: John Lane, 1917), 13.

46. See Trilling's essay included in this casebook, 85.

47. Nicola Shulman, *A Rage for Rock Gardening: The Story of Reginald Farrer, Gardener, Writer and Plant Collector* (London: Short Books, 2002), 73, 99.

48. Reginald Farrer, "Jane Austen, ob. July 18, 1917," *Quarterly Review* 452 (July 1917): 1–30. Reprinted in this casebook, 58.

49. Ibid., 75.

50. Ibid.

51. Ibid., 62.

52. Ibid.

53. Ibid., 75.

54. Ibid., 60.

55. Ibid., 61.

56. Ibid., 75.

57. Ibid., 77.

58. Ibid., 77.

59. Ibid., 78. These insights also anticipate subsequent criticism, including John Dussinger's perception of the triangular pattern of desire (see his essay included in this casebook), and feminist readings of *Emma* as a text celebrating female autonomy (see Claudia Johnson's essay in this casebook).

60. R. W. Chapman, *Jane Austen: Facts and Problems* (Oxford: Clarendon Press, 1948), 202.

61. Reginald Farrer, "Jane Austen, ob. July 18, 1917," *Quarterly Review* 452 (July 1917): 1–30. Reprinted in this casebook, 63.

62. *The Brontës: Their Lives, Friendships und Correspondence*, ed. T J Wise and John Alexander Symington, 4 vols (Oxford: Basil Blackwell, 1932). The letter to Williams appears in volume III, 99, under a heading "Charlotte on Jane Austen."

63. Marvin Mudrick, *Jane Austen: Irony as Defense and Discovery* (Princeton, N.J.: Princeton University Press, 1952), 1, 3.

64. Ibid., vii.

65. Chapman's distress at the work of Harding, Mudrick, and Reuben Brower is expressed explicitly in *Jane Austen: A Critical Bibliography* (Oxford: Clarendon Press, 1953).

66. Mudrick's epigraph is from Harding, "Regulated Hatred: An Aspect of the Work of Jane Austen," which first appeared in *Scrutiny* viii (March 1940): 347. Harding's essay has been republished in a collection of his writings on Austen, *Regulated Hatred and Other Essays on Jane Austen*, ed. Monica Lawlor (London: Athlone Press, 1998).

67. Mary Lascelles, *Jane Austen and Her Art* (Oxford: Oxford University Press, 1939); Q. D. Leavis, "A Critical Theory of Jane Austen's Writings," *Scrutiny* 10 (1941–42): 61–87, 114–42, 272–94; 12 (1944–45): 104–19.

68. Lascelles, v.

69. Wayne C. Booth, *The Rhetoric of Fiction* (Chicago: Chicago University Press, 1961), 243–64, reprinted in this casebook.

70. Austen's use of free indirect speech became more widely recognised after Norman Page's analysis of the technique in *The Language of Jane Austen* (Oxford: Basil Blackwell, 1972), 123–36. Its importance to the English novel is discussed by Frances Ferguson in the essay included in this casebook.

71. See 117, this volume.

72. Booth cites Katherine Mansfield in *Novels and Novelists*, ed. J. Middleton Murry (London: Constable, 1930), 304.

73. For more recent analyses of "Friendship" in Austen's novel, see Ruth Perry, "Interrupted Friendships in *Emma*," *Tulsa Studies in Women's Literature* 5 (Fall

1986): 185–202. Mary Ann O'Farrell examines the importance of the "author-friend" in "Jane Austen's Friendship," chapter 2 of *Janeites: Austen's Disciples and Devotees*, ed. Deidre Lynch (Princeton: Princeton University Press, 2000), 45–62.

74. W. J. Harvey, "The Plot of *Emma*," *Essays in Criticism* xvii (1967): 48–63.

75. Ibid., 55.

76. K. C. Phillipps, *Jane Austen's English* (London: Andre Deutsch, 1970).

77. Leavis, *The Great Tradition*, 8–9.

78. Edgar F. Shannon, "*Emma*: Character and Construction," *PMLA* 71 (1956): 637–50; Mark Schorer, "The Humiliation of Emma Woodhouse," *Literary Review* 2 (Summer 1959): 547–63.

79. A. Walton Litz, *Jane Austen: A Study of Her Artistic Development* (London: Chatto and Windus, 1965), 132–49.

80. Leavis, *Great Tradition*, 5.

81. Marilyn Butler, *Jane Austen and the War of Ideas* (Oxford: Clarendon Press, 1975), 164.

82. Ibid., 269, 273.

83. Ibid., 274.

84. Alistair Duckworth, *The Improvement of the Estate* (1971), the paperback edition (Baltimore and London: Johns Hopkins, 1994), viii.

85. Sandra M. Gilbert and Susan Gubar, *The Madwoman in the Attic* (New Haven and London: Yale University Press, 1979), 159. For more recent interest in Austen's exuberant humour, see Jill Heydt-Stevenson, "'Slipping into the Ha-ha': Bawdy Humour and Body Politics in Jane Austen's Novels," *Nineteenth-Century Literature* 55 (2000): 309–39, and *Austen's Unbecoming Conjunctions: Subversive Laughter, Embodied History* (New York: Palgrave, 2005).

86. Ibid., 160.

87. Dale Spender, *Mothers of the Novel: One Hundred Good Women Novelists before Jane Austen* (London and New York: Pandora, 1986); Jane Spencer, *The Rise of the Woman Novelist: From Aphra Behn to Jane Austen* (Oxford: Basil Blackwell, 1986). The challenge was not exclusively feminist: see, for example, Michael Mckeon, *The Origins of the English Novel, 1600–1740* (Baltimore: Johns Hopkins University Press, 1989).

88. Nancy Armstrong, *Desire and Domestic Fiction: A Political History of the Novel* (New York: Oxford University Press, 1987), 135.

89. For Trilling's comment, and Johnson's response, see their essays included in this casebook.

90. See Booth's essay, included in this casebook, 114.

91. Mary Waldron, "Men of Sense and Silly Wives: The Confusions of Mr. Knightley," from *Jane Austen and the Fiction of her Time* (Cambridge: Cambridge University Press, 1999), 112–34, reprinted in this casebook.

92. Joseph Litvak, "Reading Characters; Self, Society, and Text in *Emma*," first published in *PMLA* 100 (1985): 763–73, reprinted in this casebook.

93. Ibid., 164.

94. Reginald Farrer, "Jane Austen, ob. July 1817," *Quarterly Review* 452 (1917): 1–30, reprinted in this casebook, 94.

95. See, for example, essays by Booth and Trilling for positive views of Mr. Knightley's sensible influence.

96. John Wiltshire, *Jane Austen and the Body* (Cambridge: Cambridge University Press, 1992), 153. An extract from the chapter on *Emma* is reprinted in this casebook.

97. Edward Copeland, *Women Writing about Money: Women's Fiction in England, 1790–1820* (Cambridge: Cambridge University Press, 1995); "Money," in *The Cambridge Companion to Jane Austen*, ed. Edward Copeland and Juliet McMaster (Cambridge: Cambridge University Press, 1997), 131–48; *Jane Austen's Business*, ed. Juliet McMaster and Bruce Stovel (Basingstoke: Macmillan, 1996).

98. Mudrick, vii.

99. Edward Said, *Culture and Imperialism* (London: Chatto and Windus, 1993); Moira Ferguson, "*Mansfield Park*: Slavery, Colonialism and Gender," *Oxford Literary Review* 13 (1991): 118–39.

100. Gayle Wald, "*Clueless* in the Neo-Colonial World Order," in *The Postcolonial Austen*, ed. Rajeswari Sunder Rajan and You-me Park (London: Routledge, 2000), 218–33, reprinted in this casebook, 252. For recent work on Austen's adaptation to the screen, see also *Jane Austen in Hollywood*, ed. Linda Troost and Sayre Greenfield (Lexington: University of Kentucky Press, 1998), and *Jane Austen on Screen*, ed. Gina Macdonald and Andrew F. Macdonald (Cambridge: Cambridge University Press, 2003).

101. Southam, "*Emma*: England, Peace and Patriotism," reprinted in this casebook, 272.

102. Ibid., 271. Compare also with Farrer's attraction to *Emma* in 1917, written during the First World War.

103. Trilling, "*Emma* and the Legend of Jane Austen," included in this casebook, 99.

Opinions of *Emma*

JANE AUSTEN

◆ ◆ ◆

C APTAIN AUSTEN.[1]—liked it extremely, observing that though there might be more Wit in P. & P.—& an higher Morality in M. P.—yet altogether, on account of it's peculiar air of Nature throughout, he preferred it to either.

Mrs. F. A.[2]—liked & admired it very much indeed, but must still prefer P. & P.—

Mrs. J. Bridges—preferred it to all the others.

Miss Sharp—better than M. P.—but not so well as P. & P.—pleased with the Heroine for her Originality, delighted with Mr. K—& called Mrs. Elton beyond praise.—dissatisfied with Jane Fairfax.

Cassandra—better than P. & P.—but not so well as M. P.—

Fanny K.[3]—not so well as either P. & P. or M. P.—could not bear *Emma* herself.—Mr. Knightley delightful.—Should like J. F.—if she knew more of her.—

Mr. & Mrs. J. A.[4]—did not like it so well as either of the 8 others. Language different from the others; not so easily read.—

Edward[5]—preferred it to M. P.—*only*. —Mr. K. liked by every body.

Miss Bigg—not equal to either P. & P.—or M. P.—objected to the sameness of the subject (Match-making) all through.—Too much of Mr. Elton & H. Smith. Language superior to the others.—

My Mother—thought it more entertaining than M. P.—but not so interesting as P. & P.—No characters in it equal to Ly Catherine & Mr. Collins.—

Miss Lloyd[6]—thought it as *clever* as either of the others, but did not receive so much pleasure from it as from P. & P.—& M. P.—

Mrs. & Miss Craven—liked it very much, but not so much as the others.—

Fanny Cage—liked it very much indeed & classed it between P. & P.—& M. P.—

Mr. Sherer—did not think it equal to either M. P.—(which he liked the best of all) or P. & P.—Displeased with my pictures of Clergymen.—

Miss Bigg—on reading it a second time, liked Miss Bates much better than at first, & expressed herself as liking all the people of Highbury in general, except Harriet Smith—but could not help still thinking *her* too silly in her Loves.

The family at Upton Gray—all very much amused with it.—Miss Bates a great favourite with Mrs. Beaufoy.

Mr. & Mrs. Leigh Perrot—saw many beauties in it, but could not think it equal to P. & P.—Darcy & Elizabeth had spoilt them for anything else.— Mr. K. however, an excellent Character; Emma better luck than a Matchmaker often has.—Pitied Jane Fairfax—thought Frank Churchill better treated than he deserved.—

Countess Craven—admired it very much, but did not think it equal to P. & P.—which she ranked as the very first of it's sort.—

Mrs. Guiton—thought it too natural to be interesting.

Mrs. Digweed—did not like it so well as the others, in fact if she had not known the Author, could hardly have got through it.—

Miss Terry—admired it very much, particularly Mrs. Elton.

Henry Sanford—very much pleased with it—delighted with Miss Bates, but thought Mrs. Elton the best-drawn Character in the Book.—Mansfield Park however, still his favourite.

Mr. Haden—*quite* delighted with it. Admired the Character of Emma.—

Miss Isabella Herries—did not like it—objected to my exposing the sex in the character of the Heroine—convinced that I had meant Mrs. & Miss Bates for some acquaintance of theirs—People whom I never heard of before.—

Miss Harriet Moore—admired it very much, but M. P. still her favourite of all.—

Countess Morley—delighted with it.—

Mr. Cockerelle—liked it so little, that Fanny would not send me his opinion.—

Mrs. Dickson—did not much like it—thought it *very* inferior to P. & P.—
Liked it the less, from there being a Mr. & Mrs. Dixon in it.—

Mrs. Brandreth—thought the 3rd vol: superior to anything I had ever
written—quite beautiful!—

Mr. B. Lefroy—thought that if there had been more Incident, it would be
equal to any of the others.—The Characters quite as well drawn &
supported as in any, & from being more everyday ones, the more
entertaining.—Did not like the Heroine so well as any of the others.
Miss Bates excellent, but rather too much of her. Mr. & Mrs. Elton
admirable & John Knightley a sensible Man.—

Mrs. B. Lefroy—rank'd *Emma* as a composition with S. & S.—not so *Brilliant* as P.
& P.—nor so *equal* as M. P.—Preferred Emma herself to all the heroines.—
The Characters like all the others admirably well drawn & supported—
perhaps rather less strongly marked than some, but only the more
natural for that reason.—Mr. Knightley Mrs. Elton & Miss Bates her
favourites.—Thought one or two of the conversations too long.—

Mrs. Lefroy—preferred it to M. P.—but liked M. P. the least of all.

Mr. Fowle—read only the first & last Chapters, because he had heard it was
not interesting.—

Mrs. Lutley Sclater—liked it very much, better than M. P.—& thought
I had "brought it all about very cleverly in the last volume."—

Mrs. C. Cage wrote thus to Fanny—"A great many thanks for the loan of
Emma, which I am delighted with. I like it better than any. Every
character is thoroughly kept up. I must enjoy reading it again with
Charles. Miss Bates is incomparable, but I was nearly killed with those
precious treasures! They are Unique, & really with more fun than I can
express. I am at Highbury all day, & I can't help feeling I have just got
into a new set of acquaintance. No one writes such good sense. & so
very comfortable.

Mrs. Wroughton—did not like it so well as P. & P.—Thought the Authoress wrong, in such times as these, to draw such Clergymen as Mr.
Collins & Mr. Elton.

Sir J. Langham—thought it much inferior to the others.—

Mr. Jeffery (of the Edinburgh Review) was kept up by it three nights.

Miss Murden—certainly inferior to all the others.

Capt. C. Austen[7] wrote—"Emma arrived in time to a moment. I am
delighted with her, more so I think than even with my favourite Pride
& Prejudice, & have read it three times in the Passage."

Mrs. D. Dundas—thought it very clever, but did not like it so well as either
of the others.

Notes

1. Francis William; his brother Charles is below.
2. Francis's wife.
3. Knight.
4. James Austen.
5. James Edward.
6. Martha.
7. Charles John.

Additional Notes from the Editor

The following notes identify some of the readers who offered their opinions of *Emma*. For assistance in gathering this information, I am indebted to Deirdre Le Faye for her invaluable book, *Jane Austen's Letters*, 3rd ed. (Oxford: Oxford University Press, 1995), and to R. W. Chapman (ed.) for *Minor Works*, volume 6 of *The Novels of Jane Austen* (Oxford: Oxford University Press, 1954; rev. B. C. Southam, 1967).

Captain Austen: Francis William Austen (1774–1865), Jane's elder brother.

Mrs. F. A.: Mary Austen (née Gibson), first wife of Francis Austen, whom she married in 1806.

Mrs. J. Bridges: Charlotte Bridges (née Hawley), wife of Revd. Brook-John Bridges. Revd. Bridges' sister Elizabeth married Jane's brother Edward Austen (Knight) in 1791.

Miss Sharp: The former governess of Fanny Knight, Jane's niece (see below).

Cassandra: Cassandra Austen (1773–1845), Jane's elder sister. She was Jane's close confidante and main correspondent.

Fanny K: Frances Catherine Knight (1793–1882), Jane's niece. She was the daughter of Jane's brother Edward.

Mr. and Mrs. J. A.: James Austen (1765–1819), Jane's eldest brother, and Mary (née Lloyd) Austen (1771–1843), his second wife.

Edward: James Edward Austen-Leigh (1798–1874), Jane's nephew. He was the author of *A Memoir of Jane Austen* (1870).

Miss Bigg: Alethea Bigg, of Manydown Park in Hampshire, a close friend of Jane's.

My Mother: Cassandra Austen (née Leigh) (1739–1827), Jane's mother.

Miss Lloyd: Martha Lloyd (1765–1843), sister of James Austen's wife, Mary. Martha was a close friend of the Austen family and married Francis Austen in 1828.

Mrs. and Miss Craven: Catherine Craven (née Hughes) and Charlotte-Elizabeth Craven, wife and daughter of the Revd. John Craven. They were family friends of the Austens.

Fanny Cage: Fanny Cage (1793–1874), related by marriage to Jane's brother Edward.

Mr. Sherer: Revd. Joseph Godfrey Sherer (1770–1824). He was the vicar of Godmersham in Kent, where Jane's brother Edward had his estate.

Miss Bigg: Perhaps Alethea (see above), or another member of the Bigg family of Manydown.

The family at Upton Gray: The Beaufoy family of Upton Gray in Hampshire.

Mr. and Mrs. Leigh Perrot: James (1735–1817) and Jane (née Cholmeley) Leigh-Perrot, Jane Austen's uncle and aunt. James was the younger brother of Jane Austen's mother, Cassandra.

Countess Craven: Former actress Louisa Brunton. Her beauty and talents had captivated Lord Craven, and they married in 1807.

Mrs. Guiton: Perhaps Mrs. Guiton of Little Park Place, near Fareham in Hampshire.

Mrs. Digweed: Jane Digweed (née Terry), wife of Harry Digweed. The Digweeds lived near the Austens at Steventon in Hampshire.

Miss Terry: Mary Terry, sister of Mrs. Digweed (see above).

Henry Sanford: Friend of Jane's brother Henry.

Mr. Haden: A London surgeon.

Miss Isabella Herries: Acquaintance of Jane's brother Henry. Jane met Miss Herries in 1815 while staying at Henry's house in London.

Miss Harriet Moore: Another friend of Henry Austen's. Jane met Miss Moore in London.

Countess Morley: Wife of the Earl of Morley. Jane probably met the Countess through her brother Henry Austen.

Mrs. Dickson: Probably the wife of naval officer Captain Archibald Dickson.

Mr. B. Lefroy: Benjamin Lefroy (1791–1827), husband of Jane's niece Anna (see below).

Mrs. B. Lefroy: Anna Lefroy (née Austen), daughter of Jane's brother James. Anna married Benjamin Lefroy in 1814.

Mrs. Lefroy: One of the Lefroy family, but *not* Anne Lefroy, Jane's great friend and the subject of her poem "To the Memory of Mrs. Lefroy."

Mr. Fowle: Revd. Fulwar-Craven Fowle (1764–1840). Revd. Fowle's brother, Thomas, had been engaged to Cassandra Austen until his death in 1797.

Mrs. Lutley Sclater: Penelope Lutley-Sclater (1750–1840), a family acquaintance who lived at Tangier Park in Hampshire.

Mrs. C. Cage: Charlotte Cage (née Graham), wife of Revd. Charles Cage and mother of Fanny Cage (see above).

Sir J. Langham: Sir James Langham (1776–1833). He was related to the Sanford family, who were friends of Henry Austen's.

Mr. Jeffrey: Francis Jeffrey (1773–1850), the formidable contemporary critic and editor of the *Edinburgh Review*.

Miss Murden: Jane Murden, related to the Fowle family (see above).

Capt. C. Austen: Charles John Austen (1779–1852), Jane's youngest brother.

Mrs. D. Dundas: Janet-Whitley Dundas, friend of the Fowle family (see above).

Emma; a Novel. By the Author of Sense and Sensibility, Pride and Prejudice, &c. 3 vols. 12mo. London. 1815.

WALTER SCOTT

◆　　◆　　◆

T HERE ARE SOME VICES in civilized society so common that they are hardly acknowledged as stains upon the moral character, the propensity to which is nevertheless carefully concealed, even by those who most frequently give way to them; since no man of pleasure would willingly assume the gross epithet of a debauchee or a drunkard. One would almost think that novel-reading fell under this class of frailties, since among the crowds who read little else, it is not common to find an individual of hardihood sufficient to avow his taste for these frivolous studies. A novel, therefore, is frequently "bread eaten in secret"; and it is not upon Lydia Languish's toilet alone that Tom Jones and Peregrine Pickle are to be found ambushed behind works of a more grave and instructive character.[1] And hence it has happened, that in no branch of composition, not even in poetry itself, have so many writers, and of such varied talents, exerted their powers. It may perhaps be added, that although the composition of these works admits of being exalted and decorated by the higher exertions of genius; yet such is the universal charm of narrative, that the worst novel ever written will find some gentle reader content to yawn over it, rather than to open the page of the historian, moralist, or poet. We have heard, indeed, of one work of fiction so unutterably stupid, that the proprietor, diverted by the rarity of the incident, offered the book, which consisted of two volumes in duodecimo, handsomely bound, to any person who would declare, upon his honour, that he had read the whole from beginning to end. But although this offer was made to the passengers on board an Indiaman, during a tedious outward-bound voyage, the *Memoirs of Clegg the Clergyman,*[2] (such was the title of this unhappy composition,) completely baffled the most dull and determined student on board, and bid fair for an exception to the general rule above-mentioned,—when the love of glory prevailed with the boatswain, a man of strong and solid parts, to hazard the attempt, and he actually conquered and carried off the prize!

The judicious reader will see at once that we have been pleading our own cause while stating the universal practice, and preparing him for a display of more general acquaintance with this fascinating department of literature, than at first sight may seem consistent with the graver studies to which we are compelled by duty: but in truth, when we consider how many hours of languor and anxiety, of deserted age and solitary celibacy, of pain even and poverty, are beguiled by the perusal of these light volumes, we cannot austerely condemn the source from which is drawn the alleviation of such a portion of human misery, or consider the regulation of this department as beneath the sober consideration of the critic.

If such apologies may be admitted in judging the labours of ordinary novelists, it becomes doubly the duty of the critic to treat with kindness as well as candour works which, like this before us, proclaim a knowledge of the human heart, with the power and resolution to bring that knowledge to the service of honour and virtue. The author is already known to the public by the two novels announced in her title-page, and both, the last especially, attracted, with justice, an attention from the public far superior to what is granted to the ephemeral productions which supply the regular demand of watering-places and circulating libraries. They belong to a class of fictions which has arisen almost in our own times, and which draws the characters and incidents introduced more immediately from the current of ordinary life than was permitted by the former rules of the novel.

In its first appearance, the novel was the legitimate child of the romance; and though the manners and general turn of the composition were altered so as to suit modern times, the author remained fettered by many peculiarities derived from the original style of romantic fiction. These may be chiefly traced in the conduct of the narrative, and the tone of sentiment attributed to the fictitious personages. On the first point, although

> The talisman and magic wand were broke,
> Knights, dwarfs, and genii vanish'd into smoke,

still the reader expected to peruse a course of adventures of a nature more interesting and extraordinary than those which occur in his own life, or that of his next-door neighbours. The hero no longer defeated armies by his single sword, clove giants to the chine, or gained kingdoms. But he was expected to go through perils by sea and land, to be steeped in poverty, to be tried by temptation, to be exposed to the alternate vicissitudes of adversity and prosperity, and his life was a troubled scene of suffering and achievement. Few novelists, indeed, adventured to deny to the hero his final hour of tranquility and happiness, though it was the prevailing fashion never to relieve him out of his last and most dreadful distress until the finishing chapters of his history; so that although his prosperity in the record of his life was short, we were bound to believe it was long and uninterrupted when the author had done with him. The heroine was usually condemned to equal hardships and hazards. She was regularly exposed to being forcibly carried off like a Sabine virgin by some frantic admirer. And even if she escaped the terrors of masked ruffians, an insidious ravisher, a cloak wrapped forcibly around her head, and a coach with the blinds up driving she could not conjecture whither, she had still her share of wandering, of poverty, of obloquy, of seclusion, and of imprisonment, and was frequently extended upon a bed of sickness, and reduced to her last shilling before the author condescended to shield her from persecution. In all these dread contingencies the mind of the reader was expected to sympathize, since by incidents so much beyond the bounds of his ordinary experience, his wonder and interest ought at once to be excited. But gradually he became familiar with the land of fiction, the adventures of which he assimilated not with those of real life, but with each other. Let the distress of the hero or heroine be ever so great, the reader reposed an imperturbable confidence in the talents of the author, who, as he had plunged them into distress, would in his own good time, and when things, as Tony Lumkin says, were in a concatenation accordingly, bring his favourites out of all their troubles.[3] Mr. Crabbe has expressed his own and our feelings excellently on this subject.

> For should we grant these beauties all endure
> Severest pangs, they've still the speediest cure;
> Before one charm be wither'd from the face,
> Except the bloom which shall again have place,
> In wedlock ends each wish, in triumph all disgrace.
> And life to come, we fairly may suppose,
> One light bright contrast to these wild dark woes.[4]

In short, the author of novels was, in former times, expected to tread pretty much in the limits between the concentric circles of probability and possibility; and as he was not permitted to transgress the latter, his narrative, to make amends, almost always went beyond the bounds of the former. Now, although it may be urged that the vicissitudes of human life have occasionally led an individual through as many scenes of singular fortune as are represented in the most extravagant of these fictions, still the causes and personages acting on these changes have varied with the progress of the adventurer's fortune, and do not present that combined plot, (the object of every skilful novelist) in which all the more interesting individuals of the dramatis personæ have their appropriate share in the action and in bringing about the catastrophe. Here, even more than in its various and violent changes of fortune, rests the improbability of the novel. The life of man rolls forth like a stream from the fountain, or it spreads out into tranquillity like a placid or stagnant lake. In the latter case, the individual grows old among the characters with whom he was born, and is contemporary,—shares precisely the sort of weal and woe to which his birth destined him,—moves in the same circle,—and, allowing for the change of seasons, is influenced by, and influences the same class of persons by which he was originally surrounded. The man of mark and of adventure, on the contrary, resembles, in the course of his life, the river whose mid-current and discharge into the ocean are widely removed from each other, as well as from the rocks and wild flowers which its fountains first reflected; violent changes of time, of place, and of circumstances, hurry him forward from one scene to another, and his adventures will usually be found only connected with each other because they have happened to the same individual. Such a history resembles an ingenious, fictitious narrative, exactly in the degree in which an old dramatic chronicle of the life and death of some distinguished character, where all the various agents appear and disappear as in the page of history, approaches a regular drama, in which every person introduced plays an appropriate part, and every point of the action tends to one common catastrophe.

We return to the second broad line of distinction between the novel, as formerly composed, and real life,—the difference, namely, of the sentiments. The novelist professed to give an imitation of nature, but it was, as the French say, *la belle nature*. Human beings, indeed, were presented, but in the most sentimental mood, and with minds purified by a sensibility which often verged on extravagance. In the serious class of novels, the hero was usually

"A knight of love, who never broke a vow."

And although, in those of a more humorous cast, he was permitted a license, borrowed either from real life or from the libertinism of the drama, still a distinction was demanded even from Peregrine Pickle, or Tom Jones; and the hero, in every folly of which he might be guilty, was studiously vindicated from the charge of infidelity of the heart. The heroine was, of course, still more immaculate; and to have conferred her affections upon any other than the lover to whom the reader had destined her from their first meeting, would have been a crime against sentiment which no author, of moderate prudence, would have hazarded, under the old *régime*.

Here, therefore, we have two essential and important circumstances, in which the earlier novels differed from those now in fashion, and were more nearly assimilated to the old romances. And there can be no doubt that, by the studied involution and extrication of the story, by the combination of incidents new, striking and wonderful beyond the course of ordinary life, the former authors opened that obvious and strong sense of interest which arises from curiosity; as by the pure, elevated, and romantic cast of the sentiment, they conciliated those better propensities of our nature which loves to contemplate the picture of virtue, even when confessedly unable to imitate its excellences.

But strong and powerful as these sources of emotion and interest may be, they are, like all others, capable of being exhausted by habit. The imitators who rushed in crowds upon each path in which the great masters of the art had successively led the way, produced upon the public mind the usual effect of satiety. The first writer of a new class is, as it were, placed on a pinnacle of excellence, to which, at the earliest glance of a surprized admirer, his ascent seems little less than miraculous. Time and imitation speedily diminish the wonder, and each successive attempt establishes a kind of progressive scale of ascent between the lately deified author, and the reader, who had deemed his excellence inaccessible. The stupidity, the mediocrity, the merit of his imitators, are alike fatal to the first inventor, by shewing how possible it is to exaggerate his faults and to come within a certain point of his beauties.

Materials also (and the man of genius as well as his wretched imitator must work with the same) become stale and familiar. Social life, in our civilized days, affords few instances capable of being painted in the strong dark colours which excite surprize and horror; and robbers, smugglers, bailiffs, caverns, dungeons, and mad-houses, have been all introduced until they ceased to interest. And thus in the novel, as in every style of composition which appeals to the public taste, the more rich and easily worked mines being exhausted, the adventurous author must, if he is desirous of success, have recourse to those which were disdained by his predecessors as unproductive, or avoided as only capable of being turned to profit by great skill and labour.

Accordingly a style of novel has arisen, within the last fifteen or twenty years, differing from the former in the points upon which the interest hinges; neither alarming our credulity nor amusing our imagination by wild variety of incident, or by those pictures of romantic affection and sensibility, which were formerly as certain attributes of fictitious characters as they are of rare occurrence among those who actually live and die. The substitute for these excitements, which had lost much of their poignancy by the repeated and injudicious use of them, was the art of copying from nature as she really exists in the common walks of life, and presenting to the reader, instead of the splendid scenes of an imaginary world, a correct and striking representation of that which is daily taking place around him.

In adventuring upon this task, the author makes obvious sacrifices, and encounters peculiar difficulty. He who paints from *le beau idéal*, if his scenes and sentiments are striking and interesting, is in a great measure exempted from the difficult task of reconciling them with the ordinary probabilities of life: but he who paints a scene of common occurrence, places his composition within that extensive range of criticism which general experience offers to every reader. The resemblance of a statue of Hercules we must take on the artist's judgment; but every one can criticize that which is presented as the portrait of a friend, or neighbour. Something more than a mere signpost likeness is also demanded. The portrait must have spirit and character, as well as resemblance; and being deprived of all that, according to Bayes, goes "to elevate and surprize," it must make amends by displaying depth of knowledge and dexterity of execution. We, therefore, bestow no mean compliment upon the author of *Emma,* when we say that, keeping close to common incidents, and to such characters as occupy the ordinary walks of life, she has produced sketches of such spirit and originality, that we never miss the excitation which depends upon a narrative of uncommon events, arising from the consideration of minds, manners, and sentiments, greatly above our own. In this class she stands almost alone; for the scenes of Miss Edgeworth are laid in higher life, varied by more romantic incident, and by her remarkable power of embodying and illustrating national character.[5] But the author of *Emma* confines herself chiefly to the middling classes of society; her most distinguished characters do not rise greatly above well-bred country gentlemen and ladies; and those which are sketched with most originality and precision, belong to a class rather below that standard. The narrative of all her novels is composed of such common occurrences as may have fallen under the observation of most folks; and her dramatis personæ conduct themselves upon the motives and principles which the readers may recognize as ruling their own and that of most of their acquaintances. The kind of moral, also, which these novels inculcate, applies equally to the paths of common life, as will best appear from a short notice of the author's former works, with a more full abstract of that which we at present have under consideration.

Sense and Sensibility, the first of these compositions, contains the history of two sisters. The elder, a young lady of prudence and regulated feelings, becomes gradually attached to a man of an excellent heart and limited talents, who happens unfortunately to be fettered by a rash and ill-assorted engagement. In the younger sister, the influence of sensibility and imagination predominates; and she, as was to be expected, also falls in love, but with more unbridled and wilful passion. Her lover, gifted with all the qualities of exterior polish and vivacity, proves faithless, and marries a woman of large fortune. The interest and merit of the piece depend altogether upon the behaviour of the elder sister, while obliged at once to sustain her own disappointment with fortitude, and to support her sister, who abandons herself, with unsuppressed feelings, to the indulgence of grief. The marriage of the unworthy rival at length relieves her own lover from his imprudent engagement, while her sister, turned wise by precept, example, and experience, transfers her affection to a very respectable and somewhat too serious admirer, who had nourished an unsuccessful passion through the three volumes.

In *Pride and Prejudice* the author presents us with a family of young women, bred up under a foolish and vulgar mother, and a father whose good abilities lay hid under such a load of indolence and insensibility, that he had become contented to make the foibles and follies of his wife and daughters the subject of dry and humorous sarcasm, rather than of admonition, or restraint. This is one of the portraits from ordinary life which shews our author's talents in a very strong point of view. A friend of ours, whom the author never saw or heard of, was at once recognized by his own family as the original of Mr. Bennet, and we do not know if he has yet got rid of the nickname. A Mr. Collins, too, a formal, conceited, yet servile young sprig of divinity, is drawn with the same force and precision. The story of the piece consists chiefly in the fates of the second sister, to whom a man of high birth, large fortune, but haughty and reserved manners, becomes attached, in spite of the discredit thrown upon the object of his affection by the vulgarity and ill-conduct of her relations. The lady, on the contrary, hurt at the contempt of her connections, which the lover does not even attempt to suppress, and prejudiced against him on other accounts, refuses the hand which he ungraciously offers, and does not perceive that she has done a foolish thing until she accidentally visits a very handsome seat and grounds belonging to her admirer. They chance to meet exactly as her prudence had begun to subdue her prejudice; and after some essential services rendered to her family, the lover becomes encouraged to renew his addresses, and the novel ends happily.

Emma has even less story than either of the preceding novels. Miss Emma Woodhouse, from whom the book takes its name, is the daughter of a gentleman of wealth and consequence residing at his seat in the immediate vicinage of a country village called Highbury. The father, a good-natured, silly valetudinary, abandons the management of his household to Emma, he himself being only occupied by his summer and winter walk, his apothecary, his gruel, and his whist table. The latter is supplied from the neighbouring village of Highbury with precisely the sort of persons who occupy the vacant corners of a regular whist table, when a village is in the neighbourhood, and better cannot be found within the family. We have the smiling and courteous vicar, who nourishes the ambitious hope of obtaining Miss Woodhouse's hand. We have Mrs. Bates, the wife of a former rector, past every thing but tea and whist; her daughter, Miss Bates, a good-natured, vulgar, and foolish old maid; Mr. Weston, a gentleman of a frank disposition and moderate fortune, in the vicinity, and his wife an amiable and accomplished person, who had been Emma's governess, and is devotedly attached to her. Amongst all these personages, Miss Woodhouse walks forth, the princess paramount, superior to all her companions in wit, beauty, fortune, and accomplishments, doated upon by her father and the Westons, admired, and almost worshipped by the more humble companions of the whist table. The object of most young ladies is, or at least is usually supposed to be, a desirable connection in marriage. But Emma Woodhouse, either anticipating the taste of a later period of life, or, like a good sovereign, preferring the weal of her subjects of Highbury to her own private interest, sets generously about making matches for her friends without thinking of matrimony on her own account. We are informed that she had been eminently successful in the case of Mr. and Miss Weston; and when the novel commences she is exerting her influence in favour of Miss Harriet Smith, a boarding-school girl without family or fortune, very good humoured, very pretty, very silly, and, what suited Miss Woodhouse's purpose best of all, very much disposed to be married.

In these conjugal machinations Emma is frequently interrupted, not only by the cautions of her father, who had a particular objection to any body committing the rash act of matrimony, but also by the sturdy reproof and remonstrances of Mr. Knightley, the elder brother of her sister's husband, a sensible country gentleman of thirty-five, who had known Emma from her cradle, and was the only person who ventured to find fault with her. In spite, however, of his censure and warning, Emma lays a plan of marrying Harriet Smith to the vicar; and though she succeeds perfectly in diverting her simple friend's thoughts from an honest farmer who had made her a very suitable offer, and in flattering her into a passion for Mr. Elton, yet, on the other hand, that conceited divine totally mistakes the nature of the encouragement held out to him, and attributes the favour which he found in Miss Woodhouse's eyes to a lurking affection on her own part. This at length encourages him to a presumptuous declaration of his sentiments; upon receiving a repulse, he looks abroad else where, and enriches the Highbury society by uniting himself to a dashing young woman with as many thousands as are usually called ten, and a corresponding quantity of presumption and ill breeding.

While Emma is thus vainly engaged in forging wedlock fetters for others, her friends have views of the same kind upon her, in favour of a son of Mr. Weston by a former marriage, who bears the name, lives under the patronage, and is to inherit the fortune of a rich uncle. Unfortunately Mr. Frank Churchill had already settled his affections on Miss Jane Fairfax, a young lady of reduced fortune; but as this was a concealed affair, Emma, when Mr. Churchill first appears on the stage, has some thoughts of being in love with him herself; speedily, however, recovering from that dangerous propensity, she is disposed to confer him upon her deserted friend Harriet Smith. Harriet has, in the interim, fallen desperately in love with Mr. Knightley, the sturdy, advice-giving bachelor; and, as all the village supposes Frank Churchill and Emma to be attached to each other, there are cross purposes enough (were the novel of a more romantic cast) for cutting half the men's throats and breaking all the women's hearts. But at Highbury Cupid walks decorously, and with good discretion, bearing his torch under a lanthorn, instead of flourishing it around to set the house on fire. All these entanglements bring on only a train of mistakes and embarrassing situations, and dialogues at balls and parties of pleasure, in which the author displays her peculiar powers of humour and knowledge of human life. The plot is extricated with great simplicity. The aunt of Frank Churchill dies; his uncle, no longer under her baneful influence, consents to his marriage with Jane Fairfax. Mr. Knightley and Emma are led, by this unexpected incident, to discover that they had been in love with each other all along. Mr. Woodhouse's objections to the marriage of his daughter are overpowered by the fears of house-breakers, and the comfort which he hopes to derive from having a stout son-in-law resident in the family; and the facile affections of Harriet Smith are transferred, like a bank bill by indorsation, to her former suitor, the honest farmer, who had obtained a favourable opportunity of renewing his addresses. Such is the simple plan of a story which we peruse with pleasure, if not with deep interest, and which perhaps we might more willingly resume than one of those narratives where the attention is strongly riveted, during the first perusal, by the powerful excitement of curiosity.

The author's knowledge of the world, and the peculiar tact with which she presents characters that the reader cannot fail to recognize, reminds us something of the merits of the Flemish school of painting. The subjects are not often elegant, and certainly never grand; but they are finished up to nature, and with a precision which delights the reader. This is a merit which it is very difficult to illustrate by extracts, because it pervades the whole work, and is not to be comprehended from a single passage. The following is a dialogue between Mr. Woodhouse, and his elder daughter Isabella, who shares his anxiety about health, and has, like her father, a favourite apothecary. The reader must be informed that this lady, with her husband, a sensible, peremptory sort of person, had come to spend a week with her father.

> While they were thus comfortably occupied, Mr. Woodhouse was enjoying a full flow of happy regrets and fearful affection with his daughter.
>
> "My poor dear Isabella," said he, fondly taking her hand, and interrupting, for a few moments, her busy labours for some one of her five children—"How long it is, how terribly long since you were here! And how tired you must be after your journey! You must go to bed early, my dear—and I recommend a little gruel to you before you go.—You and I will have a nice basin of gruel together. My dear Emma, suppose we all have a little gruel."
>
> Emma could not suppose any such thing, knowing, as she did, that both the Mr. Knightleys were as unpersuadable on that article as herself,—and two basins only were ordered. After a little more discourse in praise of gruel, with some wondering at its not being taken every evening by every body, he proceeded to say, with an air of grave reflection,
>
> "It was an awkward business, my dear, your spending the autumn at South End instead of coming here. I never had much opinion of the sea air."
>
> "Mr. Wingfield most strenuously recommended it, sir—or we should not have gone. He recommended it for all the children, but particularly for the weakness in little Bella's throat,—both sea air and bathing."

"Ah! my dear, but Perry had many doubts about the sea doing her any good; and as to myself, I have been long perfectly convinced, though perhaps I never told you so before, that the sea is very rarely of use to any body. I am sure it almost killed me once."

"Come, come," cried Emma, feeling this to be an unsafe subject, "I must beg you not to talk of the sea. It makes me envious and miserable,—I who have never seen it! South End is prohibited, if you please. My dear Isabella, I have not heard you make one inquiry after Mr. Perry yet; and he never forgets you."

"Oh! good Mr. Perry—how is he, sir?"

"Why, pretty well; but not quite well. Poor Perry is bilious, and he has not time to take care of himself—he tells me he has not time to take care of himself—which is very sad—but he is always wanted all round the country. I suppose there is not a man in such practice any where. But then, there is not so clever a man any where."

"And Mrs. Perry and the children, how are they? do the children grow?—I have a great regard for Mr. Perry. I hope he will be calling soon. He will be so pleased to see my little ones."

"I hope he will be here to-morrow, for I have a question or two to ask him about myself of some consequence. And, my dear, whenever he comes, you had better let him look at little Bella's throat."

"Oh! my dear sir, her throat is so much better that I have hardly any uneasiness about it. Either bathing has been of the greatest service to her, or else it is to be attributed to an excellent embrocation of Mr. Wingfield's, which we have been applying at times ever since August."

"It is not very likely, my dear, that bathing should have been of use to her—and if I had known you were wanting an embrocation, I would have spoken to—"

"You seem to me to have forgotten Mrs. and Miss Bates," said Emma. "I have not heard one inquiry after them."

"Oh! the good Bateses—I am quite ashamed of myself—but you mention them in most of your letters. I hope they are quite well. Good old Mrs. Bates—I will call upon her to-morrow, and take my children.—They are always so pleased to see my children.—And that excellent Miss Bates—such thorough worthy people!—How are they, sir!"

"Why, pretty well, my dear, upon the whole. But poor Mrs. Bates had a bad cold about a month ago."

"How sorry I am! But colds were never so prevalent as they have been this autumn. Mr. Wingfield told me that he had never known them more general or heavy—except when it has been quite an influenza."

"That has been a good deal the case, my dear; but not to the degree you mention. Perry says that colds have been very general, but not so heavy as he has very often known them in November. Perry does not call it altogether a sickly season."

"No, I do not know that Mr. Wingfield considers it *very* sickly, except—"

"Ah! my poor dear child, the truth is, that in London it is always a sickly season. Nobody is healthy in London, nobody can be. It is a dreadful thing to have you forced to live there!—so far off!—and the air so bad!"

"No, indeed—*we* are not at all in a bad air. Our part of London is so very superior to most others!—You must not confound us with London in general, my dear sir. The neighbourhood of Brunswick Square is very different from almost all the rest. We are so very airy! I should be unwilling, I own, to live in any other part of the town;—there is hardly any other that I could be satisfied to have my children in:—but *we* are so remarkably airy—Mr. Wingfield thinks the vicinity of Brunswick Square decidedly the most favourable as to air."

"Ah! my dear, it is not like Hartfield. You make the best of it—but after you have been a week at Hartfield, you are all of you different creatures; you do not look like the same. Now I cannot say, that I think you are any of you looking well at present."

"I am sorry to hear you say so, sir; but I assure you, excepting those little nervous head aches and palpitations which I am never entirely free from any where, I am quite well myself; and if the children were rather pale before they went to bed, it was only because they were a little more tired than usual, from their journey and the happiness of coming. I hope you will think better of their looks to-morrow; for I assure you Mr. Wingfield told me, that he did not believe he had ever sent us off all together, in such good case. I trust, at least, that you do not think Mr. Knightley looking ill,"—turning her eyes with affectionate anxiety towards her husband.

"Middling, my dear; I cannot compliment you. I think Mr. John Knightley very far from looking well."

"What is the matter, sir?—Did you speak to me?" cried Mr. John Knightley, hearing his own name.

"I am sorry to find, my love, that my father does not think you looking well—but I hope it is only from being a little fatigued. I could have wished, however, as you know, that you had seen Mr. Wingfield before you left home."

"My dear Isabella,"—exclaimed he hastily—"pray do not concern yourself about my looks. Be satisfied with doctoring and coddling yourself and the children, and let me look as I chuse."

"I did not thoroughly understand what you were telling your brother," cried Emma, "about your friend Mr. Graham's intending to have a bailiff from Scotland, to look after his new estate. But will it answer? Will not the old prejudice be too strong?"

And she talked in this way so long and successfully that, when forced to give her attention again to her father and sister, she had nothing worse to hear than Isabella's kind inquiry after Jane Fairfax;—and Jane Fairfax, though no great favourite with her in general, she was at that moment very happy to assist in praising (vol. i, 212–20)

(*Emma*, 100 101).

Perhaps the reader may collect from the preceding specimen both the merits and faults of the author. The former consists much in the force of a narrative conducted with much neatness and point, and a quiet yet comic dialogue, in which the characters of the speakers evolve themselves with dramatic effect. The faults, on the contrary, arise from the minute detail which the author's plan comprehends. Characters of folly or simplicity, such as those of old Woodhouse and Miss Bates, are ridiculous when first presented, but if too often brought forward or too long dwelt upon, their prosing is apt to become as tiresome in fiction as in real society. Upon the whole, the turn of this author's novels bears the same relation to that of the sentimental and romantic cast, that cornfields and cottages and meadows bear to the highly adorned grounds of a show mansion, or the rugged sublimities of a mountain landscape. It is neither so captivating as the one, nor so grand as the other, but it affords to those who frequent it a pleasure nearly allied with the experience of their own social habits; and what is of some importance, the youthful wanderer may return from his promenade to the ordinary business of life, without any chance of having his head turned by the recollection of the scene through which he has been wandering.

One word, however, we must say in behalf of that once powerful divinity, Cupid, king of gods and men, who in these times of revolution, has been assailed, even in his own kingdom of romance, by the authors who were formerly his devoted priests. We are quite aware that there are few instances of first attachment being brought to a happy conclusion, and that it seldom can be so in a state of society so highly advanced as to render early marriages among the better class, acts, generally speaking, of imprudence. But the youth of this realm need not at present be taught the doctrine of selfishness. It is by no means their error to give the world or the good things of the world all for love; and before the authors of moral fiction couple Cupid indivisibly with calculating prudence, we would have them reflect, that they may sometimes lend their aid to substitute more mean, more sordid, and more selfish motives of conduct, for the romantic feelings which their predecessors perhaps fanned into too powerful a flame. Who is it, that in his youth has felt a virtuous attachment, however romantic or however unfortunate, but can trace back to its influence much that his character may possess of what is honourable, dignified, and disinterested? If he recollects hours wasted in unavailing hope, or saddened by doubt and disappointment; he may also dwell on many which have been snatched from folly or libertinism, and dedicated to studies which might render him worthy of the object of his affection, or pave the way perhaps to that distinction necessary to raise him to an equality with her. Even the habitual indulgence of feelings totally unconnected with ourself and our own immediate interest, softens, graces, and amends the human mind; and after the pain of disappointment is past, those who survive (and by good fortune those are the greater number) are neither less wise nor less worthy members of society for having felt, for a time, the influence of a passion which has been well qualified as the "tenderest, noblest and best."

Notes

1. In R. B. Sheridan's play, *The Rivals* (1775), Lydia Languish hides her novels, including Henry Fielding, *Tom Jones* (1749), and Tobias Smollett, *The Adventures of Peregrine Pickle* (1751), and displays books of sermons and religions writings to give a more acceptable impression to her older relatives.

2. London, 1778.

3. Tony Lumpkin is a comic character in Oliver Goldsmith's popular play, *She Stoops to Conquer* (1773).

4. George Crabbe, "The Poor of the Borough: Ellen Orford," 113–119, *The Borough: A Poem in Twenty-Four Letters* (1810), Letter 20.

5. Maria Edgeworth's *Tales of Fashionable Life* had been published in 1812.

Jane Austen, ob. July 18, 1817

REGINALD FARRER

◆　◆　◆

To lounge away the time as they could, with sofas and chitchat,
and *Quarterly Reviews.*

—*Mansfield Park,* Chapter X.

THE CONCLUDING STORMS of a great conflict had hardly died
down, when her world, almost unaware, bade farewell to Jane Austen;
now, amid the closing cataclysms of a conflict yet more gigantic, we celebrate
the hundredth year of her immortality. Time is the woodsman who fells the
smaller trees and coppice in the forest of literature, and allows us at last to see
the true proportions of its enduring giants; and the century that has passed
since Jane Austen's death now sees her preeminence securely established. An
early editor could only dare timidly to suggest that perhaps she might be
found not wholly unworthy of a place in the same shelf with Miss Burney and
Miss Edgeworth. Alas for both these, gone by now into the spare bedroom,
and become the dusty curiosities of literature! Not even Jane Austen's devotion has availed to save Fanny Burney from a too-general oblivion, whereas
Jane Austen herself has long since taken rank as the centre of a cult as ardent
as a religion. There is no *via media*, indeed, where Jane Austen is concerned; by
those who might have lent features to her fools she is vividly disliked,* and by

---

* Women often appreciate her imperfectly, because she appreciated *them* so perfectly, and
so inexorably revealed them.

those for whom her fools were drawn, she is no less fervently adored. In water-logged trench, in cold cave of the mountains, in sickness and in health, in dulness, tribulation and fatigue, an ever-increasing crowd of worshippers flies insatiably for comfort and company perennially refreshing, to Hartfield and Randalls, Longbourn, Northanger, Sotherton and Uppercross.

Such positions in literature are not achieved by log-rolling. Macaulay blunders, indeed, in his praise, and in the instances he selects for it; but he undoubtedly hits the bull's eye with his usual essential accuracy, when he lights on the fact that Jane Austen is comparable only with Shakespeare.[1] For both attain their solitary and special supremacy by dint of a common capacity for intense vitalisation; both have the culminating gift of immediately projecting a living human being who is not only *a* human being, but also something much greater than any one person, a quintessentialised instance of humanity, a generalisation made incarnate and personal by genius. But the dramatist has the easier task; the novelist, unaided by actors or stage, has to impress his own imagination straight upon ours. And it is of this secret that Jane Austen is so capital a mistress; a prefatory line or two, an initial sentence, and there goes Mrs. Allen or Mrs. Price, a complete and complex identity, walking independently away down the ages. Even in their circumstances, too, Shakespeare and Jane Austen run curiously parallel. Our two greatest creators exist for us only in their work; and, when we search into their personal lives and tastes and tragedies, we glean nothing but a little chopped dull chaff of details, in which all trace of the sacred germ is lacking. In Jane Austen's case, indeed, the disappearance of the creator into his creation is made but the completer for the abundance of superficial details with which we are provided. When the dry bones of her facts are fitted together, there results for us only a lay-figure, comfortable and comely, but conveying no faintest suggestion of the genuine Jane Austen.

She was obviously ill-served by her circumstances. Behind the official biographies, and the pleasant little empty letters, and the accounts of how good she was to her mother and wouldn't use the sofa, we feel always that she really lived remote in a great reserve. She praised and valued domesticity indeed, sincerely loved her own family, and made domestic instincts a cardinal virtue in all her heroes. But the praise and value are rather official than personal; her only real intimate at home was her sister Cassandra, and it is significant that only upstairs, behind her shut door, did she read her own work aloud, for the benefit of her chosen circle in the younger generation. Yet more significant, though, is the fact that nowhere does she give any picture of united family happiness; the successful domestic unity will certainly not be successfully sought at Longbourn or Mansfield,

Northanger or Kellynch. This, to any one who understands Jane Austen's preoccupation with truth, and her selection of material only from among observed facts tested by personal experience, speaks volumes, in its characteristically quiet way, for her position towards her own family. She was in it; but she was not really of it.

Even on the point of her intimacy with Cassandra there is something curiously suggestive in the fact that, after her first two novels, she never again gives us a picture of two intimately united sisters. Maria and Julia are allies only till their interests clash; Isabella is nothing to Emma; only time and trials teach Fanny to surmount her first startled disapproval of Susan; and the best that Anne can feel for Mary Musgrove is that she "is not so repulsive and unsisterly as Elizabeth" (*Persuasion*, 43). On the other hand, in three out of these four books, the author's delight is transferred to the relations between brother and sister—Wentworth and "Sophy," Henry and Eleanor, William and Fanny, and, above all, for depth of tried alliance, Crawford and Mary. Finally, she does not even die for us of anything particular, but fades out, with Victorian gentility, in a hazy unspecified decline. How much more fortunate, in her different class, is Charlotte Brontë, of whom no detail is hidden from her admirers by any such instinct for muffling things up in discretions and evasions! Even in popular language this distinction holds; no one dreams of calling the lesser writer anything but "Charlotte Brontë," while there still exists a whole sect of Jane Austen's devotees, no Laodiceans either, who to this day will always talk of her as "Miss Austen." Which is as if one were to speak currently of Mr. Milton, and Monsieur de Molière.

These fantasies of propriety, together with her own misleadingly modest allusion to the "little piece of ivory" on which she worked, have done much to perpetuate the theory, still held among the profane, that she is a "limited" writer. It is by no means so that her faithful see their radiant and remorseless Jane; and, though criticism depends, in the last resort, chiefly on what the critic himself brings to his subject (so that what each man comes seeking, that he will most surely find), Jane Austen's personality may be much more profitably reconstructed in her work, than from the superficial details of her life, doled out to us by her biographer. A writer's fame, in fact, relies for its permanent value on his own transpiring personality; in every line he is inevitably "giving himself away," and the future of his work depends on whether what he has to give possesses the salted quality of eternity. And impersonality comes as the first ingredient in the specific for immortality. The self-revelation of the writer must be as severely implicit as it is universally pervasive; it must never be conscious or obtruded.

There is, indeed, a section of writers, as of readers, who believe in frequent appearances of the author before his curtain, to make deductions from his text, and point out conclusions. This is a pandering to laziness in the reader; every meaning should be clearly discoverable in the text, without its being necessary for the author himself to dig it out for us. And to such readers as these, who want their pabulum already peptonised, Jane Austen deliberately avoids appeal. As in her own life she evaded the lionising that lesser women covet, and would assuredly have approved Cassandra's destruction of her private letters, so in her work she no less carefully avoids overt appearance on her stage. She is there all the time, indeed, but never *in propria persona*, except when she gaily smiles through the opener texture of *Northanger Abbey*, or, with her consummate sense of art, mitigates for us the transition out of her paradises back into the grey light of ordinary life, by letting the word "I" demurely peer forth at last, as the fantasmagoria in *Mansfield Park*, *Emma* or *Northanger Abbey* begins to thin out to its final pages. Otherwise she is the most aloof of writers, and does not work "for such dull elves" (as she says herself) as will not so far come to meet the author as to make out for themselves his conclusions and deductions.

This elimination of the author is only part of the intense concentration which the greatest writers develop in their subject. The essence of conviction, in the game of make-believe, is to convince yourself first of all, finally and absolutely. This can only be done by forgetting yourself entirely, by blotting out the whole irrelevant world from your purview, and centralising, with a single-eyed undeviating passion of conviction, upon the tale you are setting out to live. It is at this point that all living writers (with the exception of Rhoda Broughton) fail. They are telling stories in which they have either no flesh-and-blood belief of their own, or else too much; telling them with an eye to their audience and to themselves and their own pet notions, telling them, that is, objectively, not subjectively, and piling up masses of detail and explanation in order to obscure the inner lack of any completed identity between the author and his matter.

It is precisely here that Jane Austen so magnificently succeeds. Wars may be raging to their end as the background of *Persuasion*, or social miseries strike a new facet of *Emma*; otherwise all the vast anguish of her time is non-existent to Jane Austen, when once she has got pen in hand, to make us a new kingdom of refuge from the toils and frets of life. Her kingdoms are hermetically sealed, in fact, and here lies the strength of their impregnable immortality; it is not without hope or comfort for us nowadays, to remember that *Mansfield Park* appeared the year before Waterloo, and *Emma* the year after. For Jane Austen is always concerned only with the universal, and not with the particular. And it is according as they invest their souls in the former or the latter that authors eternally survive or rapidly pass away. Fashions change, fads and fancies come and go, tyrannies and empires erupt and collapse; those who make events and contemporary ideas the matter of their work have their reward in instant appreciation of their topical value. And with their topical value they die.* Art is a mysterious entity, outside and beyond daily life, whether its manifestation be by painting or sculpture or literature. If it use outside events at all, it must subdue them to its medium, and become their master, not their mere vehicle. So a hundred thousand novels come and go; but Jane Austen can never be out of date, because she never was in any particular date (that is to say, never imprisoned in any), but is coextensive with human nature.

Talk of her "limitations" is vain, and based on a misapprehension. When we speak of her as our greatest artist in English fiction we do not mean that she has the loudest mastery of any particular mood, the most clamant voice, the widest gamut of subjects: we mean that she stands supreme and alone among English writers in possession of the secret which so many French ones possess—that is, a most perfect mastery of her weapons, a most faultless and precise adjustment of means to end. She is, in English fiction, as Milton in English poetry, the one completely conscious and almost unerring artist. This is to take only the technical side of her work; her scale and scope are different matters. There is, in some quarters, a tendency to quarrel with Jane Austen because in her books there is nothing that she never intended to be there, no heroic hectorings, no Brontesque ebulliencies, no mountain or moor or "bonny beck"[2] (to use Charlotte Brontë's own phrase)—surely one of the monumental ineptitudes of criticism, seeing that the most elementary axiom of art is the artist's initial right to choose his own medium. We have no more right, in fact, to cavil at Jane Austen for not writing *The Duchess of Malfi* than at Webster for not writing *Northanger Abbey*.

At the same time, it must never be thought that limitation of scene implies limitation of human emotion. The measure of perfection has no relation to the size of its material. Perfection is one and incommensurable. Class-limitation, in fact, is no limitation of sympathy; and a breaking heart is a breaking heart, no more nor less, whether it find vent in the ululations of Tamburlaine, or in the "almost screamed with agony" of Marianne

---

* After Mr. Gray of Sackville Street, Jane Austen specifies no tradesman, except Broadwood, nor even dwells on any detail of fashion.

Dashwood (*Sense and Sensibility*, 182). Jane Austen's heroes and heroines and subject-matter are, in fact, universal human nature, and conterminous with it, though manifested only in one class, with that class's superficial limitations, in habits and manner of life.

And here another error vitiates the caviller's thought. Readers fall into two groups—the objective and the subjective. And it is only the objective class who, because emotion is not vehemently expressed by Jane Austen, will fail to realise with what profound effect it is implied. She does not expound feeling; she conveys it. With her artist's instinct, she knows that exposition by the writer destroys conviction in the reader. She has at heart, all through her life, that maxim of the French which English writers find it so impossible to assimilate—"Glissez toujours, n'appuyez pas": do your work rightly, and trust the intelligence of the reader to do the rest. When Anne again meets Wentworth there is nothing shown in the text but the little flutter given to the sentence by the repetition of the descriptive adjective in:—"The room seemed full, full of persons and voices" (*P*, 59); but the sensitised reader is left fairly staggering in the gale of Anne's emotion, revealed in that tiny hint more intimately than by all the paragraphs of passionate prose in which other writers would exhaustively set out the emotions of Wentworth and Anne, until no emotion at all was left in the reader. For the objective writer toils and toils outside his subject, accumulating convincing details until conviction is destroyed; the subjective gives the bare and encyclopædic essential in a line or a word, and then goes on. And of all great writers Jane Austen is the most evocative, doing in half a dozen words (applied in exactly the proper measure, in exactly the proper place) what the sedulous subtleties of Henry James are unable to convey so clearly in as many fine-spun pages. Knightley, for instance, staying "vigorously" (*Emma*, 433) on, away from Emma in Brunswick Square, gives us in one syllable more of Knightley and more of Emma than whole long paragraphs of analysis.

And among the secrets of Jane Austen's inexhaustible charm is that her work, especially in her second period, is so packed with such minute and far-reaching felicities that the thousandth reading of *Emma* or *Persuasion* will be certain to reveal to you a handful of such brilliant jewels unnoticed before. If she has nothing to say to those who want to sit passive while the whole story is put down plain before them like meat on a plate, she has all the more delights to unfold for those who know that the whole point of reading lies in eager cooperation with a sympathetic writer. The more rigid, in fact, the elimination of the non-essential, the more blazing the certitude with which the essential is projected. Jane Austen is even of an Elizabethan economy in her stage-settings. Modern writers pretend to reveal their characters by dint of descriptions copious as an upholsterer's catalogue; she produces her details sparingly, bit by bit, only where each is dramatically necessary to the course of character or action; often, by one of her most characteristic exquisitenesses, they are only revealed in the conversation of her persons. And, in the result, with what a life-long intimacy do we come at last to know her houses and her rooms, her gardens and shrubberies! This indirect method, too, she often chooses, to give emotions and impressions and personal pictures. Elizabeth Bennet's own delightfulness is sensibly enhanced by that of Mrs. Gardiner, since she was so special a favourite there; while Elizabeth Elliot's "something so formal and *arrangé* in her air; and she sits so upright," (*P*, 215) though it comes quite at the end of the book, gives us an instant intimate vision of Lady Russell, besides flashing at us the whole essence of Elizabeth herself.

As for landscape, so often the stumbling-block of novelists, Jane Austen cannot be said to make any very serious use of it in her first period; but in the second, although she is far too craft-wise to fancy you can vitalise a character by dint of emotionalising its countryside and garden, she quite definitely (though still with finest economy) avails herself more and more of the outer world, not only for its value as a picture in itself—we may spend a vivid day at Sotherton—but also as playing its part in the development of her people. The squalor of Portsmouth, the autumn landscapes of Lyme and Uppercross, have a definite place in the evolution of Fanny and Anne; while the July storm which darkens the dark climax of *Emma* is the pathetic fallacy pure and simple. It is only towards the end of her own life, that is, with the deepening of her own sympathies, that her faultless sense of fitness and relevance so far widens also as to give greater latitude to her methods of inspiring sympathy.

For it is but fair to her cruder critics to admit that Jane Austen has no taste for expressed erotics, and will thereby always seem insipid to the large crowd of readers, chiefly women, who are responsible for that perennial ill-repute of fiction against which Jane Austen herself personally launches the novelist's Magna Carta in *Northanger Abbey*, because they read fiction principally as an erotic stimulant, and judge its merits accordingly, by the ardour of its descriptions and expressions. In this aspect of life Jane Austen has no interest. Her concern is primarily with character unfolded through love, not with that love's crudities of appetite and incident. In the supreme moments, in point of fact, humanity becomes inarticulate, and thus no longer gives material for art. Jane Austen, knowing this, is too honest to forge us false coin of phrases, and too much an artist to pad out her lines with asterisks and dashes and ejaculations. She accepts the condition, asks her reader to accept it also, and contents herself with dealing with the emotions on either side of the crucial outbreak. It is notorious how she avoids detail in her proposal-scenes; certainly not from "ladylike" cowardice, nor from any incapacity, but merely in her artist's certainty that the epical instants of life are not to be adequately expressed in words. "What did she say? Just what she should, of course: a lady always does" (*E*, 431). Jane Austen, with whimsical gaiety of candour, here lays down her position once for all, and frankly tells her reader that there are matters into which neither he nor she can decently pry. That she *could* tear a passion to tatters with the best of them, indeed, is shown by Marianne Dashwood; that she never repeated the picture shows her sense of its unfitness and fatal facility, by comparison with the subtler treatments of emotion in which alone she was interested. Any red-blooded writer can state passions, it takes a genius to suggest them; and Jane Austen is preeminently a clear-brained writer rather than a red-blooded one. Yet no one is left doubting Emma's feeling for Knightley, or Anne's for Wentworth, though nothing at all is said of physical attractions, and the whole effect is made by implication. But made it indubitably is, and indelibly.

On the feelings of her men, of course, Jane Austen has nothing to say at first hand, is too honest an artist to invent, and too clean a woman to attempt the modern female trick of gratifying her own passions by inventing a lover, and then identifying herself with his desires, in so far as she can concoct them. Yet it would be quite a mistake to call her men pallid or shadowy. In point of fact, they are usually carried out with all her vivid certainty, yet considered only in relation to her women, and thus, by comparison, quieter in colour, deliberately subordinate in her scheme. Even the earlier heroes will be found perfectly adapted to their place in her books, when once that place is understood; as for the later ones, they stand most definitely on legs of their own, so far as their movements in the story require. Perhaps the best of all is Knightley, not only in relation to Emma but also in himself.

Nor must it be brought against Jane Austen that she does not lard her work with sociology, religion or metaphysics. Such divagations may make a story more stirring; they certainly make it more ephemeral. And, against such writers as believe the novel is Heaven's appointed jam for the powder of their own opinions, Jane Austen decisively heads the other school, which believes that "the book, the whole book, and nothing but the book" is the novelist's best motto. She herself pours scorn on the notion that *Pride and Prejudice* would really be better if padded out with "solemn nonsense about Bonaparte"[3]; and where for once (in order to prove Fanny's brains) she ventures on irrelevant flights of rhetoric, she for once lamentably falls to earth, in those two speeches of Fanny's in the Vicarage shrubbery—deliverances false in fact, trite in thought, turgid and sententious in expression. Normally, however, she remains undistracted from the purpose of her book; and, from the first sentence, submerges herself in the single thought of the story's development, with that wholeheartedness of delight in creation for its own sake which is the prerogative of the highest genius alone, alone awakening in the reader an answering rapture of conviction and absorption. Thus it is that, to her faithful, Jane Austen has become flesh and blood of their mind's inmost fabric. Who commonly quotes Charlotte Brontë or George Eliot? But every turn and corner of life is illuminated or defined for us by some sentence of Jane Austen's; and every dim character in our "dusty mortal days" has something of one or another in the long gallery of her creations. Thus to become the very texture of humanity's mind and talk from generation to generation, is the attainment of the supreme visualisers only; talent, at the best, can merely photograph, either from the real or from an ideal.

SO FAR we have looked only at the literary aspect of Jane Austen. The secret of her immortality is to be found in that underlying something which is the woman herself; for, of all writers, she it is who pursues truth with most utter and undeviable devotion. The real thing is her only object always. She declines to write of scenes and circumstances that she does not know at first hand; she refuses recognition, and even condonement, to all thought or emotion that conflicts with truth, or burkes it, or fails to prove pure diamond to the solvent of her acid. She is, in fact, the most merciless, though calmest, of iconoclasts; only her calm has obscured from her critics the steely quality, the inexorable rigour of her judgment. Even Butler, her nearest descendant in this generation, never seems really to have recognised his affinity. For Jane Austen has no passion, preaches no gospel, grinds no axe; standing aloof from the world, she sees it, on the whole, as silly. She has no animosity for it; but she has no affection. She does not want to better fools, or to abuse them; she simply sets herself to glean pleasure from their folly. Nothing but the first-rate in life is good enough for her tolerance; remember Anne Elliot's definition of "good company," and her cousin's rejoinder, "That is not good company; that is the best" (*P*, 150).

   Everything false and feeble, in fact, withers in the demure greyness of her gaze; in "follies and nonsense, whims and inconsistencies" (*Pride and Prejudice*, 57), she finds nothing but diversion, dispassionate but pitiless. For, while no novelist is more sympathetic to real values and sincere emotion, none also is so keen on detecting false currency, or so relentless in exposing it. At times, even, her antagonism to conventionalities and shams betrays her almost to a touch of passion. Yet, if ever she seems cruel, her anger is but just impatience against the slack thought and ready-made pretences that pass current in the world and move her always to her quiet but destructive merriment; as in the famous outburst about Miss Musgrove's "large fat sighings over a son whom alive no one had cared for" (*P*, 68)—a *cri de cœur* for which the author for once feels immediately bound to come before the curtain, to mitigate it with a quasi-apology quite devoid of either conviction or recantation. Nor will she hear of any reserves in honesty and candour; not only the truth, but the whole truth, must be vital to any character of whom she herself is to approve. Civilised urbane discretion, and assent to social falsehoods, make strong points in Anne's private distrust of William Elliot, and in Fanny's disapproval of Henry Crawford, artfully thrown in contrast as he is against the breezy impetuous young frankness of William Price.

She is consumed with a passion for the real, as apart from the realistic; and the result is that her creations, though obviously observed, are no less obviously generalised into a new identity of their own. She acknowledges no individual portrait, such as those in which alone such essentially unimaginative writers as Charlotte Brontë can deal. And in this intense preoccupation with character, she is frankly bored with events; the accident at Lyme shows how perfunctorily she can handle a mere occurrence, being concentrated all the time on the emotions that engender it, and the emotions it engenders. Her very style is the mirror of her temperament. Naturally enough, she both writes and makes her people speak an English much more flowing and lucid than is fashionable in ordinary writers and ordinary life; but, allowing for this inevitable blemish, the note of her style is the very note of her nature, in its lovely limpidity, cool and clear and flashing as an alpine stream, without ebulliencies or turbidness of any kind. It is not for nothing that "rational" is almost her highest word of praise. Good sense, in the widest meaning of the word, is her be-all and end-all; the perfect σωφροσύνη which is also the perfect αὐταρκεῖα.

For her whole sex she revolts against "elegant females," (*PP*, 109) and sums up her ideal woman, not as a "good-natured unaffected girl" (a phrase which, with her, connotes a certain quite kindly contempt), but as a "rational creature" (*PP*, 109). The pretences of *Vanity Fair*, for instance, to be an historical novel, fade into the thinnest of hot air when one realises, with a gasp of amazement, that Amelia Sedley is actually meant to be a contemporary of Anne Elliot. And thus one understands what a deep gulf Victorianism dug between us and the past; how infinitely nearer to Jane

Austen are the sane sensible young women of our own day than the flopping vaporous fools who were the fashion among the Turkish-minded male novelists of Queen Victoria's fashions.* Take Catherine Morland, a country parson's daughter, suffered to run quite wild,† and compare her list of reading with the incredible Pinkertonian education in "accomplishments." Imagine Miss Pinkerton allowing Amelia Sedley to read *Othello*; or Amelia wishing to do so, or understanding any of it if she did! At the same time, the famous outburst in *Northanger Abbey* shows that, in those days as well as later, "imbecility in females is a great enhancement of their personal charms." It is by a most curious irony of fate, indeed, that the ignorant attribute to Jane Austen and her heroines just that very primness and futility of which she, and they, are most contemptuous.

Her heroines, indeed, are out-of-door creatures, by no means fettered by conventional ignorance or innocence; and they all have minds of their own so clear and firm that, while their good-feeling remains unalienated, their judgments equally remain unconciliated. "A knowledge, which she often wished less, of her father's character" (*P*, 34) is part of lovely gentle Anne; and even self-righteous Fanny owns to herself that *her* father was still worse than she had expected—"he swore and he drank, he was dirty and gross" (*Mansfield Park*, 389)—with a succinct yet comprehensive candour that would certainly not have marked any Victorian heroine's attitude towards her "dear papa." And, how much nearer we are to-day to Anne and Fanny than to the generation immediately behind us, is shown by the fact that Pastor Manders' ejaculation in *Ghosts*,[4] that it is Oswald's duty to love and honour his impossible dead father, represented such an accepted axiom to the Victorians that its obvious irony in the play was felt to be a blasphemy; whereas to us of to-day the irony has lost all point, because the axiom itself is seen as clearly to be mere nonsense, as it was seen long ago, by Fanny and Anne and Eleanor Tilney.

In fact, all the women whom Jane Austen commends are absolutely honest and well-bred in mind. Breeding is not a matter of birth or place, but

---

* It is but fair to add that male delight in female imbecility is as eternal as Jane Austen herself declared; and that Scott's heroines (with the exception of Diana Vernon) are generally of an insipid feebleness sinking to the lowest Victorian standards.

† Jane Austen seems to have postulated so much of intelligence in her girls, as to *prefer* for them a haphazard rather than a regular education. Elizabeth Bennet, also, was left to choose for herself whether she would learn or not; while Miss Lee's pompous curriculum at Mansfield is openly laughed at, and shown to lead to no good result, to no real education in character.

of attitude towards life; Jane Austen's standard, like Anne Elliot's behaviour, is as "consciously right as it is invariably gentle" (*P*, 153); and, one may add, as unselfconscious about its quality as real breeding is always bound to be. Her tone of perfect quiet assurance, and taking-for-grantedness, has nowhere been equalled. Many writers, even of the great (especially nowadays, and especially among women), are too painfully at ease in their Sions of castle or country-house,* with a naïve excessiveness, a solemn rapture of emphasis, that shows their inmost feeling to be really Mary Crawford's at finding herself in Mansfield Vicarage garden. Even Thackeray gloats over the silver coffeepots at Castle Gaunt; even Henry James lingers too lovingly amid the material details of what Gertrude Atherton would call "aristocratic" life; Jane Austen alone is as indifferent and as much at ease, wherever she goes, as those only can be who are to the manner and the matter born and bred. Note, with what decision, for instance, but with what a lack of betraying emphasis, she reserves "vulgar" forms, such as "quiz" and "beau," and "you was," to the exclusive use of her vulgar characters. And how it is only her underbred women—Isabella Thorpe, Mrs. Elton, Lucy Steele— who use the bare surname of a man; Jane and Elizabeth Bennet, even in their most intimate private dialogues, never talk of "Bingley" or "Darcy" until the familiarity has been justified by betrothal. And again, the middle-class sisters, Lady Bertram and Mrs. Norris, are to each other, respectively, "Sister" and "Lady Bertram," throughout their book. These are samples of the small unobtruded points that give Jane Austen's readers such unending delight.

LADY SUSAN is the first of her books to call for comment. It is not good; it is crude and hard, with the usual hardness of youth. Yet it is so important to the study of its author's career and temperament that it would be disastrous to omit it from future editions, in deference to any fancied wishes of her "shade."[5] The faults of youth are really only the excesses of what are to be excellences in the matured writer; and the cold unpleasantness of *Lady Susan* is but the youthful exaggeration of that irreconcilable judgment which is the very backbone of Jane Austen's power, and which, harshly evident in the first book, is the essential strength of all the later ones, finally protruding its bony structure nakedly again in *Persuasion*. But *Lady Susan* also links on to *Mansfield Park*. For where and when did Jane Austen come into contact with the "Smart Set" of her time? Biographies give no slightest hint; but we must

---

* Mary Crawford "had seen scores of great houses, and cared for none of them."

not forget Miss Mitford's impression of Jane Austen as a pretty little empty-headed husband-hunting fool. However violently at variance may be this verdict from all we can divine of Jane Austen, it was evidently this un-suspectedly gay creature who foregathered at one time with the "Souls," in intellectual attraction and moral repulsion. For out of the same set, brilliant and heartless, which is the very scene of *Lady Susan*, are ultimately to be projected Henry and Mary Crawford.

With *Sense and Sensibility* we approach the maturing Jane Austen. But it has the almost inevitable frigidity of a reconstruction, besides an equally inevitable uncertainty in the author's use of her weapons. There are *longueurs* and clumsinesses; its conviction lacks fire; its development lacks movement; its major figures are rather incarnate qualities than qualitied incarnations. Never again does the writer introduce a character so entirely irrelevant as Margaret Dashwood, or marry a heroine to a man so remote in the story as Colonel Brandon. This is not, however, to say that *Sense and Sensibility*, standing sole, would not be itself enough to establish an author's reputation. The opening dialogue, for instance, between John and Fanny Dashwood—obviously belonging to the second version of the story—ranks among the finest bits of revelation that even Jane Austen has given us; and criticism stands blissfully silent before Sir John Middleton, Mrs. Jennings, and the juxtaposition of Lady Middleton and Fanny Dashwood, "who sympathised with each other in an insipid propriety of demeanour and a general want of understanding." But its tremendous successors set up a standard beside which *Sense and Sensibility* is bound to appear grey and cool; nobody will choose this as his favourite Jane Austen, whereas each one of the others has its fanatics who prefer it above all the rest.

But now comes the greatest miracle of English Literature. Straight on the heels of *Lady Susan* and *Sense and Sensibility* this country parson's daughter of barely twenty-one breaks covert with a book of such effortless mastery, such easy and sustained brilliance, as would seem quite beyond reach of any but the most mature genius. Yet, though *Pride and Prejudice* has probably given more perfect pleasure than any other novel (Elizabeth, to Jane Austen first, and now to all time, "is as delightful a creature as ever appeared in print," literature's most radiant heroine, besides being the most personally redo-lent of her creator), its very youthful note of joyousness is also the ne-gation of that deeper quality which makes the later work so inexhaustible. Without ingratitude to the inimitable sparkle of this glorious book, even *Northanger Abbey*, in its different scale, must be recognised as of a more sump-tuous vintage. *Pride and Prejudice* is, in fact, alone among the Immortal Five, a story pure and simple, though unfolded in and by character, indeed, with a dexterity which the author never aimed at repeating. For, as Jane Austen's power and personality unfold, character becomes more and more the very fabric of her works, and the later books are entirely absorbed and dominated by their leading figures; whereas Darcy and Elizabeth are actors among others in their comedy, instead of being the very essence of it, like Anne or Emma. And to the reader, the difference is that, whereas he can never come to an end of the subtle delights that lurk in every sentence of the later books, there does come a point at which he has *Pride and Prejudice* completely assimilated.

Perhaps Jane Austen never quite recovered this first fine careless rapture; still, the book has other signs of youth. It has a vice-word, "tolerably," and its dialogue retains traces of Fanny Burney. Compare the heavy latinised paragraphs of the crucial quarrel between Darcy and Elizabeth (the sentence which proved so indelible a whip-lash to Darcy's pride is hardly capable of delivery in dialogue at all, still less by a young girl in a tottering passion) with the crisp and crashing exchanges in the parallel scene between Elton and Emma. The later book provides another comparison. Throughout, when once its secret is grasped, the reader is left in no doubt that subconsciously Emma was in love with Knightley all the time. In *Pride and Prejudice* the author has rather fumbled with an analogous psychological situation, and is so far from making clear the real feeling which underlies Elizabeth's deliberately fostered dislike of Darcy, that she has uncharacteristically left herself open to such a monstrous misreading as Sir Walter Scott's, who believed that Elizabeth was subdued to Darcy by the sight of Pemberley. In point of fact, we are expressly told that her inevitable feeling, "this might have been mine," is instantly extinguished by the belief that she could not bear it to be hers, at the price of having Darcy too; while her subsequent remark to Jane is emphatically a joke, and is immediately so treated by Jane herself ("another entreaty that she would be serious," (*PP*, 373) etc.), wiser than some later readers of the scene.

Sir Walter's example should be a warning of how easy it is to trip even amid the looser mesh of Jane Austen's early work. Rapid reading of her is faulty reading. As for Mr. Collins and Lady Catherine, whom some are ungrateful enough to call caricatures, it must definitely be said that they are figures of fun, indeed, but by no means figures of farce. At the same time both are certainly touched with a youthful sheer delight in their absurdity which gives to them an objective ebullience not to be found in more richly comic studies such as Lady Bertram or Mr. Woodhouse. Nor does Jane Austen ever again repeat the parallelism between two sisters, that makes the fabric of the two early books. Already, in her incisive treatment of

Charlotte Lucas, the later Jane Austen is foreshadowed; and *Pride and Prejudice* contains the first example of her special invention, the middle-aged married woman whose delightful presence in the middle-distance of the picture reflects an added pleasantness on the different leading figures with which Mrs. Gardiner, Mrs. Grant, Mrs. Weston, and Mrs. Croft are brought in contact, as foils and confidants. Had Macaulay happed on these examples, the proof of his contention would have been as unquestionable as its truth.

In *Northanger Abbey* Jane Austen takes a big stride forward. Developing her taste for technical problems, she here tackles a very difficult one—in an artist's consciousness of the problem, indeed, but with youth's indomitable unconsciousness of its full difficulty. A lesser writer, or a maturer, would have either jibbed at such a task as that of interweaving two motives, of parody and serious drama, or would have crashed heavily through their thin ice. In buoyancy of youth and certainty of power, Jane Austen skims straight across the peril, and achieves a triumph so complete that easy readers run the risk of missing both triumph and problem, in mere joy of the book. She even allows herself to dally here with her own delight, and personally steps forward in the tale with her three great personal outbreaks, on Novels, on Folly in Females, and on the Vanity of Feminine Motives in Dress. As for the reader, the closer his study of the dovetailing of the two motives, the profounder his pleasure. Parody rules, up to the arrival of Catherine at Northanger, which is the pivot of the composition; after which the drama, long-brewing out of the comic motive, runs current with it, and soon predominates. The requisite hyphen is provided by John and Isabella Thorpe, as differently important in one aspect of the tale as in the other. Each moment of the drama artfully echoes some note of the parody that had prevailed before; and the General's final outburst is just what had been fore-shadowed long before, in burlesque, of Mrs. Allen. Catherine herself suffers by this very nicety of poise and adjustment; she is really our most delightful of all *ingénues*, but her story is kept so constantly comic that one has no time to concentrate on its chief figure.

Fun, too, tends to overshadow the emotional skill with which the movement is developed. Even the processes by which Catherine so plausibly hardens herself into her grotesque belief that General Tilney killed his wife, even her stupefaction before the commonplaceness of the murdered martyr's room, pale beside the sudden comic tragedy of her awakening,* so

---

* Jane Austen loves to have her heroine taken in, either by herself or some one else; so that author and reader can enjoy a private smile together.

convincing as it is, so completely blending the two motives of the book, and, in itself, so vibrant with an emotion as genuine as its generating causes are ridiculous. "She raised her eyes to him more fully than she had ever done before," is an early, but very notable, instance of Jane Austen's peculiar power of conveying intense feeling with a touch. In fact, *Northanger Abbey* marks the point of transition between the author's first period and her second. Already character is a serious rival to the story; henceforth it becomes more and more the main motive, till finally we reach *Persuasion*, than which no known novel of anything like equal calibre is so entirely devoid of any "story" at all.

And now, in Jane Austen's life comes an unexpected gap. The family is moving; it goes to Bath; it goes to Portsmouth. In all those ten odd years she produces nothing, except the beginning of *The Watsons*, which she soon dropped in an unexplained distaste, for which critics have vainly sought a reason. Was it, perhaps, because these were the crucial years of the Napoleonic war, during which its stress was most felt, and concentration on novel-writing was found to be impossible? Much more probably she was simply fretted with removals and uncongenial surroundings; and unhappy, not only in general circumstances, but also with what gleam of personal romance came abortive into her own life. Anne Elliot's distaste for Bath has a more personal note than is usual in her creator's work, and the Portsmouth scenes of *Mansfield Park* a peculiarly *vécu* quality. Altogether one cannot but feel that in her thirties our heroine was not in health of body and spirit, nor in any environment sufficiently settled and sympathetic, to generate those floods of delight which she had hitherto poured forth. And then the family settles at Chawton. Immediately Jane Austen gets to work again; and with astounding fecundity pours forth the three supreme efforts of her maturity in the last three or four years before her death, presumably of cancer, at the age of forty-two. And not one of the three is a novel of laughter, like those of the earlier period.

Mansfield Park is Jane Austen's *gran rifiuto*, perhaps under the influence of the unhappiness through which she had been passing. None of her books is quite so brilliant in parts, none shows a greater technical mastery, a more audacious facing of realities, a more certain touch with character. Yet, alone of her books, *Mansfield Park* is vitiated throughout by a radical dishonesty, that was certainly not in its author's own nature. One can almost hear the clerical relations urging "dear Jane" to devote "her undoubted talent to the cause of righteousness"; indeed, if dates allowed, one could even believe that Mr. Clarke's unforgettable suggestion about the country clergyman had formed fruit in this biography of Edmund Bertram. In any case, her purpose of edification, being not her own, is always at cross-purposes with her unprompted joy in creation. She is always getting so interested in her subject, and so joyous in her management of it, that when her official purpose comes to mind, the resulting high sentiment or edifying speech is a wrench alike to one's attention and credulity. And this dualism of motive destroys not only the unity of the book, but its sincerity. You cannot palter with truth; one false assumption puts all the drawing and colouring out of gear.

For example, Jane Austen has vividly and sedulously shown how impossible a home is Mansfield for the young, with the father an august old Olympian bore, the mother one of literature's most finished fools, and the aunt its very Queen of Shrews; then suddenly, for edification, she turns to saying that Tom Bertram's illness converted him to a tardy appreciation of domestic bliss. Having said which, she is soon overmastered by truth once more, and lets slip that he couldn't bear his father near him, that his mother bored him, and that consequently these domestic blisses resolved themselves into better service than you'd get in lodgings, and the ministrations of the uninspiring Edmund. Worse still, because more vital in the book, is her constant deliberate weighting of the balance against Crawford and Mary, who obviously have her artist's affection as well as her moralist's disapproval (as is proved by the very violence of her outbreaks of injustice against them). The consequent strain is such that she defeats her own end by making us take their side against Edmund and Fanny. She throws away the last chance of imposing her view, when she makes Mary, *ex hypothesi* worldly, calculating and callous, not only accept a penniless dull little nobody as her brilliant brother's wife, but even welcome her with a generous cordiality of enthusiasm which sets Fanny's cold self-righteous attitude of criticism to the Crawfords in a more repellent light than ever.

The *dénouement* is an inevitable failure, accordingly. It is the harshest of those precipitate *coups de théâtre* by which Jane Austen, impatient of mere happenings, is too apt to precipitate the conclusions of her books, and jerk her reader's belief with a sudden peripety for which no previous symptom of character had prepared him. Indeed, *Pride and Prejudice* and *Northanger Abbey* are the only two of her books which work out to an inevitable end by means of character, and character alone. But the elopement of Crawford and Maria is a specially flagrant fraud on the reader, a dishonest bit of sheer bad art, meant to clear the field for Fanny, and wrench away the story from its obvious proper end, in the marriages of Edmund and Mary, Crawford and Fanny. However much an author may dislike letting his "pen dwell on guilt and misery," (*MP*, 461) this is no excuse for making Henry forfeit the woman he loves (and is winning), for the sake of another about whom he does not care two straws. Crawford was no mere boy, to be rushed by any married woman into a scandal so fatal to his plans; and without some sufficient explanation one utterly declines to believe he ever did so. Yet Jane Austen inartistically shirks giving any reason for a perversity otherwise incredible. It was not that she would not; her fundamental honesty told her she could not.

Yet Henry, after all, had a very lucky miss of Fanny. How he could ever seriously have wanted to marry her, in fact, becomes a puzzle, for she is the most terrible incarnation we have of the female prig-pharisee. Those who still survive of the Victorian school, which prized a woman in proportion as she was "little" and soft and silly, keep a special tenderness in their hearts for Fanny Price. Alas, poor souls, let them only have married her! Gentle and timid and shrinking and ineffectual as she seems, fiction holds no heroine more repulsive in her cast-iron self-righteousness and steely rigidity of prejudice; though allowance must be made, of course, as Jane Austen always implies it, and at least once definitely states it, for the jealousy that taints her whole attitude to Mary. Fate has not been kind to Mary Crawford. Her place in the book, her creator's spasms of bias against her, combine to obscure the fact that she is by far the most persistently brilliant of Jane Austen's heroines. It is mere unfair Fanny-feeling to pretend she has neither heart nor morals, but she predominates in brains; and, of all her creator's women, she would be the most delightful as a wife—to any man of brains himself, with income and position. For even dear Elizabeth might sometimes seem a trifle pert beneath the polluted shades of Pemberley, and dear Emma have her moments of trying to direct destiny at Donwell as disastrously as she'd already done at Hartfield.

On the whole, then, *Mansfield Park*, with its unparalleled flights counteracted by its unparalleled lapses, must count lower as an achievement than *Emma*, with its more equal movement, at a higher level of workmanship. Had it not been for its vitiating purpose, indeed, *Mansfield Park* would have taken highest rank. Amazing, even in Jane Austen, is the dexterity of the play scenes, and the day at Sotherton; amazing even in a French realist would be the unflinching veracity with which the Portsmouth episode is treated. Only those who have tried to write, perhaps, can fully realise the technical triumphs of Jane Austen. At Sotherton she has practically her whole cast on the stage at once, yet she juggles so accurately that each character not only keeps its own due importance but continues to evolve in exactly the proper relation to all the other ones. And this *tour de force* is bettered by the play scenes, prolonged over a whole period as they are, with an even larger crowd manœuvred simultaneously in a complicated maze of movement, that never for an instant fails to get each person into its right prominence at the required moment, without prejudice to the general figure of the dance and the particular positions of the other performers. It is a tragedy that skill so mature should here have been ruined by distracting purposes. All through *Mansfield Park*, in fact, Jane Austen is torn between the theory of what she ought to see, and the fact of what she does see. The vision is her own, the suggestion another's; and while, in talking of what she does see, she is here at her finest, in forcing herself to what she ought to see she is here at her worst; to say nothing of the harm done to her assumptions by her insight, and to her insight by her assumptions. ·

But now we come to the Book of Books, which is the book of Emma Woodhouse.* And justly so named, with Jane Austen's undeviating flair for the exact title. For the whole thing *is* Emma; there is only one short scene in which Emma herself is not on the stage; and that one scene is Knightley's conversation about her with Mrs. Weston. Take it all in all, *Emma* is the very climax of Jane Austen's work; and a real appreciation of *Emma* is the final test of citizenship in her kingdom. For this is not an easy book to read; it should never be the beginner's primer, nor be published without a prefatory synopsis. Only when the story has been thoroughly assimilated, can the infinite delights and subtleties of its workmanship begin to be appreciated, as you realise the manifold complexity of the book's web, and find that every sentence, almost every epithet, has its definite reference to equally unemphasised points before and after in the development of the plot. Thus it is that, while twelve readings of *Pride and Prejudice* give you twelve periods of pleasure repeated, as many readings of *Emma* give you that pleasure, not repeated only, but squared and squared again with each perusal, till at every fresh reading you feel anew that you never understood anything like the widening sum of its delights. But, until you know the story, you are apt to find its movement dense and slow and obscure, difficult to follow, and not very obviously worth the following.

For this is *the* novel of character, and of character alone, and of one dominating character in particular. And many a rash reader, and some who are not rash, have been shut out on the threshold of Emma's Comedy by a dislike of Emma herself. Well did Jane Austen know what she was about,

---

* "Heavens, let me not suppose that she dares go about Emma. Wood-houseing me!"— (*Emma*, 284)—a typical instance of a remark which, comic in itself, has a second comic intention, as showing Emma's own ridiculousness.

when she said, "I am going to take a heroine whom no one but myself will much like." And, in so far as she fails to make people like Emma, so far would her whole attempt have to be judged a failure, were it not that really the failure, like the loss, is theirs who have not taken the trouble to understand what is being attempted. Jane Austen loved tackling problems; her hardest of all, her most deliberate, and her most triumphantly solved, is Emma.

What is that problem? No one who carefully reads the first three opening paragraphs of the book can entertain a doubt, or need any prefatory synopsis; for in these the author gives us quite clear warning of what we are to see. We are to see the gradual humiliation of self-conceit, through a long self-wrought succession of disasters, serious in effect, but keyed in Comedy throughout. Emma herself, in fact, *is never to be taken seriously.* And it is only those who have not realised this who will be "put off" by her absurdities, her snobberies, her misdirected mischievous ingenuities. Emma is simply a figure of fun. To conciliate affection for a character, not because of its charms, but in defiance of its defects, is the loftiest aim of the comic spirit; Shakspeare achieved it with his besotted old rogue of a Falstaff, and Molière with Celimène. It is with these, not with "sympathetic" heroines, that Emma takes rank, as the culminating figure of English high-comedy. And to attain success in creating a being whom you both love and laugh at, the author must attempt a task of complicated difficulty. He must both run with the hare and hunt with the hounds, treat his creation at once objectively and subjectively, get inside it to inspire it with sympathy, and yet stay outside it to direct laughter on its comic aspects. And this is what Jane Austen does for Emma, with a consistent sublimity so demure that indeed a reader accustomed only to crude work might be pardoned for missing the point of her innumerable hints, and actually taking seriously, for example, the irony with which Emma's attitude about the Coles's dinner party is treated, or the even more convulsing comedy of Emma's reflexions after it. But only Jane Austen is capable of such oblique glints of humour; and only in *Emma* does she weave them so densely into her kaleidoscope that the reader must be perpetually on his guard lest some specially delicious flash escape his notice, or some touch of dialogue be taken for the author's own intention.

Yet, as Emma really does behave extremely ill by Jane Fairfax, and even worse by Robert Martin, merely to laugh would not be enough, and every disapproval would justly be deepened to dislike. But, when we realise that each machination of Emma's, each imagined piece of penetration, is to be a thread in the snare woven unconsciously by herself for her own enmeshing in disaster, then the balance is rectified again, and disapproval can lighten to laughter once more. For this is another of Jane Austen's triumphs here—the way in which she keeps our sympathies poised about Emma. Always some charm of hers is brought out, to compensate some specially silly and ambitious naughtiness; and even these are but perfectly natural, in a strong-willed, strong-minded girl of only twenty-one, who has been for some four years unquestioned mistress of Hartfield, unquestioned Queen of Highbury. Accordingly, at every turn we are kept so dancing up and down with alternate rage and delight at Emma that finally, when we see her self-esteem hammered bit by bit into collapse, the nemesis would be too severe, were she to be left in the depths. By the merciful intention of the book, however, she is saved in the very nick of time, by what seems like a happy accident, but is really the outcome of her own unsuspected good qualities, just as much as her disasters had been the outcome of her own most cherished follies.

In fact, Emma is intrinsically honest (it is not for nothing that she is given so unique a frankness of outlook on life); and her brave recognition of her faults, when confronted with their results, conduces largely to the relief with which we hail the solution of the tangle, and laugh out loud over "Such a heart, such a Harriet" (*E*, 475)! The remark is typical, both of Emma and of Emma's author. For this is the ripest and kindliest of all Jane Austen's work. Here alone she can laugh at people, and still like them; elsewhere her amusement is invariably salted with either dislike or contempt. *Emma* contains no fewer than four silly people, more or less prominent in the story; but Jane Austen touches them all with a new mansuetude, and turns them out as candidates for love as well as laughter. Nor is this all that must be said for Miss Bates and Mr. Woodhouse. They are actually inspired with sympathy. Specially remarkable is the treatment of Miss Bates, whose pathos depends on her lovableness, and her lovableness on her pathos, till she comes so near our hearts that Emma's abrupt brutality to her on Box Hill comes home to us with the actuality of a violent sudden slap in our own face. But then Miss Bates, though a twaddle, is by no means a fool; in her humble, quiet, unassuming happiness, she is shown throughout as an essentially wise woman. For Jane Austen's mood is in no way softened to the second-rate and pretentious, though it is typical of *Emma* that Elton's full horror is only gradually revealed in a succession of tiny touches, many of them designed to swing back sympathy to Emma; even as Emma's own bad behaviour on Box Hill is there to give Jane Fairfax a lift in our sympathy at her critical moment, while Emma's repentance afterwards is just what is wanted to win us back to Emma's side again, in time for the coming catastrophe. And even Elton's "broad handsome face," in which "every feature works," (*E*, 111) pales before that of the lady who "was, in short, so very ready to have him." (*E*, 182) "He called her Augusta; how delightful!" (*E*, 272)

Jane Austen herself never calls people she is fond of by these fancy names, but reserves them for such female cads or cats as Lydia Bennet, Penelope Clay, Selina Suckling, and "the charming Augusta Hawkins." (*E*, 181) It is characteristic, indeed, of her methods in *Emma*, that, though the Sucklings never actually appear, we come to know them (and miss them) as intimately as if they did. Jane Austen delights in imagining whole vivid sets of people, never on the stage, yet vital in the play; but in *Emma* she indulges herself, and us, unusually lavishly, with the Sucklings at Maple Grove, the Dixons in Ireland, and the Churchills at Enscombe. As for Frank, he is among her men what Mary Crawford is among her women, a being of incomparable brilliance, moving with a dash that only the complicated wonderfulness of the whole book prevents us from lingering to appreciate. In fact, he so dims his cold pale Jane by comparison that one wonders more than ever what he saw in her. The whole Frank-Jane intrigue, indeed, on which the story hinges, is by no means its most valuable or plausible part. But Jane Fairfax is drawn in dim tones by the author's deliberate purpose. She had to be dim. It was essential that nothing should bring the secondary heroine into any competition with Emma. Accordingly Jane Fairfax is held down in a rigid dulness so conscientious that it almost defeats another of her *raisons d'être* by making Frank's affection seem incredible.

But there is very much more in it than that. Emma is to behave so extremely ill in the Dixon matter that she would quite forfeit our sympathy, unless we were a little taught to share her unregenerate feelings for the "amiable, upright, perfect Jane Fairfax." (*E*, 243) Accordingly we are shown Jane Fairfax always from the angle of Emma; and, despite apparently artless words of eulogy, the author is steadily working all the time to give us just that picture of Jane, as a cool, reserved, rather sly creature, which is demanded by the balance of emotion and the perspective of the picture.* It is curious, indeed, how often Jane Austen repeats a favourite composition; two sympathetic figures, major and minor, set against an odious one. In practice, this always means that, while the odious is set boldly out in clear lines and brilliant colour, the minor sympathetic one becomes subordinate

---

* Remember, also, that Jane Austen did herself personally hate everything that savoured of reserve and disingenuousness, "trick and littleness."

to the major, almost to the point of dulness. The respective positions of Emma, Jane, and Mrs. Elton shed a flood of light back on the comparative paleness of Eleanor Tilney, standing in the same minor relation to Catherine, as against Isabella Thorpe; and the trouble about *Sense and Sensibility* is that, while Marianne and Elinor are similarly set against Lucy, Elinor, hypothetically the minor note to Marianne, is also, by the current and intention of the tale, raised to an equal if not more prominent position,* thus jangling the required chord, so faultlessly struck in *Northanger Abbey*, and in *Emma* only marred by the fact that Jane Fairfax's real part is larger than her actual sound-value can be permitted to be.

Sentimentality has busied itself over the mellowing influences of approaching death, evident in *Persuasion*. The only such evidences are to be found in its wearinesses and unevennesses, and in the reappearance of that bed-rock hardness which only in *Lady Susan* stands out so naked. Jane Austen herself felt its faults more strongly than subsequent generations have done. She was depressed about the whole book. And what she meant, however much one may disagree, is plain. *Persuasion* has its uncertainties; the touch is sometimes vague, too heavy here, too feeble there—Mrs. Smith is introduced with too much elaboration, Anne Elliot with too little; balance is lost, and the even, assured sweep of *Emma* changes to a fitful wayward beauty. This is at once the warmest and the coldest of Jane Austen's works, the softest and the hardest. It is inspired, on the one hand, by a quite new note of glacial contempt for the characters she doesn't like, and, on the other, by an intensified tenderness for those she does. The veil of her impersonality wears thin; *Persuasion* is no Comedy, like *Emma*, and contains no woven pattern of Austenian irony. The author allows herself to tell her tale almost openly, and, in her strait treatment of Lady Russell and the Dowager Viscountess, shows very plainly her own characteristic attitude towards the artificial claims of rank—with such decision, indeed, that one wonders why, with *Persuasion* to his hand, Mr. Goldwin Smith should have been at pains to note a mere flash of "radical sympathy" in "poor Miss Taylor" (where, in point of fact, there is no trace of it). As for Mrs. Clay, she is introduced with so much more emphasis than her ultimate place in the story warrants, that it looks as if she had originally been meant to play a much larger part in it. And worst of all is the violent and ill-contrived exposure of William Elliot, which is also wholly unnecessary, since we are expressly told that not even

---

* The first version of the book was called *Elinor and Marianne*; which quite clearly, coming from Jane Austen, shows that Elinor was meant to be the dominant figure.

for Kellynch could Anne have brought herself to marry the man associated with it. In fact, the whole Clay-Elliot imbroglio that cuts the non-existent knot at the end of the book is perhaps the clumsiest of Jane Austen's *coups de théâtre*, though not deliberately false as that of Mansfield Park.

And yet, when everything is said and done in criticism, those who love *Persuasion* best of all Jane Austen's books have no poor case to put forward. For *Persuasion* is primarily Anne Elliot. And Anne Elliot is a puzzling figure in our literature. She is not a *jeune fille*, she is not gay or happy, brilliant or conspicuous; she is languidly, if not awkwardly brought on the stage, unemphasised, unemphatic. And yet Anne Elliot is one of fiction's greatest heroines. Gradually her greatness dawns. The more you know of her, the more you realise how perfectly she incarnates the absolute lady, the very counterpart, in her sex, of the καλοκάγαθòς among men. And yet there is so little that is obvious to show for all this. For the book is purely a cry of feeling; and, if you miss the feeling, you miss all. It sweeps through the whole story in a vibrating flood of loveliness; yet nothing very much is ever said. Jane Austen has here reached the culminating point in her art of conveying emotion without expression. Though *Persuasion* moves very quietly, without sobs or screams, in drawing rooms and country lanes, it is yet among the most emotional novels in our literature.

Anne Elliot suffers tensely, hopelessly, hopefully; she never violates the decencies of silence, she is never expounded or exposed. And the result is that, for such as can feel at all, there is more intensity of emotion in Anne's calm (at the opposite pole to Marianne's "sensibility") than in the wildest passion-tatterings of Maggie Tulliver or Lucy Snowe; and that culminating little heart-breaking scene between Harville and Anne (quite apart from the amazing technical skill of its contrivance) towers to such a poignancy of beauty that it takes rank with the last dialogue of mother and daughter in the *Iphigeneia*, as one of the very sacred things of literature that one dares not trust oneself to read aloud. And any other ending would be unbearable. So completely, in fact, do Anne and her feelings consume the book that the object of them becomes negligible. Wentworth, delightful jolly fellow that he is (with his jolly set of sailor-friends, whom Anne so wanted for hers), quite fades out of our interest, and almost out of our sight.

It is not so with the rest of the people, however. I have had curious testimony to their singular actuality. A great friend of mine, a man who never opens a book by any chance, if a newspaper be to hand, finding himself shut up for weeks in a tiny Chinese town on the borders of Tibet, was driven at last, in sheer desperation of dulness, to Jane Austen. I watched the experiment with awe and anguish. I might have spared myself.

Emma baffled him indeed, but *Pride and Prejudice* took him by storm. And then, to my terror, he took up *Persuasion*; for surely of all her works, the appeal of *Persuasion* is the most delicate and elusive. But again I might have spared my fears. *Persuasion* had the greatest success of all; for days, if not weeks, my friend went mouthing its phrases, and chewing the cud of its felicities. "That Sir Walter," he would never weary of repeating, "he's a *nib!*" And when I tried to find out what had so specially delighted him in *Persuasion*, he suddenly and finally summed up the whole of Jane Austen and her work:— "Why, all those people, they're—they're *real!*"

Notes

1. Thomas Babington Macaulay, unsigned article, "The Diaries and Letters of Mme D'Arblay," *Edinburgh Review* (January 1843), lxxvi, 561 2. Reprinted in B. C. Southam, ed., *Jane Austen: The Critical Heritage, Vol. 1. 1811–1870* (London: Routledge & Kegan Paul, 1968), 122–123.

2. Charlotte Brontë to G. H. Lewes, 12 January, 1848, Reprinted in *Critical Heritage*, I. 126.

3. To Cassandra Austen, 4 February, 1813, *Jane Austen's Letters*, ed. Deirdre Le Faye, 3rd. ed. (Oxford: Oxford University Press, 1995), 203.

4. Henrik Ibsen, *Ghosts* (1881).

5. "Shade," is a reference to Austen's comment on *Pride and Prejudice*, of 4 February 1813, *Jane Austen's Letters*, 203.

Emma and the Legend
of Jane Austen

LIONEL TRILLING

◆ ◆ ◆

IT IS POSSIBLE to say of Jane Austen, as perhaps we can say of no other
writer, that the opinions which are held of her work are almost as interesting, and almost as important to think about, as the work itself. This
statement, even with the qualifying "almost," ought to be, on its face, an
illegitimate one. We all know that the reader should come to the writer with
no preconceptions, taking no account of any previous opinion. But this, of
course, he cannot do. Every established writer exists in the aura of his
legend—the accumulated opinion that we cannot help being aware of, the
image of his personality that has been derived, correctly or incorrectly, from
what he has written. In the case of Jane Austen, the legend is of an unusually
compelling kind. Her very name is a charged one. The homely quaintness of
the Christian name, the cool elegance of the surname, seem inevitably to
force upon us the awareness of her sex, her celibacy, and her social class.
"Charlotte Brontë" rumbles like thunder and drowns out any such special
considerations. But "Jane Austen" can by now scarcely fail to imply femininity, and, at that, femininity of a particular kind and in a particular social
setting. It dismays many new readers that certain of her admirers call her
Jane, others Miss Austen. Either appellation suggests an unusual, and
questionable, relation with this writer, a relation that does not consort with

the literary emotions we respect. The new reader perceives from the first that he is not to be permitted to proceed in simple literary innocence. Jane Austen is to be for him not only a writer but an issue. There are those who love her; there are those—no doubt they are fewer but they are no less passionate—who detest her; and the new reader understands that he is being solicited to a fierce partisanship, that he is required to make no mere literary judgment but a decision about his own character and personality, and about his relation to society and all of life.

And indeed the nature of the partisanship is most intensely personal and social. The matter at issue is: What kind of people like Jane Austen? What kind of people dislike her? Sooner or later the characterization is made or implied by one side or the other, and with extreme invidiousness. It was inevitable that there should arise a third body of opinion, which holds that it is not Jane Austen herself who is to be held responsible for the faults that are attributed to her by her detractors, but rather the people who admire her for the wrong reasons and in the wrong language and thus create a false image of her. As far back as 1905 Henry James was repelled by what a more recent critic, Professor Marvin Mudrick, calls "gentle-Janeism" and he spoke of it with great acerbity.[1] James admired Jane Austen; his artistic affinity with her is clear, and he may be thought to have shared her social preferences and preoccupations. Yet James could say of her reputation that it had risen higher than her intrinsic interest warranted: the responsibility for this, he said, lay with "the body of publishers, editors, illustrators, producers of magazines, which have found their 'dear,' our dear, everybody's dear Jane so infinitely to their material purpose."[2] In our own day, Dr. Leavis's admiration for Jane Austen is matched in intensity by his impatience with her admirers.[3] Mr. D. W. Harding in a well-known essay[4] has told us how the accepted form of admiration of Jane Austen kept him for a long time from reading her novels, and how he was able to be at ease with them only when he discovered that they were charged with scorn of the very people who set the common tone of admiration. And Professor Mudrick, in the preface to his book on Jane Austen,[5] speaks of the bulk of the criticism of her work as being "a mere mass of cozy family adulation, self-glorif[ication] . . . and nostalgic latterday enshrinements of the gentle-hearted chronicler of Regency order." It is the intention of Professor Mudrick's book to rescue Jane Austen from coziness and nostalgia by representing her as a writer who may be admired for her literary achievement, but who is not to be loved, and of whom it is to be said that certain deficiencies of temperament account for certain deficiencies of her literary practice.

The impatience with the common admiring view of Jane Austen is not hard to understand and sympathize with, the less so because (as Mr. Harding and Professor Mudrick say) admiration seems to stimulate self-congratulation in those who give it, and to carry a reproof of the deficient sensitivity, reasonableness, and even courtesy, of those who withhold their praise. One may refuse to like almost any author and incur no other blame from his admirers than that of being wanting in taste in that one respect. But not to like Jane Austen is to put oneself under suspicion of a general personal inadequacy and even—let us face it—of a want of breeding.

This is absurd and distasteful. And yet we cannot deal with this unusual— this extravagantly personal—response to a writer simply in the way of condemnation. No doubt every myth of a literary person obscures something of the truth. But it may also express some part of the truth as well. If Jane Austen is carried outside the proper confines of literature, if she has been loved in a fashion that some temperaments must find objectionable and that a strict criticism must call illicit, the reason is perhaps to be found not only in the human weakness of her admirers, in their impulse to self-flattery, or in whatever other fault produces their deplorable tone. Perhaps a reason is also to be found in the work itself, in some unusual promise that it seems to make, in some hope that it holds out.

OF JANE AUSTEN'S six great novels *Emma* is surely the one that is most fully representative of its author. *Pride and Prejudice* is of course more popular. It is the one novel in the canon that "everybody" reads, the one that is most often reprinted. *Pride and Prejudice* deserves its popularity, but it is not a mere snobbery, an affected aversion from the general suffrage, that makes thoughtful readers of Jane Austen judge *Emma* to be the greater book—not the more delightful but the greater. It cannot boast the brilliant, unimpeded energy of *Pride and Prejudice*, but that is because the energy which it does indeed have is committed to dealing with a more resistant matter. In this it is characteristic of all three novels of Jane Austen's mature period, of which it is the second. *Persuasion*, the third and last, has a charm that is traditionally, and accurately, called "autumnal," and it is beyond question a beautiful book. But *Persuasion*, which was published posthumously and which may not have been revised to meet the author's full intention, does not have the richness and substantiality of *Emma*. As for *Mansfield Park*, the first work of the mature period, it quite matches *Emma* in point of substantiality, but it makes a special and disturbing case. Greatly admired in its own day—far more than *Emma*— *Mansfield Park* is now disliked by many readers who like everything else that Jane Austen wrote. They are repelled by its heroine and by all that she seems to imply of the author's moral and religious preferences at this moment of her life, for Fanny Price consciously devotes herself to virtue and piety, which she achieves by a willing submissiveness that goes against the modern grain. What is more, the author seems to be speaking out against wit and spiritedness (while not abating her ability to represent these qualities), and virtually in praise of dullness and acquiescence, and thus to be condemning her own peculiar talents. *Mansfield Park* is an extraordinary novel, and only Jane Austen could have achieved its profound and curious interest, but its moral tone is antipathetic to contemporary taste, and no essay I have ever written has met with so much resistance as the one in which I tried to say that it was not really a perverse and wicked book. But *Emma*, as richly complex as *Mansfield Park*, arouses no such antagonism, and the opinion that holds it to be the greatest of all Jane Austen's novels is, I believe, correct.

Professor Mudrick says that everyone has misunderstood *Emma*, and he may well be right, for *Emma* is a very difficult novel. We in our time are used to difficult books and like them. But *Emma* is more difficult than any of the hard books we admire. The difficulty of Proust arises from the sheer amount and complexity of his thought, the difficulty of Joyce from the brilliantly contrived devices of representation, the difficulty of Kafka from a combination of doctrine and mode of communication. With all, the difficulty is largely literal; it lessens in the degree that we attend closely to what the books say; after each sympathetic reading we are the less puzzled. But the difficulty of *Emma* is never overcome. We never know where to have it. If we finish it at night and think we know what it is up to, we wake the next morning to believe it is up to something quite else; it has become a different book. Reginald Farrer speaks at length of the difficulty of *Emma* and then goes on to compare its effect with that of *Pride and Prejudice*. "While twelve readings of *Pride and Prejudice* give you twelve periods of pleasure repeated, as many readings of *Emma* give you that pleasure, not repeated only, but squared and squared again with each perusal, till at every fresh reading you feel anew that you never understood anything like the widening sum of its delights."[6] This is so, and for the reason that none of the twelve readings permits us to flatter ourselves that we have fully understood what the novel is doing. The effect is extraordinary, perhaps unique. The book is like a person—not to be comprehended fully and finally by any other person. It is perhaps to the point that it is the only one of Jane Austen's novels that has for its title a person's name.

For most people who recognize the difficulty of the book, the trouble begins with Emma herself. Jane Austen was surely aware of what a complexity she was creating in Emma, and no doubt that is why she spoke of her as "a heroine whom no one will like except myself." Yet this puts it in a minimal way—the question of whether we will like or not like Emma does not encompass the actuality of the challenge her character offers. John Henry Newman stated the matter more accurately, and very charmingly, in a letter of 1837.[7] He says that Emma is the most interesting of Jane Austen's heroines, and that he likes her. But what is striking in his remark is this sentence: "I feel kind to her whenever I think of her." This does indeed suggest the real question about Emma, whether or not we will find it in our hearts to be kind to her.

Inevitably we are attracted to her, we are drawn by her energy and style, and by the intelligence they generate. Here are some samples of her characteristic tone:

"Never mind, Harriet, I shall not be a poor old maid; it is poverty only which makes celibacy contemptible to a generous public!"

(*Emma*, 85)

Emma was sorry; to have to pay civilities to a person she did not like through three long months!—to be always doing more than she wished and less than she ought!

(*E*, 166)

"I do not know whether it ought to be so, but certainly silly things do cease to be silly if they are done by sensible people in an impudent way. Wickedness is always wickedness, but folly is not always folly."

(*E*, 212)

"Oh! I always deserve the best treatment, because I never put up with any other."

(*E*, 474)

[On an occasion when Mr. Knightley comes to a dinner party in his carriage, as Emma thinks he should, and not on foot:] "There is always a look of consciousness or bustle when people come in a way which they know to be beneath them. You think you carry it off very well, I dare say, but with you it is a sort of bravado, an air of affected unconcern; I always observe it whenever I meet you under these circumstances. *Now* you have nothing to try for. You are not afraid of being supposed ashamed. You are not striving to look taller than any body else. *Now* I shall really be happy to walk into the same room with you."

(*E*, 213)

We cannot be slow to see what is the basis of this energy and style and intelligence. It is self-love. There is a great power of charm in self-love, although, to be sure, the charm is an ambiguous one. We resent it and resist it, yet we are drawn by it, if only it goes with a little grace or creative power. Nothing is easier to pardon than the mistakes and excesses of self-love: if we are quick to condemn them, we take pleasure in forgiving them. And with good reason, for they are the extravagance of the first of virtues, the most basic and biological of the virtues, that of self-preservation.

But we distinguish between our response to the self-love of men and the self-love of women. No woman could have won the forgiveness that has been so willingly given (after due condemnation) to the self-regard of, say, Yeats and Shaw. We understand self-love to be part of the moral life of all men; in men of genius we expect it to appear in unusual intensity and we take it to be an essential element of their power. The extraordinary thing about Emma is that she has a moral life as a man has a moral life. And she doesn't have it as a special instance, as an example of a new kind of woman, which is the way George Eliot's Dorothea Brooke has her moral life, but quite as a matter of course, as a given quality of her nature.

And perhaps that is what Jane Austen meant when she said that no one would like her heroine—and what Newman meant when he said that he felt kind to Emma whenever he thought of her. She needs kindness if she is to be accepted in all her exceptional actuality. Women in fiction only rarely have the peculiar reality of the moral life that self-love bestows. Most commonly they exist in a moonlike way, shining by the reflected moral light of men. They are "convincing" or "real" and sometimes "delightful," but they seldom exist as men exist—as genuine moral destinies. We do not take note of this; we are so used to the reflected quality that we do not observe it. It is only on the rare occasions when a female character like Emma confronts us that the difference makes us aware of the usual practice. Nor can we say that novels are deficient in realism when they present women as they do: it is the presumption of our society that women's moral life is not as men's. No change in the modern theory of the sexes, no advance in status that women have made, has yet contradicted this. The self-love that we do countenance in women is of a limited and passive kind, and we are troubled if it is as assertive as the self-love of men is permitted, and expected, to be. Not men alone, but women as well, insist on this limitation, imposing the requirement the more effectually because they are not conscious of it.

But there is Emma, given over to self-love, wholly aware of it and quite cherishing it. Mr. Knightley rebukes her for heedless conduct and says, "I leave you to your own reflections." And Emma wonderfully replies:

"Can you trust me with such flatterers? Does my vain spirit ever tell me I am wrong?" (*E*, 330). She is "Emma, never loth to be first" (*E*, 71), loving preeminence and praise, loving power and frank to say so.

Inevitably we are drawn to Emma. But inevitably we hold her to be deeply at fault. Her self-love leads her to be a self-deceiver. She can be unkind. She is a dreadful snob.

Her snobbery is of the first importance in her character, and it is of a special sort. The worst instance of it is very carefully chosen to put her thoroughly in the wrong. We are on her side when she mocks Mrs. Elton's vulgarity, even though we feel that so young a woman (Emma is twenty) ought not set so much store by manners and tone—Mrs. Elton, with her everlasting barouche-landau and her *"caro sposo"* and her talk of her spiritual "resources," is herself a snob in the old sense of the word, which meant a vulgar person aspiring to an inappropriate social standing. But when Emma presumes to look down on the young farmer, Robert Martin, and undertakes to keep little Harriet Smith from marrying him, she makes a truly serious mistake, a mistake of nothing less than national import.

Here it is to be observed that *Emma* is a novel that is touched—lightly but indubitably—by national feeling. Perhaps this is the result of the Prince Regent's having expressed his admiration for *Mansfield Park* and his willingness to have the author dedicate her next book to him: it is a circumstance which allows us to suppose that Jane Austen thought of herself, at this point in her career, as having, by reason of the success of her art, a relation to the national ethic. At any rate, there appears in *Emma* a tendency to conceive of a specifically English ideal of life. Knightley speaks of Frank Churchill as falling short of the demands of this ideal: "No, Emma, your amiable young man can be amiable only in French, not in English. He may be very aimable, have very good manners, and be very agreeable; but he can have no English delicacy towards the feelings of other people: nothing really amiable about him" (*E*, 149). Again, in a curiously impressive moment in the book, we are given a detailed description of the countryside as seen by the party at Donwell Abbey, and this comment follows: "It was a sweet view—sweet to the eye and the mind. English verdure, English culture [agriculture, of course, is meant], English comfort, seen under a sun bright without being oppressive" (*E*, 360). This is a larger consideration than the occasion would appear to require; there seems no reason to expect this vision of "England's green and pleasant land." Or none until we note that the description of the view closes thus: ". . . and at the bottom of this bank, favourably placed and sheltered, rose the Abbey-Mill Farm, with meadows in front, and the river making a close and handsome curve around it" (*E*, 360). Abbey-Mill Farm is the property of young Robert Martin, for whom Emma has expressed a principled social contempt, and the little burst of strong feeling has the effect, among others, of pointing up the extremity of Emma's mistake.

It is often said, sometimes by way of reproach, that Jane Austen took no account in her novels of the great political events of her lifetime, nor of the great social changes that were going on in England. "In Jane Austen's novels," says Arnold Hauser in his *Social History of Art*, "social reality was the soil in which characters were rooted but in no sense a problem which the novelist made any attempt to solve or interpret."[8] The statement, true in some degree, goes too far. There is in *some* sense an interpretation of social problems in Jane Austen's contrivance of the situation of Emma and Robert Martin. The yeoman class had always held a strong position in English class feeling, and, at this time especially, only stupid or ignorant people felt privileged to look down upon it. Mr. Knightley, whose social position is one of the certainties of the book, as is his freedom from any trace of snobbery, speaks of young Martin, who is his friend, as a "gentleman farmer," and it is clear that he is on his way to being a gentleman pure and simple. And nothing was of greater importance to the English system at the time of the French Revolution than the relatively easy recruitment to the class of gentlemen. It made England unique among European nations. Here is Tocqueville's view of the matter as set forth in the course of his explanation of why England was not susceptible to revolution as France was:

It was not merely parliamentary government, freedom of speech, and the jury system that made England so different from the rest of contemporary Europe. There was something still more distinctive and more far-reaching in its effects. England was the only country in which the caste system had been totally abolished, not merely modified. Nobility and commoners joined forces in business enterprises, entered the same professions, and—what is still more significant—intermarried. The daughter of the greatest lord in the land could marry a "new" man without the least compunction....

Though this curious revolution (for such in fact it was) is hidden in the mists of time, we can detect traces of it in the English language. For several centuries the word "gentleman" has had in England a quite different application from what it had when it originated.... A study of the connection between the history of language and history proper would certainly be revealing. Thus if we follow the mutation in time and place of the English word "gentleman" (a derivative of our *gentilhomme*), we find its connotation being steadily widened in England as the classes draw nearer to each other and intermingle. In each successive century we find it being applied to men a little lower in the social scale. Next, with the English, it crosses to America. And now in America, it is applicable to all male citizens, indiscriminately. Thus its history is the history of democracy itself.[9]

Emma's snobbery, then, is nothing less than a contravention of the best—and safest—tendency of English social life. And to make matters worse, it is a principled snobbery. "A young farmer . . . is the very last sort of person to raise my curiosity The yeomanry are precisely the order of people with whom I feel that I can have nothing to do. A degree or two lower, and a creditable appearance might interest me; I might hope to be useful to their families in some way or other. But a farmer can need none of my help, and is therefore in one sense as much above my notice as in every other he is below it" (*E*, 29). This is carefully contrived by the author to seem as dreadful as possible; it quite staggers us, and some readers will even feel that the author goes too far in permitting Emma to make this speech.

Snobbery is the grossest fault that arises from Emma's self love, but it is not the only fault. We must also take account of her capacity for unkindness. This can be impulsive and brutal, as in the witticism directed to Miss Bates at the picnic, which makes one of the most memorable scenes in the whole range of English fiction; or extended and systematic, as in her conspiracy with Frank Churchill to quiz Jane Fairfax. Then we know her to be a gossip, at least when she is tempted by Frank Churchill. She finds pleasure in dominating and has no compunctions about taking over the rule of Harriet Smith's life. She has been accused, on the ground of her own estimate of herself, of a want of tenderness, and she has even been said to be without sexual responsiveness.

Why, then, should anyone be kind to Emma? There are several reasons, of which one is that we come into an unusual intimacy with her. We see her in all the elaborateness of her mistakes, in all the details of her wrong conduct. The narrative technique of the novel brings us very close to her and makes us aware of each misstep she will make. The relation that develops between ourselves and her becomes a strange one—it is the relation that exists between our ideal self and our ordinary fallible self. We become Emma's helpless conscience, her unavailing guide. Her fault is the classic one of *hubris*, excessive pride, and it yields the classic result of blindness, of an inability to interpret experience to the end of perceiving reality, and we are aware of each false step, each wrong conclusion, that she will make. Our hand goes out to hold her back and set her straight, and we are distressed that it cannot reach her.

There is an intimacy anterior to this. We come close to Emma because, in a strange way, she permits us to—even invites us to—by being close to herself. When we have said that her fault is *hubris* or self-love, we must make an immediate modification, for her self-love, though it involves her in self-deception, does not lead her to the ultimate self-deception—she believes she is clever, she insists she is right, but she never says she is good. A consciousness is always at work in her, a sense of what she ought to be and do. It is not an infallible sense, anything but that, yet she does not need us, or the author, or Mr. Knightley, to tell her, for example, that she is jealous of Jane Fairfax and acts badly to her; indeed, "she never saw [Jane Fairfax] without feeling that she had injured her" (*E*, 167). She is never offended—she never takes the high self-defensive line—when once her bad conduct is made apparent to her. Her sense of her superiority leads her to the "insufferable vanity" of believing "herself in the secret of everybody's feelings" and to the "unpardonable arrogance" of "proposing to arrange everybody's destiny" (*E*, 412–413), yet it is an innocent vanity and an innocent arrogance which, when frustrated and exposed, do not make her bitter but only ashamed. That is why, bad as her behavior may be, we are willing to be implicated in it. It has been thought that in the portrait of Emma there is "an air of confession," that Jane Austen was taking account of "something offensive" that she and others had observed in her own earlier manner and conduct, and whether or not this is so, it suggests the quality of intimacy which the author contrives that we shall feel with the heroine.

Then, when we try to explain our feeling of kindness to Emma, we ought to remember that many of her wrong judgments and actions are directed to a very engaging end, a very right purpose. She believes in her own distinction and vividness and she wants all around her to be distinguished and vivid. It is indeed unpardonable arrogance, as she comes to see, that she should undertake to arrange Harriet Smith's destiny, that she plans to "form" Harriet, making her, as it were, the mere material or stuff of a creative act. Yet the destiny is not meanly conceived, the act is meant to be truly creative—she wants Harriet to be a distinguished and not a commonplace person, she wants nothing to be commonplace, she requires of life that it be well shaped and impressive, and alive. It is out of her insistence that the members of the picnic shall cease being dull and begin to be witty that there comes her famous insult to Miss Bates. Her requirement that life be vivid is too often expressed in terms of social deportment—she sometimes talks like a governess or a dowager—but it is, in its essence, a poet's demand.

She herself says that she lacks tenderness, although she makes the self-accusation in her odd belief that Harriet possesses this quality; Harriet is soft and "feminine," but she is not tender. Professor Mudrick associates the deficiency with Emma's being not susceptible to men.[10] This is perhaps so; but if it is, there may be found in her apparent sexual coolness something that is impressive and right. She makes great play about the feelings and about the fineness of the feelings that one ought to have; she sets great store by literature (although she does not read the books she prescribes for herself) and makes it a condemnation of Robert Martin that he does not read novels. Yet although, like Don Quixote and Emma Bovary, her mind is shaped and deceived by fiction, she is remarkable for the actuality and truth of her sexual feelings. Inevitably she expects that Frank Churchill will fall in love with her and she with him, but others are more deceived in the outcome of this expectation than she is—it takes but little time for her to see that she does not really respond to Churchill, that her feeling for him is no more than the lively notice that an attractive and vivacious girl takes of an attractive and vivacious young man. Sentimental sexuality is not part of her nature, however much she feels it ought to be part of Harriet Smith's nature. When the right time comes, she chooses her husband wisely and seriously and eagerly.

There is, then, sufficient reason to be kind to Emma, and perhaps for nothing so much as the hope she expresses when she begins to understand her mistakes, that she will become "more acquainted with herself." And, indeed, all through the novel she has sought better acquaintance with herself, not wisely, not adequately, but assiduously. How modern a quest it is, and how thoroughly it confirms Dr. Leavis's judgment that Jane Austen is the first truly modern novelist of England. "In art," a critic has said, "the decision to be revolutionary usually counts for very little. The most radical changes have come from personalities who were conservative and even convention-al. . . ."[11] Jane Austen, conservative and even conventional as she was, perceived the nature of the deep psychological change which accompanied the establishment of democratic society—she was aware of the increase of the psychological burden of the individual, she understood the new necessity of conscious self-definition and self-criticism, the need to make private judgments of reality.[12] And there is no reality about which the modern person is more uncertain and more anxious than the reality of himself.

BUT THE CHARACTER OF EMMA is not the only reason for the difficulty of the novel. We must also take into account the particular genre to which the novel in some degree belongs—the pastoral idyll. It is an archaic genre which has the effect of emphasizing by contrast the brilliant modernity of Emma, and its nature may be understood through the characters of Mr. Woodhouse and Miss Bates.

These two people proved a stumbling-block to one of Jane Austen's most distinguished and devoted admirers, Sir Walter Scott. In his review of *Emma* in the *Quarterly Review*, Scott said that "characters of folly and simplicity, such as old Woodhouse and Miss Bates" are "apt to become tiresome in fiction as in real society."[13] But Scott is wrong. Mr. Woodhouse and Miss Bates are remarkably interesting, even though they have been created on a system of character portrayal that is no longer supposed to have validity—they exist by reason of a single trait which they display whenever they appear. Miss Bates is possessed of continuous speech and of a perfectly free association of ideas which is quite beyond her control; once launched into utterance, it is impossible for her to stop. Mr. Woodhouse, Emma's father, has no other purpose in life than to preserve his health and equanimity, and no other subject of conversation than the means of doing so. The commonest circumstances of life present themselves to him as dangerous—to walk or to drive is to incur unwarrantable risk, to eat an egg not coddled in the prescribed way is to invite misery; nothing must ever change in his familial situation; he is appalled by the propensity of young people to marry, and to marry *strangers* at that.

Of the two "characters of folly and simplicity," Mr. Woodhouse is the more remarkable because he so entirely, so extravagantly, embodies a principle—of perfect stasis, of entire inertia. Almost in the degree that Jane Austen was interested in the ideal of personal energy, she was amused and attracted by persons capable of extreme inertness. She does not judge them harshly, as we incline to do—we who scarcely recall how important a part in Christian feeling the dream of *rest* once had. Mr. Woodhouse is a more extreme representation of inertness than Lady Bertram of *Mansfield Park*. To say that he represents a denial of life would not be correct. Indeed, by his fear and his movelessness, he affirms life and announces his naked unadorned wish to avoid death and harm. To life, to mere life, he sacrifices almost everything.

But if Mr. Woodhouse has a more speculative interest than Miss Bates, there is not much to choose between their achieved actuality as fictional characters. They are, as I have said, created on a system of character portrayal that we regard as primitive, but the reality of existence which fictional characters may claim does not depend only upon what they do, but also upon what others do to or about them, upon the way they are regarded and responded to. And in the community of Highbury, Miss Bates and Mr. Woodhouse are sacred. They are fools, to be sure, as everyone knows. But they are fools of a special and transcendent kind. They are innocents—of such is the kingdom of heaven. They are children, who have learned nothing of the guile of the world. And their mode of existence is the key to the nature of the world of Highbury, which is the world of the pastoral idyll. London is but sixteen miles away—Frank Churchill can ride there and back for a haircut—but the proximity of the life of London serves but to emphasize the spiritual geography of Highbury. The weather plays a great part in *Emma;* in no other novel of Jane Austen's is the succession of the seasons, and cold and heat, of such consequence, as if to make the point which the pastoral idyll characteristically makes, that the only hardships that man ought to have to endure are meteorological. In the Forest of Arden we suffer only "the penalty of Adam,/The seasons' difference," and Amiens' song echoes the Duke's words:

> Here shall he see
> No enemy
> But winter and rough weather.[14]

Some explicit thought of the pastoral idyll is in Jane Austen's mind, and with all the ambivalence that marks the attitude of *As You Like It* toward the dream of man's life in nature and simplicity. Mrs. Elton wants to make the strawberry party at Donwell Abbey into a *fête champête*: "It is to be a morning scheme, you know, Knightley; quite a simple thing. I shall wear a large bonnet, and bring one of my little baskets hanging on my arm. Here,— probably this basket with pink ribbon. Nothing can be more simple, you see. And Jane will have such another. There is to be no form or parade—a sort of gipsy party.—We are to walk about your gardens, and gather the strawberries ourselves, and sit under trees;—and whatever else you may like to provide, it is to be all out of doors—a table spread in the shade, you know. Every thing as natural and simple as possible. Is not that your idea?" (*E*, 355) To which Knightley replies: "Not quite. My idea of the simple and natural will be to have the table spread in the dining-room. The nature and the simplicity of gentlemen and ladies, with their servants and furniture, I think is best observed by meals within doors. When you are tired of eating strawberries in the garden, there will be cold meat in the house" (*E*, 355).

That the pastoral idyll should be mocked as a sentimentality by its association with Mrs. Elton, whose vulgarity in large part consists in flaunting the cheapened version of high and delicate ideals, and that Knightley should answer her as he does—this is quite in accordance with our expectation of

Jane Austen's judgment. Yet it is only a few pages later that the members of the party walk out to see the view and we get that curious passage about the sweetness of the view, "sweet to the eye and to the mind." And we cannot help feeling that "English verdure, English culture, English comfort, seen under a sun bright without being oppressive" make an England seen—if but for the moment—as an idyll.

The idyll is not a genre which nowadays we are likely to understand. Or at least not in fiction, the art which we believe must always address itself to actuality. The imagination of felicity is difficult for us to exercise. We feel that it is a betrayal of our awareness of our world of pain, that it is politically inappropriate. And yet one considerable critic of literature thought otherwise. Schiller is not exactly of our time, yet he is remarkably close to us in many ways and he inhabited a world scarcely less painful than ours, and he thought that the genre of the idyll had an important bearing upon social and political ideas. As Schiller defines it, the idyll is the literary genre that "presents the idea and description of an innocent and happy humanity."[15] This implies remoteness from the "artificial refinements of fashionable society"; and to achieve this remoteness poets have commonly set their idylls in actually pastoral surroundings and in the infancy of humanity. But the limitation is merely accidental—these circumstances "do not form the object of the idyll, but are only to be regarded as the most natural means to attain this end. The end is essentially to portray man in a state of innocence, which means a state of harmony and peace with himself and the external world." And Schiller goes on to assert the political importance of the genre: "A state such as this is not merely met with before the dawn of civilization; it is also the state to which civilization aspires, as to its last end, if only it obeys a determined tendency in its progress. The idea of a similar state, and the belief in the possible reality of this state, is the only thing that can reconcile man with all the evils to which he is exposed in the path of civilization. . . ."

It is the poet's function—Schiller makes it virtually the poet's political duty—to represent the idea of innocence in a "sensuous" way, that is, to make it seem real. This he does by gathering up the elements of actual life that do partake of innocence, and that the predominant pain of life leads us to forget, and forming them into a coherent representation of the ideal.[16]

But the idyll as traditionally conceived has an aesthetic deficiency of which Schiller is quite aware. Works in this genre, he says, appeal to the heart but not to the mind. "We can only seek them and love them in moments in which we need calm, and not when our faculties aspire after movement and exercise. A morbid mind will find its *cure* in them, a sound soul will not find its *food* in them. They cannot vivify, they can only soften." For the idyll excludes the idea of activity, which alone can satisfy the mind—or at least the idyll as it has been traditionally conceived makes this exclusion, but Schiller goes on to imagine a transmutation of the genre in which the characteristic calm of the idyll shall be "the calm that follows accomplishment, not the calm of indolence—the calm that comes from the equilibrium reestablished between the faculties and not from the suspending of their exercise. . . ."

It is strange that Schiller, as he projects this new and as yet unrealized idea, does not recur to what he has previously said about comedy. To the soul of the writer of tragedy he assigns the adjective "sublime," which for him implies reaching greatness by intense effort and strength of will; to the soul of the writer of comedy he assigns the adjective "beautiful," which implies the achievement of freedom by an activity which is easy and natural. "The noble task of comedy," he says, "is to produce and keep up in us this freedom of mind." Comedy and the idyll, then, would seem to have a natural affinity with each other. Schiller does not observe this, but Shakespeare knew it—the curious power and charm of *As You Like It* consists of bringing the idyll and comedy together, of making the idyll the subject of comedy, even of satire, yet without negating it. The mind teases the heart, but does not mock it. The unconditioned freedom that the idyll hypothecates is shown to be impossible, yet in the demonstration a measure of freedom is gained.

So in *Emma* Jane Austen contrives an idyllic world, or the closest approximation of an idyllic world that the genre of the novel will permit, and brings into contrast with it the actualities of the social world, of the modern self. In the precincts of Highbury there are no bad people, and no adverse judgments to be made. Only a modern critic, Professor Mudrick, would think to call Mr. Woodhouse an idiot and an old woman: in the novel he is called "the kindhearted, polite old gentleman" (*E*, 295). Only Emma, with her modern consciousness, comes out with it that Miss Bates is a bore, and only Emma can give herself to the thought that Mr. Weston is *too* simple and openhearted, that he would be a "higher character" if he were not quite so friendly with everyone. It is from outside Highbury that the peculiarly modern traits of insincerity and vulgarity come, in the person of Frank Churchill and Mrs. Elton. With the exception of Emma herself, every person in Highbury lives in harmony and peace—even Mr. Elton would have been all right if Emma had let him alone!—and not merely because they are simple and undeveloped: Mr. Knightley and Mrs. Weston are no less innocent than Mr. Woodhouse and Miss Bates. If they please us and do not bore us by a perfection of manner and feeling which is at once lofty and homely, it is because we accept the assumptions of the idyllic world which they inhabit—we have been led to believe that man may actually live "in harmony and peace with himself and the external world."

The quiet of Highbury, the unperturbed spirits of Mr. Woodhouse and Miss Bates, the instructive perfection of Mr. Knightley and Mrs. Weston, constitute much of the charm of *Emma*. Yet the idyllic stillness of the scene and the loving celebration of what, for better or worse, is fully formed and changeless, is of course not what is decisive in the success of the novel. On the contrary, indeed: it is the idea of activity and development that is decisive. No one has put better and more eloquently what part this idea plays in Jane Austen's work than an anonymous critic writing in the *North British Review* in 1870:[17]

> Even as a unit, man is only known to [Jane Austen] in the process of his formation by social influences. She broods over his history, not over his individual soul and its secret workings, nor over the analysis of its faculties and organs. She sees him, not as a solitary being completed in himself, but only as completed in society. Again, she contemplates virtues, not as fixed quantities, or as definable qualities, but as continual struggles and conquests, as progressive states of mind, advancing by repulsing their contraries, or losing ground by being overcome. Hence again the individual mind can only be represented by her as a battle-field where contending hosts are marshalled, and where victory inclines now to one side and now to another. A character therefore unfolded itself to her, not in statuesque repose, not as a model without motion, but as a dramatic sketch, a living history, a composite force, which could only exhibit what it was by exhibiting what it did. Her favourite poet Cowper taught her,
> By ceaseless action all that is subsists.[18]

The mind as a battlefield: it does not consort with some of the views of Jane Austen that are commonly held. Yet this is indeed how she understood the mind. And her representation of battle is the truer because she could imagine the possibility of victory—she did not shrink from the idea of victory—and because she could represent harmony and peace.

The anonymous critic of the *North British Review* goes on to say a strange and startling thing—he says that the mind of Jane Austen was "saturated" with a "Platonic idea." In speaking of her ideal of "intelligent love"—the phrase is perfect—he says that it is based on the "Platonic idea that the giving and receiving of knowledge, the active formation of another's character, or the more passive growth under another's guidance, is the truest and strongest foundation of love."[19] It is an ideal that not all of us will think possible of realization and that some of us will not want to give even a theoretical assent to. Yet most of us will consent to think of it as one of the most attractive of the idyllic elements of the novel. It proposes to us the hope of victory in the battle that the mind must wage, and it speaks of the expectation of allies in the fight, of the possibility of community—not in actuality, not now, but perhaps again in the future, for do we not believe, or almost believe, that there was community in the past?

The impulse to believe that the world of Jane Austen really did exist leads to notable error. "Jane Austen's England" is the thoughtless phrase which is often made to stand for the England of the years in which our author lived, although any serious history will make it sufficiently clear that the England of her novels was not the real England, except as it gave her the license to imagine the England which we call hers. This England, especially as it is represented in *Emma*, is an idyll. The error of identifying it with the actual England ought always to be remarked. Yet the same sense of actuality that corrects the error should not fail to recognize the remarkable force of the ideal that leads many to make the error. To represent the possibility of controlling the personal life, of becoming acquainted with ourselves, of creating a community of "intelligent love"—this is indeed to make an extraordinary promise and to hold out a rare hope. We ought not be shocked and repelled if some among us think there really was a time when such promises and hopes were realized. Nor ought we be entirely surprised if, when they speak of the person who makes such promises and holds out such hopes, they represent her as not merely a novelist, if they find it natural to deal with her as a figure of legend and myth.

Notes

1. Marvin Mudrick, *Jane Austen: Irony as Defense and Discovery* (Princeton, N.J.: Princeton University Press, 1952), vii.

2. Henry James, *The Question of Our Speech; The Lesson of Balzac: Two Lectures* (Boston: Houghton Mifflin, 1905).

3. F. R. Leavis, *The Great Tradition* (London: Chatto and Windus, 1948).

4. "Regulated Hatred: An Aspect of the Work of Jane Austen," *Scrutiny* VIII (March 1940).

5. *Jane Austen: Irony as Defense and Discovery.*

6. "Jane Austen," *Quarterly Review* 228 (July 1917) Reprinted in this casebook, 75.

7. 19 January 1837, *The Letters and Diaries of John Henry Newman, Vol VI, January 1837– December 1838*, ed. Gerard Tracey (Oxford: Clarendon Press, 1984), 16.

8. Arnold Hauser, *The Social History of Art*, 2 vols (London: Routledge and Kegan Paul, 1951), II, 825–826.

9. Alexis de Tocqueville, *The Old Regime and the French Revolution*, Anchor edition (Garden City, N.Y.: Doubleday, 1955), 82–83. Tocqueville should not be understood as saying that there was no class system in England but only that there was no caste system, caste differing from class in its far greater rigidity. In his sense of the great advantage that England enjoyed, as compared with France, in having no caste system, Tocqueville inclines to represent the class feelings of the English as being considerably more lenient than in fact they were. Still, the difference between caste and class and the social and political importance of the "gentleman" are as great as Tocqueville says.

10. Mudrick, *Jane Austen: Irony as Defense and Discovery*, 181–206.

11. Harold Rosenberg, "Revolution and the Idea of Beauty," *Encounter* (December 1953).

12. See Abram Kardiner, *The Psychological Frontiers of Society* (New York: Columbia University Press, 1945), 410. In commenting on the relatively simple society which is described in James West's *Plainville, U.S.A.*, Dr. Kardiner touches on a matter which is dear, and all too dear, to Emma's heart—speaking of social mobility in a democratic, but not classless, society, he says that the most important criterion of class is "manners," that "knowing how to behave" is the surest means of rising in the class hierarchy. Nothing is more indicative of Jane Austen's accurate awareness of the mobility of her society than her concern not so much with manners themselves as with her characters' concern with manners.

13. Walter Scott, unsigned review of *Emma* in *Quarterly Review* XIV (188–201) 188–201, included in this casebook, 55.

14. William Shakespeare, *As You Like It* II, i, 5–6; II, v, 40–43.

15. "On Simple and Sentimental Poetry," in *Essays Aesthetical and Philosophical* (London: Bohn, 1875).

16. Schiller, in speaking of the effectiveness that the idyll should have, does not refer to the pastoral-idyllic element of Christianity which represents Christ as an actual shepherd.

17. Richard Simpson, *North British Review* lxxii (April 1870): 129–52. Reprinted in B. C. Southam, ed., *Jane Austen: The Critical Heritage, Vol. 1: 1811–1870* (London: Routledge & Kegan Paul, 1968), 241–265.

18. William Cowper, *The Task*, Book I, 367. Reprinted in *Critical Heritage* I, 249–250.

19. Emma's attempt to form the character of Harriet is thus a perversion of the relation of Mrs. Weston and Mr. Knightley to herself—it is a perversion, says the *North British* critic, adducing Dante's "*amoroso uso de sapienza*," because it is without love.

Control of Distance in Jane Austen's *Emma*

WAYNE C. BOOTH

◆ ◆ ◆

Sympathy and Judgment in *Emma*

HENRY JAMES ONCE described Jane Austen as an instinctive novelist whose effects, some of which are admittedly fine, can best be explained as "part of her unconsciousness." It is as if she "fell-a-musing" over her work-basket, he said, lapsed into "wool-gathering," and afterward picked up "her dropped stitches" as "little masterstrokes of imagination."[1] The amiable accusation has been repeated in various forms, most recently as a claim that Jane Austen creates characters toward whom we cannot react as she consciously intends.[2]

Although we cannot hope to decide whether Jane Austen was entirely conscious of her own artistry, a careful look at the technique of any of her novels reveals a rather different picture from that of the unconscious spinster with her knitting needles. In *Emma* especially, where the chances for technical failure are great indeed, we find at work one of the unquestionable masters of the rhetoric of narration.

At the beginning of *Emma*, the young heroine has every requirement for deserved happiness but one. She has intelligence, wit, beauty, wealth, and position, and she has the love of those around her. Indeed, she thinks herself completely happy. The only threat to her happiness, a threat of which she is unaware, is herself: charming as she is, she can neither see her own excessive pride honestly nor resist imposing herself on the lives of others. She is deficient both in generosity and in self-knowledge. She discovers and corrects her faults only after she has almost ruined herself and her closest friends. But with the reform in her character, she is ready for marriage with the man she loves, the man who throughout the book has stood in the reader's mind for what she lacks.

It is clear that with a general plot of this kind Jane Austen gave herself difficulties of a high order. Though Emma's faults are comic, they constantly threaten to produce serious harm. Yet she must remain sympathetic or the reader will not wish for and delight sufficiently in her reform.

Obviously, the problem with a plot like this is to find some way to allow the reader to laugh at the mistakes committed by the heroine and at her punishment, without reducing the desire to see her reform and thus earn happiness. In *Tom Jones* this double attitude is achieved, as we have seen, partly through the invention of episodes producing sympathy and relieving any serious anxiety we might have, and partly through the direct and sympathetic commentary. In *Emma*, since most of the episodes must illustrate the heroine's faults and thus increase either our emotional distance or our anxiety, a different method is required. If we fail to see Emma's faults as revealed in the ironic texture from line to line, we cannot savor to the full the comedy as it is prepared for us. On the other hand, if we fail to love her, as Jane Austen herself predicted we would[3]—if we fail to love her more and more as the book progresses—we can neither hope for the conclusion, a happy and deserved marriage with Knightley following upon her reform, nor accept it as an honest one when it comes.[4] Any attempt to solve the problem by reducing either the love or the clear view of her faults would have been fatal.

Sympathy through Control of Inside Views

The solution to the problem of maintaining sympathy despite almost crippling faults was primarily to use the heroine herself as a kind of narrator, though in third person, reporting on her own experience. So far as we know, Jane Austen never formulated any theory to cover her own practice; she invented no term like James's "central intelligence" or "lucid reflector" to describe her method of viewing the world of the book primarily through Emma's own eyes. We can thus never know for sure to what extent James's accusation of "unconsciousness" was right. But whether she was inclined to speculate about her method scarcely matters; her solution was clearly a brilliant one. By showing most of the story through Emma's eyes, the author insures that we shall travel with Emma rather than stand against her. It is not simply that Emma provides, in the unimpeachable evidence of her own conscience, proof that she has many redeeming qualities that do not appear on the surface; such evidence could be given with authorial commentary, though perhaps not with such force and conviction. Much more important, the sustained inside view leads the reader to hope for good fortune for the character with whom he travels, quite independently of the qualities revealed.

Seen from the outside, Emma would be an unpleasant person, unless, like Mr. Woodhouse and Knightley, we knew her well enough to infer her true worth. Though we might easily be led to laugh at her, we could never be made to laugh sympathetically. While the final unmasking of her faults and her humiliation would make artistic sense to an unsympathetic reader, her marriage with Knightley would become irrelevant if not meaningless. Unless we desire Emma's happiness and her reform which alone can make that happiness possible, a good third of this book will seem irredeemably dull.

Yet sympathetic laughter is never easily achieved. It is much easier to set up a separate fool for comic effects and to preserve your heroine for finer things. Sympathetic laughter is especially difficult with characters whose faults do not spring from sympathetic virtues. The grasping but witty Volpone can keep us on his side so long as his victims are more grasping and less witty than he, but as soon as the innocent victims, Celia and Bonario, come on stage, the quality of the humor changes; we no longer delight unambiguously in his triumphs. In contrast to this, the great sympathetic comic heroes often are comic largely because their faults, like Uncle Toby's sentimentality, spring from an excess of some virtue. Don Quixote's madness is partly caused by an excess of idealism, an excess of loving concern for the unfortunate. Every crazy gesture he makes gives further reason for loving the well-meaning old fool, and we can thus laugh at him in somewhat the same spirit in which we laugh at our own faults—in a benign, forgiving spirit. We may be contemptible for doing so; to persons without a sense of humor such laughter often seems a wicked escape. But self-love being what it is, we laugh at ourselves in a thoroughly forgiving way, and we laugh in the same way at Don Quixote: we are convinced that his heart, like ours, is in the right place.

Nothing in Emma's comic misunderstandings can serve for the same effect. Her faults are not excesses of virtue. She attempts to manipulate

Harriet not from an excess of kindness but from a desire for power and admiration. She flirts with Frank Churchill out of vanity and irresponsibility. She mistreats Jane Fairfax because of Jane's good qualities. She abuses Miss Bates because of her own essential lack of "tenderness" and "good will."

We have only to think of what Emma's story would be if seen through Jane Fairfax's or Mrs. Elton's or Robert Martin's eyes to recognize how little our sympathy springs from any natural view, and to see how inescapable is the decision to use Emma's mind as a reflector of events—however beclouded her vision must be. To Jane Fairfax, who embodies throughout the book most of the values which Emma discovers only at the end, the early Emma is intolerable.

But Jane Austen never lets us forget that Emma is not what she might appear to be. For every section devoted to her misdeeds—and even they are seen for the most part through her own eyes—there is a section devoted to her self-reproach. We see her rudeness to poor foolish Miss Bates, and we see it vividly. But her remorse and act of penance in visiting Miss Bates after Knightley's rebuke are experienced even more vividly. We see her successive attempts to mislead Harriet, but we see at great length and in high color her self-castigation (*Emma*, 134, 141, 421). We see her boasting proudly that she does not need marriage, boasting almost as blatantly of her "resources" as does Mrs. Elton (*E*, 85). But we know her too intimately to take her conscious thoughts at face value. And we see her, thirty-eight chapters later, chastened to an admission of what we have known all along to be her true human need for love. "If all took place that might take place among the circle of her friends, Hartfield must be comparatively deserted; and she left to cheer her father with the spirits only of ruined happiness. The child to be born at Randalls must be a tie there even dearer than herself; and Mrs. Weston's heart and time would be occupied by it. . . . All that were good would be withdrawn" (*E*, 422).

Perhaps the most delightful effects from our sustained inside view of a very confused and very charming young woman come from her frequent thoughts about Knightley. She is basically right all along about his preeminent wisdom and virtue, and she is our chief authority for taking *his* authority so seriously. And yet in every thought about him she is misled. Knightley rebukes her; the reader knows that Knightley is in the right. But Emma?

> Emma made no answer, and tried to look cheerfully unconcerned, but was really feeling uncomfortable, and wanting him very much to be gone. She did not repent what she had done; she still thought herself a better

judge of such a point of female right and refinement than he could be; but yet she had a sort of habitual respect for his judgment in general, which made her dislike having it so loudly against her; and to have him sitting just opposite to her in angry state, was very disagreeable.

(*E*, 65)

Even more striking is the lack of self-knowledge shown when Mrs. Weston suggests that Knightley might marry Jane Fairfax.

Her objections to Mr. Knightley's marrying did not in the least subside. She could see nothing but evil in it. It would be a great disappointment to Mr. John Knightley [Knightley's brother]; consequently to Isabella. A real injury to the children—a most mortifying change, and material loss to them all;—a very great deduction from her father's daily comfort— and, as to herself, she could not at all endure the idea of Jane Fairfax at Donwell Abbey. A Mrs. Knightley for them all to give way to!—No, Mr. Knightley must never marry. Little Henry must remain the heir of Donwell.

(*E*, 227–8)

Self-deception could hardly be carried further, at least in a person of high intelligence and sensitivity.

Yet the effect of all this is what our tolerance for our own faults produces in our own lives. While only immature readers ever really identify with any character, losing all sense of distance and hence all chance of an artistic experience, our emotional reaction to every event concerning Emma tends to become like her own. When she feels anxiety or shame, we feel analogous emotions. Our modern awareness that such "feelings" are not identical with those we feel in our own lives in similar circumstances has tended to blind us to the fact that aesthetic form can be built out of patterned emotions as well as out of other materials. It is absurd to pretend that because our emotions and desires in responding to fiction are in a very real sense disinterested, they do not or should not exist. Jane Austen, in developing the sustained use of a sympathetic inside view, has mastered one of the most successful of all devices for inducing a parallel emotional response between the deficient heroine and the reader.

Sympathy for Emma can be heightened by withholding inside views of others as well as by granting them of her. The author knew, for example, that it would be fatal to grant any extended inside view of Jane Fairfax. The inadequacies of impressionistic criticism are nowhere revealed more clearly than in the suggestion often made about such minor characters that their authors would have liked to make them vivid but didn't know how.[5] Jane Austen knew perfectly well how to make such a character vivid; Anne in *Persuasion* is a kind of Jane Fairfax turned into heroine. But in *Emma*, Emma must shine supreme. It is not only that the slightest glance inside Jane's mind would be fatal to all of the author's plans for mystification about Frank Churchill, though this is important. The major problem is that any extended view of her would reveal her as a more sympathetic person than Emma herself. Jane is superior to Emma in most respects except the stroke of good fortune that made Emma the heroine of the book. In matters of taste and ability, of head and of heart, she is Emma's superior, and Jane Austen, always in danger of losing our sympathy for Emma, cannot risk any degree of distraction. Jane could, it is true, be granted fewer virtues, and then made more vivid. But to do so would greatly weaken the force of Emma's mistakes of heart and head in her treatment of the almost faultless Jane.

Control of Judgment

But the very effectiveness of the rhetoric designed to produce sympathy might in itself lead to a serious misreading of the book. In reducing the emotional distance, the natural tendency is to reduce—willy-nilly—moral and intellectual distance as well. In reacting to Emma's faults from the inside out, as if they were our own, we may very well not only forgive them but overlook them.[6]

There is, of course, no danger that readers who persist to the end will overlook Emma's serious mistakes; since she sees and reports those mistakes herself, everything becomes crystal clear at the end. The real danger inherent in the experiment is that readers will overlook the mistakes as they are committed and thus miss much of the comedy that depends on Emma's distorted view from page to page. If readers who dislike Emma cannot enjoy the preparation for the marriage to Knightley, readers who do not recognize her faults with absolute precision cannot enjoy the details of the preparation for the comic abasement which must precede that marriage.

It might be argued that there is no real problem, since the conventions of her time allowed for reliable commentary whenever it was needed to place Emma's faults precisely. But Jane Austen is not operating according to the conventions, most of which she had long since parodied and outgrown; her technique is determined by the needs of the novel she is writing. We can see this clearly by contrasting the manner of *Emma* with that of

Persuasion, the next, and last-completed, work. In *Emma* there are many breaks in the point of view, because Emma's beclouded mind cannot do the whole job. In *Persuasion*, where the heroine's viewpoint is faulty only in her ignorance of Captain Wentworth's love, there are very few. Anne Elliot's consciousness is sufficient, as Emma's is not, for most of the needs of the novel which she dominates. Once the ethical and intellectual framework has been established by the narrator's introduction, we enter Anne's consciousness and remain bound to it much more rigorously than we are bound to Emma's. It is still true that whenever something must be shown that Anne's consciousness cannot show, we move to another center; but since her consciousness can do much more for us than Emma's, there need be few departures from it.

The most notable shift for rhetorical purposes in *Persuasion* comes fairly early. When Anne first meets Captain Wentworth after their years of separation that follow her refusal to marry him, she is convinced that he is indifferent. The major movement of *Persuasion* is toward her final discovery that he still loves her; *her* suspense is thus strong and inevitable from the beginning. The reader, however, is likely to believe that Wentworth is still interested. All the conventions of art favor such a belief: the emphasis is clearly on Anne and her unhappiness; the lover has returned; we have only to wait, perhaps with some tedium, for the inevitable outcome. Anne learns (*Persuasion*, 61) that he has spoken of her as so altered "he should not have known her again!" "These were words which could not but dwell with her. Yet she soon began to rejoice that she had heard them. They were of sobering tendency; they allayed agitation; they composed, and consequently must make her happier." And suddenly we enter Wentworth's mind for one time only: "Frederick Wentworth had used such words, or something like them, but without an idea that they would be carried round to her. He had thought her wretchedly altered, and, in the first moment of appeal, had spoken as he felt. He had not forgiven Anne Elliot. She had used him ill"—and so he goes on, for five more paragraphs. The necessary point, the fact that Frederick believes himself to be indifferent, has been made, and it could not have been made without some kind of shift from Anne's consciousness.

At the end of the novel, we learn that Wentworth was himself deceived in this momentary inside view: "He had meant to forget her, and believed it to be done. He had imagined himself indifferent, when he had only been angry" (*P*, 241). We may want to protest against the earlier suppression as unfair, but we can hardly believe it to be what Miss Lascelles calls "an oversight."[7] It is deliberate manipulation of inside views in order to destroy our conventional security. We are thus made ready to go along with Anne in her long and painful road to the discovery that Frederick loves her after all.

The only other important breaks in the angle of vision of *Persuasion* come at the beginning and at the end. Chapter one is an excellent example of how a skilful novelist can, by the use of his own direct voice, accomplish in a few pages what even the best novelist must take chapters to do if he uses nothing but dramatized action. Again at the conclusion the author enters with a resounding reaffirmation that the Wentworth-Elliot marriage is as good a thing as we have felt it to be from the beginning.

> Who can be in doubt of what followed? When any two young people take it into their heads to marry, they are pretty sure by perseverance to carry their point, be they ever so poor, or ever so imprudent, or ever so little likely to be necessary to each other's ultimate comfort. This may be bad morality to conclude with, but I believe it to be truth; and if such parties succeed, how should a Captain Wentworth and an Anne Elliot, with the advantage of maturity of mind, consciousness of right, and one independent fortune between them, fail of bearing down every opposition?[8]
>
> (*P*, 248)

Except for these few intrusions and one in chapter xix, Anne's own mind is sufficient in *Persuasion*, but we can never rely completely on Emma. It is hardly surprising that Jane Austen has provided many correctives to insure our placing her errors with precision.

The chief corrective is Knightley. His commentary on Emma's errors is a natural expression of his love; he can tell the reader and Emma at the same time precisely how she is mistaken. Thus, nothing Knightley says can be beside the point. Each affirmation of a value, each accusation of error is in itself an action in the plot. When he rebukes Emma for manipulating Harriet, when he attacks her for superficiality and false pride, when he condemns her for gossiping and flirting with Frank Churchill, and finally when he attacks her for being "insolent" and "unfeeling" in her treatment of Miss Bates, we have Jane Austen's judgment on Emma, rendered dramatically. But it has come from someone who is essentially sympathetic toward Emma, so that his judgments against her are presumed to be temporary. His sympathy reinforces ours even as he criticizes, and her respect for his opinion, shown in her self-abasement after he has criticized, is one of our main reasons for expecting her to reform.

If Henry James had tried to write a novel about Emma, and had cogitated at length on the problem of getting her story told dramatically, he could not have done better than this. It is possible, of course, to think of *Emma* without Knightley as *raisonneur*, just as it is possible to think of *The Golden Bowl*, say, without the Assinghams as *ficelles* to reflect something not seen by the Prince or Princess. But Knightley, though he receives less independent space than the Assinghams and is almost never seen in an inside view, is clearly more useful for Jane Austen's purposes than any realistically limited *ficelle* could possibly be. By combining the role of commentator with the role of hero, Jane Austen has worked more economically than James, and though economy is as dangerous as any other criterion when applied universally, even James might have profited from a closer study of the economies that a character like Knightley can be made to achieve. It is as if James had dared to make one of the four main characters, say the Prince, into a thoroughly good, wise, perceptive man, a thoroughly clear rather than a partly confused "reflector."

Since Knightley is established early as completely reliable, we need no views of his secret thoughts. He has no secret thoughts, except for the unacknowledged depths of his love for Emma and his jealousy of Frank Churchill. The other main characters have more to hide, and Jane Austen moves in and out of minds with great freedom, choosing for her own purposes what to reveal and what to withhold. Always the seeming violation of consistency is in the consistent service of the particular needs of Emma's story. Sometimes a shift is made simply to direct our suspense, as when Mrs. Weston suggests a possible union of Emma and Frank Churchill, at the end of her conversation with Knightley about the harmful effects of Emma's friendship with Harriet (*E*, 41). "Part of her meaning was to conceal some favourite thoughts of her own and Mr. Weston's on the subject, as much as possible. There were wishes at Randalls respecting Emma's destiny, but it was not desirable to have them suspected."

One objection to this selective dipping into whatever mind best serves our immediate purposes is that it suggests mere trickery and inevitably spoils the illusion of reality. If Jane Austen can tell us what Mrs. Weston is thinking, why not what Frank Churchill and Jane Fairfax are thinking? Obviously, because she chooses to build a mystery, and to do so she must refuse, arbitrarily and obtrusively, to grant the privilege of an inside view to characters whose minds would reveal too much. But is not the mystery purchased at the price of shaking the reader's faith in Jane Austen's integrity? If she simply withholds until later what she might as well relate now—if her procedure is not dictated by the very nature of her materials—why should we take her seriously?

If a natural surface were required in all fiction, then this objection would hold. But if we want to read *Emma* in its own terms, the real question about these shifts cannot be answered by an easy appeal to general principles. Every author withholds until later what he "might as well" relate now. The question is always one of desired effects, and the choice of any one effect always bans innumerable other effects. There is, indeed, a question to be raised about the use of mystery in *Emma*, but the conflict is not between an abstract end that Jane Austen never worried about and a shoddy mystification that she allowed to betray her. The conflict is between two effects both of which she cares about a good deal. On the one hand she cares about maintaining some sense of mystery as long as she can. On the other, she works at all points to heighten the reader's sense of dramatic irony, usually in the form of a contrast between what Emma knows and what the reader knows.

As in most novels, whatever steps are taken to mystify inevitably decrease the dramatic irony, and, whenever dramatic irony is increased by telling the reader secrets the characters have not yet suspected, mystery is inevitably destroyed. The longer we are in doubt about Frank Churchill, the weaker our sense of ironic contrast between Emma's views and the truth. The sooner we see through Frank Churchill's secret plot, the greater our pleasure in observing Emma's innumerable misreadings of his behavior and the less interest we have in the mere mystery of the situation. And we all find that on second reading we discover new intensities of dramatic irony resulting from the complete loss of mystery; knowing what abysses of error Emma is preparing for herself, even those of us who may on first reading have deciphered nearly all the details of the Churchill mystery find additional ironies.

But it is obvious that these ironies could have been offered even on a first reading, if Jane Austen had been willing to sacrifice her mystery. A single phrase in her own name—"his secret engagement to Jane Fairfax"—or a short inside view of either of the lovers could have made us aware of every ironic touch.

The author must, then, choose whether to purchase mystery at the expense of irony. For many of us Jane Austen's choice here is perhaps the weakest aspect of this novel. It is a commonplace of our criticism that significant literature arouses suspense not about the "what" but about the "how." Mere mystification has been mastered by so many second-rate writers that her efforts at mystification seem second-rate.

But again we must ask whether criticism can be conducted effectively by balancing one abstract quality against another. Is there a norm of dramatic irony for all works, or even for all works of a given kind? Has anyone ever formulated a "law of first and second readings" that will tell us just how many of our pleasures on page one should depend on our knowledge of what happens on page the last? We quite properly ask that the books we call great be able to stand up under repeated reading, but we need not ask that they yield identical pleasures on each reading. The modern works whose authors pride themselves on the fact that they can never be read but only re-read may be very good indeed, but they are not made good by the fact that their secret pleasures can only be wrested from them by repeated readings.

In any case, even if one accepted the criticism of Jane Austen's efforts at mystification, the larger service of the inside views is clear: the crosslights thrown by other minds prevent our being blinded by Emma's radiance.

The Reliable Narrator and the Norms of *Emma*

If mere intellectual clarity about Emma were the goal in this work, we should be forced to say that the manipulation of inside views and the extensive commentary of the reliable Knightley are more than is necessary. But for maximum intensity of the comedy and romance, even these are not enough. The "author herself"—not necessarily the real Jane Austen but an implied author, represented in this book by a reliable narrator—heightens the effects by directing our intellectual, moral, and emotional progress. She performs, of course, most of the functions described in chapter vii. But her most important role is to reinforce both aspects of the double vision that operates throughout the book: our inside view of Emma's worth and our objective view of her great faults.

The narrator opens *Emma* with a masterful simultaneous presentation of Emma and of the values against which she must be judged: "Emma Woodhouse, handsome, clever, and rich, with a comfortable home and happy disposition, seemed to unite some of the best blessings of existence; and had lived nearly twenty-one years in the world with very little to distress or vex her." This "seemed" is immediately reinforced by more directly stated reservations. "The real evils of Emma's situation were the power of having rather too much her own way, and a disposition to think a little too well of herself; these were the disadvantages which threatened alloy to her many enjoyments. The danger, however, was at present so unperceived, that they did not by any means rank as misfortunes with her."

None of this could have been said by Emma, and if shown through her consciousness, it could not be accepted, as it must be, without question. Like most of the first three chapters, it is non-dramatic summary, building up, through the ostensible business of getting the characters introduced, to Emma's initial blunder with Harriet and Mr. Elton. Throughout these chapters, we learn much of what we must know from the narrator, but she turns over more and more of the job of summary to Emma as she feels more and more sure of our seeing precisely to what degree Emma is to be trusted. Whenever we leave the "real evils" we have been warned against in Emma, the narrator's and Emma's views coincide: we cannot tell which of them, for example, offers the judgment on Mr. Woodhouse that "his talents could not have recommended him at any time," or the judgment on Mr. Knightley that he is "a sensible man," "always welcome" at Hartfield, or even that "Mr. Knightley, in fact, was one of the few people who could see faults in Emma Woodhouse, and the only one who ever told her of them."

But there are times when Emma and her author are far apart, and the author's direct guidance aids the reader in his own break with Emma. The beautiful irony of the first description of Harriet, given through Emma's eyes (*E*, 23) could no doubt be grasped intellectually by many readers without all of the preliminary commentary. But even for the most perceptive its effect is heightened, surely, by the sense of standing with the author and observing with her precisely how Emma's judgment is going astray. Perhaps more important, we ordinary, less perceptive readers have by now been raised to a level suited to grasp the ironies. Certainly, most readers would overlook some of the barbs directed against Emma if the novel began, as a serious modern novelist might well begin it, with this description:

> [Emma] was not struck by any thing remarkably clever in Miss Smith's conversation, but she found her altogether very engaging—not inconveniently shy, not unwilling to talk—and yet so far from pushing, shewing so proper and becoming a deference, seeming so pleasantly grateful for being admitted to Hartfield, and so artlessly impressed by the appearance of every thing in so superior a style to what she had been used to, that she must have good sense and deserve encouragement. Encouragement should be given. Those soft blue eyes . . . should not be wasted on the inferior society of Highbury . . .
>
> (*E*, 23)

And so Emma goes on, giving herself away with every word, pouring out her sense of her own beneficence and general value. Harriet's past friends, "though very good sort of people, must be doing her harm." Without knowing them, Emma knows that they "must be coarse and unpolished, and very unfit to be the intimates of a girl who wanted only a little more knowledge and elegance to be quite perfect." And she concludes with a beautiful burst of egotism: "She would notice her; she would improve her; she would detach her from her bad acquaintance, and introduce her into good society; she would form her opinions and her manners. It would be an interesting, and certainly a very kind undertaking; highly becoming her own situation in life, her leisure, and powers." Even the most skillful reader might not easily plot an absolutely true course through these ironies without the prior direct assistance we have been given. Emma's views are not so outlandish that they could never have been held by a female novelist writing in her time. They cannot serve effectively as signs of her character unless they are clearly disavowed as signs of Jane Austen's views. Emma's unconscious catalogue of her egotistical uses for Harriet, given under the pretense of listing the services she will perform, is thus given its full force by being framed explicitly in a world of values which Emma herself cannot discover until the conclusion of the book.

The full importance of the author's direct imposition of an elaborate scale of norms can be seen by considering that conclusion. The sequence of events is a simple one: Emma's faults and mistakes are brought home to her in a rapid and humiliating chain of rebukes from Knightley and blows from hard fact. These blows to her self-esteem produce at last a genuine reform (for example, she brings herself to apologize to Miss Bates, something she could never have done earlier in the novel). The change in her character removes the only obstacle in the way of Knightley's proposal, and the marriage follows. "The wishes, the hopes, the confidence, the predictions of the small band of true friends who witnessed the ceremony, were fully answered in the perfect happiness of the union."

It may be that if we look at Emma and Knightley as real people, this ending will seem false. G. B. Stern laments, in *Speaking of Jane Austen*, "Oh, Miss Austen, it was not a good solution; it was a bad solution, an unhappy ending, could we see beyond the last pages of the book." Edmund Wilson predicts that Emma will find a new protégée like Harriet, since she has not been cured of her inclination to "infatuations with women." Marvin Mudrick even more emphatically rejects Jane Austen's explicit rhetoric; he believes that Emma is still a "confirmed exploiter," and for him the ending must be read as ironic.[9]

But it is precisely because this ending is neither life itself nor a simple bit of literary irony that it can serve so well to heighten our sense of a complete and indeed perfect resolution to all that has gone before. If we look at the values that have been realized in this marriage and compare them with those realized in conventional marriage plots, we see that Jane Austen means what she says: this will be a happy marriage because there is simply nothing left to make it anything less than perfectly happy. It fulfils every value embodied in the world of the book—with the possible exception that Emma may never learn to apply herself as she ought to her reading and her piano! It is a union of intelligence: of "reason," of "sense," of "judgment." It is a union of virtue: of "good will," of generosity, of unselfishness. It is a union of feeling: of "taste," "tenderness," "love," "beauty."[10]

In a general way, then, this plot offers us an experience superficially like that offered by most tragicomedy as well as by much of the cheapest popular art: we are made to desire certain good things for certain good characters, and then our desires are gratified. If we depended on general criteria derived from our justified boredom with such works, we should reject this one. But the critical difference lies in the precise quality of the values appealed to and the precise quality of the characters who violate or realize them. All of the cheap marriage plots in the world should not lead us to be embarrassed about our pleasure in Emma and Knightley's marriage. It is more than just the marriage: it is the rightness of this marriage, as a conclusion to all of the comic wrongness that has gone before. The good for Emma includes both her necessary reform and the resulting marriage. Marriage to an intelligent, amiable, good, and attractive man is the best thing that can happen to this heroine, and the readers who do not experience it as such are, I am convinced, far from knowing what Jane Austen is about—whatever they may say about the "bitter spinster's" attitude toward marriage.

Our modern sensibilities are likely to be rasped by any such formulation. We do not ordinarily like to encounter perfect endings in our novels—even in the sense of "perfectedness" or completion, the sense obviously intended by Jane Austen. We refuse to accept it when we see it: witness the many attempts to deny Dostoevski's success with Alyosha and Father Zossima in *The Brothers Karamazov*. Many of us find it embarrassing to talk of emotions based on moral judgment at all, particularly when the emotions have any kind of affirmative cast. Emma herself is something of a "modern" in this regard throughout most of the book. Her self-deception about marriage is as great as about most other important matters. Emma boasts to Harriet of her indifference to marriage, at the same time unconsciously betraying her totally inadequate view of the sources of human happiness.

If I know myself, Harriet, mine is an active, busy mind, with a great
many independent resources; and I do not perceive why I should be
more in want of employment at forty or fifty than one-and-twenty.
Woman's usual occupations of eye and hand and mind will be as open to
me then, as they are now; or with no important variation. If I draw less,
I shall read more; if I give up music, I shall take to carpet-work.

Emma at carpet-work! If she knows herself indeed.

And as for objects of interest, objects for the affections, which is, in
truth, the great point of inferiority, the want of which is really the great
evil to be avoided in not marrying [a magnificent concession, this] I shall
be very well off, with all the children of a sister I love so much, to care
about. There will be enough of them, in all probability, to supply every
sort of sensation that declining life can need. There will be enough for
every hope and every fear; and though my attachment to none can
equal that of a parent, it suits my ideas of comfort better than what is
warmer and blinder. My nephews and nieces!—I shall often have a niece
with me.

(*E*, 85–86)

Without growing solemn about it—it is wonderfully comic—we can recognize that the humor springs here from very deep sources indeed. It can be
fully enjoyed, in fact, only by the reader who has attained to a vision of
human felicity far more profound than Emma's "comfort" and "want" and
"need." It is a vision that includes not simply marriage, but a kind of loving
converse not based, as is Emma's here, on whether the "loved" person will
serve one's irreducible needs.

The comic effect of this repudiation of marriage is considerably increased
by the fact that Emma always thinks of marriage for others as their highest
good, and in fact unconsciously encourages her friend Harriet to fall in love
with the very man she herself loves without knowing it. The delightful
denouement is thus what we want not only because it is a supremely good
thing for Emma, but because it is a supremely comic outcome of Emma's
profound misunderstanding of herself and of the human condition. In the
schematic language of chapter v, it satisfies both our practical desire for
Emma's well-being and our appetite for the qualities proper to these artistic
materials. It is thus a more resounding resolution than either of these elements separately could provide. The other major resolution of the work—
Harriet's marriage with her farmer—reinforces this interpretation. Emma's

sin against Harriet has been something far worse than the mere meddling of a busybody. To destroy Harriet's chances for happiness—chances that depend entirely on her marriage—is as close to viciousness as any author could dare to take a heroine designed to be loved. We can laugh with Emma at this mistake only because Harriet's chance for happiness is restored (*E*, 473).

Other values, like money, blood, and "consequence," are real enough in *Emma*, but only as they contribute to or are mastered by good taste, good judgment, and good morality. Money alone can make a Mrs. Churchill, but a man or woman "is silly to marry without it." Consequence untouched by sense can make a very inconsequential Mr. Woodhouse; untouched by sense or virtue it can make the much more contemptible Mr. and Miss Elliot of *Persuasion*. But it is a pleasant thing to have, and it does no harm unless, like the early Emma, one takes it too seriously. Charm and elegance without sufficient moral force can make a Frank Churchill; unschooled by morality it can lead to the baseness of Henry Crawford in *Mansfield Park* or of Wickham in *Pride and Prejudice*. Even the supreme virtues are inadequate in isolation: good will alone will make a comic Miss Bates or a Mr. Weston, judgment with insufficient good will a comic Mr. John Knightley, and so on.

I am willing to risk the commonplace in such a listing because it is only thus that the full force of Jane Austen's comprehensive view can be seen. There is clearly at work here a much more detailed ordering of values than any conventional public philosophy of her time could provide. Obviously, few readers in her own time, and far fewer in our own, have ever approached this novel in full and detailed agreement with the author's norms. But they were led to join her as they read, and so are we.

Explicit Judgments on Emma Woodhouse

We have said in passing almost enough of the other side of the coin—the judgment of particular actions as they relate to the general norms. But something must be said of the detailed "placing" of Emma, by direct commentary, in the hierarchy of values established by the novel. I must be convinced, for example, not only that tenderness for other people's feelings is an important trait but also that Emma's particular behavior violates the true standards of tenderness, if I am to savor to the full the episode of Emma's insult to Miss Bates and Knightley's reproach which follows. If I refuse to blame Emma, I may discover a kind of intellectual enjoyment in the episode, and I will probably think that any critic who talks of "belief" in tenderness as operating in such a context is taking things too seriously. But I can never enjoy the episode in its full intensity or grasp its formal coherence. Similarly, I must agree not only that to be dreadfully boring is a minor fault compared with the major virtue of "good will," but also that Miss Bates's exemplification of this fault and of this virtue entitle her to the respect which Emma denies. If I do not—while yet being able to laugh at Miss Bates—I can hardly understand, let alone enjoy, Emma's mistreatment of her.

But these negative judgments must be counteracted by a larger approval, and, as we would expect, the novel is full of direct apologies for Emma. Her chief fault, lack of good will or tenderness, must be read not only in relationship to the code of values provided by the book as a whole—a code which judges her as seriously deficient; it must also be judged in relationship to the harsh facts of the world around her, a world made up of human beings ranging in degree of selfishness and egotism from Knightley, who lapses from perfection when he tries to judge Frank Churchill, his rival, down to Mrs. Elton, who has most of Emma's faults and none of her virtues. In such a setting, Emma is easily forgiven. When she insults Miss Bates, for example, we remember that Miss Bates lives in a world where many others are insensitive and cruel. "Miss Bates, neither young, handsome, rich, nor married, stood in the very worst predicament in the world for having much of the public favour; and she had no intellectual superiority to make atonement to herself, or frighten those who might hate her, into outward respect" (*E*, 21). While it would be a mistake to see only this "regulated hatred" in Jane Austen's world, overlooking the tenderness and generosity, the hatred of viciousness is there, and there is enough vice in evidence to make Emma almost shine by comparison.

Often, Jane Austen makes this apology-by-comparison explicit. When Emma lies to Knightley about Harriet, very close to the end of the book, she is excused with a generalization about human nature: "Seldom, very seldom, does complete truth belong to any human disclosure; seldom can it happen that something is not a little disguised, or a little mistaken; but where, as in this case, though the conduct is mistaken, the feelings are not, it may not be very material.—Mr. Knightley could not impute to Emma a more relenting heart than she possessed, or a heart more disposed to accept of his" (*E*, 431–32).

The Implied Author as Friend and Guide

With all of this said about the masterful use of the narrator in *Emma*, there remain some "intrusions" unaccounted for by strict service to the story itself. "What did she say?" the narrator asks, at the crucial moment in the major love scene. "Just what she ought, of course. A lady always does.—She said enough to show there need not be despair—and to invite him to say more himself" (*E*, 431). To some readers this has seemed to demonstrate the author's inability to write a love scene, since it sacrifices "the illusion of reality."[11] But who has ever read this far in *Emma* under the delusion that he is reading a realistic portrayal which is suddenly shattered by the unnatural appearance of the narrator? If the narrator's superabundant wit is destructive of the kind of illusion proper to this work, the novel has been ruined long before.

But we should now be in a position to see precisely why the narrator's wit is not in the least out of place at the emotional climax of the novel. We have seen how the inside views of the characters and the author's commentary have been used from the beginning to get the values straight and to keep them straight and to help direct our reactions to Emma. But we also see here a beautiful case of the dramatized author as friend and guide. "Jane Austen," like "Henry Fielding," is a paragon of wit, wisdom, and virtue. She does not talk about her qualities; unlike Fielding she does not in *Emma* call direct attention to her artistic skill. But we are seldom allowed to forget about her for all that. When we read this novel we accept her as representing everything we admire most. She is as generous and wise as Knightley; in fact, she is a shade more penetrating in her judgment. She is as subtle and witty as Emma would like to think herself. Without being sentimental she is in favor of tenderness. She is able to put an adequate but not excessive value on wealth and rank. She recognizes a fool when she sees one, but unlike Emma she knows that it is both immoral and foolish to be rude to fools. She is, in short, a perfect human being, within the concept of perfection established by the book she writes; she even recognizes that human perfection of the kind *she* exemplifies is not quite attainable in real life. The process of her domination is of course circular; her character establishes the values for us according to which her character is then found to be perfect. But this circularity does not affect the success of her endeavor; in fact it insures it.

Her "omniscience" is thus a much more remarkable thing than is ordinarily implied by the term. All good novelists know all about their characters—all that they need to know. And the question of how their narrators are to find out all that they need to know, the question of "authority," is a relatively simple one. The real choice is much more profound than this would imply. It is a choice of the moral, not merely the technical, angle of vision from which the story is to be told.

Unlike the central intelligences of James and his successors, "Jane Austen" has learned nothing at the end of the novel that she did not know at the beginning. She needed to learn nothing. She knew everything of importance already. We have been privileged to watch with her as she observes her favorite character climb from a considerably lower platform to join the exalted company of Knightley, "Jane Austen," and those of us readers who are wise enough, good enough, and perceptive enough to belong up there too. As Katherine Mansfield says, "[T]he truth is that every true admirer of the novels cherishes the happy thought that he alone—reading between the lines—has become the secret friend of their author."[12] Those who love "gentle Jane" as a secret friend may undervalue the irony and wit; those who see her in effect as the greatest of Shaw's heroines, flashing about her with the weapons of irony, may undervalue the emphasis on tenderness and good will. But only a very few can resist her.

The dramatic illusion of her presence as a character is thus fully as important as any other element in the story. When she intrudes, the illusion is not shattered. The only illusion we care about, the illusion of traveling intimately with a hardy little band of readers whose heads are screwed on tight and whose hearts are in the right place, is actually strengthened when we are refused the romantic love scene. Like the author herself, we don't care about the love scene. We can find love scenes in almost any novelist's works, but only here can we find a mind and heart that can give us clarity without oversimplification, sympathy and romance without sentimentality, and biting irony without cynicism.

Notes

1. "The Lesson of Balzac," *The Question of Our Speech* (Boston: Houghton Mifflin, 1905), 63. A fuller quotation can be found in R. W. Chapman's indispensable *Jane Austen: A Critical Bibliography* (Oxford, 1955). Some important Austen items published too late to be included by Chapman are: (1) Ian Watt, *The Rise of the Novel* (Berkeley, C.A.: University of California Press, 1957); (2) Stuart M. Tave, review of Marvin Mudrick's *Jane Austen: Irony as Defense and Discovery* (Princeton, N.J.: Princeton University Press, 1952) in *Philological Quarterly*, XXXII (July, 1953), 256–57; (3) Andrew H. Wright, *Jane Austen's Novels: A Study in Structure* (London: Chatto and Windus, 1953), 36–82; (4) Christopher Gillie, "*Sense and Sensibility*: An Assessment," *Essays in Criticism*, IX (January, 1959), 1–9, esp. 5–6; (5) Edgar F. Shannon, Jr., "*Emma*: Character and Construction," *PMLA*, LXXI (September, 1956), 637–50.

2. See, for example, Mudrick, *Jane Austen: Irony as Defense and Discovery*, 91, 165; Frank O'Connor, *The Mirror in the Roadway* (London: Hamish Hamilton, 1957), 30.

3. "A heroine whom no one but myself will much like" (James Edward Austen Leigh, *Memoir of His Aunt* [London, 1870; Oxford, 1926], 157).

4. The best discussion of this problem is Reginald Farrer's "Jane Austen," *Quarterly Review*, (July, 1917), 1–30; reprinted in this case book. For one critic the book fails because the problem was never recognized by Jane Austen herself: Mr. E. N. Hayes, in what may well be the least sympathetic discussion of *Emma* yet written, explains the whole book as the author's failure to see Emma's faults. "Evidently Jane Austen wished to protect Emma. . . . The author is therefore in the ambiguous position of both loving and scorning the heroine" (*"Emma*: A Dissenting Opinion," *Nineteenth-Century Fiction*, [June, 1949], 18, 19).

5. A. C. Bradley, for example, once argued that Jane Austen intended Jane Fairfax to be as interesting throughout as she becomes at the end, but "the moralist in Jane Austen stood for once in her way. The secret engagement is, for her, so serious an offence, that she is afraid to win our hearts for Jane until it has led to great unhappiness" ("Jane Austen," in *Essays and Studies, by Members of the English Association*, II [Oxford: Clarendon Press, 1911], 23).

6. I know of only one full-scale attempt to deal with the "tension between sympathy and judgment" in modern literature, Robert Langbaum's *The Poetry of Experience* (London: Chatto and Windus, 1957). Langbaum argues that in the dramatic monologue, with which he is primarily concerned, the sympathy engendered by the direct portrayal of internal experience leads the reader to suspend his moral judgment. Thus, in reading Robert Browning's portraits of moral degeneration—e.g., the duke in "My Last Duchess" or the monk in "Soliloquy of a Spanish Cloister"—our moral judgment is overwhelmed "because we prefer to participate in the duke's power and freedom, in his hard core of character fiercely loyal to itself. Moral judgment is in fact important as the thing to be suspended, as a measure of the price we pay for the privilege of appreciating to the full this extraordinary man" (83). While I think that Langbaum seriously underplays the extent to which moral judgment remains even after psychological vividness has done its work, and while he perhaps defines "morality" too narrowly when he excludes from it such things as power and freedom and fierce loyalty to one's own character, his book is a stimulating introduction to the problems raised by internal portraiture of flawed characters.

7. Mary Lascelles, *Jane Austen and Her Art* (Oxford: Oxford University Press, 1939), 204.

8. It seems to be difficult for some modern critics, accustomed to ferreting values out from an impersonal or ironic context without the aid of the author's voice, to make use of reliable commentary like this when it is provided. Even a highly

perceptive reader like Mark Schorer, for example, finds himself doing unnecessary acrobatics with the question of style, and particularly metaphor, as clues to the norms against which the author judges her characters. In reading *Persuasion*, he finds these clues among the metaphors "from commerce and property, the counting house and the inherited estate" with which it abounds ("Fiction and the Matrix of Analogy," *Kenyon Review* [Autumn, 1949], 540). No one would deny that the novel is packed with such metaphors, although Schorer is somewhat overingenious in marshaling to his cause certain dead metaphors that Austen could not have avoided without awkward circumlocution (esp. 542). But the crucial question surely is: What precisely are these metaphors of the countinghouse doing in the novel? *Whose* values are they supposed to reveal? Accustomed to reading modern fiction in which the novelist very likely provides no direct assistance in answering this question, Schorer leaves it really unanswered; at times he seems almost to imply that Jane Austen is unconsciously giving herself away in her use of them (e.g., 543).

But the novel is really very clear about it all. The introduction, coming directly from the wholly reliable narrator, establishes unequivocally and without "analogy" the conflict between the world of the Elliots, depending for its values on selfishness, stupidity, and pride—and the world of Anne, a world where "elegance of mind and sweetness of character" are the supreme values. The commercial values stressed by Schorer are only a selection from what is actually a rich group of evils. And Anne's own expressed views again and again provide direct guidance to the reader.

9. The first two quotations are from Wilson's "A Long Talk about Jane Austen," *A Literary Chronicle: 1920–1950* (New York, 1952). The third is from Mudrick, *Jane Austen*, 206.

10. It has lately been fashionable to underplay the value of tenderness and good will in Jane Austen, in reaction to an earlier generation that overdid the picture of "gentle Jane." The trend seems to have begun in earnest with D. W. Harding's "Regulated Hatred: An Aspect of the Work of Jane Austen," *Scrutiny*, VIII (March, 1940), 346–62. While I do not feel as strongly aroused against this school of readers as does R. W. Chapman (see his *A Critical Bibliography*, 52, and his review of Mudrick's work in the *T.L.S.* [September 19, 1952]), it seems to me that another swing of the pendulum is called for: when Jane Austen praises the "relenting heart," she means that praise, though she is the same author who can lash the unrelenting heart with "regulated hatred."

11. Edd Winfield Parks, "Exegesis in Austen's Novels," *South Atlantic Quarterly* LI (January 1952), 117.

12. *Novels and Novelists*, ed. J. Middleton Murry (London: Constable, 1930), 304.

Emma

"Woman, Lovely Woman, Reigns Alone"

CLAUDIA L. JOHNSON

◆ ◆ ◆

THERE WAS A TIME, and not too long ago, when Jane Austen was considered to be above—or was it really below?—the anxieties of authorship. For Richard Simpson, as for many of Austen's Victorian admirers, it was necessary to presume an "unconsciousness of [Austen's] artistic merits" in order to regard her, in his own words, as "dear Aunt Jane," a kindly spinster who never minded being interrupted while at work because her "powers were a secret to herself," and who was gratefully surprised to earn even the little money she did because she rated her own abilities too low to expect acknowledgment.[1] Encouraged by members of Austen's own family, who in the "Biographical Notice" and the *Memoir* protest with obtrusive defensiveness that Austen put her family before her art, such views have survived well into our own century. Taking particular care to "redeem" Austen from "any possible suspicion of superiority or conceit," R. Brimley Johnson asserts that Austen's "taste was strong against any parade of authorship, and her affection would have accused herself of both conceit and selfishness, had she required privacy for work, or allowed herself to be so absorbed as to neglect any social or domestic duty." R. W. Chapman later affirmed that "the sweetest reward of her labours" was nothing more ambitious or independent than "to have pleased her family." And as late as 1957, in the biographical sketch prefixed to his widely available edition of *Emma*, Lionel Trilling's stress on Austen's commitment to a charmed family circle assures us that Austen never upset the parlor or the dining room with overweening authorial preoccupations as unladylike as they are egotistical.[2]

For our current recognition of Austen's artistic self-consciousness we have to thank, not the discovery of any new information, but rather a disposition to pay attention to what has always been before us. Austen's account of the profits generated by her novels, for example, is now acknowledged to indicate an interest in matters as vulgar as commercial success. Her somewhat testy preface to *Northanger Abbey* is now permitted to betray lingering mortification at the refusal of Crosby & Co. to print this, her first formally submitted novel, and to convey a wish that readers properly consider the historical provenance of her work. And of course the remarks scattered throughout the letters and her collection of opinions about *Mansfield Park* and *Emma* plainly attest to an intense curiosity about responses to her novels outside the family circle. To all appearances, she deemed no opinion about her novels too stupid or malapropos to copy out and preserve for future reference.

Austen's concern about the fate of her novels with the public was deeply felt and often manifested itself in decidedly personal attitudes towards her heroines, about whose popularity with the public she was a good judge. Elizabeth Bennet, she was certain, was so delightful a creature that if readers did not like her, it was no fault of her own. But with Emma, Austen knew she was taking a risk. Authorial solicitude on her behalf, however, has proved a mixed blessing. Her statement "I am going to take a heroine whom no-one but myself will much like" has been treated more as an invitation to search out what is objectionable about Emma than as a calculated challenge to the judgments of her audience, for the criticism of Emma is freighted with alarming animosities.[3] Concerning this Austenian heroine, more than any other, commentary conspicuously gives the lie to the naive assumption that literary criticism is the business of disinterested professionals whose discussions evolve from ideologically neutral historical, aesthetic, or merely commonsensical criteria. If Austen enters the canon because she seemed to deny or devalue her authority, Emma has been the heroine critics have loved to scold precisely because it never occurs to her to apologize for the control she takes over the destinies of others. Because Emma is often charged with the same transgressions—being "arrogant, self-important, and controlling" or "narcissistic and perfectionist"—from which critics diligently attempted to exempt Austen, it is worth considering them at some length.[4] The absolution of one and the arraignment—sometimes indulgent and sometimes not—of the other alike derive from a profound discomfort with female authority, and female authority itself is the subject of *Emma*.

Determining the common denominator in much *Emma* criticism requires no particular cleverness. Emma offends the sexual sensibilities of many of her critics. Transparently misogynist, sometimes even homophobic, subtexts often bob to the surface of the criticism about her. Even those critics who do not specifically address the subject of gender employ loaded oppositions about moral and social values, supposedly endorsed by the author herself, which imply a sexual hierarchy reified in marriage. For example, A. Duckworth's contention that "Emma in the end chooses society rather than self, an inherited order rather than a spontaneous and improvised existence," implicitly opposes and prefers the orderly, patriarchal, rational, masculine, and, above all, right to the disorderly, subjectivist, imaginative, feminine, and self-evidently wrong.[5] In much *Emma* criticism, however, psychosexual concepts are not merely implicit. To many of this novel's most distinguished critics, Emma's want of feminine softness and compliancy is her most salient and most grievous shortcoming. Marvin Mudrick's assertion that Emma is a "confirmed exploiter" is an erotic complaint disguised as a moral one. His "Emma has no tenderness" really means that she is not sexually submissive to and contingent upon men: hers is "a dominating and uncommitting personality." Curiously enough, though, because he does not notice his own assumption of a masculine monopoly on desirable qualities, Mudrick inadvertently justifies Emma's dereliction from "femininity." If Mr. Woodhouse "is really" that most contemptible of creatures, "an old woman," we can hardly wonder that his daughter opts for the emotional detachment and the penchant for managing that could place her beyond such scorn. But though Mudrick complains that Emma "plays God," what he really means is that she plays man, and he, as well as others, will not permit her thus to elude the contempt that is woman's portion, do what she may. Wilson, who alludes ominously to Emma's "infatuations with women," and Mudrick himself, who darkly hints about her preference of "the company of women" whom "she can master and direct," treat Emma's "coldness" as though it were a culpably perverse refusal of their own sexual advances. To critics at a loss to account for how Emma could like Harriet more than she likes Mr. Elton, what other than an unacceptable attachment to women could possibly account for a failure to be impressed with and "humanly" committed to men?[6]

Readers who have not cared to ponder Emma's sexuality have still entangled her in unexamined and curiously revealing attitudes which are, if anything, more pernicious in their linkage of sex and politics. Blowing the whistle on readers who doubt that marriage will cure Emma, Wayne Booth, for example, declares with the preemptive dogmatism peculiar to outraged decency, "Marriage to an intelligent, amiable, good, and attractive man is the best thing that can happen to this heroine, and the readers who do not experience it as such are, I am convinced, far from knowing what Jane Austen is about."[7] Never implying that this high-strung young lady really needs a good man, Trilling argues that Emma's objectionable behavior derives from a sexual peculiarity more subversive than a mere passing disinterest in marriage: "The extraordinary thing about Emma," he claims, "is that she has a moral life as a man has a moral life." Emma's anomalous status as a moral agent is owing entirely to her self-love, a sentiment which in turn derives from "the first of virtues, the most basic and biological of the virtues, that of self-preservation." Untroubled by the Darwinian premise that nature, in the guise of biology, has in depriving women of the survival instinct, de facto barred them from the moral life, Trilling, it is true, does not chide Emma for her manly trespasses. But this is only because they are so reassuringly uncalculated and exceptional as to deserve his curiosity and his indulgence. Trilling also appeals to the "biological nature of moral fact" in his essay on *The Bostonians*, after all, and in that novel challenges to male hegemony that are based on *principle* meet with a very different response.[8]

In fairness not merely to the aforementioned readers but also to the originality of *Emma* itself, it must be observed that if in detaching herself from the romantic plot Emma neglects the feminine roles twentieth-century critics would assign to her, these roles were insisted upon if anything more self-consciously and strenuously in the fiction of Austen's period. There they appear in a handful of permutations which vary according to the persuasions of the author. In anti-Jacobin novels, bad girls are undone by radical seducers, while good girls are obedient daughters and chaste wives. Even in novels by radical men—such as *Fleetwood, Anna St. Ives*, and *Man As He is*—heroines sometimes prove themselves worthy of courageously progressive suitors or husbands by possessing the same mildness, modesty, and educability which would recommend them to reactionary gentlemen. In novels by radical women, however, they can figure as the victims of a husband's or father's greed, or perhaps even of a radical lover's cold egotism. Emma's very difference makes her and her novel exceptional, for even in the case of that one wholly traditional bond at the center of Emma's life—her tender love for her father—the intellectual, physical, and even moral frailty of this paternal figure necessitates a dependence upon female strength, activity, and good judgment. Possessing these qualities in abundance, Emma does not think of herself as an incomplete or contingent being whose destiny is to be determined by the generous or blackguardly actions a man will make towards her. A caricature of comme il faut propriety, even Mrs. Elton defers, nominally at least, to the rule of her husband, her "lord and master" (*Emma*, 455). But Emma does not need the mediation of marriage because she already possesses an independence and consequence that marriage to a "lord and master" would, if anything, probably diminish: "I believe few married women are half as much mistress of their husband's house, as I am of Hartfield" (*E*, 84). Further, Emma is so accustomed to rule that, as Mr. Knightley jokes to Mrs. Weston, she has absorbed the office of husband unto herself, giving her governess a "good education" in "the very material matrimonial point of submitting your own will, and doing as you were bid" (*E*, 38).

In Austen's other novels, women independent enough to manage their own estates and dictate to others are widows, like Mrs. Smith and Lady Catherine. By contrast, single rich women, such as Sophia Grey, are prey to roving fortune hunters. Unlike her predecessors, Emma alone has "none of the usual inducements" to marriage: "Fortune I do not want; employment I do not want; consequence I do not want" (*E*, 84). Sometimes held up as evidence of frigidity or some comparably pathological character flaw, Emma's businesslike reasoning about marriage is actually all of a piece with that of other characters in *Emma*, from the lowly Harriet to the mighty Churchills, whose possession or lack of "fortune," "employment," and "consequence" bears on their matrimonial decisions. Knightley himself applauds Miss Taylor's marriage to Mr. Weston precisely because it enables her "to be secure of a comfortable provision" (*E*, 11). And far from feeling insulted by being so regarded, Mr. Weston considers Miss Taylor's lack of fortune and consequence a complementary blessing in its own right. The social and economic superiority of his first wife put him at a sentimental disadvantage. Such was her condescension that his "warm heart and sweet temper made him think every thing due to her in return for the great goodness of being in love with him" (*E*, 15), long after she is cast off by her family, and long after the young couple runs through her fortune. Marrying "poor Miss Taylor" gives him "the pleasantest proof of its being a great deal better to chuse than to be chosen, to excite gratitude rather than to feel it" (*E*, 17)—better as well, we assume, to have someone else feel that everything is due to him for *his* great goodness in having chosen beneath him. There is no call to hint at the sinister here: Mr. Weston is not the less amiable for enjoying his benevolence. Unlike us, Austen is not embarrassed by power, and she depicts it with the quiet pervasiveness and nonchalance that suggest how effortlessly she took it and the sentiments relative to it for granted. What makes Emma unusual, then, is not that she, as Trilling would have it, is a woman freakishly endowed with self-love, but rather that she is a woman who possesses and enjoys power, without bothering to demur about it.

In the animadversions of even the most sympathetic of Emma's critics, then, the political import of sexual difference is clearly exposed, for what they present as pertaining to female nature really pertains to female rule. Emma assumes her own entitlement to independence and power—power not only over her own destiny, but, what is harder to tolerate, power over the destinies of others—and in so doing she poaches on what is felt to be male turf. The royal dedication of *Emma* is often cited to account for the patriotism of its outbursts about English verdure, English reticence, and English social structure. But if it is appropriate to speak of *Emma* as a patriotic novel—and I believe it is—then it must be acknowledged that its patriotism is of a very unusual sort. Austen privately expressed hesitations about the Prince Regent in strong terms, and she inscribed the dedication to him only after realizing she had no choice.[9] When we recall further that Austen disapproved of His Royal Highness specifically because of his notorious infidelity to his wife, the inscription of a novel predominated by female power can conceivably look more like an act of quiet cheek than of humble submission. In stunning contrast with *Mansfield Park*, where husbands dominate their households with as little judiciousness as decency, in *Emma* woman *does* reign alone. Indeed, with the exception of Knightley, all of the people in control are women: Mrs. Churchill's whims as well as her aches and pains are felt, discussed, and respected miles away from her sofa; at least some, if not all, people in the neighborhood accept Mrs. Elton's ministrations as "Lady Patroness"; and Emma's consciousness that she is considered "first" in consequence at Highbury may peeve her critics, but it does not faze her neighbors, and no one—least of all Mr. Knightley— questions her right to preeminence.

In its willingness to explore positive versions of female power, *Emma* itself is an experimental production of authorial independence unlike any of Austen's other novels. As we have seen, the novels up through *Mansfield Park* are textured with highly politicized allusions, themes, plots, and characters. But the texture of *Emma* is remarkably spare. There is a hue and cry about an "infamous fraud upon the rights of men and women" (*E*, 254). But the crime in question is a conspiracy to deprive them of their dinner, not their dignity as autonomous agents. Austen does not allude to the tradition of political fiction as regularly in *Emma* as she does elsewhere, but such relative silence does not signify an abandonment of the political tradition. In fact, the case is quite the opposite. At the height of her powers, Austen steps into her own authority in *Emma*, and she participates in the political tradition of fiction, not by qualifying or critiquing it from within, but rather by trying to write from its outsides. *Emma* is assuredly unlike the anarchistic and egalitarian novels of William Godwin, Thomas Holcroft, and Mary Wollstonecraft in fundamentally accepting English class structure, and in being able to discriminate positive authority figures. Emma is frequently brought to task for her "snobbism." But if she offends democratic sympathies when she declares that "a farmer can need none of my help, and is therefore in one sense as much above my notice as in every other he is below it" (*E*, 29), she is merely describing with unwonted bluntness a mode of social organization which the most attractive of Austen's heroes—Darcy, for one—thrive on and honor without raising our dander. Knightley himself opposes Emma's plans to match Harriet with Mr. Elton, certainly not because Harriet should make up her own mind, but rather because, though "men of sense" and "men of family" will rightly scorn to marry her, she is good enough for a farmer such as Robert Martin (*E*, 64).

But at the same time, *Emma* is a world apart from conservative fiction in accepting a hierarchical social structure not because it is a sacred dictate of patriarchy—*Mansfield Park* had spoiled this—but rather because within its parameters class can actually supersede sex. Thus *Emma* recuperates a world Austen savages in novels such as *Mansfield Park* and *Northanger Abbey*, in order to explore what was precluded in those novels, the place such a world can afford to women with authority. Though it may favor male rule, the social system sustained in *Emma* recognizes the propriety of female rule as well, and it is to this system that Emma, in the absence of any social superiors, owes her preeminence. Now this of course is not to say that Emma's ideas about her social status and the prerogatives attached to it are always sound in themselves or consistent in their application. It is to say rather that Emma's sense of the privileges and duties attached to her station is legitimate. This position has been almost impossible for criticism to accept. Domineering matrons like Mrs. Ferrars or Lady Catherine are bad enough. But we expect heroines to be like Fanny Price, to disclaim power "*in propria persona*" (*Mansfield Park*, 398) and to attend with admirable patience to the directions of others even when they are wrong. We scarcely notice how, though Edmund pointedly marks the chilliness of Fanny's east room, he never troubles himself to order a fire to burn there, because modest young heroines themselves are not supposed to notice, much less resent, such negligence—and we customarily accept what they see, and what they cannot see, as sound.

Emma's self-assurance—"I always deserve the best treatment, because I never put up with any other" (*E*, 474)—is thus doubly unnerving because it exceeds the purely personal and is reinforced by a social privilege which commands a respect easier to extend to a man of Sir Thomas's stature than to a woman of Lady Catherine's, let alone Emma's. Furthermore, because we tend to read Austen's novels much as Mary Bennet would, as dramas of moral correction—where Marianne is properly punished for impetuosity, Elizabeth for her prejudice (and so on)—Emma's power is generally presented as the problem she must overcome. In no novel are Austen's methods particularly instructional, but *Emma* most conspicuously lacks the clarity of emphasis and the conclusory arguments that mark didactic fiction, omissions that have in fact disturbed many readers. One recent critic has vigorously complained that Emma's humiliation is too brief and too private, and that she is never vigorously "punished" for her wrongdoing; and many readers have been troubled that Emma shows no sign of "reform" by the end of the novel. The leisurely eddying of *Emma*'s pace, combined with the insistent ordinariness—not to say vapidity—of so much of its material, makes strident moralizing sound a bit strained.[10] As a result, the identification and assessment of the faults which are supposed to make humiliation and reform necessary have a hyperbolic ring to them. When one critic lists among Emma's reprehensible "mortifications" of others' feelings her curt refusal of Mr. Elton's inebriated proposal, one feels this is scraping the bottom of the barrel indeed.[11] Since the steady absorption of feminist perspectives into the corpus of Austenian criticism, the incommensurateness of action and reaction has been noted, and some readers, who presumably cannot understand why Mr. Elton's feelings are deemed worthier of indulgence than Emma's—have ventured to confess that they could never figure out exactly what Emma did to merit so much indignation in the first place.

What indeed? Austen anticipates the question as early as the fifth chapter, when Knightley and Mrs. Weston debate the wisdom of Emma's rule with the maturity and candor of opposition that mark so many of the disagreements in this novel. Emma has long been the subject of their quarrels, and Knightley has long been accustomed to monitor Emma with ready reproof. True to form, he warns that Emma's association with Harriet is "a bad thing" (*E*, 36). But though they proceed from an anxiety for improvement that we can appreciate only later, even the very worst of Knightley's criticisms turn out to be fretfully minute: Emma, he complains, has never finished her reading lists; she has not applied her talents steadily; no one has ever gotten the better of her precocity; her new young friend will harm

Emma by flattering her vanity, and Emma in turn will harm her by swelling her silly head (*E*, 37, 38). Mrs. Weston does not share Knightley's dire predictions about Emma's projects, because she considers her judgment worth relying on: "[w]here Emma errs once, she is in the right a hundred times" (*E*, 40). Here is no blind dependence on the infallibility of Emma's authority, but instead a confidence in its basic soundness: "She has qualities which may be trusted; she will never lead any one really wrong; she will make no lasting blunder" (*E*, 40).

Emma amply corroborates Mrs. Weston's faith in the fitness of Emma's rule, but often so tactfully as to be almost imperceptible. This tact, however, is necessary first of all because Emma's best actions are of the sort which she, unlike Mrs. Elton, disdains to trumpet. A few strokes of the pen, for example, show that in her attentions to the poor and afflicted of her parish, Emma is intelligent, generous, compassionate, and—whatever she is in her studies—steady. Further, although Knightley thinks her "rather negligent" in contributing to the "stock" of Miss Bates's "scanty comforts" (*E*, 155), Emma's "own heart" ranks visits there an obligation. She is not shown to fuss over sending that hindquarter of pork to the Bateses—though her father would mull and send less—and when she does explain to Knightley that respect for her father's peace prevents her from making her carriage of use to her neighbors, he smiles with conviction (*E*, 228). Because she nowhere styles herself "Lady Patroness," we can only assume that Emma considers the performance of untold acts of kindness a duty attached to her social position requiring no announcement or praise.

Considering the contrast between Emma and Mrs. Elton can enable us to distinguish the use of social position from the abuse of it, a proper sense of office from a repulsive officiousness; and in the process it offers a glimpse of the conservative model of social control working well. The principle of difference between the two women and their rules is not finally reducible to class. What makes Mrs. Elton intolerable is not that she is new money and Emma is old, and that Mrs. Elton thus only pretends to prerogatives of status Emma comes by honestly. Mrs. Elton's exertions of leadership set our teeth on edge because of their insistent publicity, not because of their intrinsic fraudulence. Emma may be convinced that in attending their party she "must have delighted the Coles—worthy people, who deserved to be made happy!" (*E*, 231), but she keeps the satisfactions of condescension to herself. But by tirelessly asserting her centrality in the minds of others, Mrs. Elton bullies her auditors into frustrated acquiescence: "Nobody can think less of dress in general than I do—but upon such an occasion as this, when everybody's eyes are so much upon me, and in compliment to the

Westons—who I have no doubt are giving this ball chiefly to do me honour—
I would not wish to be inferior to others" (E, 324). Determined to advertise her sagacity, Mrs. Elton furthermore has a vested interest in airing what
places others at a disadvantage, uncannily seizing on painful features of
others' lives, and forcing them to the center of attention: "I perfectly understand your situation, however, Miss Woodhouse—(looking towards
Mr. Woodhouse)—Your father's state of health must be a great drawback"
(E, 275). But Emma has ready stores of "politeness" (E, 157) which enable her
to respect what is delicate by leaving it unsaid. She feels gratified when Jane
Fairfax divulges the hardships of living at home; but she exclaims "Such a
home, indeed! such an aunt!" (E, 363) only to herself.

More than nicety is at issue here. Just as the impoliteness Lady Catherine
and Darcy evinced towards others in persistently apprising them of their
inferiority constituted a socially significant wrong, a theft of the self-
satisfaction to which all are entitled, so do Mrs. Elton's bruited exertions of
authority triumph improperly in the dejection of others—as when she,
intervening as friend as well as patron, hastens Jane's assignment as a
governess, or just as bad, when she colludes with her husband to humiliate
Harriet publicly for her upstart pretensions. At her worst, Emma transgresses in much the same way when she mocks Miss Bates at Box Hill, or
when she discloses her suspicions about Jane Fairfax to Frank Churchill.
Shameful though these infractions are, they stand out precisely because
they are so infrequent, and if Mrs. Elton's presence on the scene helps us
to identify and to deplore them, it also helps appreciate how much better
Emma handles herself by comparison. Generally Emma is, if anything, admirably forbearing: she endures page after page of "quiet prosings" and
often vexing developments without letting slip the slightest impatience,
and she brooks Mrs. Elton's presumption without so much as a sarcasm or
protest. Unlike Mrs. Elton, Emma has a proper regard for public opinion
that—with a few very important exceptions—restrains her impulse to
abuse. Feelings of "pride or propriety" make Emma "resolve on not being
the last to pay her respects" (E, 270) to the new bride, and when her
neighbors celebrate Mrs. Elton's attractions, Emma lets the praise pass
"from one mouth to another as it ought to do, unimpeded" (E, 281) by her
own dissent. Because Emma does not wish to be "exposed to odious suspicions, and imagined capable of pitiful resentment" (E, 291), she behaves
even more politely than she is inclined, while Mrs. Elton degenerates into
the blatancy of incivility. The neighborhood that did not exist in *Mansfield
Park* is everywhere in *Emma*. Emma herself defers to its civilizing restraints
and in the process shows conservative ideology working at its best. Henry

Tilney had pleaded that the watchful eyes of "voluntary spies" whose good opinion we value will repress the insolence of power, but General Tilney, as we recall, did not care how he treated his little guest or who knew it. But Emma is an authority figure responsive to the morally corrective influence of public opinion. This is what makes her feel the truth of Knightley's reproach at Box Hill, and this is what makes her resolute, swift, and feeling in her amends.[12]

Emma is so remarkable a novel at least in part for its ability to include what is politely left unsaid. The excellence of Emma's rule is often disclosed tactfully, because if it were vaunted brusquely à la Mrs. Elton, it would show her father at too great a disadvantage. Mr. Woodhouse's twofold hostility to disruption and indigestion so unfits him for the duties incumbent upon the head of a respected household that Emma is often obliged to ignore or to oppose him quietly for decency's sake, and in the process she displays powers of delicacy and forbearance which are the more impressive given the vivacity of her own temper and the incisiveness of her wit. When a most unpatricianlike selfishness on Mr. Woodhouse's part would exclude even as old and indispensable a friend as Mr. Knightley from dinner, Emma's "sense of right" interferes to procure him the proper invitation (*E*, 98). Similarly, while Mr. Woodhouse's anxiety for the health of others compels him to take food away from the guests at his table, Emma takes the duties of "patriarchal hospitality" upon her own shoulders without stinting: she "allowed her father to talk—but supplied her visitors in a much more satisfactory style" (*E*, 25). Thus the narrative style of *Emma* shows, but does not call attention to, the courtesy with which Emma manages the household around her. Her diplomacy is characteristically inobtrusive, as when she steers hypochondriacal companions away from topics, such as the insalubriousness of sea air, likely to occasion disputes not the less rancorous for their manifest pettiness; or when she intercedes to separate warring conversants, as when John Knightley indulges in one of his many eruptions of peevishness against Mr. Woodhouse himself (*E*, 105–6).

This kind of superintendence is one of the prerogatives of rule, and it comes as spontaneously to Emma as it does, say, to Sir Thomas. Other than voyaging to Antigua in order to squeeze more money out of his slave plantations—an enterprise which, even if it does highlight his decisiveness, hardly shows him to unequivocal advantage—Sir Thomas's principal activities are much the same as Emma's: he manages his household—with less aplomb—and he oversees the destinies of those around him. This he accomplishes principally by encouraging or discouraging specific marriages. That this is Emma's activity as well, and that this constitutes socially

significant activity, are points that merit emphasis. Progressives and re-
actionaries fought their ideological battles in the arenas of family and
neighborhood, and the whos, whys, and why-nots of matchmaking were
not the idle concerns of meddlesome women with nothing better to do.
In Austen's fiction the making and prohibiting of matches preoccupies
country squires like Sir John Middleton and great gentry like Darcy himself
just as much as it does well-meaning gossips like Mrs. Jennings; and in this
context, Mr. Woodhouse's opposition to marriage—"[H]e lamented that
young people would be in such a hurry to marry—and to marry strangers
too" (*E*, 177)—is particularly comical. And even though, of all Austen's
positive male authority figures, Mr. Knightley is remarkably the least offi-
cious and encroaching in this respect, as in all others, his recommendation
that Emma mind her own business—"Leave him [Elton] to chuse his own
wife. Depend upon it, a man of six or seven-and-twenty can take care of
himself" (*E*, 14)—is slightly disingenuous, and he later retracts it. Far from
being above applying his own understanding to other people's business, he
oversees the personal affairs of his neighbors more closely than Emma does,
and his indignation over Emma's "interference" with Harriet Smith is due in
part to the embarrassment he feels for his own, now futile, interference with
Robert Martin.

Emma is always taken to task for her scheme to improve Harriet, and this
disapproval exposes the importance we ascribe to the sex differential in
matters pertaining to authority. The satisfaction Emma takes in this project
is surely not unlike the self-approbation generally allowed to reflect well on
Sir Thomas when he decides to take Fanny from the squalor of Portsmouth
to the splendor of Mansfield. While he observes Fanny's comportment at the
ball "with much complacency," feeling "proud of his niece" and "pleased
with himself" for the "education and manners she owed to him" (*MP*, 276),
Emma, with the "real good-will of a mind delighted with its own ideas"
contemplates the patron-ward relationship with the same sense of personal
gratification: "*She* would notice her; she would improve her; she would
detach her from her bad acquaintance, and introduce her into good society;
she would form her opinions and her manners" (*E*, 24–25). If anything,
Emma's exertions of power on another's behalf are considerably more
generous than his. Sir Thomas admits Fanny into his household only on
the condition that she be accorded a semimenial status, and when she turns
on him in defiance of his authority and to assert her independence from his
intentions, he makes her feel his ire. But Emma realizes that bringing
Harriet to Hartfield accords her a status which Emma herself is now ob-
ligated to respect. Accordingly, when Harriet just as inevitably turns on

Emma and threatens to supplant her in Knightley's affections, Emma's own "strong sense of justice by Harriet" prompts her to admit that Harriet "had done nothing to forfeit the regard and interest which had been so voluntarily formed and maintained" (*E*, 408), and acknowledging her own responsibility for Harriet's aspirations, Emma declines to oppose, however heartily she may lament them.

But Emma's faults with respect to Harriet are imputed to be more serious than mere bossiness. Even granting, as characters in the novel do, that Emma's wish to improve Harriet's situation is not intrinsically wrong, Emma is held to be deluded in supposing Harriet worth the trouble at all, and in treating her as anything more than an irredeemably silly girl who ought to remain in the set to which she was born. Thus not only are Emma's attempts to "author" people according to her intentions held at fault, but so are her related efforts to "read" them: Emma is rebuked alternately as a dominatrix or as an "imaginist" and "female Quixote." The categories of authoring and reading may seem to have an unsuitably (post) modern ring to them, but historical considerations confirm them in decisively political ways. *Northanger Abbey*, for example, makes it clear that women's voices as writers and readers affront the moral authority of men—fathers, brothers, generals, clergymen. Austen's heroines typically bring about crises when they utter what their more conventional male sweethearts do not want to imagine or to hear: with the example of gothic fiction before her, Catherine strikes Henry dumb when she "imagines" his father's crimes; Mary unnerves Edmund when she speaks lightly of illicit sex, as a woman ought never to speak. "Imaginism" of Emma's sort, then, is not a private matter; it refuses to rest content with placid surfaces defenders of public order call reality, and it arrogates to itself the right to penetrate— "There was no denying that those [Knightley] brothers had penetration" (*E*, 135)—secrets some would not wish to see brought to light. In the high-Tory antiromance *The Heroine*, Eaton Stannard Barrett, as we have seen, attempted to exorcize precisely this socially disruptive potential of women authors and readers—and not just of gothic novels either, since Frances Burney's *Evelina* (1778) does just as much damage as Regina Maria Roche's *Children of the Abbey* (1798)—by undermining their authority. To accomplish this, he relegates them from the outset to the realm of insanity. Here Cherubina, crazed from an overdose of ladies' novels, imagines that she is a warrior poised for battle, that her servants are her vassals, and that her house is her castle. Ceremoniously arming herself, she even rallies her troops with patriotic cant about the degraded aristocracy, oppressed people, and glorious cause of liberty. A young lady who questions her father's paternity is already an outrage, but one who suffers disruptively viraginous delusions of grandeur to which she expects the world to submit cannot be tolerated. As if to underscore the dangerous affinity between the insanity of Cherubina's airs and the insanity of political rabble-rousing of all sorts, Barrett has Cherubina conclude her harangue to her imagined troops with a recognition of her talents as a politician: "I judged that the same qualities which have made me so good a heroine, would, if I were a man, have made me just as illustrious a patriot."[13] For a Tory conservative such as Barrett, female authority and female imagination, unchecked by responsible male authorities, have the power to turn the world upside down. He defuses this threat by defining it as illusory, by invoking a construction of reality which women's novels and women readers challenge every time they distrust the stories their mentors tell them and suggest a connection between their imaginative literature and real life: Cherubina ends up in a madhouse, where she is cured by a commonsensical mentor/suitor who impresses upon her the absolute distinction between romance and reality.

To consider Emma a female Quixote in this tradition is to imply a more simpleminded and transparent distinction between romance and reality than *Emma* anywhere permits. *The Heroine* is a travesty of female writing and reading, while *Emma*, like *Northanger Abbey* before it, is a cagey celebration of it. Such is the consummate mastery of Austen's plotting here that Emma's misapprehensions seem utterly plausible when we read the novel for the first time, and she appears willfully to "mis-read" the sunny clarity of truth only when our own repeated readings of this romance, the stuff of literary criticism, have laid her misconstructions bare. But even more to the point, *Emma* invites us to consider how the two poles of romance and reality, considered so inflexibly discrete in *The Heroine*, actually interpenetrate. In this respect *Emma* recalls and refines the aesthetic self-consciousness of the juvenilia and *Northanger Abbey*. Not surprisingly, given that *Emma* is after all a novel and Emma a character in it, Highbury is teeming with highly conventionalized tales of love, which are often referred to as "histories" and "stories," and which have left their living traces in the orphaned offspring who appear to comprise a rather large proportion of the community. In addition to Harriet herself, to whose "history" we will return, Jane Fairfax herself emerges from a matrix of several "interesting" sentimental histories. The hapless daughter of a love match between a lieutenant who dies in battle and a devoted bride who dies of grief, hers now is a tale of female difficulty. As such, her "history" would not be out of place next to Mary Wollstonecraft's *The Wrongs of Woman, or Maria* and Burney's *The Wanderer, or Female Difficulties*. As Emma rather shrewdly intuits, Jane's covert story is a tale of guilty passion presented amid an assortment of eroticized details that derive from the gothic. Emma considers this "fair heroine" (*E*, 220) as a persecuted, yet guilty nun, "leading a life of privation and penance" (*E*, 217) among family and neighbors, rather than mixing with the world. To Emma, she appears to be steeling herself "with the fortitude of a devoted noviciate" (*E*, 165) for the "mortification" now necessary because she, as Emma infers, has tasted the "dangerous pleasure" of being the beloved of her best friend's husband.[14]

Although their "histories" are not elaborated as methodically, the experiences of other characters have an aura of romance about them as well. Mr. Weston's first marriage appears to have been a romance of high life, in which the dashing Captain takes to wife a high-spirited and spoiled woman who alienates her wealthy relations, obliges her sweet-tempered husband to live beyond their means, who repines at their poverty, and who finally dwindles to a death that melts the hearts of erstwhile resentful relatives. The offspring of this impecunious match, Frank Churchill, is a "child of good fortune" (*E*, 448), and thus his story—like Emma's—is in many respects the reverse of Jane's, for it confounds the dictates of poetic justice and gives him more happiness than he deserves (*E*, 447). Even Miss Hawkins, likewise an orphan whose story ends up better perhaps than she deserves, is given the false history of the social climber, for her credit as well as Elton's require improving the "story" (*E*, 181) of her scanty fortune by rounding it *up* to ten thousand pounds (*E*, 181). Congratulating herself for her success in masterminding marriages, as it would appear for the time being, Emma believes that the matches which form so effortlessly under her guidance must entail a revision of *Midsummer Night's Dream*: a "Hartfield edition of Shakespeare" would require "a long note" on the line, "The course of true love never did run smooth" (*E*, 75). Emma's annotations may be wrong, but in thinking of a text to begin with, and this text in particular, she has not foolishly confounded the disparate categories of romance and reality, for the reality of Highbury is itself constituted by many different stories— adventures, distresses, robberies, rescues—not all of which ever get told or even noticed with the emphasis they could.

Emma's misapprehension of Harriet's "history" (*E*, 23) is generally agreed to be the most conspicuous example of her quixotic preference of romance to reality, and her example discloses why novelists like Barrett, let alone decent young men like Henry Tilney, consider female imaginism worse than foolish, downright dangerous. The "natural daughter of somebody" (*E*, 22), Harriet does indeed present quite a story, and as Austen and her contemporaries well knew, the telling or the suppression of it serves discernible political interests. As a child of a guilty connection, supported with minimal respectability but unacknowledged, Harriet inhabits a story about the failures of responsible paternity, a story which radical novelists, such as Inchbald in *Nature and Art* and Hays in *Victim of Prejudice*, did not let lie. Austen herself folded stories like Harriet's into the center of *Sense and Sensibility*, where the second Eliza, assumed to be the "natural daughter" (*Sense and Sensibility* 66) of Colonel Brandon, is herself about to give birth to yet another natural child after being seduced and abandoned by Willoughby. There, we remember, Lady Middleton could not tolerate even mentioning, much less associating with, a natural daughter, even one of reputedly genteel parentage. Although in 1813 Austen judged the topic sensitive enough to warrant deleting a sarcasm at Lady Middleton's expense from the second edition of *Sense and Sensibility*, Emma is ready enough to accept the breach of marital vows as a fact of life: Mr. Churchill's promiscuous production of "half a dozen natural children" (*E*, 393), she muses, may cut Frank out of his inheritance. In undertaking Harriet's improvement, then, Emma irreverently rocks the boat and refuses to mind her own business. Like Mrs. Smith in *Sense and Sensibility*, she wishes to exert morally corrective authority, and her attempt appears more impressive when we remember the prevalence and the potency of attitudes like Lady Middleton's.

To hold that Emma has quixotically "mis-read" Harriet's history, or that she herself "created what she saw" out of whole cloth instead of accepting the less interesting definiteness of "objective" truth, is thus to beg a lot of questions about the equity of the social system and the position of women generally in that system. It is to imply that Emma ought to have believed that her neighbors commit no sexual indiscretions and to assume that Harriet has no story. But even though it apotheosizes "true gentility, untainted in blood and understanding" (*E*, 358), *Emma* doesn't make matters quite so easy, for reality in *Emma* is not organized along the same lines and in accordance with the same interests Barrett had projected in *The Heroine*. To be sure, Emma *has* in some ways misread Harriet's story: Harriet turns out not to have been the daughter of a gentleman, as Emma had insisted. But Emma herself undercuts much of the import of this realization. When she admits that "even" Mr. Elton would not deserve a wife who lacks "the blood of gentility" (*E*, 482), she also, in a typically Austenian twist, avers that Harriet's blood was "likely to be as untainted, perhaps, as the blood of many a gentleman" (*E*, 482). If the gentility of "many a gentleman" is a fiction as well, Emma's imaginative trespass in Harriet's case proves to be not so egregious.

In some ways, then, *Emma* suggests that Emma has not misread Harriet after all, and that, on the contrary, other people have. Though initially the solitary and outspoken opponent of Emma's schemes for Harriet, Knightley ends up making some powerful concessions: "[Y]ou would have chosen for him better than he has chosen for himself.—Harriet Smith has some first-rate qualities which Mrs. Elton is totally without" (*E*, 331). Although Elton's own pride would balk at this acknowledgement, Knightley's observation proves persuasive. Having been so imperturbably confident of his power to tempt a woman of Emma's fortune to change her situation, he is stung by Emma's plan for him: "I am not, I think, quite so much at a loss" (*E*, 132). But the bride he triumphantly brings to Highbury belies this indignant claim: while his mate is perfectly suited to him in conceit and mean-spiritedness, her "history" of gentility turns out to be only slightly less spurious and "romantic" than Harriet's, although it is rapidly gaining the privileged footing of reality.

The same flexibility in the social fabric that makes Harriet a legitimate subject for Emma's solicitude has already accommodated Mr. Weston, and is now, alas, giving place to the clergyman's wife—whose father, like Harriet's and Mr. Weston's, was also in trade. What is accepted as real and what is dismissed as imaginary, under these circumstances, then, is a matter of social position, which is always itself in the process of changing. But if this consideration vindicates Emma in one quarter, it turns against her in another, for the fluidity of social boundaries confounds the authoritarian readings of a Barrett, and to some extent, in a different way, of an Emma as well. Emma herself has always been spotty in recognizing this feature of her society. Even as she considers the Coles to occupy a different level of being than herself and observes their steps up the social ladder with some resentment, she recommends Mr. Weston as a model of gentlemanliness without blinking; even as she taxes Robert Martin with the onerous charge of being a coarse farmer, she readily makes exceptions of his educated sisters. If Emma's ideas about the disposition of social status in her world are none too consistent, it is with good cause. The same mechanisms which make rises possible make falls possible as well, and therefore can threaten Emma with the loss of her own authority. The women in *Emma* who do not and cannot reign bring Emma to this humbling consciousness. During her penitent visit to Miss Bates, Emma pauses in sobered contemplation, not of the condition of mankind in general, but of woman's situation in particular: "The contrast between Mrs. Churchill's importance in the world, and Jane Fairfax's, struck her; one was every thing, the other nothing—and she sat musing on the difference of woman's destiny" (*E*, 384).

Emma's exclusion of men from her reverie indicates her readiness not to omit herself from that category of persons whose status as "every thing" or "nothing" seems gratuitous and so undependable. The penultimate chapters of *Emma* present a different heroine from the one who at the outset appeared to assume the permanence of her power and in that assumption had become a rather unfeeling reader. Pondering the difference of woman's destiny, however, Emma remorsefully relinquishes "all her former fanciful and unfair conjectures" (*E*, 384) about Jane and Mr. Dixon well before she actually learns about their untruth. Figuring forth the vulnerability of handsome, clever, and accomplished young ladies to the indignities of powerlessness, penury, and dependence, Jane's story, unlike Harriet's, is not a gratifying one to Emma, and Jane's unwillingness to impart it makes her a closed book that keeps others, most notably Emma herself, at an unflatteringly inaccessible distance, and one even Mr. Knightley, who loves an "open temper" (*E*, 289), cannot like. By preferring to read Jane's story as a tale of guilty passion, Emma had maintained for herself the prerogative either of censure or of generous exoneration that placed her apart from and above Jane. As Emma herself recognizes, in having done so she has "transgressed the duty of woman by woman" (*E*, 231). As a single woman in need of work, Jane must sell herself in slavery, not as human flesh, but as human intellect, she is quick to add. But governesses were typically suspected of an interest in selling their flesh as well. As Mary Ann Radcliffe argued in her *The Female Advocate* (1799), women seeking any sort of livelihood are typically treated like prostitutes, because prostitution is the only sale which they are recognized as capable of transacting, the only thing they have ever really been taught to do. By indulging in precisely these sorts of suspicions, Emma has herself confirmed, rather than opposed, thinking which transgresses "the duty of woman by woman" and betrayed a basic solidarity in order to take up the ugly role of rich and haughty women in tales of female difficulty, whose insolence, neglect, or spite prompt them to exacerbate the pain of those they should comfort: "Of all the sources of evil surrounding the former [i.e., Jane], since her coming to Highbury, she was persuaded that she must herself have been the worst. She must have been a perpetual enemy. They never could have been all three together, without her having stabbed Jane Fairfax's peace in a thousand instances" (*E*, 421).

But once again, with this history as with Harriet's, the highly qualified texture of *Emma* makes it impossible definitively to conclude that Emma had been quixotically wrong. Even the mild Mrs. Weston views Jane's secret engagement as her "one great deviation from the strict rule of right" (*E*, 400), and Jane herself considers it an illicit act "contrary to all my sense of right" (*E*, 419). Curiously enough, however, Emma herself finally sees

Jane Fairfax's story in light of another Shakespearean history, this time from *Romeo and Juliet*: "If a woman can ever be excused for thinking only of herself, it is in a situation like Jane Fairfax's.—Of such, one may almost say, that 'the world is not their's, nor the world's law'" (*E*, 400). Although Emma's assertion is carefully hedged, it must be noted that she not only relinquishes the moral authority she had been so quick to wield at Jane's expense; she also attempts to place stories such as Jane's beyond the reach of censure which conservative novelists insisted upon when they vigorously execrated men and women who exempted themselves from the rules of social control. Austen herself makes the same attempt Emma does when she imparts to Jane Fairfax "the kindness" of felicity Jane's own "conscience tells me ought not to be" (*E*, 419), or when she makes careless characters like Frank Churchill happier than they deserve to be.

Toward the end of the novel, when "the great Mrs. Churchill" quite abruptly "was no more" (*E*, 387), and when as a result Jane's "days of insignificance and evil" (*E*, 403) come to an equally unexpected halt, the arbitrariness and the instability of the "difference of woman's destiny" is further confirmed, for now the great Miss Woodhouse herself is on the verge of dwindling into "nothing." As beloved friends around her pair off and depart to form new ties of intimacy within their own domestic circles, Emma is left isolated and alone, the mistress of an empty mansion, her domain painfully contracted. Considering the substance of Knightley's rebuke at Box Hill, the apparent desolation closing in on Emma seems particularly poignant. Having considered Miss Bates in every respect except celibacy her immutable opposite, Emma had allowed that this "old maid" was "the proper sport of boys and girls" (*E*, 85). But Miss Bates too was once significant, "her notice," as Knightley reminds Emma, once "an honour" (*E*, 375). To a sobered Emma, who fears her days of insignificance are about to begin, the "difference" between her destiny and that of Miss Bates is not so great, for the future which seems to stretch out before both of them consists of the solitary care of an aging parent. Already Emma can gingerly intimate that the coming death of her father holds forth an "increase of melancholy!" (*E*, 450) she shrinks from facing alone, and the best that Emma is prepared to imagine for her future is a pious cheer altogether worthy of the kindly maiden aunt who bears a similar charge: "[H]owever inferior in spirit and gaiety might be the following and every future winter of her life to the past, it would yet find her more rational, more acquainted with herself, and leave her less to regret when it were gone" (*E*, 423).

The "resources"—beauty, wit, employment, money—which Emma thinks can preserve her from sharing Miss Bates's ignominious destiny as a poor old maid finally amount to very little. It is single womanhood itself, the lack of a circle of people to be "first" with, that turns out to be the evil, and not a powerlessness to "frighten those who might hate her, into outward respect" (*E*, 21). Much to her humbled bewilderment, Emma herself has gone from considering herself the confident author of other people's stories to realizing that she has instead been the hoodwinked and quite powerless subject of another very stale one, the "old story, probably—a common case" (*E*, 427) of an eminently flatterable provincial girl deceived by a duplicitous and mobile man who is pulling all the strings she herself could not. This necessarily reminds us that Emma's "reign" has always been subject to the restrictions common to her sex. Mrs. Elton may be insufferable when she avers that "to those who had no resources" a move from the beau monde of Bristol to Highbury might be a sacrifice; "but my resources," she goes on, "made me quite independent" (*E*, 276–77). But her boast here, as elsewhere, calls attention to a real problem. *Emma* is set into motion by the distinctively feminine boredom Emma suffers after Miss Taylor's departure. The merest "half a mile" (*E*, 6) between Hartfield and Randalls spans an impossibly huge chasm, and not just to Emma either. To her timid father, the distance is too short to warrant the alarming step of ordering the carriage, and to John Knightley, who loathes nothing so much as "another man's house" (*E*, 113), it is great enough to entail a trek no hearth-loving man would want to undertake. Having "ventured once alone" to Randalls, Emma deems it "not pleasant" (*E*, 26) for "solitary female walking" (*E*, 18), and the incidence of gypsy assaults upon unprotected schoolgirls proves her uneasiness to be more than an excess of delicacy. By showing how a matter as simple as getting from one nearby house to another to see a dear friend is for Emma almost prohibitively complicated, *Emma* tactfully shows conditions which make even "the best blessings of existence" (*E*, 5) moot. Considered in this light, Emma's wish to have "a Harriet Smith" (*E*, 26) is not the heavy wrong Mr. Knightley is inclined to think. As Mrs. Weston explains, "perhaps no man can be a good judge of the comfort a woman feels in the society of one of her own sex" (*E*, 36), a woman, moreover, confined to unvarying "intellectual solitude" (*E*, 7). Emma finally terms her fiasco with Harriet "the worst of all her womanly follies" (*E*, 463), not because women are prone to follies in general and therefore will always need the guidance of Mr. Knightleys, but rather because the conditions of isolation and restriction that exposed Emma to danger to begin with are those to which women are uniquely exposed.

If *Emma* begins with the assumption of a broad arena for legitimate and useful female rule independent from masculine supervision, then, it does not end with the assertion of its sufficiency. By the conclusion of her story,

Emma is brought low, and marriage saves her. To scholars who see Austen as a political conservative this upshot is particularly grateful because it appears to rein her in. Indeed, Mr. Knightley does look like the benevolent, all-seeing monitor crucial to the conservative fiction of Austen's day. Hovering like a chaperon around the edges of every major scene—the portrait party at Hartfield, the dinner at the Coles, the word game at the Abbey, the outing at Box Hill—he is always on the lookout for wrongdoing and nonsense, always alert in his benefactions for the poor and innocent. Knightley himself confesses that with Emma his role as moral censor has been particularly obnoxious: "I have blamed you, and lectured you, and you have borne it as no other woman in England would have borne it" (E, 430), and he is probably right. Alternately beaming with heartfelt approval when Emma acquits herself properly, and frowning with pain whenever she misbehaves, he has been half paternal and half pedagogical in his watchfulness.

But this story is no less a "human disclosure" than any of the other stories in Emma. Accordingly, it does not tell all either; something is "a little disguised, or a little mistaken" (E, 431). Knightley is not, first of all, above imaginistic misreadings of his own, nor can he be. As his readiness to denounce Frank Churchill as an "[a]bominable scoundrel" (E, 426) attests, Mr. Knightley is just as apt as Emma to misconstrue where his interest is at stake, investing his upstart rival with the extremely literary character of the heartless cad. But Frank goes from "villain" to "not desperate" to a "very good sort of fellow" (E, 433) in a matter of moments as soon as Knightley learns that Emma never loved him. Furthermore, Knightley is not nearly so wise and all seeing as he appears to think. He extols "the beauty of truth and sincerity in all our dealings with each other" (E, 446), but many things—fortunately—have escaped his monitorship, Emma's worst faults among them. Knightley never learns, for example, that Emma did not stop with Mr. Elton, but proceeded to match Harriet and Frank; nor does he learn that Harriet, for her part, learned enough about gentility to disdain the very idea, and to prefer him instead, which is, after all, more than Emma had the wisdom to do. Emma, of course, must keep at least some of these humiliating little secrets to herself. To do any less would be an Eltonian trespass on Harriet's feelings. But even after Harriet's marriage takes the pressure off, Emma is still disingenuous about the "full and perfect confidence" she can now look forward to practicing as a conjugal "duty" (E, 475). She has had more to "blush" (E, 446) about than Harriet all along, and only moments later, Emma is blushing again, this time at the name of Dixon: "'I can never think of it,' she cried, 'without extreme shame'" (E, 477). One wonders how Mr. Knightley would judge Emma's readiness not only to form scandalous thoughts about his favorite, but exultantly to impart them as well. But Emma's part in Jane's story is never disclosed, and Emma herself gets by with no more than some private embarrassment whenever she receives "a little more praise than she deserved" (*E*, 475). Austen's refusal to expose and to arraign a heroine reprehensible by conventional standards shows how she parts company with conservative counterparts, and given the morally privileged position monitor figures of Knightley's ilk enjoy in their fiction, Austen's determination to establish a discrepancy between what he knows and what we know about Emma is daring.

But Knightley is a far more extraordinary character than a monitor manqué. He himself does not set much store by his monitorship, and even though he always does lecture and blame, nothing ever comes of it. Monitors like Edgar Mandlebert in *Camilla* and Edmund in *Mansfield Park* enforce their advice by threatening to withdraw affection and approval if they are not immediately obeyed—"advice" being for them, as we have seen in *Mansfield Park*, merely a decent term for "command." They stand as fair-weather friends who may turn on naughty charges at any minute. But Knightley and Emma stand on an equal footing, and this necessarily modifies the dynamic of advice giving, endowing it with more of the friendly directness that marks the advice scenes between Mrs. Gardiner and Elizabeth. For Knightley, advice is not a function of power. He does not assume that the parental liberty he takes in reproaching due him—indeed it is a "privilege rather endured than allowed" (*E*, 374). Being who and what she is, Emma dishes out almost as much as she gets, and when she does not follow his advice—which is almost always—he does not turn away.

Knightley, no less than Darcy, is thus a fantastically wishful creation of benign authority, in whom the benefits and attractions of power are preserved and the abuses and encroachments expelled. As such he is the very reverse of Coelebs in Hannah More's *Coelebs in Search of a Wife*. To the extent that *Coelebs* tells young ladies to comport themselves modestly like sweet helpmates if they want to catch a husband, it holds forth the promise to girls across the kingdom that their skill at housewifery and their strenuous exertions of self-subordination will all pay off in the end, making them more desirable to the best sort of men than lively women, wits, and flirts. But *Emma* does the opposite. Here choosy men prefer saucy women—not women who place themselves at the margins, letting themselves be noticed only so they may show that they are not so vain as to crave attention, but women who love even the unflattering limelight, and who do not hesitate to pen themselves the subject of other people's news to Maple Grove and

Ireland: "Mr. Frank Churchill and Miss Woodhouse flirted together excessively" (*E*, 368). In the character of Isabella, Austen shows that the good
little wife cannot hold a candle to Emma: ". . . poor Isabella, passing her life
with those she doated on, full of their merits, blind to their faults, and
always innocently busy, might have been a model of right feminine happiness" (*E*, 140). The "might" here does more than underscore the difference
between how Mr. Woodhouse deplores the destiny of "poor Isabella" and
how more conventional people would envy it. It also places the statement
outside narrative endorsement. Chattering vacuously, oblivious to how she
and her children endure the same curse of "living with an ill-tempered
person" (*E*, 121) which she complacently pities in Mr. Churchill, Isabella
has probably fewer claims to ready wit than Harriet herself. And to a man
as discriminating as Knightley she presents "striking inferiorities" which
serve only to throw Emma's "brilliancy" (*E*, 433) into higher relief. Wifely
virtues are not meet for Emma; her hand, as he says somewhat proudly, "is
the strongest" (*E*, 297), and he likes it that way.

The conclusion of *Emma* shares the polyvalence characteristic of the
endings in Austen's later novels. The tenderness of Emma's filial piety—
strong enough to make her hesitate to marry at all—proves her to be reassuringly devoted to precisely those relationships which political conservatives wanted to protect. Moreover, Emma's devolution to marriage with a
man seventeen years her senior puts an end to her "reign alone," and brings
her back within the confines of that relationship which she had offended so
many readers by slighting. But problems still remain. Because Emma and
Knightley are social equals, marriage itself does not present the same difficulty it had in *Pride and Prejudice*. There, in order to secure the value of
Elizabeth's reward—Pemberley and Darcy—Austen had to preserve the
mythic prestige of the same institutions that had earlier depressed Elizabeth's significance. But because *Emma* deals more specifically with female
rule, a conclusion like that of *Pride and Prejudice* is inadmissible: it would too
conspicuously diminish the social prestige on which the heroine has rightly
drawn all along. In order to secure Emma's prestige and the prerogative that
comes with it, the ending of *Emma* turns back on the very outlines it seems to
confirm. Mr. Knightley himself avers, "A man would always wish to give a
woman a better home than the one he takes her from" (*E*, 428), and Mr.
Weston's feelings show that such generosity, far from being sublimely
disinterested, confers an obligation which later affords "a man" the sweet
pleasure of his wife's gratitude. But while Donwell Abbey is surely "a better
home" than Hartfield, *Emma* closes by deferring Knightley's wish indefinitely
to a time none wish to hasten—that is to say, until Mr. Woodhouse's death.

As Emma well knows, Knightley's move into Hartfield is extraordinary considering his own power and independence: "How very few of those men in a rank of life to address Emma would have renounced their own home for Hartfield!" (*E*, 467). The conclusion which seemed tamely and placidly conservative thus takes an unexpected turn, as the guarantor of order himself cedes a considerable portion of the power which custom has allowed him to expect. In moving to Hartfield, Knightley is sharing *her* home, and in placing himself within her domain, Knightley gives his blessing to her rule.

Without working off so many of the politicized texts which commonly undergird Austen's earlier fiction, *Emma* accomplishes the same social criticism as they did, by figuring forth figures of positive and unashamed authority more interested in promoting than repressing satisfaction, and by establishing the priority of social arrangements which, without being revolutionary or anarchistic, nevertheless fall outside the model drearily exemplified, say, in *Mansfield Park*. Their probity being utterly certain, Emma and Knightley do not have to bend to the yoke of conventions that do not suit them, and neither, within limits of course, does Austen. *Emma* ends with a marriage, it is true, but it also celebrates a "small band of true friends" (*E*, 484), and gets away without defining a new domestic circle. Emma and Knightley yet have their separate concerns, their separate realms, their separate rule. This atypicality makes social climbers like Mrs. Elton nervous— "Shocking plan, living together [at Hartfield]. It would never do" (*E*, 469). But eccentricity is one of the privileges of the elite, and in this case it permits the hero and heroine to be husband and wife, yet live and rule together with the autonomy of friends.

Notes

1. In B.C. Southam, ed. *Jane Austen: The Critical Heritage, Vol. I: 1811–1870* (London: Routledge & Kegan Paul, 1968), 263, 265.

2. R. Brimley Johnson, *Jane Austen* (London: Sheed and Ward, 1927), 74, 72–3; R. W. Chapman, *Facts and Problems* (Oxford: Clarendon Press, 1948), 134; *Emma*, ed., Lionel Trilling (Boston: Houghton Mifflin, 1957), xxv–xxvi, included in this casebook.

3. *Memoir of Jane Austen*, 157.

4. Bernard Paris, *Character and Conflict in Jane Austen's Novels: A Psychological Approach* (Detroit: Wayne State University Press, 1978), 69, 73.

5. Alistair Duckworth, *The Improvement of the Estate* (Baltimore, Md.: Johns Hopkins University Press, 1971), 148.

6. Marvin Mudrick, *Jane Austen: Irony as Defense and Discovery* (Princeton, N.J.: Princeton University Press, 1952), 181–206; Edmund Wilson, "A Long Talk About Jane Austen," *New Yorker* 20 (24 June 1944): 69.

7. Wayne C. Booth, *The Rhetoric of Fiction* (Chicago: University of Chicago Press, 1961), 260, included in this casebook, 114.

8. Trilling, introduction to *Emma*, x; *The Opposing Self* (New York: Viking, 1955), 116. Such attitudes cannot be dismissed as the crudeness of a bygone era, for a tacit belief that for women, at least, biology is destiny still underpins recent criticism about *Emma*. P. J. M. Scott, for example, insists that "Miss Woodhouse"—as she is repeatedly called—is "frightened of the wedded state"; *Jane Austen: A Reassessment* (New York: Barnes and Noble, 1982), 64.

9. *Jane Austen's Letters*, 504 (16 February 1813); F. B. Pinion, *A Jane Austen Companion* (New York: St. Martin's Press, 1973, rev. ed. 1976), 21.

10. Scott, *Reassessment*, 67–68.

11. Stuart M. Tave, *Some Words of Jane Austen* (Chicago: University of Chicago Press, 1973), 246. I am much indebted to Tave's now classic study which so illuminates the distinctive features of Austen's language.

12. For a complementary discussion of the ethical importance of the community, see Julia Prewitt Brown, *Jane Austen's Novels: Social Change and Literary Form* (Cambridge: Harvard University Press, 1979).

13. Eaton Stannard Barrett, *The Heroine* (London, 1813), 3 vols., vol. 3, 168–69, 171.

14. For a discussion of the gothic elements in the characterization of Jane Fairfax, see Judith Wilt, "The Powers of the Instrument, or Jane, Frank, and the Pianoforte," in *Persuasions, The Jane Austen Society of North America*, no. 15 (16 December 1983): 41–47.

Reading Characters

Self, Society, and Text in Emma

JOSEPH LITVAK

◆ ◆ ◆

IN *THE MADWOMAN IN THE ATTIC,* Sandra M. Gilbert and Susan Gubar describe the fate of the Austenian heroine as a "fall into literacy" (Gilbert and Gubar, 139). To fall into literacy is to "fall from authority into the acceptance of one's status as a mere character" (GG, 161), to be at once silenced and confined—in the words of one chapter title, to be "Shut Up in Prose." Yet Gilbert and Gubar show how heroines like Elizabeth Bennet, Emma Woodhouse, and Anne Elliot subvert the patriarchal structures in which they are inscribed, imaging Jane Austen's own quiet subversion of the repressive ideology her novels seem to endorse. In reclaiming authority, both Austen and these characters assert their "irrepressible interiority" and their "belief in female subjectivity" (GG, 179).

Austen's novels are indeed subtly subversive, but this subversion does not take place in the name of interiority, subjectivity, or even authority, if authority means nothing more than "freedom, autonomy, and strength" (GG, 177). These virtues look surprisingly like those of the phallic pen to which Gilbert and Gubar, asking "with what organ can females generate texts?" (GG, 7), seek a feminist alternative. Moreover, despite the acuity of their individual analyses, Gilbert and Gubar force themselves into the peculiar position of implying that authorship—a role superior to that of the "mere character"—involves a redemption from "literacy," that the ideal author is somehow external to her text, beyond or above textuality. Significantly, this attitude places them in the unlikely company of certain male critics whose mistrust of "literacy," or literariness, derives from an ideology with which feminism would seem to have little in common.

In an almost canonical gesture, critics of *Emma* stigmatize linguistic playfulness, or merely a fondness for the written word, as a threat to moral well-being. Marvin Mudrick typifies this stance, indicting in both the novel and its heroine—"whom," Austen predicted, "no one but myself will much like" (Austen-Leigh, 157)—what he calls the "triumph of surface," where the scandal of "wit adrift from feeling" finds its objective correlative in Emma's latent lesbianism (Mudrick, 203).[1] Admittedly, Gilbert and Gubar differ from Austen's male critics in their reasons for wanting to separate self and text. Whereas the latter equate literariness with frivolity and narcissism, the former view it as an effect of living in the "tight place" to which women are condemned (GG, 113). Pushed dangerously close to the contaminating world of signs, the Austenian heroine, like Austen herself, must exercise extraordinary ingenuity to keep her autonomous selfhood intact. Both the feminist critics and the conservatives, however, despite their manifest political differences, subscribe to the ideology of character implicit in Malcolm Bradbury's observation that *Emma* persuades us "to see the full human being as full, fine, morally serious, totally responsible, entirely involved, and to consider every human action as a crucial committing act of self-definition" (Bradbury, 231).

As D. A. Miller has noted, Austen's quiet authority tends to intimidate even her shrewdest readers (Miller, 59).[2] Yet when characters in her work suggest not the plenitude invoked by Bradbury but, rather, the artifice and materiality of *written* characters, moralism encounters significant obstacles. To locate these linguistic residues, these scandals of "literacy," is to identify traces of Austen's own rebellion against an overly reassuring moral ideology, traces that intimate a subversiveness far more interesting than that imagined by Gilbert and Gubar.[3]

A brief passage from *Mansfield Park* (1814) will serve as a prelude to the tensions at work in *Emma* (1816) and as proof that, even in what looks like her most authoritarian novel, Austen can disrupt her own orthodoxy. The description concerns Fanny Price's attempt, late in the novel, to introduce her sister to the pleasures of reading:

[A]fter a few days, the remembrance of her books grew so potent and stimulative, that Fanny found it impossible not to try for books again.

There were none in her father's house; but wealth is luxurious and daring—and some of hers found its way to a circulating library. She became a subscriber—amazed at being any thing *in propria persona*, amazed at her own doings in every way; to be a renter, a chuser of books! And to be having any one's improvement in view of her choice! But so it was. Susan had read nothing, and Fanny longed to give her a share in her own first pleasures, and inspire a taste for the biography and poetry which she delighted in herself.

(*Mansfield Park*, 398)

The exultant tone of Austen's *style indirect libre* imitates Fanny's joy on realizing herself as what Bradbury calls a "full human being." Yet the giddiness of the passage may also betoken Austen's response to an inconspicuous but "potent and stimulative" contradiction. For the embarrassing fact that the passage just barely conceals is that Fanny comes into her own only by entering a system of exchange, a circulating library. To be "any thing *in propria persona*," Fanny must spend her wealth, dispersing it into a larger economy; to consolidate her personhood, she has to insert herself into a constantly fluctuating literary structure. It is precisely her fall into "literacy," or literariness, that establishes Fanny's selfhood.

This passage merits attention not because it speaks of reading and writing: these themes occur often enough—and often innocently—in Austen's novels. Its interest, rather, lies in the way its literary references hint at some more than merely thematic literariness, some nagging but unspecifiable linguistic opacity in the novel itself. By collapsing the distance, moreover, between self and text—between a saving inwardness and a dangerously verbal sociability—the passage confounds categories that the novel posits elsewhere as opposites.

In *Emma*, this unsettling of polarities finds its wittiest advocate in the heroine herself, who, in a characteristic move, complains that Mr. Knightley, the novel's "normative and exemplary figure" (Duckworth, 148), finds their respective judgments "not near enough to give me a chance of being right, if we think differently" (D, 99). Yet Emma's attempt to substitute difference for opposition is more than just a clever piece of sophistry. Emma is frequently "wrong," as she is here, but perhaps she is "right" to question the absoluteness with which Knightley does in fact view the distinction between them. Perhaps, moreover, her "wrongness" is often closer to being "right"—that is, to yielding knowledge of the fictions that sustain social existence—than Knightley and his scholarly advocates will admit. Patriarchal criticism of *Emma*, of course, takes Knightley's side, portraying the narrative as a conflict in which "right" seeks to appropriate "wrong" and to recast it (her) in its (his) own image. It is possible, however, to pursue an apparently perverse but more critically productive tactic: we can give Emma some respect and construe the conflict dialectically, treating it less as an opposition and more as a difference.

We might try, then, to read the novel as a contest between Emma and Knightley, a contest between two equally compelling interpretations of the self—especially the female self—and society. Knightley states his views succinctly when he objects to Emma's adoption of Harriet Smith as her protégée: "I am much mistaken if Emma's doctrines give any strength of mind, or tend at all to make a girl adapt herself rationally to the varieties of her situation in life.—They only give a little polish" (*Emma*, 39). Despite the stark opposition that Knightley's terms suggest, the difference between the two implicit pedagogies cannot be simplified as the difference between a serious and a playful education or between a moral and an aesthetic one. For if Knightley's "strength of mind" borders on the conformist virtue of "adaptability," Emma's "polish," while it signals a politics of superficiality, is by no means superficial.

Whenever characters in *Emma* seem merely to be playing with words, the stakes are in fact much higher. One particularly instructive episode revolves around "puzzles," anagrams that the contestants must unscramble. Here the chief competitors are not Knightley and Emma but Knightley and Frank Churchill, whose recalcitrance, as we will see, Emma refines. Knightley dislikes Frank Churchill, not only because the younger man seems to be a rival for Emma's affections but also because Frank presumes to "read every body's character" (*E*, 150). Having just let slip a possible clue to his involvement with Jane Fiarfax, and regretting his carelessness, Frank uses the word game as a pretext for apology:

> Frank Churchill placed a word before Miss Fairfax. She gave a slight glance around the table, and applied herself to it. Frank was next to Emma, Jane opposite to them—and Mr. Knightley so placed as to see them all; and it was his object to see as much as he could, with as little apparent observation. The word was discovered, and with a faint smile pushed away.
>
> (*E*, 347–48)

As Knightley's stance here shows, his resentment of Frank stems in part from his fear that Frank may usurp the role of master reader: it is Knightley alone who shall reserve the right "to read every body's character," to be "so placed as to see them all." Knightley's motives here are typical: if *Emma*, as many critics have noted, is a detective novel, then Knightley, even more than Emma herself, aspires to the role of chief detective. For while Emma is content to fantasize about various romantic scenarios involving Frank Churchill, Knightley will not rest until he has seen into the heart of the mystery surrounding Frank and Jane. For Knightley, reading fosters "strength of mind," but it is also a mode of surveillance.

By acting *un*interested, Knightley would appear *dis*interested as well. But his surreptitious behavior undermines the notion of disinterested reading. Seeing without appearing to observe, reading without appearing to read, Knightley at once admits and suppresses this duplicity. Later in the novel, the fervor with which he praises the "disinterestedness" of Jane's love for Frank (*E*, 428), when in fact her own pecuniary and perhaps erotic interest in that relationship seems considerable, betrays Knightley's extraordinary interest in disinterestedness, a virtue he is apt to see even where it does not exist.[4] Earlier in the novel, the vehemence with which he denounces Frank, whom he does not even know yet, strikes Emma as "unworthy the real liberality of mind which she was always used to acknowledge in him" (*E*, 151). Of course, the most memorable illustration of Knightley's partiality is his comically nitpicking reading of Frank's long letter to Mrs. Weston, a reading whose reductiveness Emma labors to mitigate. However "impressive and admirable" Knightley may be (Mudrick, 200), he is hardly an innocent interpreter.[5]

Knightley continues his detective work, recalling the incriminating remark that Frank has tried to explain away by recourse to an alleged "dream":

> The word was *blunder*; and as Harriet exultingly proclaimed it, there was a blush on Jane's cheek which gave it a meaning not otherwise ostensible. Mr. Knightley connected it with the dream; but how it could all be, was beyond his comprehension. How the delicacy, the discretion of his favourite could have been so lain asleep! He feared there must be some decided involvement. Disingenuousness and double-dealing seemed to meet him at every turn. These letters were but the vehicle for gallantry and trick. It was a child's play, chosen to conceal a deeper game on Frank Churchill's part.
>
> (*E*, 348)

Joseph Wiesenfarth observes that the "word 'blunder' runs like a discord through the novel, indicating mistakes that are made in the games of words as well as in the more serious and dangerous games of matchmaking"

(Wiesenfarth, 210). The recurrence of the word points indeed to the centrality of misinterpretation and misbehavior in this would-be bildungsroman. Yet the problems that a proper education—or at least one overseen by Knightley— would correct may be more fundamental than mere "mistakes": the discord that runs through the novel may signify a certain perverse malfunctioning that can be neither corrected nor even regulated. For what disturbs Knightley here is that his attempts at interpretive mastery of Frank Churchill's game meet with resistance; he encounters not just the temporary unintelligibility of scrambled letters but the much greater recalcitrance of "disingenuousness and double-dealing." As we have seen, Knightley's own posture partakes of a certain disingenuousness as well. Yet he cannot accept Frank's "puzzles" as more than just structurally puzzling. What should have been mere "child's play" has turned out "to conceal a deeper game," and Knightley can tolerate only a socially sanctioned and therefore superficial "depth," only a legible illegibility.[6] The social mechanism favored by Knightley contains and neutralizes subjectivity by encoding it within a cultural alphabet, so that one may read character by reading the characters, or letters, that a character forms.

The first sign of malfunctioning appears when Jane's blush gives the word *blunder* a "meaning," but one "not otherwise ostensible." Thus finding the affair "beyond his comprehension," Knightley experiences the same blockage that awaits the reader who approaches Jane Austen's novels unprepared for their frequent literariness, expecting only the easeful wisdom of "gentle Jane." Frank's "deeper game" defies Knightley's authority, refusing to confirm the older man as the paternal or patriarchal supervisor of children at play. For such, in Knightley's view, is the purpose of games. Since they presuppose rules, they emblematize the governability of society. To the extent that they include a moment of limited opacity, games permit the illusion that each player's individual self possesses a unique interiority. To the extent that they subordinate this individuality to an ultimately decipherable code, games ensure the transparency of the self. The real winner, thus, is the ideology of institutional control—or what Knightley will refer to euphemistically as the "beauty of truth and sincerity in all our dealings with each other" (*E*, 446).

At least in this round, however, that ideology loses: the most that Knightley can infer is "some decided involvement," probably of Frank Churchill with Jane Fairfax. Frank would appear triumphant for the time being despite his blunder, because he has rewritten the rules of the game so that the game itself is no longer the same. To assume, as Knightley does, that "these letters were but the vehicle for gallantry and trick" is not to understand the new game but, rather, to concede its mystery.

Vehicles and conveyance loom large in the next problematic passage as well. In one of her rare utterances, the shadowy Jane Fairfax, talking with Knightley's brother, delivers a surprisingly impassioned hymn to the postal service:

> "The post office is a wonderful establishment!" said she.—"The regularity and dispatch of it! If one thinks of all that it has to do, and all that it does so well, it is really astonishing!"
>
> "It is certainly very well regulated."
>
> "So seldom that any negligence or blunder appears! So seldom that a letter, among the thousands that are constantly passing about the kingdom, is even carried wrong—and not one in a million, I suppose, actually lost! And when one considers the variety of hands, and of bad hands too, that are to be deciphered, it increases the wonder!"
>
> (*E*, 296)

Certain "literary" institutions seem to inspire a significant rhetorical excess in Austen's novels: Jane's praise of the post office is as suspiciously feverish as Fanny's delight in belonging to the library. Offering her own version of the Lacanian dictum that "a letter always arrives at its destination," Jane may very well be denying her fear that letters do not always arrive where and when they should. If Lacan's formulation insists on the inevitability of a certain system or structure, then Jane's hyperbolic encomium both re-presses and reveals grave doubts about the inevitability of any system or structure whatsoever. We will learn, of course, that Jane is concerned about the "regularity" of her clandestine correspondence with Frank Churchill and that, indeed, their engagement is broken off as a result of a serious blunder on the part not of the post office but of Frank himself: he simply forgets to mail an all-important letter. Yet the postal service is merely a synecdoche for the much larger system of communication on which the novel centers—namely, the social text in which the characters keep construing and misconstruing one another—so that any anxiety about mail deliveries may be taken as an anxiety about the semiotic efficiency or governability of society as a whole.

Jane's desire, then, that blunders never appear—her need to assert that of all the letters "constantly passing about the kingdom . . . not one in a million [is] actually lost"—originates in the same ideology as does Knightley's impatience with Frank's "deeper game." Bad handwriting is to Jane what "disinterestedness and double-dealing" are to Knightley: both complicate the operation of "deciphering," compromising any institution that would call itself "very well regulated." Yet Jane has said not that blunders never appear, only that they "seldom" appear. Even she can acknowledge the possibility of handwriting so bad, so shamefully illegible, that no strategy of deciphering could contain it. Should it "spread," such handwriting could eventually disrupt the entire system of coding and decoding, of writing and reading—in short, of communication—by which a Mr. Knightley might define society.

But what would such handwriting look like? Insofar as it resisted deciphering, it might be too cipher-bound to admit of interpretation. What would it mean, though, to be cipher-bound, or even to be a cipher? Paraphrasing a poem by Anne Finch, Gilbert and Gubar write: "[A]ll females are 'Cyphers'—nullities, vacancies—existing merely and punningly to increase male 'Numbers' (either poems or persons) by pleasuring either men's bodies or their minds, their penises or their pens" (GG, 9). Bad or excessively "ciphered" handwriting would thus represent a sort of *degré zéro de l'écriture*, writing so "ladylike" in its vacuousness that it would refuse to add up to anything like a meaning. It is tempting to view the devaluation of women as ending up ironically subverting patriarchal arithmetic. Yet just how would that subversion come about? For answers, we might turn again to *Mansfield Park*, whose heroine, as Leo Bersani points out, "almost is *not*" (Ber, 273). Fanny's aunt, Lady Bertram, may come even closer to the condition of nothingness: one of the other characters refers to her as "more of a cipher now" (*Mansfield Park*, 162) than when her husband, away on business, is at home. That phrase typifies the sarcasm that Austen reserves for particularly insipid characters, but it also suggests something more interesting. For how can anyone be more—or less—of a cipher? Either one is a cipher or one is not. In replacing a definition of the cipher or one is not. In replacing a definition of the cipher as a mere zero with an understanding of ciphers as quantities susceptible of increase and decrease, Austen reminds us of the radical instability of the term. For ciphers are not just numbers but figures as well, and the word *cipher* itself imitates the shiftiness of verbal figures. Just as figures of speech mean something other than themselves, so ciphers are figures both in the mathematical sense and in the more elusive rhetorical sense: "symbolic characters," according to *Webster's New International Dictionary*, ciphers are letters as well as numbers, but letters that call their own literality into question. No longer mere zeros, ciphers designate that species of "bad handwriting" known as figurative language, which, by exceeding the literal, may prevent letters from arriving at their destinations.[7] Figurative language marks the blundering that threatens the orderly delivery of messages.

One such subversive slippage from mathematical exactness to rhetorical uncertainty takes up almost all of chapter 9 in the first volume of *Emma*, a chapter that has to do precisely with ciphers. We have seen Knightley criticize Emma's educational principles because "[t]hey only give a little polish," but here we observe the decisive role of ciphers in transforming the curriculum of a finishing school into a politics of superficiality. A moralistic reading will assume that the chapter—not to mention the novel as a whole—has been written from the viewpoint of Mr. Knightley, the "custodian of Jane Austen's judgment" (Litz, 168). But a reading more sensitive to Austen's figures will discover elements that evade such deciphering. In the following passage, which describes the academic program Emma has devised for Harriet, we may discern both authoritarian and subversive discourses:

> Her views of improving her little friend's mind, by a great deal of useful reading and conversation, had never yet led to more than a few first chapters, and the intention of going on tomorrow. It was much easier to chat than to study; much pleasanter to let her imagination range and work at Harriet's fortune, than to be labouring to enlarge her comprehension or exercise it on sober facts; and the only literary pursuit which engaged Harriet at present, the only mental provision she was making for the evening of life, was the collecting and transcribing all the riddles of every sort that she could meet with, into a thin quarto of hot-pressed paper, made up by her friend, and ornamented with cyphers and trophies.
>
> (*E*, 69)

Knightley has already mentioned Emma's long-standing propensity for drawing up lists of books to read, only to abandon her ambitious plans. "I have done with expecting any course of steady reading from Emma," he announces, explaining that "she will never submit to any thing requiring industry and patience, and a subjection of the fancy to the understanding" (*E*, 37). In acknowledging that Emma and Harriet can never get beyond "a few first chapters," this later passage seems to confirm his opinion. It supports the numerous interpretations of *Emma* as a negative portrait of the artist, as an exorcism of the "imaginist" (*E*, 335) or solipsist in Austen herself.[8] Indeed, the gently mocking description of Harriet's sole "literary pursuit" seems, more seriously, to indict Emma, who would rather "let her imagination range and work at Harriet's fortune," enmeshing her in flimsy little novels of sensibility, than develop in both her pupil and herself enough *Sitzfleisch* to follow her ambitious syllabus.

Emma is, admittedly, acting like a bad novelist. Yet the "badness" of her "novels" corresponds less to the immaturity and capriciousness of one who has not read enough than to the semiotic aberrance of someone with "bad handwriting." For though Emma's curriculum may not involve much reading, she and Harriet spend a great deal of time writing—specifically, "collecting and transcribing all the riddles of every sort that [Harriet] could meet with, into a thin quarto of hot-pressed paper, made up by her friend, and ornamented with cyphers and trophies." Here, of course, Knightley could find all the evidence he needs to convict Emma of pedagogical malpractice: not only does the copying of riddles seem like a stultifying waste of time; the very cover of the riddle book emblematizes the meaninglessness of mere decoration. But, as we have suggested, while "cyphers" may escape the stratagems of meaning, they are hardly without significance. We might remember Austen's "merely" ornamental analogy for her own art—a "little bit (two Inches wide) of Ivory" (*Letters*, 323). Interestingly enough, the "cyphers" on Harriet's riddle book exist alongside "trophies," pictures of prizes. Trophies imply victory—which in turn implies conflict—and relate etymologically to tropes. As we will see, this chapter stages a battle between figurative language and figuring out, between ciphers and deciphering, between Emma's deep superficiality and Knightley's superficial depth.

"Depth," here, signifies subversive complexity, not just "strength of mind," which, as Knightley intimates, presupposes the ability to "submit" and "subject" oneself. Yet if the ciphers on the cover of the riddle book suggest the first kind of depth, they do so otherwise than by pointing to a plot below—and more politically serious than—what Gilbert and Gubar call "Jane Austen's Cover Story." For ciphers, as the dictionary reminds us, can be "texts in secret writing," monograms of some systematically dissimulated referent—in short, riddles. Here one *can* judge a book by its cover: the ciphers on the cover of Harriet's book cover the ciphers inside, which turn out to represent not ultimate truth but merely more covering.

Now, such a conception of the relation between surface and depth may seem less than subversive. In fact, it might appear entirely compatible with Knightley's belief that because games permit illusions of depth they guarantee—in their function as "child's play"—patriarchal control. How is it, then, that ciphers serve the antiauthoritarian cause? How, in Emma's hands, do they become figures of disruption? How does the play of surfaces in which they are implicated become deep in the subversive sense, rather than in either the authoritarian sense or even the sense that Gilbert and Gubar's notion of a feminist subtext might imply? If the chapter supports authoritarian as well as subversive readings and at the same time dramatizes the conflict between them, that conflict is not between figurative language and literal language but between two interpretations of figurative language. Where the "Knightleian" interpretation grounds figurative language in social rules, the "Emmaesque" interpretation sees it as inherently ungroundable, even in any politically acceptable subtext. Although Knightley himself does not appear in the chapter, we may identify as his proxy the eligible young bachelor Mr. Elton, whom Emma is busy imagining as Harriet's suitor and whose amorous riddle supplies Emma with an irresistible opportunity for creative misreading. Let us look at the pre-text out of which she constructs one of her best "bad novels":

> To Miss———.
> CHARADE.
> My first displays the wealth and pomp of kings,
>   Lords of the earth! their luxury and ease.
> Another view of man, my second brings,
>   Behold him there, the monarch of the seas!
>
> But, ah! united, what reverse we have!
>   Man's boasted power and freedom, all are flown;
> Lord of the earth and sea, he bends a slave,
>   And woman, lovely woman, reigns alone.
>
> Thy ready wit the word will soon supply,
>   May its approval beam in that soft eye!
>
> (*E*, 71)

The misreading begins even before Emma reads the charade, as soon as she tells Harriet: "Take it, it is for you. Take your own" (*E*, 71). Ownership is indeed at issue both in the interpretation of this riddle and in the novel as a whole, and in failing to see herself as the rightful "owner" of Elton's riddle, Emma is at odds with the novel's ethic of property and propriety.[9] The riddle itself is profoundly concerned with "wealth and pomp," "power and freedom." Announcing his interest in "courtship," Elton at the same time, as Paul H. Fry cogently notes, betrays a preoccupation with "Power (court) and Wealth (naval commerce)...that prove[s] to the unblinkered eye that [he] will never marry Harriet Smith" (Fry, 132). A reading less willful than Emma's would, of course, have paid more attention to the way in which Elton's characters express his character. Yet to be at once a reading and a writing—to exemplify productive error—Emma's reading has to be not only a reading of emblems but also an emblem in its own right. In a sense, Emma reads the riddle all too well. For if Elton's flattering rhetoric hints conventionally at a "reverse" of conventional power structures, Emma's misreading enacts that very "reverse," reading his figures unconventionally.

Offering an alternative to the patriarchal view of reading as a regimen for "strengthening the mind" and forming character, Emma's misreading arises from a radically different understanding of character. Whereas the patriarchal program would form character by inserting the self into the slots of convention, the subversive counterprogram begins by defining the self as a slot. On the one hand, Elton's caption, "To Miss _____ ," merely indicates that the whole business of courtship is a sort of prefabricated "text," a series of conventional performances: if the offering of flirtatious riddles is the first stage of the game, then the rules require that the young riddler honor the modesty topos by leaving the young woman's name blank, as in some contemporary novel, and that she, moreover, regard herself as playing a game, acting a part in a ready-made fiction. According to this view, one forms one's character by recognizing one's status as character in a novel not of one's own design.[10] On the other hand, "To Miss _____ " could be rewritten figuratively as "To Miss Blank." Not only does this rewriting magnify the conventionality—we might even say the "emptiness"—of Elton's formula, but it also invokes the very sign of emptiness or lack on which the subversive discourse turns. For a blank is a kind of zero or cipher. Yet if a cipher is not just a zero but a sign of figurality as well, then "To Miss Blank" conjoins femininity itself with the disruptive irregularity of figurative language. From a patriarchal perspective, woman is a zero waiting to fill a blank space; from a subversive perspective, "Miss Cipher" is the name for the irreducible figurality of the self, whether male or female.

Emma's misreading, then, produces a "novel" in "bad handwriting," a "novel" whose female characters personify this illegibility. Such a reading, however, neither proclaims the "enigma of woman" nor ascribes to women the power of self-authoring. To appreciate its full force—to know what the association of women with ciphers involves—we must find out why Emma fills the blank with Harriet's name rather than her own. Why, after she has subjected the riddle to a thorough analysis, does Emma persist in the delusion that it was intended for Harriet? How, in getting part of the riddle "wrong," does Emma produce an interpretation that is curiously "right"? If the conventional view of character insists that one accept one's place in a predetermined social text, then the subversive view of the self as a rhetorical figure—not just as a figure or character in a novel—can be charged with narcissistic implications: to see oneself as a trope may be to revel in aesthetic self-admiration. And indeed, precisely this charge has been leveled against Emma. Darrell Mansell, for example, writes that Harriet "never amounts to much more than a projection of Emma's own personality onto a blank, reflecting surface" (Mansell, 152). Though Harriet does belong to that group of Austenian characters who, as Leo Bersani would say, almost are not, the mere fact of her blankness does not render Emma's relationship with her narcissistic. Something more complex than narcissism characterizes this relationship. For in misreading "Miss _____," Emma at once puts Harriet where she herself should be and assumes Harriet's place. Filling the blank with "Smith" instead of "Woodhouse," Emma not only cedes her slot to Harriet but also installs herself in Harriet's habitual position—that of blankness.

The Emma described as "clever" in the first sentence of the novel thus discloses an element of Harriet in herself. It is almost as if, for a moment, Emma and Harriet had become a composite character, so that Emma's assumption that the riddle was intended for Harriet seems oddly appropriate. We might say that the difference between a rhetorical figure and a figure in a novel is the difference between composite and unitary characters, except that to define the self as a rhetorical figure is to suggest the compositeness—the overdetermination—of all characters. As characters in a novel, Harriet and Emma fall short of uniqueness and unity because, substituting for each other, they "mean" something other than themselves, just as a rhetorical figure means something other than itself. Even Elton's riddle supports this theory of the overdetermined self, since its closing couplet speaks of the loved one's "ready wit," clearly an Emma-like attribute, and of her "soft eye," which, Emma says, is "Harriet exactly" (*E*, 72). Now, the incompatibility of these epithets may signal the insincerity, or merely the inaccuracy, that results from "going by the book," as Elton has done. Later, when Emma has learned Elton's true intentions, she corroborates this view, musing indignantly, "To be sure, the charade, with its 'ready wit'—but then, the 'soft eyes'—in fact it suited neither; it was a jumble without taste or truth" (*E*, 134). Repentant, she seems to disavow her first reading. Yet even in this implicit concession to Knightley—even as she repudiates her "novel"—Emma articulates the most subversive insight of her misreading. For what that misreading discovers is that the real "jumble" is not so much the riddle as the self. Now she blames Elton's want of taste for the very fascination that underlies her relationship with Harriet—a fascination not with the self but with the otherness of the self, with the heterogeneity that Emma-as-Harriet and Harriet-as-Emma embody. No wonder Emma realizes "that Mr. Knightley must marry no one but herself" (*E*, 408) only after Harriet has confessed *her* love for Knightley: Harriet's discourse is the discourse of the other, the other lodged within Emma herself.

Occupied by rival ideologies, chapter 9 typifies the ambiguity that un-settles the narrative at several junctures. Read from Knightley's point of view, the chapter demonstrates what can happen without a "subjection of the fancy to the understanding." Read from Emma's point of view, it allegorizes a theory of the self that rejects the hierarchical terms of the first ideology, organizing the self horizontally and contingently rather than vertically and paradigmatically. Moreover, although the Emma-Elton-Harriet imbroglio is exposed fairly early in the novel, the misreading per-formed in chapter 9 anticipates other setbacks in what looks like Knightley's gradual conquest of Emma. One such instance occurs during the famous excursion to Box Hill, in the course of which Emma insults Miss Bates. There, the politics of superficiality presents itself once again in the form of characters and word games. Amid the general unpleasantness of the outing, Mr. Weston offers a conundrum, asking the party, "What two letters of the alphabet are there, that express perfection?" (*E*, 371). The answer is "M. and A.—Em-Ma," and "Emma found a great deal to laugh at and enjoy in it" (*E*, 371). Knightley, however, takes the conundrum as an opportunity to reprove Emma, saying "*Perfection* should not have come quite so soon" (*E*, 371). With characteristic moral seriousness, he reads the characters to read Emma's character, finding in what Austen calls a "very indifferent piece of wit" an image for that character's imperfection or incompletion (*E*, 371). Two letters have been left out of Emma's name, and Knightley wishes to see Emma's character made whole. Yet the badness of the pun partakes also of the "badness" we have come to associate with figurative language, and it is precisely this "badness" that Emma "enjoys." For Mr. Weston has reminded her that character need not be a homogeneous entity, that it is an aggregate of many different characters, that the self is no more a fixed identity than the name, a construct susceptible to fragmentation and re-arrangement.

In recalling the otherness of the self, moreover, Emma sees herself through otherness, as another sees her. What Knightley would chastise as narcissistic self-absorption is in fact an acknowledgment that one is em-bedded in a "text" more intricate than one's own name. If Knightley con-ceives the social text as conferring on the self a predetermined—hence illusory—subjectivity, Emma's social text figures collective existence as an endless collaborative process of reading and writing, in which the self emerges as a site of overlapping interpretations. Emma's valetudinarian father writes melodramatic letters about her misadventure with the gypsies, for "if he did not invent illnesses for her, she could make no figure in a message" (*E*, 336). The social text that Emma inhabits comprises any number of such "inventions": like everyone else in this world, she is always "making a figure" in one message or another, because she is always being reinvented, or reread, both by herself and by other selves.

Even marriage—the apotheosis of the "beauty of truth and sincerity in all our dealings with each other," the paradigm of "every thing that is decided and open" (*E*, 460)—is marked by the fictiveness and the evasions of the social. For despite Knightley's declaration that he and Emma have finally arrived at a state of mutual transparency, at the end of the novel she is still practicing "disguise, equivocation [and] mystery" in not revealing that Harriet is in love with him (*E*, 475). As Mudrick observes, "There is no happy ending" (Mudrick, 206)—at least not if happiness lies in the ideal of society as an ultimately legible text composed of and by a homogeneous set of interpretive conventions. The novel ends instead with a trio of marriages whose unintelligibility, not only to outsiders but perhaps even to the partners themselves, suggests a densely woven fabric of fictions and misreadings.

Oddly enough, it is Knightley, of all people, who contemplates the need for both fictionality and error. Late in the novel, on one of the few occasions when he praises Emma unreservedly, he also pays the highest compliment to the subversive theory of the self:

> "My interference was quite as likely to do harm as good. It was very natural for you to say, what right has he to lecture me?—and I am afraid very natural for you to feel that it was done in a disagreeable manner. I do not believe I did you any good. The good was all to myself, by making you an object of the tenderest affection to me. I could not think about you so much without doating on you, faults and all; and by dint of fancying so many errors, have been in love with you ever since you were thirteen at least."
>
> (*E*, 462)

Is this speech merely a display of gallantry on the part of a conqueror whose defeated adversary has shown sufficient signs of humility? While it is possible to dismiss these remarks as Emma's reward for submitting, the last sentence in particular has a concessive force that puts it beyond the less-than-sincere rhetoric of the gracious winner. Knightley, after all, is telling Emma not just that he loves her, "faults and all," but that he himself has "fancied" or invented "many" of those "errors." If the narrative has traditionally been conceived as a linear development whereby Emma, changing under Knightley's influence, moves gradually toward a welcoming recognition of that influence, now the Pygmalion myth gets a new twist: Knightley is interested less in perfecting the "object of [his] tenderest affection" than in "fancying"—at once imagining and liking—her charming imperfections. The dissatisfaction Knightley voices when he criticizes Mr. Weston's feeble conundrum thus appears in a different light: "*Perfection* should not have come quite so soon" no longer means "Unfortunately, Emma is not yet perfect"; it might be glossed more accurately as "Thank you, Mr. Weston, but I wish to continue enjoying Emma's imperfections for a while." Demanding perfection so that he may invent further imperfections, denouncing Emma's errors so that he may fancy more of them, Knightley in fact desires nothing less than an indefinite postponement of that conquest toward which he seems to aspire.

Instead of resolving itself into a linear progression, then, the narrative turns out to be going in circles. Those who bemoan the absence of a "happy ending"—of more persuasive proof that Emma has been converted—are impatient with precisely this circularity. For the failure of the linear model implies a failure of the unilateral ethical scheme in which a morally superior Knightley transforms a morally inferior Emma. Whereas it was his job to rescue her from literariness and its attendant ethical dangers, now he too appears to be tangled up in that net. Pretending to "sober and direct" her (Mudrick, 200), he has ended up egging her on to further bouts of misguided fiction making. Knightley's words suggest how complicated the picture has become: "fancying so many errors," he is no more a mere critic than Emma is a mere fiction maker. His interpretations are flights of fancy, which she must read to produce her little novels of error, to which he in turn takes a fancy, producing additional fanciful interpretations. Austen is at her most subversive, then, not in intimating the antisocial recesses of her heroine's interiority but in locating Emma in this potentially endless circuit of fiction, interpretation, and desire, with its dynamic and reciprocal relations between men and women. When the self is an effect of its overdetermined acts and society is not one text but a continuously revolving or circulating library, the descent into literacy becomes a fortunate fall.

Notes

1. Other influential critics who demonstrate the affinity between a certain ethical conservatism and antiliterariness are A. Walton Litz and U. C. Knoepflmacher. Litz says of Emma that "ultimately she must realize that she has viewed life as a game in

which she can display her imagination and powers of perception; it is no accident that Jane Austen uses Emma's fondness for conundrums, charades, and word-games to reveal her errors of imagination" (138). According to Knoepflmacher, Frank Churchill's "letter-writing is emblematic of a failure to front the responsibilities inherent in rank, family, and love, and his persistence in employing the written, rather than the spoken, word to convey his final apologies demonstrates also that he has not benefited from the near-disaster brought about by his previous indirections" (656).

2. My reading is indebted at several crucial points to Miller's. His acute analysis of *Emma* provides a model for reading the novel as a product of conflicting narrative and ideological pressures.

3. I should point out that I do not regard my reading as value-free or as privileged with some special access to the "purely literary" aspect of Austen's novel. Rather, I intend to show the interpenetration of the literary and the political in that text. But unlike much Austen criticism, which presupposes an unproblematically mimetic relation between text and world, this essay attends to the articulations that both join and separate them. Thus, it considers not only the way in which literary pursuits like reading and writing acquire social significance but also the way in which literary devices like riddles and anagrams transform the very notion of the social. Instead of moving in one direction, from the world and our assumptions about it into the text, I propose to move in both directions, from world to text and back.

4. It might be objected that, since Knightley thinks well of Jane Fairfax and ill of Frank Churchill, his attitude should not be characterized as "patriarchal." Arguing that his likes and dislikes have nothing to do with gender, one might suggest that Knightley insists not on male supremacy but on the need for the honesty and directness he perceives in Jane (and in himself), as opposed to the manipulativeness he senses in Frank (and in Emma). But everything Knightley disdains in Frank he associates with femininity. Of Frank's handwriting, for example, he says, "I do not admire it. It is too small—wants strength. It is like a woman's writing" (297). For Knightley, *feminine* and *devious* are synonyms, and moral distinctions keep turning into sexual distinctions.

5. The thematics of power and vision in this episode would lend themselves well to the kind of analysis Jacques Lacan performs in his famous "Seminar on 'The Purloined Letter.'" If, thus far in the game, Emma sees nothing, Frank Churchill resembles those characters in Poe's story whose "glance . . . sees that the first sees nothing and deludes itself as to the secrecy of what it hides" (44). Frank may delude himself, but Knightley is deluded as well, insofar as he thinks that his own, third glance, which "sees that the first two glances leave what should be hidden exposed to whoever would seize it" (44), remains itself unexposed. I am not accusing

Knightley of failing to recognize that he is a character in a novel. My point, rather, is that by reading—without feigning disinterestedness—Knightley's own reading, we may be able to glance at the secrets that moralistic interpretation would hide. Needless to say, this fourth glance could claim no mastery either, since it too might easily become one more object in an endless chain of deconstructions.

6. Marilyn Butler writes, "Although so much of the action takes place in the inner life, the theme of the novel is skepticism about the qualities that make it up—intuition, imagination, original insight" (273). This comment might serve as an accurate description of Knightley's ideological double bind, but, as I hope to show, the novel itself is not always bound to this contradiction.

7. The word *cipher* appears in three significant places in Austen's work. Besides its occurrences in *Mansfield Park* and in the more complex passage from *Emma* that we are about to discuss, the word has an interesting function in *Northanger Abbey* (composed between 1798 and 1803), Austen's earliest major novel. In the climactic episode of that novel's parody of Gothic fiction, the heroine, Catherine Morland, discovers, among other curious objects, a chest engraved with a "mysterious cypher" (164). The subsequent action constitutes a debunking of Gothic conventions: when exposed to the light of day, for example, what looked like a hidden manuscript documenting torture and madness turns out to be a laundry list. But despite the pains Austen takes to demystify Catherine's suspicions as so much hocus-pocus picked up from Gothic novels, one detail remains unexplained—namely, the cipher. Its indelibility might represent a grudging and furtive tribute to the tradition that Austen is trying to discredit, or it could indicate, as Gilbert and Gubar argue, that Austen is not really opposed to the Gothic at all, that the novel's subject is the "terror and self-loathing that results when a woman is made to disregard her personal sense of danger" (143). In either case, even in this early novel the word *cipher* figures in a resistance to whatever effacements a complacently thematic reading of Austen would accomplish.

8. In addition to Mudrick, see, for example, John Halperin: "It is Emma's inability to subject fancy to reason that causes most of her problems and forms the core of the novel's dramatic structure" (201); Darrell Mansell: "In *Emma* . . . an artist is portrayed in the process of creating art, the art of fiction; and it is tempting to see the heroine as a kind of self-portrait of her author" (153); Susan Morgan: "The claim of the novel is that life is interesting, that fact can be as delightful as fiction, that imagination need not be in conflict with reality" (39).

9. The classic discussion of *Emma*'s emphasis on the "values of commerce and property, of the counting house and the inherited estate" (99), is Mark Schorer's "The Humiliation of Emma Woodhouse." For a more recent treatment of property and propriety as Austenian themes, see D. A. Miller (esp. 15–50).

10. For an implicitly conventionalizing reading of *Emma* in terms of speech-act theory, see Mary Vaiana Taylor.

Works Cited

Austen-Leigh, J. E. 1926. *A Memoir of Jane Austen.* Oxford: Clarendon.

Bersani, Leo. 1976. *A Future for Astyanax: Character and Desire in Literature.* Boston: Little.

Bradbury, Malcolm. 1970. "Jane Austen's *Emma.*" In *Jane Austen,* Emma: *A Casebook.* Ed. David Lodge. Nashville: Aurora. 217–31.

Butler, Marilyn. 1975. *Jane Austen and the War of Ideas.* Oxford: Clarendon.

Duckworth, Alastair M. 1971. *The Improvement of the Estate: A Study of Jane Austen's Novels.* Baltimore, Md.: Johns Hopkins University Press.

Fry, Paul H. 1979. "Georgic Comedy: The Fictive Territory of Jane Austen's *Emma.*" *Studies in the Novel* 11:129–46.

Gilbert, Sandra M., and Susan Gubar. 1979. *The Madwoman in the Attic: The Woman Writer and the Nineteenth-Century Literary Imagination.* New Haven: Yale University Press.

Halperin, John. 1975. "The Worlds of *Emma*: Jane Austen and Cowper." In *Jane Austen: Bicentenary Essays.* Ed. John Halperin. Cambridge: Cambridge University Press. 197–206.

———, ed. 1975. *Jane Austen: Bicentenary Essays.* Cambridge: Cambridge University Press.

Knoepflmacher, U. C. 1967. "The Importance of Being Frank: Character and Letter-Writing in *Emma.*" *Studies in English Literature* 7:639–58.

Lacan, Jacques. 1973. "Seminar on 'The Purloined Letter.'" *Yale French Studies* 48:38–72.

Litz, A. Walton. 1965. *Jane Austen: A Study of Her Artistic Development.* New York: Oxford University Press.

Mansell, Darrell. 1973. *The Novels of Jane Austen: An Interpretation.* New York: Barnes.

Miller, D. A. 1981. *Narrative and Its Discontents: Problems of Closure in the Traditional Novel.* Princeton, N.J.: Princeton University Press.

Morgan, Susan. 1980. *In the Meantime: Character and Perception in Jane Austen's Fiction.* Chicago: University of Chicago Press.

Mudrick, Marvin. 1952. *Jane Austen: Irony as Defense and Discovery.* Princeton, N.J.: Princeton University Press.

Schorer, Mark. 1963. "The Humiliation of Emma Woodhouse." In *Jane Austen: A Collection of Critical Essays.* Ed. Ian Watt. Englewood Cliffs, N.J.: Prentice Hall. 98–111.

Taylor, Mary Vaiana. 1978. "The Grammar of Conduct: Speech Act Theory and the Education of Emma Woodhouse." *Style* 12:357–71.

Wiesenfarth, Joseph. 1975. "*Emma*: Point Counter Point." In *Jane Austen: Bicentenary Essays.* Ed. John Halperin. Cambridge: Cambridge University Press. 207–20.

Desire

Emma In Love

JOHN DUSSINGER

❖   ❖   ❖

W HEN CHARACTERS PLAY GAMES in Austen's fiction, we are led
to believe, they may be sublimating "real-life" conflicts or actually revealing quite serious, even dangerous, intentions within the encounter. As
we ponder their behavior, moreover, we are subscribing to a more fundamental game that the author has initiated in her parodic text—namely, the
metaphor of lived experience. In this quixotic reflexivity, as the reader
watches characters play tricks on other characters, he or she forgets about
being manipulated within the linguistic frames arranged by Austen. Without
quite knowing it, once our curiosity about the players is aroused, we fall into
the role of spectators at an event and project our wishes onto the story.

To begin with, even before the reader himself can become actively engaged with the text, characters are already shown to be prying into each
other's affairs and thus stirring up trouble; and almost at once patterns of
discourse are set in motion to elicit a finite set of responses among the actors
and external witnesses involved. At one level of abstraction, the narrative
text insinuates itself like a crossword puzzle, providing just enough information to stir the reader's interest in filling in the empty spaces. Similarly,
the charades in *Emma* function reflexively as a play-within-a-play, imitating
in miniature the whole enterprise of constituting the text of the novel. In

their textual roles, then, narrators/characters intentionally or unintentionally speak in fragments—revealing themselves sufficiently to attract attention yet all the while concealing some part, not merely to keep the story going but because the *whole* story can never be told. In this way parody brings us to a solipsistic standstill in our efforts to fathom the truth of what is said.

Just as it is the precondition of reading, so desire is inherent in the discourse of character. Not surprisingly, therefore, novels tend to stress knowledge as the protagonist's goal; and to this extent the modern detective story answers a primary need of realistic fiction. Of Austen's novels, *Emma* is most obviously plotted on the heroine's ignorance of a central mystery; and her discovery of the truth coincides, we are to understand, with a new self-awareness leading to her own engagement to marry. In the other novels some element of knowledge is also at stake: Marianne Dashwood comes to see that passion is suicidal; Catherine Morland learns the real evil of General Tilney's greed; Elizabeth Bennet sees Darcy in a new light on her visit to Pemberley; Fanny Price comprehends the full impact of Mansfield during her exile in Portsmouth; and Anne Elliot finds at last that Wentworth still loves her. Knowledge and character development, essentials of the bildungsroman formula, are important to Austen's method; and Tory interpretations generally press hard the lessons the errant heroine must learn, as if this didactic gratification itself were not part of the author's game plan.

But in past readings this epistemological emphasis has ignored the dialogical text, which articulates the language of human consciousness in a rhythm of desire and boredom without end. While one part of the story satisfies the appetite for the resolution of conflict, another brings into doubt not only the possibility of fulfillment but even the freedom of the character engaged in the process of willing. It is this primary concern with the state of being that the Austen narrator/character articulates in one form or another throughout the story. Rasselas's demand, "Give me something to desire," implies the fundamental paradox of narrative dynamics: the subject cannot exist literally without *some* intention, and of course the subject is no more than a cipher without the reader's prior act of conjuring her up from the printed page. As it already expresses a desire, Rasselas's demand is tautological; and Imlac's moral psychology is in keeping with the quest motif of the romance: "Some desire is necessary to keep life in motion, and he, whose real wants are supplied, must admit those of fancy."[1] In practice, however, the fictional subject is no more free to choose his terms of desiring than the victim of passion is to alter his feelings.[2]

Desire is not merely a theme in, say, Johnson's and Austen's texts: it is inextricably woven into the fabric of narrative itself; and some authors call attention to this fact more than others, deliberately frustrating the reader's impatience for closure. Recent semiotics help to explain the phenomenon:

> Because signs are used to communicate not only a finished product, the message, but also the processes which make the ongoing production of that message possible, a text functions much like a painting, which communicates a clearly identifiable narrative message, while also displaying the diacritical marks of that message all across the canvas without allowing a clear distinction of what is form and what is substance.[3]

If the distinction between tenor and vehicle is illusory, Blanchard further points out, the dual structure of showing and telling, axiomatic in any representational theory, no longer obtains; instead of a single, unified text imaging an original, authoritative consciousness, narrative reveals the usual vagaries of overlapping codes and omissions intrinsic to speech.

Programmed within an erotic field, characters sometimes emerge to reflect on the tenuous source of their being and even to complain of their textual fate, as in Don Quixote's allusions to the evil enchanter (the author) who holds him in thrall: "I am in love, for no other reason than that it is incumbent on knights-errant to be so."[4] Austen's parodic narrators take a similar predeterministic stance toward their subject. Marianne Dashwood is duty bound as sentimental heroine, we are told, to match feelings to her situation and "would have thought herself very inexcusable had she been able to sleep at all the first night after parting from Willoughby" (*Sense and Sensibility*, 83). By contrast, opposing texts jostle for control of Catherine Morland's mind:

> Whether she thought of him so much, while she drank her warm wine and water, and prepared herself for bed, as to dream of him when there, cannot be ascertained; but I hope it was no more than in a slight slumber, or a morning doze at most; for if it be true, as a celebrated writer has maintained, that no young lady can be justified in falling in love before the gentleman's love is declared, it must be very improper that a young lady should dream of a gentleman before the gentleman is first known to have dreamt of her.
>
> (*Northanger Abbey*, 29–30)

Although "falling in love" is an attitude imitative of romance and is thus inevitably suspect, not all language of undying devotion is insincere simply because it has been used before; indeed, as Thackeray recognized,[5] there are conditions when acting a role becomes identical with the role itself, when all the world becomes truly a stage. In another context, free indirect discourse obviates the lover's standard aria and thereby communicates deep feeling without any hint of posturing. What matters is Anne Elliot's heartfelt reception of his words:

> Of what he had then written, nothing was to be retracted or qualified. *He persisted in having loved none but her. She had never been supplanted. He never even believed himself to see her equal. Thus much indeed he was obliged to acknowledge—that he had been constant unconsciously, nay unintentionally; that he had meant to forget her, and believed it to be done. He had imagined himself indifferent, when he had only been angry; and he had been unjust to her merits, because he had been a sufferer from them. Her character was now fixed on his mind as perfection itself, maintaining the loveliest medium of fortitude and gentleness.*
>
> (*Persuasion*, 241; emphasis added)

Wentworth's actual speech at the time may have been the outpouring of the individual soul, and nothing in the passage raises doubts about his sincerity; but it also belongs to a literary type, a category of the lover's discourse that Roland Barthes identifies as "The Intractable."[6]

Love is more a situation than a sentiment; and in Austen the situation is nearly always triangular, mediated through a variety of rival claims on the protagonists. Although characters appear to move at random and undergo encounters by happenstance, even the everyday world turns out to be regulated by kinetic contraries. Despite the illusions of the moment, therefore, desire is not free and unconditional; rather, as characters discover by hindsight, it arises from certain opposing tensions in discourse, subject to no higher authority than the laws of motion. As we see in the same context quoted above, for instance, Wentworth frankly acknowledges the impact a rival has in enhancing his desire for Anne in the last hours before his declaration:

> She had not mistaken him. Jealousy of Mr. Elliot had been the retarding weight, the doubt, the torment. That had begun to operate in the very hour of first meeting her in Bath; that had returned, after a short suspension, to ruin the concert; and that had influenced him in every thing he had said and done, or omitted to say and do, in the last four-and-twenty hours. It had been gradually yielding to the better hopes which

her looks, or words, or actions occasionally encouraged; it had been vanquished at last by those sentiments and those tones which had reached him while she talked with Captain Harville; and under the irresistible governance of which he had seized a sheet of paper, and poured out his feelings.

(*P*, 241)

In this passage, rendered entirely in free indirect discourse, emotion is found to be the work of the moment, a product of energy generated from impetus and resistance, tension and release. Despite the "serious" tone of this confession, moreover, the mechanical forces involved are reminiscent of Pope's epigrammatic style:

> When bold Sir *Plume* had drawn *Clarissa* down,
> *Chloe* stept in, and kill'd him with a Frown;
> She smil'd to see the doughty Hero slain,
> But at her Smile, the Beau reviv'd again.[7]

Again, the parodic disclosure of character, with all its finite dependence on signs for its existence, operates uneasily with the narrative presentation of a moral consciousness, free and unconditioned. But it is this peculiar contradictory sense of character that is distinctive of Austen's comic art.

Because it is most outspokenly "French" in spirit, a fulfillment of the promise shown already in *Lady Susan*, *Emma* is our set piece for the interpretation of desire in Austen. Daring in its untrammeled will-to-power, the narrative of self here moves through one situation after another in an amoral dialectic usually embraced by the villainous characters in the other novels and openly avowed by the Crawfords. As in the other novels where the triangular situation culminates in an ordeal testing the heroine's strength to surrender her desire, Emma must suffer pain and humiliation before she attains the pleasure of at last dominating her world; but she differs from all the other Austen heroines in having a voice in her world from the outset.

From the analysis of the magnitude and direction of desire in *Emma* our inquiry turns to the "body language" of desire, mainly references to food and drink as signs of intentionality. Generally speaking, Austen places a Fieldingesque emphasis upon the appetite as a measure of good or bad nature, as well as of good or bad physical health; and though the motif of food appears in the earliest novels, it is most symbolic in *Mansfield Park* and *Emma*. As the opening metaphor in *Tom Jones* suggests, the reader's primary role is to cannibalize the character, to taste his humor directly on the palate after the narrator-chef has dressed it: "[w]e shall represent Human Nature at first to the keen Appetite of our Reader, in that more plain and simple Manner in which it is found in the Country, and shall hereafter hash and ragoo it with all the high *French* and *Italian* Seasoning of Affectation and Vice which Courts and Cities afford."[8] Processing the text, to extend the metaphor, incorporates language emotively, just as eating food incorporates the object into the self: appetite and consuming (tasting, mastication) are primary impulses, whereas critical judgment, the finesse of comparison, is secondary.

In contrast to desire, which is verbally structured on social relations, appetite, often to our embarrassment, is a basically visceral, nonsituational, and nonverbal urge of the body. Neither wish-making nor hunger is entirely subject to the conscious will, however, but is partly autonomous in the character's emotional life. It is such blind forces within the "real-life" encounter that Austen recognizes in her intriguing phrase "the work of a moment," a sudden release of energy after a period of tension that may seal the character's fate without further ado. Textually these moments lie beyond the margins of words and are represented as interruptions—silence. Without some fragmentation of the character's speech there is no apparent energy behind the words. Of course, not all instances of fragmentation are indubitable proof of "real feeling" but may simply indicate mindlessness, as in Mrs. Allen's nervous ejaculations by the window (*Northanger Abbey*, 60) or in Mr. Elton's feeble attempt to defend Emma's portrait of Harriet (*E*, 48). Hence, by a tactical shift in narrative direction, the parodic voice not only signals the artificiality of representing the self but also the inadequacy of words to convey the *lived* self.

Emma In Love

Emma is probably the most Gallic novel in English, imbued with the acuity of La Rochefoucauld, Diderot, and Laclos, even to the extent of warping the rural English into caricatures of plain dealers, vulnerable to the sly cynicism from across La Manche. It is not Austen's particular attitudes toward French culture that matter, however, but rather the convenience of this intertextual locus for a discourse on the radical egoism of desire called for in her undercutting of romantic situations. One announced game within the narrative concerns getting the heroine to fall in love the way attractive young women are supposed to do when courted by attractive young men; and, given the strategies of the interlopers in the story, only the exertion of a penetrating intelligence (emulating the author's and external reader's)—and of course the happenstance that conditions *any* moment—will preserve her from her predicted textual fate. Mary Crawford's jocular remark that selfishness needs to be forgiven because it is incurable (*Mansfield Park*, 68) ignores, to be sure, the positive alternatives of egoism often borne out by Fanny who, besides exercising prudence, also feels compassion toward those who deserve it. In contrast to Fanny, Emma Woodhouse seems to have everything in her favor for the pursuit of happiness; and at times her self-esteem amounts to Mary's version of egoism. If Fanny's project is to become important to someone, Emma's is no less than that of being "first." The converse of Fanny in physical health, emotional temperament, social privilege, and worldly ambition, Emma nonetheless must undergo the same struggle for self-esteem in an environment felt to be competitive and often hostile; and whatever the advantage of her material comfort, she lacks her little predecessor's flawless judgment of others, which is finally the self's best defense. Yet despite her quixotic fantasies involving others, she is surprisingly accurate in assessing her own state of mind—at least more so than Mr. Knightley ever perceives. His project toward the heroine, moreover, ironically parallels Henry Crawford's toward Fanny: "I should like to see Emma in love, and in some doubt of a return; it would do her good" (*E*, 41). He is wrong, we know, in suspecting Frank Churchill to be the one to make her fall in love; and for all his perspicacity in the many offices he performs in the community, right down to the moment of his proposal to Emma he underestimates his own hold over her mind. In many ways Emma's selfishness is no more than her effort to be assertive as an individual, free from his authority; and the momentous events in Highbury are usually beyond her control.

Despite the narrator's introductory judgments of the heroine, Emma's situation from the beginning is anything but secure, as her behavior subsequently implies: her dependence on her father and her competitiveness with Mr. Knightley, her hatred of Jane Fairfax and Miss Bates, her vicarious pleasure as matchmaker, and her continual anxiety over social class. The project of being "first" entails at once a sufficient degree of self-esteem and a belief in the inferiority of the other, and to her credit Emma often has the honesty to admit her failure to meet these requirements. Even in moments of euphoric egoism, moreover, Emma appears uneasy that her own ambitions contradict the Woodhouse ideal of fixed hereditary order.

Her pervasive concern with social rank, reflected throughout the narrative, leads inevitably to making Miss Bates the *pharmakos* of the action. As Northrop Frye explains this ritual scapegoat: "The *pharmakos* is neither innocent nor guilty. He is innocent in the sense that what happens to him is far greater than anything he has done provokes, like the mountaineer whose shout brings down an avalanche. He is guilty in the sense that he is a member of a guilty society, or living in a world where such injustices are an inescapable part of existence."[9] The pressure for something like Emma's violence to Miss Bates that fateful day at Box Hill had been mounting from the outset of the story: "Emma could not resist" (*E*, 370); and notwithstanding Mr. Knightley's lecture on how she should comport herself toward the pitiable old maid, the trauma of this scene surpasses anything the hero, heroine, or narrator can formulate in language.

According to Bernard Paris, the irresistible pressure involved her dislike of Miss Bates for constantly lauding Jane, her fear of being associated with the lower elements of her society, her hatred of the woman for being too good-natured and silly, and for being a spinster burdened with a senile mother and yet apparently content in spite of it, approving of everything and everyone indiscriminately.[10] But to invoke Johnson's Hobbesian point (in *Rambler* no. 166) about the dangers of obsequiousness in receiving charity,[11] Miss Bates clearly brings the violence on herself by talking too much about gratitude, an interpretation that will be elaborated upon in my fourth chapter. Briefly stated, a lack of self-esteem is universally contemptible, whether in the giver or in the receiver. It goes without saying that all this anxious discourse on patronage and subordination reflects the unsettling effects of the new economic and political order that accompanied the French Revolution and the Napoleonic Wars.

A youthful urge to be free of a tiresome society is enough to account for Emma's abhorrence of Miss Bates, but the poor woman's obsessive speeches only make matters worse by reflecting embarrassingly on the giver/receiver roles in egoistically motivated charity. Emma especially resents the woman's fulsome gratitude and even mimics her manner (*E*, 225), as does the narrator, eliciting the reader's own aggressions toward the scapegoat. Again, the situation automatically generates responses from the various participants in the encounter. Knightley's reprimand, however, implies that one is free to feel sympathy when called upon: "She is poor; she has sunk from the comforts she was born to; and, if she live to old age, must probably sink more. Her situation should secure your compassion" (*E*, 375). But in spite of this lofty instruction, Emma is *not* free to choose the appropriate emotions for the circumstance, especially since as a woman it is her burden, after all, to have to enter into conversation with this garrulous fool. The *pride of the moment* had possessed her.

Although the narrator informs us that Emma "was very compassionate; and the distresses of the poor were as sure of relief from her personal attention and kindness, her counsel and her patience, as from her purse" (*E*, 86), the heroine's dialogue with Harriet immediately after visiting the sick cottagers reads like an antidote to the modish sentimentalism: "If we feel for the wretched, enough to do all we can for them, the rest is empty sympathy, only distressing to ourselves" (*E*, 87). Her delight at seeing Mr. Elton on his way to the same poor family drives home again the eighteenth-century moralists' stress on the superior pleasures of giving as opposed to those of receiving: "'To fall in with each other on such an errand as this,' thought Emma; 'to meet in a charitable scheme; this will bring a great increase of love on each side. I should not wonder if it were to bring on the declaration'" (*F*, 87–88). The meditation is self-serving and made at the expense of the poor as well as of the imagined lovers. To be fair, however, except for some religiously inspired selflessness, the alternative to this crisply rational "scheme" is the maudlin discourse on the poor that Austen shunned. Whatever the actual feelings involved, muddled as they must be over such a hopelessly vague and perennial evil, there is a language commensurate with what one can do to alter real circumstances. Furthermore, if her tone seems glib on this occasion, Emma at other moments is sincere enough to send the "whole hind-quarter" of the Hartfield porker to the Bateses' without consulting her father beforehand (*E*, 172); and the "child from the cottage, setting out, according to orders, with her pitcher, to fetch broth from Hartfield" (*E*, 88) also testifies to her genuine charity, comparable to Mr. Knightley's own quiet ministry. Mute actions, rather than banal sentiments, are the best evidence of charitable feelings. Thus his lecture on her duty to the poor was hardly necessary; what is more to the point is whether *anyone* in Emma's situation could honestly avoid expressing contempt for Miss Bates. In an unusually probing conversation Harriet herself ventured the comparison between Emma and Miss Bates:

> "That is as formidable an image as you could present, Harriet; and if I thought I should ever be like Miss Bates! so silly—so satisfied—so smiling—so prosing—so undistinguishing and unfastidious—and so apt to tell every thing relative to every body about me, I would marry to-morrow. But between *us*, I am convinced there never can be any likeness, except in being unmarried."
>
> "But still, you will be an old maid! and that's so dreadful!"
>
> "Never mind, Harriet, I shall not be a poor old maid; and it is poverty only which makes celibacy contemptible to a generous public!"
>
> (*E*, 84–85)

As Emma goes on about the crucial difference between being a single woman with means and one without, her vindictiveness toward Miss Bates is
clear-cut ("[S]he is only too good natured and too silly to suit me" [*E*, 85])
and yet guarded at the same time: "Poverty certainly has not contracted her
mind: I really believe, if she had only a shilling in the world, she would be
very likely to give away sixpence of it; and nobody is afraid of her: that is a
great charm" (*E*, 85). It is a strange concession for Emma to make, the most
positive ever in the story, after ridiculing her enemy's behavior; and she may
indeed fear some likeness between themselves other than in being unmarried. Whatever the hidden motives, Emma cannot exercise the requisite
charity unless she is confident that her wealth distinguishes her from the
poor woman; and Knightley never recognizes this instability.

Emma's situation resembles that described by Stendhal, who explored
the structure of egoism against the cataclysmic changes of the Napoleonic
era and identified the stock character of the *vaniteux*. Raised by sycophants
who had flattered him into the belief that he should be happier than
others, the *vaniteux* enters the word with a metaphysical handicap: "It is because the *Vaniteux* feels the emptiness mentioned in Ecclesiastes growing
inside him that he takes refuge in shallow behavior and imitation. Because
he cannot face his nothingness he throws himself on Another who seems
to be spared by the curse."[12] If in orthodox Christian morality pride and
vanity are illusory states produced by a turning away from God and a
withdrawing into the self, the major European novelists from Stendhal to
Proust, as Girard states, have shown that the contrary conditions of other-
directedness are imitative to the extreme of self-abandonment known as
bovaryism.[13] While Emma Woodhouse's possessive desire may culminate only
in painful embarrassment in contrast to Emma Bovary's suicidal narcissism,
both characters nevertheless experience the need to transcend their circumscribed conditions ("[S]o absolutely fixed, in the same place" [*E*, 143])
and to seek escape in a mediator of some kind. If Emma Bovary is shown to
have read the wrong material for dealing with the everyday situations,
Emma Woodhouse is no less romantically inclined when it comes to
"reading" the movements of others. Her fantasy of Jane Fairfax's erotic
link with Mr. Dixon, for instance, plays upon the conventional triadic
arrangement of romantic passion.

Perhaps the clearest tie between the two Emmas is their bourgeois
malaise of snobbism. The antithesis of good citizenship, snobbery is, ironically, a problem arising from a more or less egalitarian society, where class
distinctions no longer protect the individual from the anxiety of status:
significantly, the age of the prince regent and Beau Brummell abounded

with controversy over dress and manners.[14] The faithful medieval mind, absorbed with the vanity of human existence, could look upward to the divine mediator for deliverance; after the collapse of the ancien régime, the desiring subject was reduced to making a god of others in the finite world while still condemned to self-contempt. Since the mediator was no longer divine but merely possessed of some intangible social advantages like nobility, the snob was likely to hate himself in the person imitated: "Hatred is individualistic. It nourishes fiercely the illusion of an absolute difference between the Self and that Other from which nothing separates it."[15]

Deprived of the means of skirting this illusion, Emma tacitly shares her father's phobia toward social mobility in principle; and like Mrs. Elton's Maple Grove snobbery, Emma's resentment of any aspirant among the middle ranks contradicts the same ambitious individualism which both women endorse for themselves. Their emulation of Mr. Knightley is symptomatic: while Mrs. Elton tries to vulgarize him by breaching decorum of address, thus pretending an unwarranted familiarity, Emma values him all the more as a role model by keeping him on a pedestal for the public to admire at a distance. Despite the wishful thinking embodied in the comic plot, which finally assigns appropriate places to the various female contenders, there is a lingering suspicion to the very end that not even an exemplary gentleman like Mr. Knightley can protect the social hierarchy from the egalitarian rhetoric, on the one hand, and from the elitist overreaching of the nouveau riche, on the other.[16]

Emma's disapproval of Robert Martin for being a farmer, of the Coles for their former connections in "trade" (her father refuses their invitation on the grounds of his health and Mr. Cole's temperament, but clearly it is the presumption of upstarts that bothers him most), of Mrs. Goddard for being merely a teacher, and of Miss Bates for having nothing but the memory of her clergyman father, shows her own dread of the second- and third-rate; simultaneously, it betrays her own lack of a clear identity in this society. An exception to this behavior is her kindness toward Mr. Weston and an attractive loyalty to the woman who married him; nevertheless, in later scenes she privately resents his indiscriminate affability.

Throughout this story the language of desire is emphatically based on difference and hierarchy. Mr. Elton's proposal shocks Emma into evaluating her present status as the heiress of thirty thousand pounds: "Perhaps it was not fair to expect him to feel how very much he was her inferior in talent, and all the elegancies of mind. The very want of such equality might prevent his perception of it; but he must know that in fortune and consequence she was greatly his superior" (*E*, 136). Though acknowledging the inferiority of her talent to Jane's, whose social life otherwise seems pre-determined to fall well below hers, Emma needs everything at her disposal to condemn Elton's presumptuous claim on her. In the midst of what the narrator terms her "raving," however, is the important revelation that the Woodhouses stem from the "younger branch" of an old family, that Hartfield is only a "notch" in the Donwell Abbey estate, and that "their fortune, from other sources," [that is, from trade] made them "scarcely secondary to Donwell Abbey itself, in every other kind of consequence." Scarcely secondary, but *secondary* nonetheless! Not fully apparent to the heroine is her deep-seated rivalry with the hero on account of his greater power derived from family, fortune, talent, and male prerogative, even as she paradoxically upholds his standards for her own strivings. In spite of her outward self-assurance, therefore, Emma yearns with other womanly aspirants, including Mrs. Elton and Mrs. Churchill, to find the means of her own personal legitimacy in a man's power structure; and the conse-quence is her neurotic fear of bearing any resemblance to a disturbingly nimble, if impoverished, old maid.

Implicit in the dynamics of desire is a falling-off of energy, when the mind becomes temporarily depressed by nothing to wish for; and, again, the character must exert herself if only to prevent redundancy and oblivion. The failure of the Box Hill scheme, in sharp contrast to the brief happiness attained at the Crown Inn ball, is simply a moment of truth revealing the spiritual anarchy of the Highbury world, which threatens to sink under its own ennui; and not even the audacious gamesters can stem the contagion: "At first it was downright dulness to Emma. She had never seen Frank Churchill so silent and stupid. He said nothing worth hearing—looked without seeing—admired without intelligence—listened without knowing what she said. While he was so dull, it was no wonder that Harriet should be dull likewise, and they were both insufferable" (*E*, 367).

Since blaming Churchill for Harriet's dullness only shows how far afield Emma's perception can stray, a moralist might take the view that this ennui is an evil of egoism and that the hero's stoic rationalism provides immunity from this disease. Thus Mrs. Weston's earlier remark could serve as the norm here: "I do not think Mr. Knightley would be much disturbed by Miss Bates. Little things do not irritate him" (*E*, 225–26). Yet elsewhere Emma's mind can also be provident toward little things, and without any assistance from Knightley. While waiting for Harriet to finish her purchases at Ford's, Emma converts all the trivial activities outside the door into a picturesque townscape: "A mind lively and at ease, can do with seeing nothing, and can see nothing that does not answer" (*E*, 233). But neither reason nor the imagination can save Emma from the paucity of objects to contemplate on that particular day; the very necessity of mingling with unwanted company has a claustrophobic effect, forcing her into aggressive speech for release. Until this moment, access to her hostile feelings was mainly the privilege of the dilatory Harriet or of the narrator. As her own recommendation to Frank Churchill on self-command (*E*, 364) assures us, Emma knows painfully well her duty at Box Hill but cannot resist her attack anyway.

Emma is not to blame, however, for the ennui that brought on the offending words. At Donwell the day before, we recall, not even Mr. Knightley's flawless hospitality could prevent the comic world from falling apart; and Emma's most enjoyable moment was spent alone in reverie over a pastoral, harmonious world: "It was a sweet view—sweet to the eye and the mind. English verdure, English culture, English comfort, seen under a sun bright, without being oppressive" (*E*, 360). This is the daytime equivalent to Fanny Price's nocturnal repose by the window, away from the madding crowd; thus, rather than polar opposites, both heroines respond to the "luxury of silence" (*MP*, 278) and to the "comfort of being sometimes alone" (*E*, 363).

In another context, for instance in Marianne Dashwood's narcissistic moods, Austen might have invoked Johnson on activity as therapy against the insatiable desires spawned in solitude and idleness: but Emma is no solipsistic dreamer and attempts to carry out her social duties. Lacking the opportunity of private indulgence in the scenery at Box Hill, a pleasure that seems unaccountably lost on the others, she enters the play of conversation as a modus vivendi to cope with the existential emptiness felt from the beginning of the day. Emma's problem here is not self-deception, nor is it an uncritical love of games, but rather the disturbing absence of a saving illusion: "She laughed because she was disappointed; and though she liked him [Churchill] for his attentions, and thought them all, whether in friendship, admiration, or playfulness, extremely judicious, they were not winning back her heart" (*E*, 368). In the predicament of having nothing to desire, Emma resorts to a familiar aristocratic text, to erotic play, "glad to be enlivened" (*E*, 368) for the moment by imagining (self-consciously) her part as female libertine, with Miss Bates as the prescribed petit bourgeois victim of her wit. It was Mary Crawford's predicament as well; but Emma, in contrast, shares Fanny's concern, if not her talent, for feeling the emotion appropriate to the situation.

No matter that the plot's didactic contour requires it, Emma's humiliation by Knightley's rebuke discloses yet another French text in her erotic pleasure derived from pain. Despite the requirement by the Protestant ethic of a conversion, her visceral hatred of Miss Bates remains constant to the end of the novel; and her real change of heart appears mainly in the mediating friendship formed with Jane Fairfax after her discovery of the engagement, a friendship anticipated at various moments in the heroine's consciousness earlier in the story. What is most significant about the energy released in this encounter, however, is that Mr. Knightley's angry words arouse a new feeling in her that neither she nor the narrator ever interprets: *the thrill of being punished.* As long as she can remain detached, Emma's relationships with others, when not merely boring, involve mainly vicarious pleasure. Harriet, for instance, is a delightful plaything, a "walking companion," perhaps a David Hamilton daydream, with "those soft blue eyes and all those natural graces" (*E*, 23). But in contrast to her usual lackadaisical interest in others, Emma's response to Mr. Knightley's wrath is passionate—a rare feeling of ecstasy, a complete surrender of the self to the other on the model of Christian agape:

> In this ecstatic love, then, we are far from egocentric love. The lover has no thought of himself, except that he would willingly give his all for the other. Secondly, this love is almost a dark passion; it is a fire and a wound; it is violent and sacrificial; it cares nothing for reason, because it is a madness and a rapture, and lastly it has no ulterior purpose; it seeks no reward; love is the end and consummation. Love, therefore, of this kind is above all; it looks outside itself to another person, and it is beyond reason and nature.[17]

The "wound" inflicted drives her on a mission of "penitence" to Miss Bates; and during Knightley's farewell before going to London she experiences something akin to rapture (a word usually bracketed in Austen's text for feelings imitative of romantic texts) at his slightest gesture of approval:

> —It seemed as if there were an instantaneous impression in her favour, as if his eyes received the truth from her's, and all that had passed of good in her feelings were at once caught and honoured.—He looked at her with a glow of regard. She was warmly gratified—and in another moment still more so, by a little movement of more than common friendliness on his part.—He took her hand;—whether she had not herself made the first motion, she could not say—she might, perhaps, have rather offered it—but he took her hand, pressed it, and certainly was on the point of carrying it to his lips—when, from some fancy or other, he suddenly let it go.

(*E*, 385–86)

There are few scenes anywhere in Austen that come as close to depicting the heroine's utter trust in the male counterpart, without the least hint of ridicule, as this one of unfulfilled desire. Although oblivious to the fact, Mr. Knightley, in contrast to Henry Crawford's experiment on Fanny, has succeeded in his project of making Emma fall in love and be in doubt of having it returned.

The violence of this encounter has unleashed new energies and refined the heroine's awareness of herself as a sexual being through reference to quasi-religious texts on suffering and humiliation. Emma Woodhouse, of course, is not Emma Bovary; and it may be that she is simply exaggerating her guilt and indulging in masochistic dreams as an alternative to the ultimate crisis of Box Hill, the utter dearth of eros at the moment. Having savored this frightening experience of ritual bondage, however, she readily snaps back to her former self and overcompensates for her brief defeat by dreams of grandeur, feeling most in command of events just before discovering Harriet's love for Knightley. Armed with the knowledge of Jane's and Frank's engagement, she mitigates her anger at having been used by considering what the news will mean for "Harriet, poor Harriet!"—now presumably reduced to the carrion of dark passion. Furthermore, though having been duped all along by Churchill, she takes comfort in the thought that her vain flirtation had given her real power over Jane: "—Emma could now imagine why her own attentions had been slighted. This discovery laid many smaller matters open. No doubt it had been from jealousy.—In Jane's eyes she had been a rival; and well might any thing she could offer of assistance or regard be repulsed" (*E*, 403).

Emma is an imaginist, as many readers have said, but the narrative only superficially declares her need of abandoning this talent. On the contrary, she emulates her author's own intertextuality as she "reads" Jane's story. Mock heroic metaphors of torture imply all the sadism of imagining the Gothic heroine's writhing agonies: "An airing in the Hartfield carriage would have been the rack, and arrow-root from the Hartfield storeroom must have been poison" (*E*, 403). It was only a passing thought; but nevertheless, to the narrator's secret delight, it could not be stifled. The next sentence weighs the degree of power gained by her newfound knowledge against the quantity of charity to be allotted to either Jane or Harriet under the circumstances: "She understood it all; and as far as her mind could disengage itself from the injustice and selfishness of angry feelings, she acknowledged that Jane Fairfax would have neither elevation nor happiness beyond her desert. But poor Harriet was such an engrossing charge! There was little sympathy to be spared for any body else" (*E*, 403). As if rewound all the more tightly after her momentary selflessness and dependence, Emma's ego glories in the knowledge of the secret engagement and its apparently dire consequences for her protégée.

While deriving self-esteem from her exclusive grasp of events ("She understood it all" [*E*, 403]), Emma can rise to being charitable toward her rivals; but with the return of self-contempt at Harriet's traumatic declaration, she loses control and suffers the deepest jealousy ever. Like Victor Frankenstein confronting the monster of his own creation, Emma panics at the metamorphosis of the sweet, docile, and selfless object into a discriminating judge of gentlemen, who repeats the very words of an earlier lesson on the differences between a farmer and a man of quality. Now, in imitation of other Austen heroines, strength in defeat is all that Emma can hope for as she endures Harriet's detailed account of her romance with Knightley until they are happily interrupted by Mr. Woodhouse's entrance; but after all the compression of outward demeanor, when finally alone, "this was the spontaneous burst of Emma's feelings: 'Oh God! that I had never seen her!'" (*E*, 411). At this point one may surmise that she actually regrets Harriet's recovery from the "putrid sore throat." Now that the distance in triangular desire has dangerously narrowed and brought the three participants almost face to face, there is no brooking the usurper ("[T]here would be no need of *compassion* to the girl who believed herself loved by Mr. Knightley").

Whatever her personal loss in this matter, Emma resorts to a snobbish elevation of the beloved to vindicate her hatred of the rival; and the whole reverie is in free indirect discourse:

> Mr. Knightley and Harriet Smith!—It was an union to distance every wonder of the kind.—The attachment of Frank Churchill and Jane Fairfax became commonplace, threadbare, stale in the comparison, exciting no surprise, presenting no disparity, affording nothing to be said or thought.—Mr. Knightley and Harriet Smith!—Such an elevation on her side! Such a debasement on his!—It was horrible to Emma to think how it must sink him in the general opinion, to foresee the smiles, the sneers, the merriment it would prompt at his expense; the mortification and disdain of his brother, the thousand inconveniences to himself.
>
> (*E*, 413)

Aside from her obvious rivalry with her female charge, Emma dreads the possibility that the man she had always admired from a sexual distance, without the threatening necessity of marriage in adult life, should stumble into the mill of the conventional and deprive her of further imitative desire: his sterling class is her only assurance of that "absolute difference" to distinguish herself from the second- and third-rate. Her eventual sympathy with Jane, however, shows a liberal impulse that contradicts this obsession with hierarchy and assures us that the sentiments toward Harriet are greatly distorted by jealousy.

A major twist to this novel, nevertheless, is its refusal to bow to conventional plot solutions to restore a neat equilibrium between the heroine and her rival. Characters have no way of escaping the "evil of their situation." If Emma's feelings toward Harriet immediately after the fateful discovery are unrelievedly selfish, they do not improve even after Knightley's proposal abruptly allays her worst fears. Upon his spontaneous words of love, Emma's immediate reaction is to gloat over her enemy's defeat: "[T]o see . . . that Harriet was nothing; that she was every thing herself" (*E*, 430). With a perverse gush of egotism, she hugs herself for not having revealed to him the truth about Harriet's error: "[T]here was time also to rejoice that Harriet's secret had not escaped her, and to resolve that it need not and should not." Although her self-esteem had enabled her to take a charitable view of Jane's fortune, here it requires a persistent rejection of Harriet as a friend because of the imagined rivalry between them. While listening to Knightley's proposal, Emma can think only of Harriet's demise and her own determination to withhold any assistance: "[F]or as to any of that heroism of sentiment which might have prompted her to entreat him to transfer his affection from herself to Harriet, as infinitely the most worthy of the two . . . Emma had it not" (*E*, 431). Then, in a parody of religious sacrifice, which warns us against taking too seriously the whole business of the heroine's moral reform: "She felt for Harriet, with pain and with contrition; but no flight of generosity run mad, opposing all that could be probable or reasonable, entered her brain" (*E*, 431). As in the conjunction of Mars and Venus, sexual love is warfare; and the narrative leaves few doubts about how deeply felt were the "pain" and "contrition" for her vanquished enemy.

Although from this stage on Harriet is merely "dead weight" to Emma, a continually irksome reminder of past errors, the former is still full of surprises: for instance, her quick return to Robert Martin ("[I]t really was too much to hope even of Harriet, that she could be in love with more than *three* men in one year" [*E*, 450]); and the discovery of her humble origins ("The stain of illegitimacy, unbleached by nobility or wealth, would have been a stain indeed" [*E*, 428]). Hence, as Emma's self-esteem reaches new heights by the end of the story: "—The intimacy between her and Emma must sink; their friendship must change into a calmer sort of good will; and, fortunately, what ought to be, and must be, seemed already beginning, and in the most gradual, natural manner" (*E*, 482). A question never raised in the text is whether Emma would ever have gone so far as to become engaged had it not been for Harriet's misapprehension of Mr. Knightley's love; in any case, the heroine is too caught up in the mechanics of triangular desire to see that her power over the rival has obviated her former detachment. Emma's ego now depends precariously upon Mr. Knightley's favor, and the alternative is too frightening to contemplate— an utter void equivalent to death.

In view of her entrapment in the text, therefore, Emma could readily say, with Don Quixote, that she is in love because it is incumbent upon the heroine of romance to be so. If love proves to be more a situation than an idea, perhaps La Rochefoucauld best describes the motive: "It is difficult to define love; what can be said is that in the soul it is a passion to dominate another, in the mind it is mutual understanding, whilst in the body it is simply a delicately veiled desire to possess the beloved after many rites and mysteries."[18] Another maxim of the great French egoist suggests why desire is inevitably triangular in Austen: "Jealousy is in some measure just and reasonable, since it merely aims at keeping something that belongs to us or we think belongs to us, whereas envy is a frenzy that cannot bear anything that belongs to others."[19] Compassion, charity, and friendship are surely possible in Austen's fictional world; but what is most remarkable about her comic art is the moral neutrality it shows toward such traditional vices as hatred, jealousy, envy, pride, and other modes of self-aggrandizement condemned by Christian tradition. From our brief analysis of Emma as desiring subject, the reason for this neutrality should be clear: emotion (the *character*'s emotion, to give it a place in the text) is not free and spontaneous but inherently contextual and triadic in structure. "Some desire is necessary to keep life in motion"; unless a character is given the situation necessary for desire, however, there is no life. This is the vicious circle that Emma comprehends in the end and exploits unconscionably to be first. Throughout her struggle to avoid the pitfalls of romantic passion and the degradation of being among the second- and third-rate heroines of pulp fiction, Emma nevertheless emulates other texts, especially from the eighteenth-century French libertine tradition; and thus without always knowing it, she has no choice but to play the game prescribed for her.

Notes

1. Quotations from Samuel Johnson, "The History of Rasselas, Prince of Abissinia," chaps. 3 and 8, respectively, in *Rasselas, Poems, and Selected Prose*, ed. Bertrand H. Bronson (New York: Rinehart, 1952), 511, 522.

2. Cf. Roland Barthes: "What is proposed, then, is a portrait—but not a psychological portrait; instead, a structural one which offers the reader a discursive site: the site of someone speaking within himself, *amorously*, confronting the other (the loved object), who does not speak," *A Lover's Discourse: Fragments*, trans. Richard Howard (New York: Hill and Wang, 1978), 3.

3. Marc Eli Blanchard, *Description: Sign, Self, Desire: Critical Theory in the Wake of Semiotics* (The Hague: Mouton, 1980), 2.

4. Miguel de Cervantes, *Don Quixote*, ed. Joseph R. Jones and Kenneth Douglas (New York: Norton, 1981), pt. 2, chap. 32, 601.

5. Thackeray describes listening to a French singer of a sentimental ballad who not only made his audience weep but reduced himself to tears by his own performance. See *The English Humourists*, Everyman's Library (London: Dent, 1912), 233–34.

6. Barthes, *A Lover's Discourse*, 22–24.

7. Alexander Pope, *The Rape of the Lock*, ed. Geoffrey Tillotson, *The Twickenham Edition of the Poems of Alexander Pope*, 3d ed. (London: Methuen; New Haven and London: Yale University Press, 1962), 2:206 (canto 5, ll. 67–70).

8. Henry Fielding, *The History of Tom Jones, A Foundling*, ed. Fredson Bowers, *The Wesleyan Edition of the Works of Henry Fielding* (Middletown, Conn.: Wesleyan University Press, 1975), 34 (I, i).

9. Northrop Frye, *Anatomy of Criticism* (New York: Atheneum, 1968), 41.

10. Bernard Paris, *Character and Conflict in Jane Austen's Novels* (Detroit: Wayne State University Press, 1978), 85.

11. At the center of Johnson's essay is a norm hopelessly beyond the reach of the poor: although the action of giving and receiving is reciprocal among the privileged classes, "by what means can the man please . . . who has no power to confer benefits; whose temper is perhaps vitiated by misery . . . ?" *The Rambler*, ed. W. J. Bate and Albrecht B. Strauss, *The Yale Edition of the Works of Samuel Johnson* (New Haven and London: Yale University Press, 1969), 5:118.

12. René Girard, *Deceit, Desire, and the Novel*, trans. Yvonne Freccero (Baltimore: Johns Hopkins University Press, 1965), 66.

13. Ibid., 58–59.

14. Brummell invoked models from ancient Greece and Rome to justify his taste in fashions. See Beau Brummell, *Male and Female Costume*, ed. Eleanor Parker (New York: Arno, 1978).

15. Girard, *Deceit, Desire, and the Novel*, 73.

16. Some modern readers welcome this diminution of the gentleman's prerogative. Julia Prewitt Brown, for instance, remarks about Mr. Knightley's move to Hartfield: "Since he has no really important relationship to give up in leaving his estate, the sacrifice is proper." *Jane Austen's Novels: Social Change and Literary Form* (Cambridge, Mass.: Harvard University Press, 1979), 124.

17. M. C. D'Arcy, *The Mind and Heart of Love* (Cleveland, Ohio: World Publishing, 1967), 100.

18. La Rochefoucauld, *Maxims*, trans. L. W. Tancock (Baltimore: Penguin Books, 1959; reprint 1967), no. 68.

19. Ibid., no. 28.

Emma: The Picture of Health

JOHN WILTSHIRE

◆　◆　◆

EDUCATORS, NATURALLY ENOUGH, have read *Emma* as a novel
about education. More sophisticated, or more self-conscious, latter-day
authors and readers have thought it to be about authorship, or about
reading. Many accounts exist which see it as a novel about perception, or
understand it in epistemological terms, or interpret it as a novel of her-
meneutics. Some have even fancied *Emma* to be about its heroine's imagination.[1] There is hardly a critic who, once having entered the close and
intricate world the novel constructs, has not found it hospitable to a coherent and plausible reading, or who has not found something new and
interesting to observe in Highbury. But with very few exceptions, no one has
yet diagnosed *Emma* to be a novel concerned with health.

One exception is J. R. Watson's article "Mr. Perry's Patients: A View of
Emma" (1970)[2] and, taking his hint, I will begin this exploration of matters of
health in the novel by noting the predominance of this figure, the country
apothecary or local doctor, who historically is the precursor of the general
practitioner.[3] Except that predominance is hardly the word, for Mr. Perry,
though very well known to all the novel's readers, never actually appears
on its pages. He is omnipresent and very active, but scarcely seen, cloistered
with Mr. Woodhouse whilst the drama goes on elsewhere, or glimpsed

occasionally as he rides about the village, or when Emma catches sight of him "walking hastily by" as she is waiting for Harriet outside Ford's, referred to (every twenty or thirty pages): implied, but not presented. Most often he is reported on indirectly, through two or even three intermediaries, as when Harriet tells Emma how Miss Nash has told her, that Mr. Perry told *her*, that he saw Mr. Elton on the road carrying the famous portrait, and teased him that "He was very sure there must be a lady in the case." Or he appears by proxy, through Mr. Woodhouse attributing to him his own opinions about the healthiness of Cromer, or when he is appealed to about the digestive merits of wedding cake. When his speech is most fully conveyed to the reader (and his accents are briefly captured) it is still indirect speech. He makes his most confused, most blurred appearance, of course, in Frank Churchill's blunder about his setting up his carriage (*Emma*, 344) as an item of Highbury gossip that provides Frank and the reader with a good deal of amusement, but leaves Mr. Perry and his concerns still strangely indeterminate.

This effect of Mr. Perry is one consequence of the narrational choice made by the author of this novel. Emma's is the salient, and the controlling point of view. Mr. Perry is only one of a number of examples of figures who inhabit the middle distance of the text, access to whose conversation or thoughts is not given us, as a consequence of this restriction of narrative perspective. Yet this feature of Mr. Perry is not, one might argue, an accidental or unfortunate result of this procedure. Many of the allusions to him, such as Emma's reminding her father how he nursed her through the measles (or indeed, his setting up, or not setting up, his carriage) are designed to suggest his part in the social establishment of the village. Though a professional, he is, like Mr. Cole or Mr. Weston, also an entrepreneur, rising in prosperity with the rise in his reputation, and if he is able to think of a carriage, and set up as a gentleman, that is presumably because he is in constant attendance on the community's richest patient.[4] When called to the genteel poor, like the Bates, he does not, we understand, charge a fee, and thus, in another mode, makes clear his claim to gentlemanly status. All this contributes to the *effet du réel*—to the novel's careful construction of the social verisimilitudes of village life—but the mode of his presentation also plays its part in the sense of depth that is one of its more remarkable achievements.

Mr. Perry is a nodal point, not only as a relay-station of gossip, but as a key reference in the distinctive sociolect of Highbury, a speech idiom which, taking its cue from Mr. Woodhouse, is much concerned with discussion of and enquiries about sickness and health. Highbury gossip interprets his purchase of the carriage, not as a sign of his prosperity, or of his social prestige, but in terms of his own ill health. "It was owing to [Mrs. Perry's] persuasion, as she thought his being out in bad weather did him a great deal of harm" is Frank's recital of the gossip (*E*, 344–45). Economic relations and social determinants are thus displaced or partially concealed by their redefinition as matters of health. By redefining social (and gender) relations wholly as a language of the body, of seemingly self-produced, autonomous conditions, here and as we shall see, in more important instances, Highbury remains oblivious to the political and social structures that are actually organising its world. Highbury knows people, becomes familiar with them, comes to own them, in the mode of patienthood. All these inferences are tucked away in the midst of a narrative whose apparent enticement is to give a crucial clue about the romantic relation of Frank and Jane. Yet Mr. Perry's plural and eccentric position within the text helps at the same time to problematise the very questions of health and illness on which he is the deferred and obscured authority.

In *Emma*, both the high and the low, both the rich and powerful Mrs. Churchill of Enscombe, and the poor cottager whom Emma and Harriet go to visit, are noticed as sufferers from ill health. The novel is littered too with para-medical paraphernalia and talk, from Isabella's claims about the favourable air of Brunswick Square, to Harriet's treasured court-plaister, to the Hartfield arrowroot dispatched for Jane, to Emma's speculations about that special "constitution" of Frank Churchill's which makes him cross when he is hot. It could be argued that Jane Austen uses these matters of health merely as a pretext, as incidental topics of conversation or concern in the novel, whilst really focusing on the more crucial matters her critics have so thoroughly elucidated—those matters of motive and perception, of imagination and self-knowledge, the life of consciousness, that can plausibly be made the central stuff of this psychologically adroit novel. After all, health is used as a pretext in the novel itself by its characters. Jane Fairfax arrives in Highbury supposedly to try the effect of her native air on a long-standing cold (caught early in November, as it happens, in the first phase, the first strain, of her secret engagement). Frank uses his fixing of the spectacles of the deaf, sleepy—and presumably now also blinded—Mrs. Bates as a cover for dallying with Jane by the piano, or rushes out with umbrellas on the excuse that "Miss Bates must not be forgotten" to welcome Jane to the ball. Emma, finding Harriet's disappointed presence too uncomfortable after accepting Mr. Knightley's proposal, remembers that she has a bad tooth, and has long wanted to see a dentist—a convenient excuse for shipping her off to Isabella in London. Jane Austen thereby avoids her encroaching on Emma's happiness as the novel draws to a close (and Harriet's reproachful letter is reported on, but not given, for the same reason) but at the risk of (or even with the purpose of?) our making comparisons between the rights of a Harriet Smith and the constant medical attention deemed the perquisite of the more powerful.

The author can thus be caught up to the same trick as her characters, as when, to give another example, she contrives to bestow a sore throat on Harriet, getting her out of the Christmas eve visit to the Westons, so that Emma and Mr. Elton may reach a confrontation alone. But is it merely incidental—a bit of narrative scenery—that on returning back from Mrs. Goddard's, where she has found that Harriet was "very feverish and had a bad sore throat," Emma and Mr. Elton, walking "in conversation about the invalid," should be "overtaken by Mr. John Knightley, returning from the daily visit to Donwell, with his two eldest boys, whose healthy, glowing faces shewed all the benefit of a country run, and seemed to ensure a quick dispatch of the roast mutton and rice pudding they were hastening home for"? (*E*, 109) Or is this an example of a stringent narrative economy, working in terms other than plot, the inscription of tensions, here to do with health, gender and appetite, that will later need to be resolved? When the information that Frank Churchill has gone back to Richmond on the very evening of Box Hill, and therefore broken with Jane, needs to be conveyed, Miss Bates is the ventriloquist:

> "It was before tea—stay—no, it could not be before tea, because we were just going to cards—and yet it was before tea, because I remember thinking—Oh! no, now I recollect, now I have it; something happened before tea, but not that. Mr. Elton was called out of the room before tea, old John Abdy's son wanted to speak with him. Poor old John, I have a great regard for him; he was clerk to my poor father twenty-seven years; and now, poor old man, he is bed-ridden, and very poorly with the rheumatic gout in his joints—I must go and see him today; and so will Jane, I am sure, if she gets out at all. And poor John's son came to talk to Mr. Elton about relief from the parish: he is very well to do himself, you know, being head man at the Crown, ostler, and every thing of that sort, but still he cannot keep his father without some help; and so, when Mr. Elton came back, he told us what John ostler had been telling him, and then it came out about the chaise having been sent to Randall's to take Mr. Frank Churchill to Richmond. That was what happened before tea. It was after tea that Jane spoke to Mrs. Elton."
>
> (*E*, 382–83)

Hidden in Miss Bates' loosely-knit chatter is the information which explains why Jane has suddenly decided to take the job as a governess. The reader, invited to read from the point of view of Emma, for whom there is "nothing in all this either to astonish or interest" skims over poor John Abdy as an irrelevance, and, even when he or she is wise to the plot, dismisses John as a cunning decoy. But is he merely a decoy, or is the reference to him planted to further an interest of the text less overt still than the romance plot of Frank and Jane Fairfax?[5] One thing his mention does reveal (but we are too preoccupied to notice) is that Miss Bates has a moral life and exercises the sort of charity and attention towards inferiors and dependents that the reader and Emma find it still so hard, even at this moment, to give to her.

Plot contrivance and the opportunity for some mild and traditional comedy at the expense of the hypochondriac: these are certainly ways of accounting for the plethora of medical talk and incident in *Emma*. Yet Watson was able to take this further. "The comedy about health is able to illuminate character in a significant way" he suggests. "One of the ways in which the nature of certain characters in *Emma* is established is by observing the ways in which they react to illness in others, the degree of forbearance and kindness which they show; behind such trivial actions as mending Mrs. Bates's spectacles and reassuring Mr. Woodhouse there lies a necessary human law, the duty to comfort the fatherless, and the widows in their affliction."[6] The theme of health enables Jane Austen to bring out serious issues in a comic mode, he argues, particularly in revealing Emma's continuous self-abnegation in the face of her father's relentless demands. How suggestive this is as a general claim can be illustrated by the scene at the Woodhouse dinner for the Eltons where Jane Fairfax's daily walk to the post office becomes the focus of discussion.

The chapter is one in which, for a while, Emma's distinctive point of view is in abeyance. Mr. John Knightley and Jane, old acquaintances, for both of whom Highbury was home, but who have both moved in a wider, more sophisticated and harsher world than the one that presently encloses them, have met in the rain that morning, and John Knightley cross-questions (since he is in the law) Jane about her habit of walking to the post office in all weathers. For the first time in the novel we hear conversation between two intelligent equals other than Emma and John Knightley's brother. What Jane says is sensitive, wise—and downright misleading. "You have every body dearest to you always at hand, I, probably, never shall again; and therefore till I have outlived all my affections, a post-office, I think, must always have power to draw me out, in worse weather than to-day" (*E*, 294). The reader is likely to assume that Jane is alluding to the prospect of a future as a governess, especially as this shortly becomes the explicit topic of conversation, but the narrational pretext would be, of course, that she may only be thinking of separation from the Campbells and Dixons. She has, as it happens, received a letter from Frank only that morning, just as Mrs. Weston has, announcing his impending visit, or at least this is the implication of the "air of greater happiness than usual—a glow both of complexion and spirits" which Emma shortly detects in her.

Concern that Jane might have damaged her health by her foolhardiness is expressed in a brief spectrum of responses. John Knightley's interrogation is followed by Mr. Woodhouse, whose old-fashioned gallantry and courtesy, as well as his vapidity, are expressed in his concerned inquiry "My dear, did you change your stockings?" His placid assumption "My dear Miss Fairfax, young ladies are very sure to be cared for," is, in Jane's circumstances, both pathetic and ludicrous, nor as ideologically innocent as it might seem. Mrs. Elton's bullying interference is contrasted with Mrs. Weston's maternal solicitude—"Better wait an hour or two, or even half a day for your letters, than run the risk of bringing on your cough again." All this concern, all this kindness (who, despite Mrs. Elton, can doubt that it *is* kindness?) would actually prevent Jane from doing what she most wants and needs to do. Not only would Mrs. Elton's scheme of getting "one of our men" to fetch Jane's letters inevitably result in Frank being known as her correspondent, Jane would be denied an excuse for escape from her aunt and grandmother, and the suffocating atmosphere of their rooms. The kindness—even Mrs. Weston's—has an element of aggression in it, an unconscious wish to keep Jane within known bounds, and in its misdirected concern replicates the claustrophobia of her family life. The scene is a text for Arthur Kleinman's observation that the stress/support model is a woefully incomplete notion of the social reception of crisis and illness, for what is stress at one moment may be support the next, and kindness itself can also be a burden.[7] That supportive community of Highbury is also, at times, almost insupportable (though, fortified by the prospect of Frank's visit here, Jane stands up for herself).

Highbury's medicalised sociolect installs the body as the key to understanding—or at least communicating with—the person. Care for others is expressed, in a limited and sometimes damaging mode, as concern for the minor stresses and strains of their physical living. Though superficially supportive, such a mode of transacting relationships is not an enhancing or enabling one, for it positions persons too readily as patients and depends too completely upon obliviousness to or naiveté about their inner psychological and instinctive life. It is because Jane's motives are, deliberately, hidden from this community (and initially from the reader) that her body necessarily becomes the site for the construction of meanings, and that her instance thus replicates, in an amplified mode, the novel's representation of Mrs. Churchill.

Through its comfortable concern with its denizens' well-being, the novel poses a series of important questions, I suggest, about the nature of health, which are put more insistently through its gallery of sufferers from so-called "nervous" disorders. Not only does Isabella Knightley, as might be expected, complain of "those little nervous head-aches and palpitations which I am never entirely free from any where," but even placid Harriet, even Mrs. Weston, let alone Jane Fairfax, suffer from, or complain of these symptoms called "nerves." But the two grand embodiments of the nervous constitution in *Emma* are Mr. Woodhouse and Mrs. Churchill and they preside, one way or another, over the novel's action.

Nervous disorder was a common diagnosis at this period, in other places than Highbury. The King himself was a sufferer, as Fanny Burney reports in her court journal for 1788. " 'I am nervous' he cried; 'I am not ill, but I am nervous; if you would know what is the matter with me, I am nervous.' "[8] "It was . . . only in the eighteenth century," writes the medical historian W. F. Bynum, "that it became possible to suffer from the 'nerves.' "[9] George Cheyne's *The English Malady or a Treatise of Nervous Disease of All Kinds* (1733), a very popular textbook of the early part of the century, was chiefly responsible, he suggests, for putting the notion of the nerves and the nervous system as a source of human suffering into general circulation. Cheyne described the nervous patient, Bynum reports, as "a personality type found in those with 'weak, loose, and feeble, or relaxed nerves,' the result of which was extreme sensitivity to hot and cold, weak digestion, a tendency to alternative diarrhoea and costiveness, and other signs of valetudinarianism."[10] "Nervous disorders are the Diseases of the Wealthy, the Voluptuous and the Lazy," Cheyne wrote in a censorious moment, in which he none the less makes a significant point.[11] The argument of his book is that this new (and very widespread) disease entity was the product of increasing wealth and leisure among the middle classes, and this association of the nervous temperament or constitution with affluence continues through the century as "nervous" disorders make their appearance in an increasing number of textbooks. The work on irritability, sensibility and the nervous system undertaken most notably in Britain by Robert Whytt at the mid-century[12] would have grafted a new "scientific" understanding onto this already current conception, and confirmed its association with amplified or exacerbated sensibility (which was also a preserve of the leisured classes).

The typical symptoms of the nervous patient are described, for instance, in the Introduction to a book called *A View of the Nervous Temperament* published by Dr. Thomas Trotter in 1807:

> An inaptitude to muscular action, or some pain in exerting it; an irksomeness, or dislike to attend to business and the common affairs of life; a selfish desire of engrossing the sympathy and attention of others to the narration of their own sufferings; with fickleness and unsteadiness of temper, even to irascibility: and accompanied more or less with dyspeptic symptoms, are the leading characteristics of *nervous disorders*; to be referred in general, to debility, increased sensibility, or torpor of the alimentary canal.[13]

Some behavioural features distributed between Mr. Woodhouse and Mrs. Churchill are obviously predicated here. Trotter's social profile of the typical patient is equally apposite, since he suggests that "torpid habits of living" are the consequence of patients with money in the public funds having no need to work for their livelihood, "without any of those urgent motives which preserve energy of mind, so condusive to health." When he later warns that nervous patients may become dependent upon a "gossiping physician" who becomes "a kind of appendage to their establishment," Trotter could well be describing Mr. Woodhouse and Mr. Perry.

> Being singular in the selection of friends, they seldom mix in company; sedentary from habit, they go little abroad; their amusements and recreation are thus limited, and such as possess the talent of bringing news, and telling a story, are at all times welcome guests. But as the tale of their own complaints engrosses so much of their conversation, a medical gossip, before all others, is the most acceptable.[14]

As one might expect, Cheyne, Trotter, and other physicians recommended a frugal diet, exercise and fresh air to relieve the condition. Walking and gardening are recommended, for instance, to young ladies: "And while her nervous aunts are moping their evenings over the card table, she will gather health by her cheerful excursions; and preserve her bloom of countenance by the only means that can give it an additional charm."[15] It's in a similar vein that the narrator recommends Mrs. Goddard's school in Highbury, "reckoned a particularly healthy spot" where young ladies were certainly not (as in, presumably, more affluent and prestigious establishments) "screwed out of health and into vanity." Instead, Mrs. Goddard lets them "run about a great deal in the summer, and in winter dressed their chilblains with her own hands" (*E*, 21–22).

Thomas Trotter also strikes a Woodhouse-like note of solicitude about young ladies getting wet feet:

> The lady of weak health, who may wish to display an ancle, should be very guarded how she throws off her warm socks. Many evils befal the sex from cold feet: such as follow on walking abroad with thin shoes on damp roads...I have known some serious nervous ailments brought on by a young lady evading the orders of a judicious parent; and after being dressed, retiring privately to put off the additional petticoat and understockings, that she might dance the more lightly.[16]

This is "medical" advice which is actually focusing or activating ideology and gender politics: the young woman is defined equally by her propensity to sickness as by her coquetry and the two are seen to be linked as essential properties of the female.[17] "My dear, young ladies are very sure to be cared for," as Mr. Woodhouse tells Jane, but this means in effect that young women, as a given of their gender, are positioned as patients, or potential patients, at a lower level of bodily capacity and resourcefulness than young men, and, while entitled to "care," have initiative taken from them. This element in its attitude to Jane is hidden from Highbury, but not from the novel.

Various doctors suggested various organic pathologies as the substratum of nervous disorders, but increasingly they were understood as "functional" conditions, a term which is sometimes used in modern discussion, as in psychoanalysis, to designate disorders which have behavioural, and therefore "real" symptoms, but for which no organic cause can be discovered. Such conditions—akin to hysteria—are, as Bynum writes, particularly intriguing to historians (he might have added, literary critics) because "they seem to show most clearly the cultural, social, and ideological factors which influence definitions and perceptions of disease and constrain the behaviour of both patients and their doctors."[18] Though perceived as "disease" by both parties to the medical transaction, disorders of the nervous system, "temperament" or "constitution" are best, in fact, characterised as illness, whose meaning inscribed the social and cultural circumstances of the patient—as was implicitly recognised through the emphasis in doctors' accounts on the social class of sufferers.

Mr. Woodhouse is described as "a nervous man, easily depressed" and his needs influence and perhaps dictate the life of his daughter, but the

other chief sufferer from "nerves" in *Emma* exerts an even more powerful
hold on events in Highbury. Mrs. Churchill, of the great Yorkshire family,
is known only by report as "a very odd-tempered woman" (according to
the mild, forgiving Mrs. Weston). Her name alludes to Sarah Churchill,
Duchess of Marlborough, Pope's Atossa, the type of the captious great lady
("Last night, her Lord was all that's good and great / A Knave this morning,
and his Will a Cheat"[19]). Emma's idea of her is that "while she makes no
sacrifice for the comfort of the husband, to whom she owes every thing . . .
she exercises incessant caprice towards *him*" (*E*, 123). "The evil of the distance from Enscombe," a disgruntled and disbelieving Mr. Weston tells
Mrs. Elton,

> "is, that Mrs. Churchill, *as we understand*, has not been able to leave the
> sopha for a week together. In Frank's last letter, she complained, he said,
> of being too weak to get into her conservatory without having both his
> arm and his uncle's! This, you know, speaks a great deal of weakness—
> but now she is so impatient to be in town, that she means to sleep only
> two nights on the road."
>
> (*E*, 306)

The lady's nerves being soon "under continual irritation and suffering"
from the noise of London, she removes once again to Richmond.

The adopted son, Frank Churchill, is evidently her favourite. His engagement to Jane Fairfax (like Mr. Churchill's sister's marriage to Captain
Weston, an unsuitably low connection) needs must be kept secret or presumably he would be "thrown off with due decorum" like his predecessor.
"His importance at Enscombe was very evident," as Emma perceives. "He did
not boast, but it naturally betrayed itself, that he had persuaded his aunt
where his uncle could do nothing, and on her laughing and noticing it, he
owned that he believed (excepting one or two points) he could *with time*
persuade her to any thing" (*E*, 221). Emma can only partly understand his
meaning, of course. Frank has now, in February, been almost six months
engaged to Jane, and it is this "time" that he is presumably playing for. To
persuade his aunt he must keep in her good books; thus, though he wants
to be with Jane, and preparations for the ball are in full train, when she
summons, he must go.

> A letter arrived from Mr. Churchill to urge his nephew's instant return.
> Mrs. Churchill was unwell—far too unwell to do without him; she had
> been in a very suffering state (so said her husband) when writing to her

nephew two days before, though from her usual unwillingness to give pain, and constant habit of never thinking of herself, she had not mentioned it; but now she was too ill to trifle, and must entreat him to set off for Enscombe without delay.

(*E*, 258)

If in Highbury Frank plays the part of intending suitor to Emma, at Enscombe he plays the role of solicitous son. He departs, grumbling "He knew her illnesses: they never occurred but for her own convenience." He has himself, of course, acquired his step-mother's talent for manipulation.

Is Mrs. Churchill "really ill" (*E*, 316) or not? Frank offers conflicting readings of her condition, perhaps depending on the degree of inconvenience she causes him. Knowledge of this figure on the distant horizons of *Emma* is filtered through Frank's reports, and obscured by the supervening questions of his motivation, and these reports are then refracted in the light of the desires of those who receive them. When the Churchills are in London, he finds it no more easy, apparently, to come to Highbury. "His aunt could not bear to have him leave her. Such was his own account at Randall's. If he were quite sincere, if he really tried to come, it was to be inferred that Mrs. Churchill's removal to London had been of no service to the wilful or nervous part of her disorder" (*E*, 316). On this occasion Frank "could not be prevailed on by all his father's doubts, to say that her complaints were merely imaginary, or that she was as strong as ever" (*E*, 317). The mystery, or undecidability, of Mrs. Churchill's illness is not resolved, either, by her death. "Mrs. Churchill, after being disliked at least twenty-five years, was now spoken of with compassionate allowances. In one point she was fully justified. She had never been admitted before to be seriously ill. The event acquitted her of all the fancifulness and all the selfishness of imaginary complaints" (*E*, 387). She is now admitted into Highbury discourse on its own terms as "Poor Mrs. Churchill!" But Highbury is obtuse and the ambiguity persists, since she is carried off, as the narrator makes occasion to say, "by a sudden seizure of a different nature from any thing foreboded by her general state."[20] How one reads Mrs. Churchill's illness depends then upon one's own interests, position and point of view—perhaps one's own state of health. The phrase "the wilful or nervous part of her disorder" is interesting, especially considering Mr. Woodhouse. Are "nerves" then an aspect of the will, referable to the self as moral agent? When Elton flatteringly insinuates that Emma's visit must have been a "cordial" to Harriet, Emma puts him neatly in his place by replying, "My visit was of use to the nervous part of her complaint, I hope: but not even I can charm away a sore throat" (*E*, 114). Does Jane Austen, as George III apparently did, oppose "nervous" to genuine disorder?

Whatever its "real" nature, Mrs. Churchill's ill health functions well enough to keep Frank running back to her. He is prevented from making the strawberry party, too, as he says, by "a temporary increase of illness in her; a nervous seizure, which had lasted some hours" (*E*, 363). Mrs. Churchill then, has great—in fact, very precise and crucial—influence upon the action of the novel. Without her, there would be no need to keep the engagement so long a secret; without her illness Frank would be free to come and go, and enjoy himself as he pleases. Without her caprices he could himself be less "self-willed" and have no need to flirt with Emma. Her demand for attention originates a cascade of incidents, for his late arrival at Donwell provokes the crisis in Frank and Jane's relationship, generating the tense and unhappy Box Hill party, which in turn impacts upon Emma and her relationship with Mr. Knightley. She is thus the always absent origin of the novel's events.[21] High in the social hierarchy, she is high in the hierarchy of causes. Her power—based, of course, on her status as an elder and her affluence—infiltrates the smallest events of provincial Highbury.

Mrs. Churchill, the sufferer from "nerves," operates in the novel as the covert double of Mr. Woodhouse, the "nervous man" whom Emma spends so much of her time and energy attending to and comforting. If one reads the novel to emphasise the "wilful" side of their disorders, the parallels are striking. She is elderly and rich, Frank is her adopted son, she uses her illnesses to keep him at home and to prevent him from marrying, by fear that he will displease her and lose his inheritance. Mr. Woodhouse is elderly and rich, Emma is his unmarried daughter; he uses his ill health to keep her at home and to discourage the journeys abroad, the social contacts, that might lead to marriage. Her distant power over Highbury is paralleled by his local one: he is consulted in everything, in every arrangement his welfare and whims are of first concern. The parallel is disguised because Mr. Woodhouse is presented as kindly and generally liked, while Mrs. Churchill is thought to be cantankerous and generally disliked. The reader's knowledge of Mrs. Churchill is gathered from hostile witnesses—principally Mr. Weston: Mr. Woodhouse is seen only through friendly and benevolent eyes. No one in the novel would think of comparing the two. She is a minor character in far-off Yorkshire whereas he is the unconsciously presiding genius whose words open the novel and whose welfare determines its close. But the parallels generate—or so it might be argued—what Jane Austen, having chosen to construct her narrative from Emma's position, choosing Emma's as the salient point of view, can of necessity render only by subversive means. She foregrounds the sweetness of Mr. Woodhouse's character, his kindness and his courtesy, whilst the hidden Churchill homology indicates the power-relations that an impartial analysis would display as the organising dynamic. The relation is clothed in love and dutifulness, but the skeleton of its structure is Mr. Woodhouse's inevitable authority as the patriarchal elder, and his power over Emma's life.

Such a Foucauldian emphasising of power-relations can doubtless be challenged by those readers and critics who would see Mrs. Churchill's treatment of Frank rather as a contrast to Mr. Woodhouse's dependence on Emma, understanding it to work similarly to the way Mrs. Elton's bullying and patronising function as an extension or parody of Emma's own faults, a parallel which casts some light no doubt, but which turns out in the end to be specious. (And certainly Emma's sentiments towards her father are quite different from Frank's towards his aunt.) Mr. Woodhouse's fussing never actually stands in the way of Emma's activities—she manages to go to the Westons', the Coles', to take part in the ball at the Crown, despite his fears and inhibitions.[22] Yet to restrict one's notion of power to this behavioural level is certainly to limit the possibilities of the novel. Mr. Woodhouse's influence over Emma's thoughts and feelings, it could well be argued, is less direct, and more tenacious than his simple objections to rich food or late nights. All neurotic symptoms have the potential to ensnare others in their toils. And one might be inclined to disbelieve in Mr. Woodhouse's illness to precisely the same extent that one disbelieves in Mrs. Churchill's. For most parts of the novel the comedy that attends Mr. Woodhouse's foibles is certainly an encouragement to believe that his complaints are greatly exaggerated. What, apart from sensitivity to noise, fear of danger, dislike of travel and change, not to speak of "torpor of the alimentary canal"—are his symptoms? "His habits of gentle selfishness" are selfishness nonetheless; and though he is well-meaning and charitably disposed, it is scarcely possible not to notice that all the real good, all the active charity in the novel, is Emma's and Knightley's, and that a good deal of Emma's involves overriding her father's wishes. Left to himself, his benevolence has a self-cancelling quality that renders it dubious—witness Mrs. Bates's Tantalus torture with the sweetbread and asparagus. On the other hand (and here the analogy with Mrs. Churchill again appears) when after she has accepted Knightley Emma thinks about her father's future welfare, she seems to take for granted that his physical condition is declining, and that his demands upon her cannot be refused. Mr. Woodhouse's illness, however intangible, has the pressure of a social, and emotional, fact.

The reader who opens *Emma* stands, with its heroine, on the margins of a community. The narrative of the novel requires that the reader share the idiom and valuations of that community, whilst being aware, of course, that these values are far from absolute, and that, moreover, their relation to "Jane Austen's" own is obscure. One can repudiate the idiom, read with the eye of a stranger, substitute different standards and another form of speech and describe the community around Henry Woodhouse, for example, as "Emma's idiot father and his circle of ossified friends"[23] but this will not help to understand the dynamics of that community, nor to make Austen's presentation of it explicable in the new terms. One is left with no standpoint except outside a novel whose narrative technique invites precisely that one enter the ways of its world. How then to make sense of the relationships around him, to understand not only Mr. Woodhouse himself, but those (some of them evidently meant as authorial deputies) who treat Mr. Woodhouse, not merely with deference, but with kindness and affection— even love? Imagining a psychoanalytic case-study of Emma, Avrom Fleishman posits a latter-day diagnosis of her father. "It's often assumed by the layman that people with evident *hypochondria* are really well, but [Emma's] father, though not organically, is clearly mentally ill. The diagnosis of his illness is probably *premature senility*, featuring acute anxiety."[24] Dangers attend any attempt to understand Mr. Woodhouse in modern medicalised terms, such as the one I have just used, "neurotic." All the same, the text gives signs that Mr. Woodhouse's nervous inhibitions do have far reaching influence on Emma, and that they are potentially destructive, even though their presence is chiefly displayed in the process of Emma's triumphing over them. (Not always—she doesn't succeed in preventing Mr. Woodhouse's comments about doctors and bathing places from maddening John Knightley.) In fact, her management of her father's domestic life is used to throw light on his ill health at the same time as it illustrates the nature of the capabilities she brings to the task. Consider the little comic episode that ends chapter II:

> What was unwholesome to him, he regarded as unfit for any body; and he had, therefore, earnestly tried to dissuade them from having any wedding cake at all, and when that proved vain, as earnestly tried to prevent any body's eating it. He had been at the pains of consulting Mr. Perry, the apothecary, on the subject. Mr. Perry was an intelligent, gentlemanlike man, whose frequent visits were one of the comforts of Mr. Woodhouse's life; and, upon being applied to, he could not but acknowledge, (though it seemed rather against the bias of inclination,) that wedding-cake might certainly disagree with many—perhaps with most people, unless taken moderately. With such an opinion, in confirmation of his own, Mr. Woodhouse hoped to influence every visitor of

the new-married pair; but still the cake was eaten; and there was no rest
for his benevolent nerves till it was all gone.

There was a strange rumour in Highbury of all the little Perrys being
seen with a slice of Mrs. Weston's wedding cake in their hands: but Mr.
Woodhouse would never believe it.

(*E*, 19)

No doubt the cake is an overt symbol of celebration and festivity—the
wedding itself. But because it is to be eaten, and eaten with relish, it
symbolises, in a more amplified fashion, the bodily enjoyments that Mr.
Woodhouse's mode of life is devoted to reducing. He resists all walks,
outings, late nights, dances, trips, expeditions, excursions, engagements,
marriages on the pretext that these activities endanger health. His pro-
gramme is the denial of almost all bodily activity and almost all bodily
enjoyment—as amusingly illustrated in the loin of pork which he suggests
should be "boiled with a little carrot" but which the Bates, not having in
this case the benefit of his advice, have, unprompted, roasted with apples.
He does not like to be reminded of the body's demands and appetites. The
cake's richness, so irrationally distressful to him, can be read as a sign that
Miss Taylor has escaped from Hartfield and is no longer a spectator at life's
feast. What it symbolises can be amplified further, for by a simple substi-
tution of one appetite by another, a simple displacement of the genital or
sexual to the oral or gustatory, it can imply that the comic manifestations
of his valetudinarianism originate in a disturbed sexuality.[25] When Mrs.
Elton talks of him as her "beau," and of his gallantry, and of her "caro
sposo" being jealous, the sexualised banter is glaringly inappropriate, but
given such hints readers have a right to wonder whether, as John Dussinger
suggests, some malformation of sexual life may not be at the root of Henry
Woodhouse's condition: or rather, whether his condition (which is to say,
of course, his role in the novel) cannot appropriately be understood in an
holistic mode which would include sexuality as an aspect of his illness.
Certainly Emma's health is contrasted with his hypochondria, and in Emma
health and sexual appetency are linked.

For Emma is not defeated by her father's neurotic proscriptions. She is
able to get around him (for his own good) by a stratagem of her own. Her
outwitting her father here is part of a series of effects which demonstrate
that Emma's qualities—of independence, initiative, resourcefulness—can
be relied upon for everyone's and her own good, as when, faced with his
recommendation to Miss Bates of "a *little* bit of tart, a *very* little bit" Emma
"allowed her father to talk, but supplied her visitors in a much more

satisfactory style." Her stratagem here aligns her with Frank Churchill's "young person" who (as he tells the appalled Mr. Woodhouse) will sometimes slip behind a curtain and throw up a window, at a ball, a moment when Frank himself is practising tricks on the old gentleman. "I am sure it was a source of high entertainment to you, to feel that you were taking us all in," as Emma tells Frank concerning the engagement, "I think there is a little likeness between us." Her resourcefulness involves co-opting Mr. Perry, the very man Mr. Woodhouse thinks is his friend and ally, and Mr. Perry's giving the cake to his children—the sign of his own marriage and sexual fecundity. The sly joke that rounds the chapter off works by suppressing and condensing the connecting information (which would be something like this: "Dear Mr. Perry, as long as this wedding cake remains in the house it will make my father miserable. Do take it home to Mrs. Perry and give a slice each to your children"). The text as read thus enables the pleasurable saving of psychological energy that, as Freud claimed, all jokes make. Does the joke not also communicate a hostility to—at least a derision of—Mr. Woodhouse that the text nowhere explicitly admits? The laugh against him is therapeutic; it expresses—at several different levels— health triumphing in the face of a mild but stubborn perversity. And by handing the last word to him, it demonstrates the largesse of its own comic vitality.

The incident fulfils Mrs. Weston's just-expressed hopes. "Dear Emma was of no feeble character; she was more equal to her situation than most girls would have been, and had sense and energy and spirits that might be hoped would bear her well and happily through its little difficulties and privations" (*E*, 18). In fact "spirit" is the quality in Emma that is the most reliable antagonist of her father's pathology. "Spirit" or "spirits" are, in themselves, morally neutral, but in relation to him, they reveal their value. "Her father's spirits required support" and it is Emma's own spirit which can be relied upon, it seems, to surmount the impediments placed in her way by his nerves, and that make her, in so far as she is so, a free or autonomous being. The word or term is used very frequently in the novel. "With an alacrity beyond the common impulse of a spirit which yet was never indifferent to the credit of doing every thing well and attentively," she is "inspirited" by the opportunity to interfere in Harriet's love-life, just as she is "animated" by suspicions of Jane's. When she is told that Frank is to arrive soon "Emma's spirits were mounted quite up to happiness" (*E*, 189). Emma's partner in spirits and mischief in fact is Frank, who has "the constitution of the Weston" and "seemed to have all the life and spirit, cheerful feelings and social inclinations of his father" and whose talk is "the effusion of lively spirits" (*E*, 198). Much later Jane Fairfax herself speaks of "his temper and spirits—his delightful spirits."

"Spirit" is at least as important a quality of Emma as her imagination, though it has remained largely invisible to (or perhaps, taken for granted by) her commentators. As I have suggested, for Jane Austen the property is in itself morally neutral: to possess "spirit" (like Mary Crawford—or even Selina Hawkins), verve, courage, or perhaps merely a strong ego, is not necessarily to have "merit." But it is at least—in the context of *Emma*—to have potential value, and in certain conditions, to become "delightful." Intricate in its history, the word overlaps, of course, with a sense of "spirit," as in "spiritual," contradistinguished from the bodily or earthly. The novel includes one exchange which obviously uses "spirit" in the derived sense of "guide" or "monitor," when Emma asks cheekily of Mr. Knightley "Does my vain spirit ever tell me I am wrong?" and he replies "Not your vain spirit, but your serious spirit. If the one leads you wrong, I am sure the other tells you of it" (*E*, 330), though here, of course, Emma's very question demonstrates her spirit in the other sense.

In the cluster of meanings most germane to Austen's use in *Emma* (though other overtones are not excluded), the word seems to suggest a bridging or holistic conflation of the physical and the mental, for the mental alacrity it sometimes celebrates runs quickly into physical energy and activity, and "good spirits" can hardly be thought of except against a background of bodily well-being. Definition 14 in Johnson's *Dictionary* is illuminating about what Jane Austen's usage frequently implies: "That which gives vigour or cheerfulness to the mind; the purest part of the body, bordering, says Sydenham, on immateriality. In this meaning it is commonly written with the plural termination." As Johnson's citation of Dr. Thomas Sydenham (1624–89) suggests, "spirits," in the plural, carries a medical history. Often "spirits" (or "pneuma") were imagined, as in Johnson's definition, as being situated within the body, where they designated partly a physical agent and partly a force.[26] The usage derived ultimately from the animal, natural and vital spirits of Galenic physiology, conceived as highly rarefied liquids, which coursed through the veins, vessels, and ultimately the nervous system of the patient. The conception was thoroughly outmoded in medicine, but still vestigially current in other forms of writing during the later eighteenth and early nineteenth centuries. Lydia Bennet, for instance, is described as having "high animal spirits" (*Pride and Prejudice*, 45). Cowper in a poem first published in 1803 could write "To Mary": "Thy spirits have a fainter flow / I see thee daily weaker grow / 'Tis my distress that brought thee low." Maria Edgeworth's Flora Campbell, an exact contemporary of Emma, similarly has "a constant flow of good spirits and the charming domestic talent of making every trifle a source of amusement to herself and others."[27] The *Oxford English Dictionary* gives an interesting instance from 1790 which connects spirits in this residual medical sense with appearance: "[H]er spirits retired inward, her cheeks grew pale, and down she sank." Animated or good spirits and "bloom" were thus connected: the attractive appearance of the female being the outward sign of her physiological and sexual well-being.

In this period, then, "spirits" are ceasing to evoke a medical context and are in the process of being naturalised as an essential given of the emotional self. And it is this process of naturalisation and diffusion of meaning (previously also undergone by the medieval "humours") which tends to make them unproblematic and hence invisible to analysis. Their representation, too, though a crucial tactic of the novel, can pass without comment. The reason why Jane Austen's commentators remain silent on certain aspects of the text may be that whilst imagination and perception, as mental faculties or aspects of consciousness, have been the central subject of Western philosophical enquiry, "spirits," which enters our vocabulary from another, a (proto)scientific, tradition, has been naturalised, as a fact of being, understood as a constituent part of bodily nature. Of course people in our culture—the culture we still share with Austen—have, or are in, "high" and "low" spirits, just as they may be good or bad humoured—how else to describe them? But people in China or Mali would not necessarily recognise themselves in these terms. As for us, we hardly notice how "spirits" conflates psychological and physical being. Austen's critics, following Knightley, examine Emma's "errors of imagination," and stress the novel's understanding of the creative nature of perception, because through that discourse the novelist could be inserted into the mainstream epistemological tradition and given an honourable place there, but there has been no equivalently sophisticated philosophic treatment of the body. Virginia Woolf famously declared that "English has no words for the shiver and the headache,"[28] but it is possible to amplify her comment, and generalise as truly that the language has no developed discourse for translating the responses of all kinds of bodily human-being into conceptual discussion. Moreover "spirits," eagerness and activity, as demonstrated in the novel, are less easy to theorise since they essentially consist in praxis: one can therefore discourse at will about Emma's "mistakes" or misconceptions, without taking account of the animation and energy transmitted in the prose, which is equally a part of that construction in language which we identify as Emma Woodhouse. A reading aloud is needed, and is often all that is needed, to mark the rhythmic vitality with which her life is transcribed. But to enlarge in discourse on the way that Emma's spirits are represented as a factor of her (moral) life runs the risk of seeming banal to some and inconsequential to others. It would be equally a mistake to erect "spirit" into a stiffly moral value, to stand with, say, "reason," "perception" or "self-knowledge," an abstract quality to be pitted against these in a gladiatorial contest of abstractions, when the presence of Emma's spirits in the text is as hidden, is as internal, fluid and intricate as their supposed antecedent physical nature. The question certainly is closely bound up with Jane Austen's invention of free indirect speech and her utilisation of the novel form as the legitimation of female desire.

A favourite passage of writers wishing to display Austen's control of her medium, the irony that simultaneously represents Emma's thoughts, and reveals their dubiousness, the exposure of "precisely how Emma's judgment is going astray"[29] is her initial response to Harriet:

She was not struck by any thing remarkably clever in Miss Smith's conversation, but she found her altogether very engaging—not inconveniently shy, not unwilling to talk—and yet so far from pushing, shewing so proper and becoming a deference, seeming so pleasantly grateful for being admitted to Hartfield, and so artlessly impressed by the appearance of every thing in so superior a style to what she had been used to, that she must have good sense and deserve encouragement. Encouragement should be given. Those soft blue eyes and all those natural graces should not be wasted on the inferior society of Highbury and its connections. The acquaintance she had already formed were unworthy of her. The friends from whom she had just parted, though very good sort of people, must be doing her harm. They were a family of the name of Martin, whom Emma well knew by character, as renting a large farm of Mr. Knightley and residing in the parish of Donwell—very creditably she believed—she knew Mr. Knightley thought highly of them—but they must be coarse and unpolished, and very unfit to be the intimates of a girl who wanted only a little more knowledge and elegance to be quite perfect. *She* would notice her; she would improve her; she would detach her from her bad acquaintance and introduce her into good society; she would form her opinions and her manners. It would be an interesting and certainly a very kind undertaking; highly becoming her own situation in life, her leisure, and powers.

(*E*, 23–24)

The reader certainly notices, and delights in, the subterfuges of Emma's thinking here—in the agility of the transition from "very good sort of people" to "bad acquaintance" and hence to "good society," for example, and the whisking away of the internal monitor Mr. Knightley's opinions between two parentheses. The point is not that one does not remark the self-deception and snobbery, even arrogance, that these manoeuvres manifest, but that one picks up, at the same time, contrapuntally, and as a part of that very same self-deception and arrogance, the warmth, the eagerness, the panache and brio that enable these feats of psychological legerdemain to pass off successfully as if what were taking place were a process of reasonable thought. Emma's activity here is delightful to behold. Wayne Booth, the critic I have quoted, writes that Emma concludes "with a beautiful burst of egotism," that pulsing and emphatic series of final good resolutions, but in common with most of Austen's critics he is more comfortable in talking about the egoism ("Emma's unconscious catalogue of her egotistical uses for Harriet"[30]) than about the beauty. Not to reckon with what the narrator shortly conceptualises as "alacrity" and "real good-will," though, is not to read half the information conveyed in this prose.

It is not long before Mr. Knightley is pointing out the dangers to Harriet and to Emma in this friendship. His fears are dismissed or at least deflected by Mrs. Weston, who (mistakenly, as it turns out) thinks well of the friendship and, in Knightley's words, "would rather talk of her person than her mind":

> "Very well; I shall not attempt to deny Emma's being pretty."
>
> "Pretty! say beautiful rather. Can you imagine any thing nearer perfect beauty than Emma altogether—face and figure?"
>
> "I do not know what I could imagine, but I confess that I have seldom seen a face or figure more pleasing to me than hers. But I am a partial old friend."
>
> "Such an eye!—the true hazel eye—and so brilliant! regular features, open countenance, with a complexion! oh! what a bloom of full health, and such a pretty height and size; such a firm and upright figure. There is health, not merely in her bloom, but in her air, her head, her glance. One hears sometimes of a child being 'the picture of health;' now Emma always gives me the idea of being the complete picture of grown-up health. She is loveliness itself. Mr. Knightley, is not she?"

(E, 39)

To which Knightley agrees, adding, "I love to look at her." Mrs. Weston's point seems to be that any account of Emma's faults, or any analysis of her merely as a moral agent, like Knightley's here, cannot do justice to her and even seems by the way. She is in good company in pointing to other than moral properties as sources of Emma's attraction. David Hume concluded his section on "the qualities immediately agreeable to others" in *An Inquiry Concerning the Principles of Morals* (1751) with the concession that there are attractions about which ethical analysis finds nothing to say:

> But besides all the *agreeable* qualities, the origin of whose beauty we can in some degree explain and account for, there still remains something mysterious and inexplicable, which conveys an immediate satisfaction to the spectator, but how, or why, or for what reason, he cannot pretend to determine. There is a *Manner*, a grace, an ease, a gentleness, an I-know-not-what, which some men possess above others, which is very different from external beauty and comeliness, and which, however, catches our affection almost as suddenly and powerfully... This class of accomplishments, therefore, must be trusted entirely to the blind, but sure testimony of taste and sentiment; and must be considered as a part of ethics, left by nature to baffle all the pride of philosophy, and make her sensible of her narrow boundaries and slender acquisitions.[31]

A reading of Emma as a moral agent, confronting or manipulating a world (or a person) external to herself, misses this "part of nature." Mrs. Weston does not mean that Emma instantiates some general quality "Health," but that the quality, "health," cannot be better known than by Emma's embodiment of it. As far as Mrs. Weston is concerned, she *is* health, and health is realised in her beauty. What—in the largest sense—health is, is to be known in the activity of the life that is Emma's, in what I have called her spirit: not a moral quality in itself, and certainly not guaranteeing laudable or ethically admirable conduct, but appealing to an understanding of another's life on a larger ground than that of the moral philosopher and ethicist whom Knightley here represents. Mrs. Weston is not, as Mr. Knightley, separating the two in Cartesian fashion, accuses her, talking merely of Emma's person rather than of her mind: when she goes on to say that Emma "has qualities that may be trusted," it is not just her love of Emma that speaks, but her recognition that something like what Samuel Johnson called "the exuberance of content" underwrites Emma's ultimate moral victory.

Towards the end of *Emma* there is a conversation that is designed to be compared with this one. Throughout the novel Frank Churchill has commented on Jane's pale looks to Emma, often in a snide and critical fashion, but when their engagement is public and Jane has recovered, he is free to enthuse. "Did you ever see such a skin?" he exclaims "—such smoothness! such delicacy!—and yet without being actually fair.—One cannot call her fair. It is a most uncommon complexion, with her dark eye-lashes and hair—a most distinguishing complexion!—So peculiarly the lady in it.—Just colour enough for beauty' (*E*, 478). Henry Crawford and Frank Churchill, though often aligned in a certain brand of Austen criticism, are to be distinguished: the one cool, calculating, and selfish, the other warm-hearted, impulsive, and selfish. But here Frank's drooling over his "prize" (Knightley's term, unfortunately) brings him close to Henry's appraising survey of Fanny. "She is a complete angel," he resumes:

"Look at her. Is not she an angel in every gesture? Observe the turn of her throat. Observe her eyes, as she is looking up at my father.—You will be glad to hear (inclining his head, and whispering seriously) that my uncle means to give her all my aunt's jewels. They are to be new set. I am resolved to have some in an ornament for the head. Will not it be beautiful in her dark hair?"

(*E*, 479)

"The head"! For the moment Frank seems to be thinking of Jane as an artefact to be decorated and enjoyed as a prestigious possession. Mrs. Weston, despite the term "picture," is not thinking of Emma as a specular object. "Bloom" is a suspicious term, as de Beauvoir pointed out,[32] but here Mrs. Weston does not connect it, as male observers do, as a rule, with the promise of sexual responsiveness. Instead, she connects Emma's attractiveness with a child's. Austen's novels usually dismiss children and their doting parents with some acerbity, but in *Emma* Mr. Perry's children, John Knightley's boys, and, to a lesser extent, Mrs. Weston's own pregnancy are all important signifiers of vitality and "normal" healthy growth, and here the idea is that the child evades or renders null and void moral categories, living the prehistory of a properly ethical life. Emma's complexion is not to be admired, either, because it is aesthetically "beautiful." Most importantly, "the blind but sure testimony" of Mrs. Weston's "sentiment" reproduces in her praise the very inflections of Emma herself, the repetition, the emphasis, ("complete," "loveliness itself")—reproduces that emphatic and spirited rhythm which is the textual manifestation of Emma's vital subjectivity.

Notes

1. On education in *Emma*: Mark Schorer, "The Humiliation of Emma Wood-house," *The Literary Review* 2, 4 (1959): 547–63, reprinted in Ian Watt, ed., *Jane Austen: A Collection of Critical Essays* (Englewood Cliffs, N.J.: Prentice Hall, 1963); R. E. Hughes, "The education of Emma Woodhouse," *Nineteenth Century Fiction* 16 (1962); W. J. Harvey, "The plot of *Emma*," *Essays in Criticism* 17 (1967): 48–63; Marilyn Butler, "*Emma*," in *Jane Austen and the War of Ideas* (Oxford: Oxford University Press, 1975), 250–74. On authoring: Claudia L. Johnson, "*Emma*; 'Woman, Lovely Woman, Reigns Alone,' " in *Jane Austen, Women, Politics and the Novel*" (Chicago: University of Chicago Press, 1988), 121–43, included in this casebook. On reading: Adena Rosmarin, " 'Misreading' *Emma*: The Powers and Perfidies of Interpretive History," *English Literary History* 51 (1984): 315–42; Nancy Armstrong, *Desire and Domestic Fiction: A Political History of the Novel* (New York: Oxford University Press, 1987), 134–60; John A. Dussinger, *In the Pride of the Moment; Encounters in Jane Austen's World* (Columbus: Ohio State University Press, 1990), *passim*, included in this casebook. On perception: G. Armour Craig, "Jane Austen's *Emma*: The Truths and Disguises of Human Disclosure," in *In Defense of Reading*, ed. R. Brower and R. Poirier (New York: Dutton, 1962). On epistemology: John P. McGowan, "Knowledge/Power and Jane Austen's radicalism," *Mosaic: A Journal for the Interdisciplinary Study of Literature* 18 (1985): 1–15. On imagination: Stuart Tave, *Some Words of Jane Austen* (Chicago: University of Chicago Press, 1973), 205–55; Michael Williams, "Emma, Mystery and Imagination," in *Jane Austen: Six Novels and Their Methods* (New York: St Martin's Press, 1986), 117–53.

2. J. R. Watson, "Mr. Perry's Patients: A View of *Emma*," *Essays in Criticism* 20 (1970): 334–43. See also Albert E. Wilhelm, "Three Word Clusters in *Emma*," *Studies in the Novel* 7 (1975): 49–60.

3. F. B. Smith, *The People's Health* (London: Croom Helm, 1977), 115: "The pregnant lady's dealings with her doctor began during the fourth or fifth month. In the first half of the century her closest doctor would be the local gentlemanly practitioner calling himself a 'pure' surgeon, or a surgeon apothecary like Mr. Perry of Highbury in *Emma*."

4. Mr. Weston, who has bided his time before purchasing Randalls, sees the social implications: "Perry's setting up his carriage! and his wife's persuading him to do it, out of care for his health—just what will happen, I have no doubt, some time or other; only a little premature" (*Emma*, 345).

5. Rosmarin, " 'Misreading' *Emma*," 330.

6. Watson, "Mr. Perry's Patients," 334.

7. Arthur Kleinman, *Rethinking Psychiatry: From Cultural Category to Personal Experience* (New York: Free Press, 1988), 64.

8. *The Diary and Letters of Madame D'Arblay*, edited by her niece, 7 vols. (London 1854), IV, 237 (November 6, 1788).

9. W. F. Bynum, "The nervous patient in eighteenth- and nineteenth-century Britain: The psychiatric origins of British neurology," in Bynum, Roy Porter and Michael Shepherd, eds., *The Anatomy of Madness: Essays in the History of Psychiatry*, 2 vols. (London: Tavistock Publications, 1985), I, *People and Ideas*, 89–102, 91.

10. Bynum, "Nervous Patient," p. 91.

11. George Cheyne, *The English Malady, or a Treatise of Nervous Diseases of All Kinds* (1733), fifth edition, 1735, 159.

12. Robert Whytt, *Physiological Essays, II; Observations on the sensibility and irritability of the parts of men and other animals, occasioned by Dr. Haller's late treatise on these subjects* (Edinburgh 1756). See R. K. French, *Robert Whytt: The Soul and Medicine* (London: Wellcome Institute of the History of Medicine, 1969), *passim*, and George S. Rousseau, "Nerves, spirits and fibres: Towards defining the origins of sensibility," *The Blue Guitar* 2 (1976): 125–53.

13. Thomas Trotter, MD, *A View of the Nervous Temperament* (London 1807), xvi. The passage is a quotation from Trotter's previous *Medicina Nautica*, vol. III.

14. Trotter, *Nervous Temperament*, 246, 232.

15. Trotter, *Nervous Temperament*, 249.

16. Trotter, *Nervous Temperament*, 79.

17. I owe this suggestion to an unpublished paper by Professor Gerda Seaman, "Better sick than sorry: Mrs. Mitty meets Lady Lazarus."

18. Bynum, "Nervous Patient," 90.

19. Alexander Pope, *The Works*, 6 vols (Edinburgh, 1764), II, "Moral Essay II, Epistle to a Lady," ll. 42–43.

20. Williams, *Six Novels and Their Methods*, 132–3. Williams points out that the "ogress" might be "merely the *ad hoc* creation of her nephew's imagination" (132).

21. Sandra M. Gilbert and Susan Gubar, *The Madwoman in the Attic* (New Haven: Yale University Press, 1979), 173.

22. Watson, "Mr. Perry's patients," 339.

23. James Thompson, *Between Self and World: The Novels of Jane Austen* (University Park: Pennsylvania State University Press, 1988), p. 168. The term "idiot" was used by Marvin Mudrick.

24. Avrom Fleishman, "Two Faces of Emma," in *Jane Austen: New Perspectives, Women and Literature*, (New Series) vol. 3, edited by Janet Todd (New York and London: Holmes and Meier, 1983), 248–56, 248. Fleishman intends this characterisation, of course, to be absurd.

25. I owe this suggestion, as well as much more in this discussion of *Emma*, to my colleague Dr. Kay Torney. John A. Dussinger, *In the Pride of the Moment*, 162–68, notes that Mr. Woodhouse fails to decipher the erotic riddle ("Kitty, a fair but

frozen maid"), and that this "appears to conceal a sexual problem of some kind": "The cost of denying the body is seen not only in his mental block towards anything erotic but more generally in a failure of desire. . . . The Weston's wedding cake was poison to Mr. Woodhouse for reasons other than its enzymes" (167).

26. Rudolph E. Siegel, *Galen's System of Physiology and Medicine* (Basel and New York: Karger, 1968), 184.

27. Maria Edgeworth, *Tales and Novels by Maria Edgeworth*, 18 vols, (London, 1832–33), II, Moral Tales I, "Forester," 35 [1816].

28. Virginia Woolf, "On Being Ill" [1930], *The Complete Essays of Virginia Woolf*, 4 vols. (1969), IV (London: Hogarth Press, 1967), 193–202.

29. Wayne C. Booth, *The Rhetoric of Fiction* (Chicago: University of Chicago Press, 1961), 257, included in this casebook, 112. Yasmine Gooneratne, *Jane Austen* (Cambridge: Cambridge University Press, 1970), 142–4.

30. Booth, *Rhetoric*, 258, included in this casebook, 113.

31. *The Philosophical Works of David Hume*, 4 vols. (Edinburgh, 1825), IV, 345. I take this quotation from S. L. Goldberg's article, "Agents and Lives: Making Moral Sense of People" (*The Critical Review* 25 [1983]: 26–49). My whole discussion of *Emma* (as well as some of my terms), is indebted to the argument of this article, but the claim that "even subtle moralists like Dr. Johnson and Jane Austen seem . . . distant from us in the clear, sharp (and ultimately comfortable) outlines of their moral categories and language" (36) is one I take issue with.

32. Simone de Beauvoir, *The Second Sex* (1949), translated and edited by H. M. Parshley, reprinted 1986 (Harmondsworth: Penguin Books, 1986), 190–92.

Men of Sense and Silly Wives

The Confusions of Mr. Knightley

MARY WALDRON

◆ ◆ ◆

T HE "OPINIONS OF MANSFIELD PARK" which Jane Austen collected and preserved gave her evidence that, though some readers were
aware of the dispersal of the focus of reader approval present in the novel—
they were doubtful about which characters they ought to "like," and were
honest about saying so—others tended to remodel the content to suit their
expectations, and missed the novel's subtleties and built-in uncertainties.
Lady Robert Kerr, for instance, commented on "the pure morality with
which it abounds" making it "a most desirable as well as useful work"; "Mr.
Egerton the Publisher praised it for it's Morality" (*Minor Works*, vol 6. of *The
Novels of Jane Austen*, ed. R. W. Chapman (Oxford: Oxford University Press,
1954), 433). Adverse criticism often centred on the shortcomings of a
character the commentator clearly thought intended to be virtuous by the
author; Fanny Knight objected to Edmund's attraction to Mary Crawford
and his failure to face up to Henry Crawford's iniquities (*MW*, 431); Mary
Cooke, a cousin, thought "Fanny ought to have been more determined on
overcoming her own feelings, when she saw Edmund's attachment to Miss
Crawford" (*MW*, 432–33), showing herself securely attached to the Fanny
Burney/Maria Edgeworth stereotype. Austen could be excused for feeling especially frustrated by the last comment, for a reading unbiassed by

expectations of moral "usefulness" clearly reveals that the plot dynamics absolutely require Fanny to fail in this way. Austen was aware that her theory of what a novel should do ran counter for the most part to public expectation, which still believed it should have an unequivocal moral message or fail in its aim. It may have been misunderstandings about Fanny Price and Edmund that drove Austen in her next novel to invent a heroine whom no one could mistake for an attempt at a conduct-book model— "whom nobody but myself will much like."[1] She had plenty of precedent for the deluded heroine (of whom Emma is a version) by early 1814. Charlotte Lennox's *The Female Quixote* was still popular with the family; in 1800 Elizabeth Hamilton, noted by Austen as a "respectable" writer, had given the world Brigetina Botherim, a burlesque counterblast to Emma Courtney, who imagines herself the heroine of a sentimental romance and relentlessly pursues the embarrassed object of her affections (*Memoirs of Modern Philosophers*);[2] Maria Edgeworth's *Angelina, or, l'Amie Inconnue* (1801) has as its central character a girl who is deceived into sentimental friendship with a drunken trickster; Eaton Stannard Barrett's *The Heroine, or Adventures of a Fair Romance Reader*, published in 1813, was being read by Austen while her brother Henry perused the completed manuscript of *Mansfield Park*; in 1814, Mary Brunton, mentioned earlier by Austen in no very flattering terms, published *Discipline*, a novel about a rich and spoilt heiress who gets her comeuppance at the hands of an older mentor/lover.[3] Moreover, Austen had included the theme already in *Northanger Abbey, Pride and Prejudice* and *Sense and Sensibility*, though not as the major ingredient. In *Emma* she takes the familiar stereotype of deluded girl versus mentor/lover, mixes it, among others, with the theme of the dependent girl (Jane Fairfax and Harriet Smith) and the model female (Jane again) and weaves a fiction of amazing intricacy in which none of the stock characters behaves exactly as might be expected and in which the reader's sympathies are never thrust into a moral conduit.

The combination of wealth and beauty in a heroine is a frequently occurring trope in eighteenth-century fiction; she is thereby rendered vulnerable to material indulgence and personal vanity, as well as to predatory suitors. Austen carefully excludes these evils from the life of Emma. She is "handsome," but we have it on the best authority that she is not vain (Mr. Knightley; *Emma*, 39); she is rich, but not addicted to dangerous entertainments such as masquerades (like, for instance, Ellen Percy in Brunton's *Discipline*), for her few visits to Brunswick Square have not provided opportunities for metropolitan dissipation on these lines; and as an unwelcome suitor, Mr. Elton is no more than a ludicrous embarrassment. Unlike Mr. Percy, Mr. Woodhouse is not intent on selling his daughter to the highest bidder—on the contrary, the very thought of marriage is anathema to him. Put like this, it is hard to see how Emma can have any adventures which would fit into a contemporary novel.

Other characters in the story are also subverted versions of stock figures. Both Mrs. Weston and Mrs. Elton have the familiar outlines of the more mature companion who can be a protective guardian or a threat of some kind. But Mrs. Weston significantly exerts no power over Emma and does not attempt to do so; Mrs. Elton fails in her attempt. Emma shows her awareness of the stereotype when she contemptuously brushes off Mrs. Elton's offer of an introduction in Bath, imaging for herself "some vulgar, dashing widow" (*E*, 275) such as abounded in popular fiction. Perhaps she even had Edgeworth's Harriet Freke in mind. Jane Fairfax is recognisable as the model fictional girl, but turns out to have a discreditable secret, which no traditionally docile young lady was allowed; and Harriet is herself a discreditable secret, though in no way responsible for her position.

But the most confusing element in *Emma* is the character of Mr. Knightley. He at first looks very much like Mr. Maitland (Ellen Percy's mentor/lover in *Discipline*) and Robert Stuart, who plays a similar role in *The Heroine*, saving Cherry/Cherubina from her romantic-novel delusions, in which she imagines herself to be a noble foundling. Mr. Knightley is as ready as they are to hand out home truths to his "pupil"; contemporary readers could be excused for assuming him to be another pattern gentleman. Even now, there is a tendency to see him as a development of Grandison. "Austen's model for wisdom," says one recent critic, echoing a long line of commentators who have seen Knightley as carrying the moral authority of the novel.[4] Though one or two critics have found fault with him, it still seems difficult for most to relinquish the idea that Austen was advocating ideal modes of behaviour of one kind or another.[5] Some feminists perceive irony in the presentation of Mr. Knightley; Margaret Kirkham in particular sees a fairly equal distribution of praise and blame between Emma herself and Mr. Knightley. My analysis closely follows hers—with the difference that I believe that Austen would have repudiated the label of "Enlightenment feminist" if she had ever heard it.[6] Her main purpose seems to me to have been literary—to produce a critique of fictional figures who control the action of the story because the narrative assumes them to be endowed with special *vertù*; such figures are as often women as men. I think, for example, of the contrast between Lady Catherine de Bourgh, who signally fails in her attempts to control anyone but Mr. and Mrs. Collins, and both Lady Montreville in Mary Brunton's *Self-control* (1810) and Lady Delvile in Frances Burney's *Cecilia* (1782) who, in spite of their unreasonable and intransigent demands, are treated with deference and respect, by the heroines as well as by a prevailing authorial presence. Jane Austen seems consciously to reject any assumption of status as value. But so far I must agree with Kirkham—if Mr. Knightley is indeed the author's model for wisdom she must have departed from her usual practice, for nowhere in the major works do we find a male character who is beyond reproach. "Pictures of perfection" made her "sick & wicked"—and not only female ones. An examination of some of the less frequented byways of the text will reveal that, far from being somehow above it all, Mr. Knightley is involved in the same kind of social/moral confusion as Emma and all the other characters and that it is with a general fictional chaos, designed to entertain rather by confusion than by satisfying certainties, that the novel is chiefly concerned.

Austen's comments on her reading during the putative gestation of *Emma* are enlightening. Burlesque novels come in for much less criticism than serious ones. One favourite novel of this kind, *The Female Quixote*, has already been mentioned in connection with *Northanger Abbey*; it has little obvious influence on *Emma*, for Emma by no means shares the naiveté or isolation of Arabella. But a certain foreshadowing of *Emma* may be detected in Eaton Stannard Barrett's *The Heroine* ("It diverted me exceedingly," says Austen in a letter to Cassandra, "a delightful burlesque").[7] Based on a similar premiss to that of Lennox's novel, that too much reading might make a girl mad, it brings the debate on young women up to date, as well as offering some trenchant criticism of well-known novels. Like Arabella, Cherry is helped back to sanity by a clergyman; but her real saviour is Robert Stuart, who analyses her faults but loves her in spite of them. "Had I not seen your failings," he says, "I should never have discovered your perfections."[8] No reader of *Emma* can fail to see the parallel with Mr. Knightley here. Several other situations also have echoes in Austen's novel—for instance, Cherry's incredible career of delusion, in which, among other things, she blows up a ruined church with gunpowder and disguises herself as a soldier, begins when she loses her governess, who is dismissed for kissing the butler. Hilarious and disrespectful comment on popular fiction would also have appealed to Austen; Cherry is presented with the phantoms of heroes and heroines and finds to her chagrin that, for instance, in the cloud-cuckoo-land of fiction, Evelina and Lord Orville lead a cat-and-dog domestic life, and that Pamela has left Mr. B. and run off with Rasselas. However, it is quite certain that Austen would have had some fault to find in the authoritative pronouncements of Robert at the end of the novel about fiction in general. He draws the inevitable distinction between instructive and useful "fictitious biography ... such as The Vicar of Wakefield ... and Cœlebs, which draw man as he is, instead of man as he cannot be, superhuman" (an odd conclusion when we remember the manly resistance to error of all kinds of More's hero, Charles) and "Romances [which] ... teach [the mind] erroneous notions of the world, by relating adventures too improbable to happen, and depicting characters too perfect to exist." To Austen's mind this was a false distinction—"pictures of perfection" constituted the major flaw in all fiction. *Emma* very clearly grows out of this central disagreement with Barrett. Other reading may also have had its effect; in 1805 Austen read Thomas Gisborne's popular work on female education; she finds it more sensible, perhaps, than earlier works by Dr. Gregory and Dr. Fordyce, but there is enough subversion of his ideal young woman in the person of Jane Fairfax to suggest that her approval was strictly limited.[9]

The location of the novel is carefully designed to maximise the confusions and mislead readers on the watch for reliable moral lessons. Austen is at some pains to show that the world of Highbury is extremely fluid. Upwardly mobile *nouveaux riches*, such as the Coles and Mr. Weston, rub shoulders with the impoverished gentry like the Bateses and the main local landowner, Mr. Knightley. They attract no accusations of venality and vulgarity—nearly everybody likes them and values their contribution to the social life of the place. Frank Churchill is being brought up in a rather mysterious, wealthier milieu than his father's; Jane Fairfax has gained entry into good society despite her poverty, through her patronage by a moderately wealthy ex-Army officer. Generally, the niceties of rank seem to be ignored. One of Emma's delusions is that she can preserve distinctions of rank when nearly everyone around her is determined to dismiss them. Circumstances continually sideline her and erode her importance; she needs to feel important—hence her eager patronage of Harriet Smith. But at every turn Austen presents Emma's errors as mild and understandable given the confusing environment in which she has to find an identity. Her little snobberies are essentially harmless, for they have no effect.

It is also the shifting nature of Highbury society which makes it such a hotbed of gossip—chiefly gossip about marriage. The ideal of the companionate marriage was well established by the time the novel was written; arranged and dynastic marriages were rare, especially among the 'middling sort'; people were expected to make "sensible" marriages, but there was plenty of room for manoeuvre, and also for social mobility in both directions. No wonder that in Highbury, whatever else may be going on, it is marriage, actual, projected or speculated about that is on everybody's mind. This includes Mr. Knightley, who shows by his interest in Robert Martin as well as by his jealousy of Frank Churchill's apparent attraction for Emma that he is not exempt from this all-pervading preoccupation. Others are more obsessively involved; Mrs. Cole, appropriately very interested in the social cross-currents of the place in which she has such an ambiguous position, is the originator of most of the speculations—she is the leader of a kind of Greek chorus of gossipy, sociable women, which includes Miss Bates, Mrs. Perry and all the teachers at Mrs. Goddard's school, not to mention Mrs. Goddard herself, who comment, question and presumably manoeuvre, in this fascinating game of "pairs." It is not often observed that Mrs. Goddard is an important motivating force in *Emma*.[10] Like that other silent but major character, Robert Martin, she never speaks, but it is she, not primarily Emma, who introduces Harriet Smith at Hartfield, and so sets the plot in motion. We are never told why she does this—why she picks on Harriet; there are other "parlour boarders" at her school whom she could presumably have brought along to one of Mr. Woodhouse's card-parties. But she chooses Harriet, and it is this which gives Emma the signal that Harriet is somehow special, fit in some way to be singled out from other pupils. She already knows that Harriet is "the natural daughter of somebody" (*E*, 22), but she—as well as the attentive reader—suspects that Mrs. Goddard knows more, especially as she seems to think Hartfield a suitable background for her. Emma therefore has good grounds for thinking it probable that Harriet may be of gentle, though illegitimate, birth. Recognition that this, though romantic, is not an altogether fanciful speculation exonerates Emma from some of the frivolousness ascribed to her by Mr. Knightley (and ultimately by Emma herself) and those readers who see him as the fount of all wisdom in the novel. It also gives Harriet a special position in the marriage stakes in Highbury, for while most people's origins and situations are known, and their possibilities therefore apparently to some extent circumscribed, Harriet's are a mystery. Emma has some reason for thinking that in her case anything might happen. Of course she has other motives (chiefly her need to feel definitely superior to someone) which are made the subject of ironic authorial comment, and she turns out to be wrong, but the basis of her patronage of Harriet is not the foolish and irresponsible whim described by Knightley and often accepted by critics. It grows out of a pervading game of chance being played by the inhabitants of Highbury—it is almost as if Harriet is a sort of wild card held by Mrs. Goddard. Harriet is the extreme example of the doubt about everybody's true social position, the collapsing nature of old ideas about rank, which leads the central characters to fall back, almost unawares, either on unlikely romantic literary stereotypes, or on the re-actionary certainties of the conduct books. And it is not only Emma who does so.

By the time of Harriet's entry into the novel, the reader's initial relationship with Mr. Knightley has been established. He is introduced in the first chapter as a "sensible man" (*E*, 9); his brisk tone in dealing with Mr. Woodhouse's neurotic anxieties and Emma's self-congratulation about having "made the match" (*E*, 11) between Miss Taylor and Mr. Weston evinces a sane and rational prudence; his whole persona breathes confidence and common sense. From the start, we feel *safe* with Mr. Knightley. Unless we are very vigilant indeed in our reading, we agree with him that Emma is rather a silly girl, interfering in what does not concern her. We feel sure that Mr. Knightley will not be engaging in any romantic games of chance. He is apparently a typical hero/guardian on the Grandison model. But Austen enjoys exploiting the reflexes of her readers, and means to disillusion us.

His conversation with Mrs. Weston in chapter 5 should begin this process, for here Knightley is shown to be in some confusion about his relationship with Emma. His ambiguous position as Emma's elder brother and substitute father has been variously noted by critics; Glenda Hudson emphasises the fraternal element: "[H]is concern is brotherly, but there are also clues along the way of his passionate feelings for her."[11] Juliet McMaster has also noted the heightening of emotional tension in the pupil-teacher relation in Austen's novels.[12] Hudson, I believe, misjudges these "clues"; "[H]is desire for her," she says, "is in no way repressed." The language of chapter 5 seems to me to be telling us something different, for he does seem to be trying to convince himself that it is her *education* that he is anxious about. The trajectory of Knightley's detached judiciousness, launched in chapter 1, may carry us over the top of this dialogue without proper attention to the actual words. Knightley is clearly at this time influenced by a contemporary theoretical model of the ideal young woman. This model had changed considerably since the middle of the previous century. A girl was not by this time expected to be ignorant; Hannah More, for instance, is insistent that a young woman should be well informed and should not, as Gregory had advised in *A Father's Legacy to His Daughters* in 1774, conceal any knowledge she might have in the interests of flattering a man.[13] Part of the reason for Austen's qualified approval of Thomas Gisborne's *Enquiry* may have been his rejection of imbecility as the best property in the marriage market.[14] But—and here Austen may have perceived a contradiction which militated against "Nature and Probability"—a girl was not encouraged, even by Gisborne and More, to push herself, to use her knowledge to attempt to exercise power. She must be able to join in conversation when required, but to leave leadership to the men. Emma has offended against this ideal in several ways, and Knightley is deeply dissatisfied with her. As her brother/father/teacher he feels she ought to be a greater credit to him, and his disappointment, combined as it is with latent sexual attraction, expresses itself in anger—a polite and civilised anger, which strives for balance and liberality, but anger nevertheless. To begin with he asserts that she is too intelligent for her own good—"At ten years old, she had the misfortune of being able to answer questions which puzzled her sister at seventeen." Instead of using this intelligence to become bookish and contemplative and fulfil the Hannah More ideal—"I have done with expecting any course of steady reading from Emma" (*E*, 37)— she has used her talents to control her social environment and for bossing everybody about; she has committed the cardinal sin of making up her own mind instead of listening to those who might be supposed to know better. He is appalled at the influence she is trying to exert on Harriet because he believes her ideas to be superficial, ill-conceived and snobbish—"I am much mistaken if Emma's doctrines give any strength of mind, or tend at all to make a girl adapt herself rationally to the varieties of her situation in life.— They only give a little polish" (*E*, 39). Mrs. Weston tries several times to divert his mind into other channels, and for a moment he appears unprejudiced in his appreciation of Emma's looks and her lack of personal vanity, but soon he is back on the attack, although it is disguised as concern—"I wonder what will become of her" (*E*, 40). The conversation ends with both Mr. Knightley and Mrs. Weston speculating about a marriage for Emma: Mrs. Weston is concealing "wishes at Randalls respecting Emma's destiny" (*E*, 41) as the wife of Frank Churchill and says nothing; Mr. Knightley actually announces his belief that marriage is the only thing that will *subdue* her—"I should like to see Emma in love, and in some doubt of a return; it would do her good" (*E*, 41). This does not seem like the wish of a kindly benevolent mentor—it can be interpreted at one level as rather savage. It is open to the reader to doubt whether he here really knows his own mind. He protests that he has had "no . . . charm thrown over [his] senses" (*E*, 37), but his very protestation suggests that he has, and that it has set up an uncomfortable conflict in his mind. He ends the conversation abruptly by talking of the weather—a sure sign of disquiet.

It is their peculiar configuration of relationships that makes it impossible, for much of the novel, for Emma and Mr. Knightley to be anything to each other than sparring-partners. They agree about very little, but obviously find their conflicts rather stimulating than otherwise. This is indicated by Emma's revision of her estimate of Frank Churchill when talking to Mrs. Weston (*E*, 122) and afterwards to Mr. Knightley. "He ought to come . . . I shall not be satisfied, unless he comes," she says to the former, brushing aside all talk of extenuating circumstances; for Mr. Knightley she produces exactly those circumstances, purely, it would seem, for the sake of disagreeing with him (*E*, 145). At times, almost inadvertently, they achieve a kind of instinctual harmony of purpose which hints at latent kindredship of spirit—as for instance during the incipient quarrel between John Knightley and Mr. Woodhouse during the family visit to Hartfield, when they both make strenuous and concerted efforts to change the subject of conversation to something other than food and medical men (*E*, 103–6), and at the snowy Christmas Eve party at Randalls when both combine to extricate Mr. Woodhouse from a situation which John Knightley and Mr. Weston are insensitively prolonging (*E*, 128); but generally they find it most natural to fall out and refuse to compromise.

The major conflict in volume I concerns Robert Martin's proposal to Harriet Smith. Harriet, the unattached young girl whose family background is quite unknown, has been detailed by Emma to provide the romantic adventure her prudent and dutiful side tells her is impossible for herself. Harriet is to be the hidden heiress—possibly of noble blood, although ordinary gentility will do—whose origins will be revealed when she makes a suitable marriage. Emma has to make do with rather ordinary materials here (Mr. Elton would be an odd choice as a hero of romance, but so much the better adapted to Austen's purpose), but this only makes her feel that her ambitions for Harriet are not too wide of the mark—unlike Cherry/Cherubina she indulges in no very extreme imaginings. Unfortunately—or fortunately for the novel's agreeable complexity—we, the readers, have to concur with Knightley that Emma's use of Harriet for what amounts to social engineering is at best unwise. Harriet's position may be open to speculation, but she should not be manipulated. The language of the dialogue constantly directs us to the vast gulf between Harriet's thinking and Emma's and the indoctrination which takes place. Almost every idea that Harriet has by the end of chapter 4, when Emma first learns about Robert Martin, has been placed there by Emma—and we cannot approve of *that*. Consequently, when in chapter 8 Mr. Knightley confronts Emma with Martin's expected proposal—which we know has already been refused—we cannot but feel in double harness with him, for we too feel wiser than Emma and are, moreover, in the secret of her delusions about Mr. Elton. We are inclined to agree with him that Emma is being "no friend to Harriet Smith" (*E*, 63).

The dialogue which now ensues is a brilliant example of Austen's delight and skill in sporting with the reader's allegiances. Though we know, at one level, that Emma is all wrong, the scene exposes not her irrationality, but Knightley's. Emma is cool, Knightley emotional; Emma consistent, while Knightley shifts his ground several times. Because of this, their opposition is anything but straightforward; both parties to the argument are less concerned with Harriet Smith and Robert Martin than with their attachment to certain contemporary ideas about marriage and status; moreover, they obviously relish the argument for its own sake.

From the outset, Mr. Knightley makes a very sweeping assumption:

> "I have reason to think . . . that Harriet Smith will soon have an offer of marriage . . . Robert Martin is the man. . . . He is desperately in love and means to marry her."
>
> (*E*, 59)

Emma immediately scents an old-fashioned, arranged-marriage stereotype in which the girl meekly accepts the advice of her elders. The fact that she at least suspects that Harriet would be quite happy to concur makes no difference to her response: "He is very obliging . . . but is he sure that Harriet means to marry him?" (*E*, 59)—theoretically and rationally a perfectly justifiable one. But Knightley makes it clear that he regards this as merely a fashionable, feminine ritual gesture—something which an up-to-date female has to *say*, but can't really mean seriously. "Well, well," he concedes indulgently, "means to make her an offer then. Will that do?"—Without waiting for a reply, he embarks on a complacent panegyric of Martin:

> I never hear better sense from any one than Robert Martin. He always speaks to the purpose; open, straight forward, and very well judg-ing. . . . He is an excellent young man, both as son and brother. I had no hesitation in advising him to marry. He proved to me that he could afford it; and that being the case, I was convinced he could not do better. I praised the fair lady too, and altogether sent him away very happy. If he had never esteemed my opinion before, he would have thought highly of me then; and, I dare say, left the house thinking me the best friend and counsellor man ever had.
>
> (*E*, 59–60)

This is so much occupied with the excellences of Robert Martin and his own good offices that it looks, at one level, like a male conspiracy to trap

Harriet before she has time to protest. But the fact that we know that she would probably like to be so trapped obscures the smug certainties of Mr. Knightley's discourse and his complete failure to take her wishes into account; his one reference to her—"the fair lady"—only serves further to diminish her. But smugness can look like judiciousness under certain circumstances, and we cannot get away from the fact that, though he may be wrong in theory, Emma is wrong in fact. They are both so caught up in their own prejudices and preconceived ideas that neither can think clearly, and the immediate real interests of Harriet Smith are submerged. Their argument is partly based on theory and partly on their ongoing personal conflict. Each seems deliberately to produce arguments designed to incense the other.

Emma is by far the more sure of herself. She stands by her theory that Harriet is of gentle birth, and therefore superior to the yeoman, Martin. Knightley's reaction shows him to be a mass of ill-thought-out notions which he is quite prepared to reverse in the interests of getting his own way. He greets the news of Harriet's refusal with stronger and less polite anger than in conversation with Mrs. Weston; he becomes "red with surprize and displeasure . . . in tall indignation" (*E*, 60) and straight away presents a total reconstruction of his previous account of the meeting with Martin.

> "What are Harriet Smith's claims, either of birth, nature or education, to any connection higher than Robert Martin? . . . She is pretty, and she is good tempered, and that is all. My only scruple in advising the match was on his account, as being beneath his deserts, and a bad connexion for him. I felt, that as to fortune, in all probability he might do much better; and that as to a rational companion or useful helpmate, he could not do worse. But I could not reason so to a man in love."
>
> (*E*, 61)

In his previous account, Martin has been "very well judging," now his love has overcome his reason; before, "he could not do better," now "he could not do worse"; and the "fair lady" is little better than a base-born idiot. Is this the sober and rational thinker we have at one level been led to expect?

Emma, on the other hand, has some very rational arguments. "A man always imagines a woman to be ready for anybody who asks her" (*E*, 60). Mr. Knightley brushes this aside, apparently unconscious of the fact that he has done exactly that: "Nonsense! a man does not imagine any such thing." Of her illegitimacy she maintains that "She is not to pay for the offence of others" (*E*, 62)—a just and compassionate view; and she quite cogently points out that no girl of seventeen should automatically be expected to accept a first offer. But the argument which most incenses Mr. Knightley and drives him into further incoherence is her stated view of the general tastes of men in their choice of wives:

> "[S]upposing her to be, as you describe her, only pretty and good-natured, let me tell you, that in the degree she possesses them, they are not trivial recommendations to the world in general, for she is, in fact, a beautiful girl . . . and till it appears that men are much more philosophic on the subject of beauty than they are generally supposed; till they do fall in love with well-informed minds instead of handsome faces, a girl, with such loveliness as Harriet, has a certainty of being admired and sought after . . . Her good-nature, too, is not so very slight a claim, comprehending, as it does, real, thorough sweetness of temper and manner, a very humble opinion of herself, and a great readiness to be pleased with other people. I am very much mistaken if your sex in general would not think such beauty, and such temper, the highest claims a woman could possess."
>
> (*E*, 63–64)

Here Emma is voicing the dictates of some of the conduct books about the qualities which are likely to attract a husband. Mr. Knightley can hardly deny that she has some authority for her assertion. However, he again brushes aside her argument, accusing her of abusing reason, and goes on to abuse it himself, becoming further enmeshed in confusions and contradictions:

> "Nothing so easy as for a young lady to raise her expectations too high . . . Men of sense, whatever you may chuse to say, do not want silly wives. Men of family would not be very fond of connecting themselves with a girl of such obscurity—and most prudent men would be afraid of the inconvenience and disgrace they might be involved in, when the mystery of her parentage came to be revealed."
>
> (*E*, 64)

This is rather hard on Robert Martin, whose prudence has not so far been questioned, and who has actually been described as a man of sense. Can he be so in fact if he wants a wife as silly as Harriet? And if, as Knightley says next, "[H]is mind has more true gentility than Harriet Smith could understand," (*E*, 65) would not he, too, be troubled by this supposed "inconvenience and disgrace" of her birth and parentage? Has Knightley thought this through? It seems more likely that we are to suppose that he strongly needs to feel that the plan which has had his enthusiastic support will succeed, and consequently strikes out rather wildly to counter arguments against it. It is really too trivial an incident for such expense of energy and emotion in the Squire of Highbury. He can't be that concerned with the affairs of such as Harriet Smith and Robert Martin—except as they touch his relations with Emma.

For the reader of this novel, though, who is conscious of its elaborate layering, there is another factor which must have influenced Emma, and cannot but have been observed by George Knightley, though he is clearly ignoring it in his dialogue with Emma—and that is his brother John's choice of a wife. J. F. Burrows dismisses the character of Isabella as having "little part to play," and in fact very little critical notice has been taken of her.[15] But Austen never introduces redundant characters. Throughout the novel we are reminded of Isabella's "striking inferiorities" (*E*, 433), her narrow interests and limited perceptions. The silly wife is a significant trope in Austen's fiction (from Mrs. Allen to Lady Bertram there is a long string of them) and excessive mother-love sometimes a significant component of it—in this Lady Middleton and Isabella Knightley are sisters, and equally ridiculous. The difference is that Isabella is treated with less broad irony than Lady Middleton, and there is no underlying contempt for her maternal solicitude emanating from any of the characters, as there is from Elinor in the case of Lady Middleton. Nevertheless, she is clearly far from bright, and it is open to the reader to wonder why John Knightley had married her. He is obviously often irritated by her; for instance, during the Christmas visit to Hartfield her collusion in hypochondria with her father drives him into open rudeness (*E*, 106). Was he attracted by the presumed thirty thousand pounds? Or does he simply prefer a silly wife, though he is, we have to believe, a "man of sense"? Towards the end of the novel we begin to suspect the latter, for his approval of his brother's engagement to Emma is very qualified. We are never given the exact grounds for his reservations, but the reactions of Mr. Knightley and Emma say it all: "...[H]e is no complimenter," says his brother on showing John's letter, and after reading it Emma is clear that "it is very plain that he considers the good fortune of the engagement as all on my side" (*E*, 464). There can be no other explanation than that he believes that women should be ruled by men and that his brother will have difficulty in governing Emma. If her brother-in-law is in any way typical, then Emma may be exaggerating when she says, "Harriet is exactly what every man delights in," but the evidence that it is true of some men cannot be denied by Mr. Knightley. He must be conscious that Isabella would never have been *his* choice. But instead of confronting the question he evades it and begins to talk about money. His next attack is on what he suspects are Emma's plans for Mr. Elton. Elton "does not mean to throw himself away" (*E*, 66). Now a "rational" primary motive (presumably that to be expected in "men of sense") in the quest for a wife would be fortune rather than education. Is Harriet too silly or too poor to satisfy a man of sense? Knightley has shown in this quarrel that he doesn't know what he thinks; Emma has shown him that the issues may be more complex than he has assumed, but he is adamant about giving any ground or engaging in a really open debate, and what amounts to bluster has not convinced her. The sort of wise counsel expected of the fictional mentor, which might have deflected Emma from her resolve and at least protected her from Elton's upstart designs, is missing. Knightley goes off in a huff, having been caught playing the Highbury game of chance—and unsuccessfully at that. But there is yet another layer of significance in this episode. Underlying it all is Emma's exposure of a raw nerve in her suggestion that Harriet might actually suit *him* (*E*, 64); he studiously ignores this, for he does not want to examine his own wishes in this regard. A "charm" has been "thrown over his senses" which he cannot think is rationally based—for Emma does not at this time measure up to the ideal wife for a "man of sense" any more than Harriet. In high indignation with Emma and himself he turns temporarily, and perhaps more in bravado than reality, to a woman who does. He is already far removed from the certainties of a Grandison, and he is far more muddled than Maitland or Stuart could ever be.

Jane Fairfax is another example of the orphan dependant, this time shifted from the surface narrative into an undetailed and what seems at first a mysterious background. Harriet may be Emma's idea of the perfect wife for a discerning man, but Jane Fairfax comes much closer to Knightley's. Jane superficially corrects much that Knightley thinks is wrong in Emma. She is apparently the perfect conduct-book young woman—well-informed, but discreet; a responder rather than an initiator, scintillatingly accomplished, but at the same time modest and quiet. Emma sees all this, and quite genuinely admires it, but cannot like Jane, because she cannot communicate with her. The reader should note that Emma very readily accepts Mr. Knightley's view that she dislikes Jane because "she saw in her the really accomplished young woman, which she wanted to be thought herself" (*E*, 166), but also that it is difficult to like somebody who will not share experience and backs away from intimacy. Mr. Knightley's analysis is unfair and ill-informed. Emma is sometimes too willing to accept guilt (her internal discourse should never be taken for the authorial voice). But she cannot escape from her natural reactions, and because she cannot understand Jane's reticence, concludes, and quite correctly, that she is hiding something. Mr. Knightley takes a little longer to come to the same conclusion; at first, on her return to Highbury, he gives the gossips good reason to suppose that his interest in Jane constitutes a preliminary to courtship. In volume II there are several instances of concern beyond the call of mere duty on the part of Knightley—he worries publicly about Jane's health, sends her gifts of apples, and so on. It is really small wonder that this is all interpreted by the likes of Mrs. Cole as courtship, and that it gives rise to suspicion even in the sensible and unimaginative Mrs. Weston (*E*, 225). These episodes are usually seen as factors in Emma's misunderstanding of Knightley and to point up her dawning personal and sexual interest in him; it is as if most commentators on the novel feel that Mr. Knightley is too solid a character to be suspected of ordinary moves in the courtship game, or of ordinary human muddle-headedness. This is to miss the ironical complexity of the interplay of character at this stage of the novel. Knightley is still recommending Jane as a person whom Emma ought to befriend, but he is, at the same time, aware of what militates against this, and against his own real involvement with Jane. His clearly embarrassed denial of the charge which Emma finally brings herself to make several weeks later (*E*, 287) represents a crisis in the relationship between himself and Emma, for he also tells her why he could never seriously consider Jane as a wife (although we may believe him to be being less than honest about this). Implicitly accepting as justified Emma's own earlier criticism of Jane as too reserved for friendship (*E*, 171), he says:

> "Jane Fairfax is a very charming young woman—but not even Jane Fairfax is perfect. She has a fault. She has not the open temper which a man would wish for in a wife."
>
> (*E*, 288)

And again:

> "Jane Fairfax has feeling . . . Her sensibilities, I suspect, are strong—and her temper excellent . . . but it wants openness. She is reserved, more reserved, I think, than she used to be—And I love an open temper."
>
> (*E*, 289)

Here Mr. Knightley has done something quite uncharacteristic of the fictional hero/guardian—he has changed his mind. There is a coded message here to Emma that not only has he decided that she has been right in her estimate of Jane—with which he has earlier strongly disagreed—but that he has relinquished his conduct-book womanly ideal and prefers Emma's "open temper"; he is saying, in effect, that a stormy relationship with someone he can trust is better than a calm one with someone whose thoughts may be hidden from him. He is inviting Emma to go on saying exactly what she thinks and at least hinting that he will no longer invoke his own superiority to oppose her. However, she fails to notice this, for she is unable at this stage to regard Mr. Knightley in the light of a possible suitor; she is too caught up in her own stereotype of what a suitor should be. Moreover, she is not being entirely "open."

Mr. Knightley much later confesses that it is jealousy of Frank Churchill that enlightens him about his own feelings for Emma. It is clear that the whole of Highbury considers Frank the obvious husband for her. His character is based upon the Lord Chesterfield idea of the "gentleman"— one for whom manner and general agreeableness are of first importance. Knightley despises him from the start, but is sufficiently caught up in the stereotype to believe that he will be irresistibly attractive to Emma. Emma's ideas about love are literary rather than the result of observation. She is impressed with Frank's manner; he measures up to all she has heard and read about handsome and eligible young men, and she tries, with little success, to fall in love with him. In spite of her internal monologue about her feelings, the reader is aware that her "love" is more a matter of determination than tender emotion and means very little. She doesn't even like him very much, and quite soon she has to admit this to herself—"I do not look upon him to be quite the sort of man . . . His feelings are warm, but I can imagine them rather changeable" (*E*, 265). From the time of Frank Churchill's return, then, we have both protagonists relinquishing their apparently ideal mate; the difference between them is that Knightley had been able, at least indirectly, to say this to Emma, while she has not been able to enlighten *him*. He goes even further at the ball at the Crown, generously bowing to her superior judgement in the matter of Harriet, throwing aside his habitual dislike of dancing to remain in her company, and at last denying that he could ever think of her as his sister (*E*, 331). Emma completely fails to recognise these signs, and it never occurs to her to disabuse anyone about her feelings for Frank. As far as anyone knows she and Frank are still destined for each other. And nobody can ask her. Questioning an unengaged girl about the state of her affections was not permitted to any but her parents or guardians. Nor would it have been proper for Emma independently to deny emotional involvement with a man who had not yet made her an offer. The result is that Knightley, along with everyone else in Highbury, remains convinced that the pair will ultimately marry. Both are quite happy to let this continue—Emma because it makes her feel more interesting, Frank from other, even less pardonable motives. So complete is her internal rejection of Frank that in the next chapter but one she hands him over to Harriet (*E*, 341)—but only in her imagination. Knightley knows nothing of this.

This misunderstanding renders Knightley both vulnerable and powerless. He is like Fanny Price in that he has to stand silently by while he watches (as he thinks) the girl he now loves give herself up to a shallow and insensitive man, in whom he shortly discovers evidence of even worse qualities. His attempts to warn her of Frank's relationship with Jane fail, for, as the reader knows, they talk at cross-purposes—"I will answer for the gentleman's indifference," says Emma incautiously, unconsciously confirming Knightley's worst fears (*E*, 350–51). It is a mistake to conclude that Knightley here reaches the truth about Jane and Frank. The text makes clear that he is alarmed but mystified. He is quite oblivious to Emma's regrettable fantasy about Jane and Mr. Dixon. Still convinced that Frank will marry Emma (after all, she has the money, and Frank must be regarded as a "sensible" man) he believes that Frank is somehow manipulating both girls, and that Emma's chances of a happy and stable marriage are doomed. He speaks out of a sense of real concern at what he sees as her danger and is saddened to find that Emma remains in her usual relation to him; she flouts his warning as ridiculous, hinting at confidentiality between herself and Frank. Knightley naturally feels defeated: "She spoke with a confidence which staggered, with a satisfaction which silenced, Mr. Knightley" (*E*, 351). Their behaviour to each other, though their relationship is subtly changing, takes its usual form of attack and repulse. But this time the situation, at least for Knightley, is far more serious than their feud about Harriet Smith. His conviction that Emma will become the victim of such hollow flattery as Frank hands out is almost as perverse as Emma's current chimera—that Frank will marry Harriet; but perverse or not, he believes that he can no longer be involved in Emma's destiny and decides to bow out. He is not pleased to see Frank Churchill at the alfresco gathering at Donwell but keeps his distance from Emma, showing that he has at that time no thoughts of renewing the battle. This episode, like the ensuing scene at Box Hill, is a *tour de force* in the manipulation of point of view, for Emma is preoccupied with other things, and is only later to understand the significance of Frank's petulant mood on his late arrival; he has met Jane as she flies from the scene, and knows that she is reaching the end of her tolerance of the situation between them—"I met *one* as I came," he says (*E*, 364).

Mr. Knightley joins the outing to Box Hill, and there sees Emma and Frank engaged in febrile badinage which a disinterested observer would be able to recognise as semi-hysterical and enjoyable to neither. Emma hates what is going on—she is finally extremely glad to get away from such "questionable enjoyments" (*E*, 374). But they have led her to do something completely out of character—her internal moral monitor, which has until now prevented her real irritation and impatience with Miss Bates from breaking through to the surface, has failed, and she has wounded her with a silly witticism (*E*, 370). Neither Mr. Knightley nor anyone else present can know that Emma's behaviour is almost entirely controlled by the Frank-Jane quarrel which, as it reaches its crisis, is poisoning the atmosphere and leaving Emma isolated and almost desperate. The reader perceives most of the action through Emma's consciousness, but is at the same time aware of how it must look to Knightley. He thinks he sees the girl for whom he has admitted to himself feelings which have nothing much to do with current standards of female excellence on the Gisborne model being corrupted by a shallow and decadent man who means to indulge in some such caddish scheme as to marry her for her money while at the same time conducting a relationship with another woman. At this time he puts little past Frank in the way of selfish unconcern and thinks that Emma is allowing herself to be dragged down to his level. He has no reason to think that he has any hope of saving her, but his concern drives him to obey old habits of remonstrance, this time with far greater seriousness than ever before: "I must once more speak to you as I have been used to do . . . I must, I will,—I will tell you truths while I can, satisfied with proving myself your friend by very faithful counsel, and trusting that you will some time or other do me greater justice than you can do now" (*E*, 375–76). There is a finality in the "once more"; it is almost a farewell—and indeed, the next day he leaves for London, to avoid (as we find out later) the painful spectacle of the final stages of Frank's courtship of Emma. But not before he discovers that he has at last triumphed. At the time Emma's response is her usual one— combat; she "tried to laugh it off" and deny that it was "so very bad" (*E*, 374). But in reality she is devastated, and by the next day Mr. Knightley is aware of what can only be described as a victory. Her acknowledgement this time of her fault and of his justification results in what must be one of the tenderest of low-key love-scenes in all fiction:

> He looked at her with a glow of regard. She was warmly gratified—and in another moment still more so, by a little movement of more than common friendliness on his part. He took her hand;—whether she had not herself made the first motion, she could not say—she might, per-haps, have rather offered it—but he took her hand, pressed it, and

certainly was on the point of carrying it to his lips—when, from some fancy or other, he suddenly let it go.—Why he should feel such a scruple, why he should change his mind when it was all but done, she could not perceive.—He would have judged better, she thought, if he had not stopped.—The intention, however, was indubitable; and whether it was that his manners had in general so little gallantry, or however else it happened, but she thought nothing became him more. It was with him, of so simple, yet so dignified a nature.—She could not but recall the attempt with great satisfaction.

(E, 385–86)

Typically, Austen places this at a point where neither party can possibly know that it *is* a love-scene, so caught up are they in their erroneous speculations, and yet Emma's preoccupation with its implications are clear from the complexities of her inner monologue here. The reader is informed of their love for each other before the protagonists have clearly formulated it themselves.

For Emma and Knightley are now farther apart than they have ever been in their picture of the true state of affairs among their friends and between themselves. In fact, though nobody yet knows it, we are in the concluding stages of the Churchill-Fairfax story, while Emma is currently convinced that Harriet and Frank are in love with each other; disabused of this, she falls into the even greater error of supposing Mr. Knightley to be in love with Harriet. Emma is still possessed with the delusion that female vacuity is the essential requirement for a "sensible" husband, and, though finally enlightened as to her own feelings, is quite unable to see herself as a desirable wife.

For one thing she is disgusted with herself. The Box Hill episode has a lasting effect. From that time she begins a long period of penance and self-castigation which has its origin in Knightley's rebuke about Miss Bates. When she becomes aware of the true state of her feelings on hearing Harriet's pretensions, this intensifies. As many critics have indicated, the free indirect style here is deceptively like an authorial voice; but we should not be deceived. Emma's gloom and despondency after hearing the news of Jane and Frank's engagement (*E*, 422–23) have no more substance than any of her other speculations, for we know that despite the Dixon fantasy, she has done no lasting damage to Jane, whose miseries are over; and moreover, her suggestion that Jane has had "something to conceal" (*E*, 203), has turned out to be true; her communication of her suspicions to Frank is embarrassing to herself but reflects even less credit on him; the idea of a marriage between Harriet and Mr. Knightley is preposterous and need not really trouble Emma if she were not still caught up in her delusions. Even her self-accusation of neglect of the Bateses is, by her own estimate "more in thought than fact" (*E*, 377). She has not perhaps fulfilled the conduct-book ideal, but has done her best in the circumstances. Miss Bates clearly strains everyone's tolerance. But she is giving in to what she supposes is Knightley's plan of reform for her—she has no notion that by this time he regards her as more sinned against than sinning, and has moreover abandoned all thoughts of changing her in any way. He is indeed at this point preparing to come hotfoot to comfort her for her supposed disappointment in Frank Churchill.

So they have both been wrong—both confused and misled, partly by others, but partly by their own prejudices. Those who see Mr. Knightley as mentor, pure and simple, tend to overlook the enormous development his character undergoes during the course of the novel. At the beginning he is entirely the self-confident paternal/fraternal guardian and pedagogue, inflexible in his concept of true womanly behaviour, sure that he knows what is best for everybody. Gradually his position is undermined, for in the long run experience teaches him that his attitudes are too rigid, that Emma's intuitions are sometimes better than his "reasonable" assumptions and that love has little to do with rules of conduct. The revelation of Jane Fairfax as an ordinary mortal tempted into that heinous collection of offences—"an ill-placed attachment," an unsanctioned engagement and a clandestine correspondence—is a shock to his system from which he does not recover. His victory at Box Hill is nowhere near as important as it might have been earlier, for now he can be in the position of a reader reading *Emma* for a second time—knowing the secret of Jane and Frank gives everything a different gloss. It certainly cheers Emma up, and the reader, entangled so intimately in her feelings, is relieved and refreshed at her clean blast of righteous anger to Mrs. Weston—even though we know, as Mrs. Weston does not, that it is Frank's impudent use of her Dixon invention that incenses her most. But the novel ends on an ironical note, for once Emma is disabused of her latest fantasy about Harriet she is contrite, and wishes to get full value for her penitence. She is still apt to see herself in the guise of an Ellen Percy or a Cherry Wilkinson—in need of admonition. While Mr. Knightley tries to escape from the patriarchal/fraternal role, Emma shows every sign of submitting herself in conventional womanly manner to her husband's dominion whether he likes it or not—"What had she to wish for? Nothing, but to grow more worthy of him, whose intentions and judgment had been ever so superior to her own" (*E*, 475). This is the expression of her mood on hearing of Harriet's engagement to Robert Martin. A moment's clear thought would remind her, and the astute reader, that Harriet's final acceptance of Martin is better based than when Knightley announced, *tout court*, that he "means to marry her" (*E*, 59). At least she has had some experience upon which to base her choice. But now Emma wants to believe that her knight has been right all along. This is the final ironical twist in the plot, and one that somewhat damages its standing as the straightforward feminist tract described by Margaret Kirkham and others, for we see a woman who has apparently every chance of enjoying an equal relationship with her husband rejecting it out of hand. This novel is not about rewards and punishments, though it does deal in changes of heart.

But as we have found, Austen's endings are never conclusive and the language of this one leaves a number of perplexities to the reader not quite prepared to accept the fairy-tale formula. Does she really mean us to accept the victory of the patriarchal stereotype? Will Emma really become as blindly uncritical as Isabella? Or (even more unlikely) will Mr. Knightley relinquish old habits of domination and really step down? Since their relationship was born of conflict neither resolution seems probable; their prenuptial felicity looks romantic but not permanent; even in their new-found harmony they show a tendency to spar. When Emma is informed of Harriet's engagement to Robert Martin she at first finds it difficult to believe, and suggests that Mr. Knightley has made some mistake. His rejoinder, "Do you dare say this? . . . What do you deserve?" is countered by her "Oh! I always deserve the best treatment, because I never put up with any other" (*E*, 474). Light-hearted at the time, it has overtones both of the past and the shape of things to come; it is left open to the reader to reflect that Mr. Knightley may again assert his superiority and Emma refuse to accept it, that they may both again obstinately hold on to untenable opinions for the sake of argument. Five other marriages are presented in the novel for consideration alongside Emma's. John and Isabella Knightley have been sufficiently discussed. We have also seen Mrs. Weston coping with her husband's unreasonable sociability and optimism and Mr. Elton's deterioration as he adapts himself to his mean-minded wife. Frank Churchill seems to regard his future wife as an *objet d'art* upon which to hang jewellery, and we can imagine, though we do not see, Harriet's subordination to the wider Martin family at Abbey-Mill. In contrast with all of these the marriage of Emma and Mr. Knightley holds the possibility of becoming a balance of opposing but equal forces, rather than the subjection of one personality to another. Mr. Knightley's removal to Hartfield shows how little he feels threatened (as brother John might have been) by the domination of a woman. Perhaps this balance is what we are intended to understand by the novel's closing words: "[T]he perfect happiness of the union." Entertained—and perhaps obliquely instructed—as we have been by their conflicts, we have to hope that Emma and Mr. Knightley *quarrel* happily ever after—a unique conclusion for a novel of its time.

Notes

1. J. E. Austen-Leigh, *A Memoir of Jane Austen* (1870), ed. R. W. Chapman (Oxford: Oxford University Press, 1926), 157.

2. Elizabeth Hamilton, *Memoirs of Modern Philosophers* (Bath, 1800).

3. Two of these works are available in modern editions—Charlotte Lennox, *The Female Quixote* (1752), ed. Margaret Dalziel. Introduction by Margaret Ann Doody (Oxford: Oxford University Press, 1989), and Mary Brunton, *Discipline* (1814), introduced by Fay Weldon (London: Pandora, 1986). *Angelina, or l'Amie Inconnue* and is included in Marilyn Butler and Mitzi Myers (eds.), *The Works of Maria Edgeworth*, 13 vols (London: Chatto and Pickering, 1999–2003), vol. 10.

4. Laura G. Mooneyham, *Romance, Language, and Education in Jane Austen's Novels* (London: Macmillan Press, 1988); 107. Many other critics uphold this view in one way or another: Tony Tanner, *Jane Austen* (London: Macmillan, 1986), esp. 202—"Mr. Knightley and his brother, who speak only sense"; Edward Neill, "Between Defence and Destruction: 'Situations' of Recent Critical Theory and Jane Austen's *Emma*," *Critical Quarterly* 29 (1987): 39–54, esp. 44; Alison Sulloway, *Jane Austen and the Province of Womanhood* (Philadelphia: University of Pennsylvania Press, 1989), esp. 39; Roger Gard, *Jane Austen's Art of Clarity* (New Haven and London: Yale University Press, 1992); and Beth Fowkes Tobin, *Superintending the Poor: Charitable Ladies and Paternal Landlords in British Fiction, 1770–1860* (New Haven and London: Yale University Press, 1993), where comment on *Emma* sees Austen upholding traditional patriarchal values through Knightley—see chapter 3, esp. 69–70.

5. For example, J. F. Burrows, *Jane Austen's* Emma (Sydney: Sydney University Press, 1968), 13, questions his authoritative function in the novel, but stops short of denying it altogether. "It is a matter," he says in his introduction, "of accepting him as a leading but not oracular participant . . . a matter of heeding his words but not bowing to them."

6. See Margaret Kirkham, *Jane Austen: Feminism and Fiction* (Hassocks, Sussex: Harvester Press, 1983; reprinted London: Athlone Press, 1997), chapter 18, esp. 133 and also Claudia Johnson, *Jane Austen: Women, Politics and the Novel* (Chicago: University of Chicago Press, 1988), collected in this casebook. See also Kirkham, *Jane Austen: Feminism and Fiction*, introduction, xxi: "[W]e can see that Austen's subject-matter is the central subject-matter of rational, or Enlightenment feminism and that her viewpoint . . . is

strikingly similar to that shown by Mary Wollstonecraft in *A Vindication of the Rights of Woman.*"

7. *Jane Austen's Letters*, 2–3 March, 1814, 256.

8. Eaton Stannard Barrett, *The Heroine, or Adventures of a Fair Romance Reader* (London, 1813), chapter 49.

9. Thomas Gisborne, *An Enquiry into the Duties of the Female Sex* (London, 1797); "I am glad you recommended Gisborne, for having begun, I am pleased with it, and I had quite determined not to read it." *Letters*, 30 August 1805, 112.

10. My attention has been drawn to an unusual exploration of Mrs. Goddard's point of view in a recent novel: Joan Austen-Leigh, *Mrs. Goddard: Mistress of a School* (Victoria, B.C.: Room of One's Own Press, 1993).

11. Glenda A. Hudson, *Sibling Love and Incest in Jane Austen's Fiction* (London: Macmillan Press, 1992), 51.

12. Juliet McMaster, *Jane Austen In Love* (Victoria, B.C.: English Literary Studies, 1978), 61.

13. John Gregory *A Father's Legacy to His Daughters* (1774), in John Gregory et. al, *The Young Lady's Pocket Library, or Parental Monitor*, London, 1790. Reprinted, with introduction by Vivien Jones (Bristol: Thoemmes Press, 1995), and Hannah More, *Essays on Various Subjects, Principally Designed for Young Ladies* (London, 1777), 37–38. "It has been advised, and by very respectable authorities too, that in conversation women should carefully conceal any knowledge or learning they may happen to possess. I own, with submission, that I do not see either the necessity or propriety of this advice." Nevertheless, More goes on to erode her own argument by asserting that a girl with "discretion and modesty, without which all knowledge is of little worth ... will never make an ostentatious display of it." More's speciality was providing quotable phrases for all sides of the argument.

14. Gisborne, *Enquiry*, chapter 12, 271–72: "[I]f we speak of intelligent and well-informed women in general, of women, who, without becoming absorbed in the depths of erudition, and losing all esteem and relish for social duties, are distinguished by a cultivated understanding, a polished taste, and a memory stored with useful and elegant information; there appears no reason to dread from the possession of these endowments a neglect of the duties of the mistress of a family."

15. Burrows, *Jane Austen's 'Emma'*.

Filming Highbury

Reducing the Community in Emma to the Screen

LINDA TROOST AND SAYRE GREENFIELD

◆　◆　◆

S IR WALTER SCOTT, in his review of Austen's *Emma*, observes that the "author's knowledge of the world . . . reminds us something of the merits of the Flemish school of painting. The subjects are not often elegant, and certainly never grand; but they are finished up to nature, and with a precision which delights the reader" (Scott, 197). To explain the different positions of the community of Highbury in the two 1996 films of *Emma*, let us start with a comparison to two Flemish painters that spring to mind. The Miramax film of *Emma*, written and directed by Douglas McGrath and starring Gwyneth Paltrow, is like the work of Vermeer. In his pictures, we see the artist's gaze focus on the details of genteel life and on subjects that project calm self-possession. *The Music Lesson*, for example, focuses contemplatively on two people surrounded by the trappings of tasteful gentry life—a viola da gamba, a virginal, and a Turkish carpet—complementing the calm, confident, and independent subjects in the portrait, the woman's face reflected in a mirror. The Meridian telefilm of *Emma* with Kate Beckinsale (screenplay by Andrew Davies and directed by Diarmuid Lawrence), by contrast, has something of Bruegel to it, perhaps his *Wedding Feast*. This painting is communal, filled with many people, both young and old, in the actions of everyday life— eating, talking, drinking—and it opens out toward the viewers, inviting them into the society. Neither Bruegel's communal nor Vermeer's individual visions, however, can represent Austen's complex novel accurately. Nonetheless, one can see the work of these artists as the extremes toward which the cinematic versions tend. Making *Emma* into a film requires portraying Emma's social context and placing her as a focal point, but the limitations of the genre inhibit the detailed attention to both a novel can give.

One could argue that *Emma* is simultaneously the most individual and most social of Austen's six major novels. It is the only one named after its heroine and the only one that sticks entirely to one community—Highbury. Frank Churchill may head to London for his haircut and piano purchasing, but the readers never do. One might also claim that this novel has the most sympathetic portrayal of the heroine's hometown—which is odd, given that the people occupying it (Mr. Elton, Mr. Woodhouse, Miss Bates) are not terribly attractive. Yet passages of pleased observation appear in *Emma* that seem unusual for Austen:

> Emma went to the door [of Ford's] for amusement.—Much could not be hoped from the traffic of even the busiest part of Highbury;—Mr. Perry walking hastily by, Mr. William Cox letting himself in at the office door, Mr. Cole's carriage horses returning from exercise, or a stray letter-boy on an obstinate mule, were the liveliest objects she could presume to expect; and when her eyes fell only on the butcher with his tray, a tidy old woman travelling homewards from shop with her full basket, two curs quarrelling over a dirty bone, and a string of dawdling children round the baker's little bow-window eyeing the gingerbread, she knew she had no reason to complain, and was amused enough, quite enough still to stand at the door. A mind lively and at ease, can do with seeing nothing, and can see nothing that does not answer.
>
> (*E*, 233)

An image of Emma's content with the small sphere of Highbury is important, given the conclusion of the novel. This novel offers no disruption of the community, which every other Austen novel seems to entail. The function of the Highbury community is to provide the setting for the resolution: that is, Emma accepts her position within the community and does not flee from it into marriage. Contrast this conclusion with Meryton's role in *Pride and Prejudice*. Even the estate of Mansfield Park suffers a slightly greater degree of disruption at the end of the novel, as Fanny Price gets her sister Susan to take her place with Lady Bertram.

But Emma will remain within Highbury and Hartfield, and that means we must accept her in the company of Mrs. Elton and her father as part of the happy ending—we name these two figures because the end of the novel reminds the reader that these people in particular will be present—no retreat to Derbyshire as Elizabeth Bennet manages. In fact, Mr. Woodhouse (the most immobile character of all) becomes the static center-point toward which the plot resolves, as Mr. Knightley moves in with him and Emma.

Usually in romances, Austen's included, marriage is not reward enough for the heroine. She gets wealth, a higher position in society, escape from an intolerable situation—some sort of bonus to confirm the happiness of the conclusion. Not in *Emma*. At least the social setting can provide no significant reward. So, if the community of Highbury cannot provide the additional reward, what bonus beyond Mr. Knightley does Emma get? Why, just what she ought, of course: self-knowledge. Between the mental distance Emma travels and the physical immobility she accepts, we can see how carefully this novel balances between being one about a society and being one about an individual.

The two recent films unbalance the novel into two different directions, which is all right since a two-hour adaptation cannot and should not try to do everything. The community around Highbury does not clinch the happy ending in the novel because Emma has that community to begin with. By the end of the novel, Emma has only Augusta Elton (lamenting the pitiful lack of white satin at the wedding) as a significant addition to her circle, and she loses Harriet Smith, "which was not to be regretted" (*E*, 482). Though Emma finally comes to appreciate Jane Fairfax, that lady departs Highbury, to return to the Campbells and prepare for marriage to Frank Churchill. Not so in the Davies film: the community does provide the joyous conclusion. Any mention of Frank and Jane's departure is omitted, and Harriet and Robert Martin are welcomed into the company of the gentlefolk, with no sense of contact to be diminished. Though the last shot in the telefilm is of turkey thieves, reminding us there is still trouble in paradise, the images before that generally reinforce a sense of expanded community as the clincher for the happy ending.

The finale of the McGrath film is conventional and focuses attention on the beautiful heroine and her reward, Mr. Knightley, by showing the wedding. The Davies screenplay, however, concludes with a Bruegelesque harvest supper that greatly changes the focus since we now see Emma within her world with all its social classes. In addition, the three betrothed couples (of assorted social classes themselves) join in a traditional dramatic emblem of unity, a country dance. As the director notes, the dance is intended to show the "three couples, who've been cast asunder, now happily with their partners, and *backed up by a harmonious society*" (Lawrence, 60; emphasis added). We get to see a scene in which Mrs. Elton is affronted by Emma's more egalitarian social recognition of Robert Martin. A fuller acceptance of her community is exactly what Emma, in contrast to Mrs. Elton, achieves in this film. The harmony at the conclusion of the Davies production comes as a relief after all the social disjunction that film has been careful to show us. Admittedly, the McGrath film shows Emma interacting with members of other social classes in various ways—visiting the sick and the poor, grappling with gypsies—but these scenes serve to advance the plot, not to clarify Emma's place within her world; therefore, the finale need not strive for conspicuous social unity. It is the Davies film that has the fuller picture of the society that surrounds the heroine, a picture that emphasizes connections within classes as well as the disjunctions between them.

Both films depict the presence of servants at the various households, but in the McGrath version, they appear quickly, announcing visitors, often in the background and without attracting the viewer's attention. The Davies production, by contrast, positions servants as the particular objects of our gaze. Davies himself remarked that Austen's novel is "unusual" for presenting a "working model of a whole society—with some fascinating glimpses of the underclass" ("Austen's Horrible Heroine"). His filmic version of the novel expands this glimpse. We cannot overlook the servants dressed in magnificent livery, easing the relaxations of the gentry still further by their efforts. This juxtaposition appears in the Box Hill scene, as the servants struggle up the slope carrying the table and elaborate equipment for the *al fresco* lunch, and in the strawberry-picking scene, when servants provide the ladies cushions on which to kneel so that they need not make contact with garden soil. It is precisely such social divisions that require the finale of the harvest supper at Donwell, where upper class and lower class can enjoy mutual conviviality as they celebrate the "wholeness in the community" (Davies, "The Final Scene," 58). That scene is hardly one of egalitarianism, but we do get a sense that one of the improvements that Emma receives is a lessening of her snobbery, though the snobbery is inherent in the social system. Such a conclusion is not unexpected: As Carol Dole has noted, costume dramas produced in the context of modern British socialism often feel the need to comment critically about the class system (Dole, 60), much in the way that contemporary American films about the past tend to be self-conscious about slavery and racial prejudice. Not surprisingly, then, the British production of *Emma* pays great attention to the situation of the serving classes in Regency Surrey whereas the American production glosses over their existence.

More subtle than the portrayal of divisions between the classes, however, are the attempts to depict the social structure within the gentry itself. No film of *Emma* could avoid a plethora of parties and dances, for that is where much of the plot occurs. Indeed both films, like Vermeer's paintings, display much finery for us to admire. But the Davies *Emma* seems concerned with also showing us the complex structures that bind families and a community together. The McGrath version seems more concerned with showing us Gwyneth Paltrow—well, Emma herself—for in that film, the important relationships all stem from and to her.

One can see something of this difference from the percentage of the dialogue each character is allotted:

	Davies	McGrath
Emma Woodhouse	33%	41%
Mr. Knightley	12%	13%
Frank Churchill	11%	4%
Harriet Smith	10%	12%
Mr. Woodhouse	6%	3%
Mr. Elton	5%	8%
Mrs. Elton	5%	3%
Miss Bates	5%	3%
Mr. Weston	4%	2%
Jane Fairfax	3%	1%
Mrs. Weston	3%	6%
John Knightley	1.7%	0.4%
Isabella Knightley	0.6%	0.3%
Robert Martin	0.4%	0.8%
Mrs. Goddard	0.4%	0.3%
Mr. Perry	0.3%	
Mrs. Cole		0.7%
Mr. Cole		0.5%

First of all, note that Gwyneth Paltrow as Emma has a higher percentage of the lines (41%) than Kate Beckinsale as Emma (33%). More impressionistically, we would say that the camera focuses on Paltrow more in silent moments, too. As Nora Nachumi has indicated, Paltrow, the famous beauty, is more conspicuously posed for the camera than the rival Emma (135–36).

For example, when Emma is checking the mail for an invitation from the Coles, McGrath places her on a Grecian sofa flanked by two potted trees and backed by white drapery. It is not just that this Emma has more lines and gets more attention from the camera; the rest of her family have far fewer lines to interrupt the focus upon her. Mr. Woodhouse drops from 6% of the lines in the Davies film to 3% in the McGrath film. Emma's sister and brother-in-law, John and Isabella Knightley, almost vanish from the film (Kaplan, 183). Another way that the McGrath film focuses upon Emma is to reduce the secondary romance, that between Frank Churchill and Jane Fairfax. Frank is the most reduced character of all, sliding from 11% of the dialogue in one film to 4% in the other, and Jane Fairfax also diminishes from 3% to 1% of the speeches.

A small and subtle alteration in the plot between the two versions also makes the point about the tighter focus upon Emma's problems when Paltrow plays her. In the novel, after the unfortunate trip to Box Hill, Emma feels terrible about her treatment of Miss Bates and, therefore, goes to call upon her, her mother, and Jane Fairfax the next day:

> "The ladies were all at home." She had never rejoiced at the sound before. . . . There was a bustle on her approach; a good deal of moving and talking. She heard Miss Bates's voice, something was to be done in a hurry; the maid looked frightened and awkward; hoped she would be pleased to wait a moment, and then ushered her in too soon. The aunt and niece seemed both escaping into the adjoining room. Jane she had a distinct glimpse of, looking extremely ill; and, before the door had shut them out, she heard Miss Bates saying, "Well, my dear, I shall *say* you are laid down upon the bed, and I am sure you are ill enough."
>
> (*E*, 378)

As for Emma's reaction to this little scene. "She had a moment's fear of Miss Bates keeping away from her. But Miss Bates soon came—'Very happy and obliged'—but Emma's conscience told her that there was not the same cheerful volubility as before—less ease of look and manner" (*Emma*, 378). Austen teases us with our expectation that Miss Bates should be the one avoiding Emma, but in fact, Jane Fairfax is the one avoiding her. The next chapter shows Emma's repeated and frustrated attentions to Jane, and we eventually understand the reason for the refusal of these assiduities: Jane is upset with Emma for her and Frank Churchill's having "flirted together excessively" (*E*, 368) at Box Hill—this flirtation on Frank's part, unknown to Emma, being the result of a quarrel between the lovers.

This sequence of interactions between Emma, Miss Bates, and Jane Fairfax appears pretty straightforward in the Davies film (if in reduced form), including a striking visual image that corresponds to these lines in the novel:

> When Emma afterwards heard that Jane Fairfax had been seen wandering about the meadows, at some distance from Highbury, on the afternoon of the very day on which she had, under the plea of being unequal to any exercise, so peremptorily refused to go out with her in the carriage, she could have no doubt—putting every thing together— that Jane was resolved to receive no kindness from *her*.
>
> (*E*, 391)

The Davies film places more interest on the problems of Jane for their own sake—perhaps even more than the novel can, restricted as it is (more or less) to Emma's viewpoint. Certainly the shot of Jane Fairfax walking across the fields weeping while being observed sympathetically by Robert Martin makes us interested in her problems and reminds us of his blighted romance. Both these characters have been hurt, inadvertently, by Emma, and this telefilm is interested in their reactions in the way the McGrath movie is not.

The McGrath film, in contrast, makes Miss Bates the one who is trying to avoid Emma. Emma is pointedly avoided at the Bates home, and we follow her sad and humiliated figure as she walks away. Why the plot change? Because this film is really concerned with Emma's feelings and not with the effect Emma has on others. The scene at the Bates home becomes a part of Emma's education in *noblesse oblige*, a necessary step on her way to becoming a chivalric Mrs. Knightley, not a clue to Jane Fairfax's situation.

This version, to be fair, does not merely cut other characters to make way for Emma. The roles of Mr. Knightley and Harriet Smith persist at the same (or slightly expanded) level of attention and that of Mrs. Weston noticeably increases. These three characters do not diminish because these are the ones in whom Emma confides. This film relies upon scenes of tête-à-têtes to illustrate the character of Paltrow's Emma, and Mrs. Weston functions as her confidante, drawing her out so that we can see Emma's thinking processes on display. Of course, Beckinsale as Emma also appears in intimate conversations, particularly with Miss Smith, Mr. Knightley, and Mr. Churchill, but Mrs. Weston is seen mostly with her husband within the larger social occasions of parties and has only two private conversations with Emma.

As the novel frequently takes us inside Emma's head, so must the films at least occasionally accomplish this maneuver, even though the form cannot perform this task so adeptly. The speaking roles are not the only indicator of Gwyneth Paltrow's dominance of the film: even when we get inside Emma's mind in both scripts, we sense the greater concern with the solitary reactions of title character in the McGrath version and the more socially enmeshed quality of the Davies version. McGrath accomplishes the trick of admitting us to Emma's private thoughts by showing her writing in her diary and simultaneously giving us a Paltrow voice-over that explains what the young woman is writing: an entry in which she wonders whether she is in love with Frank Churchill. McGrath even gives the shot a Vermeer quality by shooting her reflected in a mirror. We get to watch Emma watch herself as she dreams. In the Davies version, on the other hand, we get to experience Emma's fantasies from her point of view: we see through her eyes (and the camera's lens) as Mr. Elton thanks Emma for uniting him with Harriet, and later we see Frank Churchill's portrait smiling at us (and Emma). We become, for a moment, Emma watching other characters. For McGrath, the reactions are solely Emma's: she remains the end point of a chain of occurrences, and the camera focuses on Paltrow. For Davies, the fantasies require the images of other characters on screen, which grants them a certain importance. Even the nightmare inflicted upon Emma—a vision of Mr. Knightley's marriage to Jane Fairfax—shifts her concern from the personal to the social. "What about little Henry?" she cries aloud in church as she clutches her nephew's hand, worried about the line of inheritance of Donwell Abbey (presumably this represents a sublimation of her own desires). Her imaginings place Emma in social situations, surrounded by family and friends. Davies's Emma is not the end-point of this film or the sole focus of the camera even in the sequences that reveal her hidden thoughts. In other words, the events that occur end with their effect upon Emma in the McGrath film, whereas the implications of events in the Davies version reflect through Emma's mind and back onto society.

One may suspect the different emphases derive from the greater American influence on the Miramax film as opposed to the Meridian/Arts and Entertainment production. The feature film promotes a rising star, Gwyneth Paltrow, whereas the telefilm sits more comfortably within the British tradition of ensemble work. Beyond this, however, the two versions of *Emma* represent two different and legitimate visions of the novel: one more concerned with what happens in the society, the other more in tune with what happens to the individual. Austen's novel has the luxury of presenting both visions simultaneously; a film, however, must limit its scope.

To phrase the difference more generically, one might say that the Davies film is a comedy, in the literary sense. It is about the reestablishment of order in society after Emma's attempts at matchmaking, about building tighter bonds within the community. The McGrath film is more of a romance, in the modern sense: Paltrow gets the dishier-looking Mr. Knightley (played by Jeremy Northam). But let us not underrate romance. Austen's novel is both comedy and romance, and in so far as it is a romance, *Emma* must reward its heroine, and it happens to do so by granting her increased understanding as well as the hero. The tighter focus of McGrath's version allows the audience to focus upon Emma and her personal improvement. Indeed, it is hard *not* to focus on Gwyneth Paltrow in this film: one is glad to see her inner character become truly worthy of her Vermeer-like exterior. In contrast, the more socially-oriented British production, with the less conventionally beautiful Kate Beckinsale playing Emma, makes the audience concentrate on a wider scene, replacing a portrait of Emma with a Bruegelesque group painting that abounds with good will.

Works Cited

Austen, Jane. *Emma*. Ed. R. W. Chapman. Rev. 3rd ed. Oxford: Oxford University Press, 1933–69.

Birtwistle, Sue, and Susie Conklin. *The Making of "Jane Austen's Emma."* London: Penguin, 1996.

Davies, Andrew. "Austen's Horrible Heroine." *The Electronic Telegraph*, November 23, 1996. www.telegraph.co.uk (accessed September 26, 1999).

Davies, Andrew. "The Final Scene: Conceiving the Idea." In Birtwistle and Conklin. 57–58.

Dole, Carol M. "Austen, Class, and the American Market." In Linda Troost and Sayre Greenfield, eds., *Jane Austen in Hollywood*. Lexington: University Press of Kentucky, 1998. 58–78.

Emma. Writer Andrew Davies. Director Diarmuid Lawrence. With Kate Beckinsale and Mark Strong. Meridian-ITV/A&E, 1996.

Kaplan, Deborah. "Mass-Marketing Jane Austen: Men, Women, and Courtship in Two Recent Versions." In Troost and Greenfield. 177–87.

Lawrence, Diarmuid. "The Final Scene: Director's Approach." In Birtwistle and Conklin. 59–60.

Nachumi, Nora. "'As If!': Translating Austen's Ironic Narrator to Film." In Troost and Greenfield. 130–39.

Scott, Walter. Unsigned review of *Emma*, in *Quarterly Review*, xiv (1815–16), 188–201. Reprinted in this case book.

Clueless in the Neo-Colonial
World Order

GAYLE WALD

◆ ◆ ◆

SELDOM HAS A contemporary U.S. "teen flick" risen to the levels of both critical and commercial popularity attained by Amy Heckering's 1995 film *Clueless*, an Americanized and updated version of Jane Austen's novel *Emma*.[1] One of four Austen film adaptations released in U.S. cinemas in the space of two years (the others were *Sense and Sensibility*, *Persuasion* and a much-hyped version of *Emma* featuring Gwyneth Paltrow), *Clueless* not only attracted generally high critical regard in the mainstream and independent film press, but in its video version the film became a fast best-seller, particularly among the young female teenagers who were its primary target audience. Indeed, in a year that also witnessed the release of Larry Clark's frankly dystopian *Kids*, a movie with which it was frequently contrasted in reviews, the fate of *Clueless* seemed almost as charmed as that of its protagonist, the ever fortunate Cher Horowitz. Modelled on Austen's heroine Emma Woodhouse, Cher lives a life that appears as orderly and abundantly provided for as her over-stocked clothes closet, as seen in the film's opening sequence. It is a life untouched by the social and familial conflict, drugged-out confusion or sexual turmoil that characterize other cinematic depictions of adolescence, including Heckerling's own classic *Fast Times at Ridgemont High* (1982). Or as cultural critic Cindy Fuchs observed in a review in the

Philadelphia *City Paper*, "As 'teen movies' go, *Clueless* is obviously, self-consciously, lightweight: there are no suicides, no violence, no generational battles... no class or money angst... no racial conflicts... no sexual crises.... The world of the film is ideal, shimmering, stable."[2]

It is this "ideal, shimmering, stable" world of *Clueless* and of its protagonist Cher (played winningly by Alicia Silverstone) that I seek to interrogate in this essay. More precisely, I'm interested in using *Clueless* to explore the role of cinematic representation in the construction of national and cultural citizenship, as well as to examine the gender, race and class dimensions of the national narratives produced by a contemporary Hollywood film explicitly addressed to an audience of adolescent and preadolescent U.S. girls. The impetus for my enquiry into *Clueless* emerges, at least in part, from silences and elisions in the critical literature on nation, Empire and U.S. cinema. While scholars have recognized the status of U.S. films as global commodities (that is, commodities whose paths of dissemination mirror the paths of global capital), mediating the production of national narratives for "foreign" as well as domestic audiences, they have been reluctant to interrogate how notions of nationhood and national identity circulate in films that do not explicitly promote jingoistic fantasies of U.S. global supremacy. At the same time, they have often failed adequately to theorize the *gendering* of nationalist discourses in U.S. cinema, overlooking in particular the possibility that these may be voiced, embodied or symbolized by female protagonists whose sphere of influence is more likely to be the home than the boardroom or the battlefield. Yet while *Clueless*, a clever adaptation of an English comedy of manners, would seem quite remote from the innumerable Hollywood action and suspense films that wear their nationalist desire on their sleeves, primarily calling upon women to establish the heterosexuality of male heroes, this essay argues that it is no less likely a site for the production or negotiation of national narratives and fantasies (Boose 1993, 587–91). Rather, what we find in *Clueless* is a representation of national citizenship that is inextricably tied to, and mediated through, the representation of commodity consumption, heterosexual romance, and class and gender "cluelessness."

Fuch's useful oxymoron of a world at once "shimmering" and "stable" anticipates my method of reading *Clueless* as a film structured around contradictions, especially concerning Cher's status as a privileged First World "consumer citizen." Like *Emma, Clueless* centralizes the narrative of its protagonist's development from eager orchestrator of others' social affairs to object of her own heterosexual romance, a process depicted as both inevitable and desirable, particularly in so far as it corresponds to Cher's loss of a cluelessness that inures her to her privileged place in the "real" world. At the same time, in pursuing this narrative end—one dictated by the precedent of Austen's text as well as by the exigencies of market and genre—*Clueless* subsumes or deflects many of the questions raised by its portrayal of Cher's national and class agency. In so doing, I argue, the film situates the subjectivity of its protagonist at the intersection of competing narratives of gender itself; for while it represents Cher as a "First World" girl who deploys her cluelessness in order to "innocently" access power, it also suggests that such cluelessness stands in the way of her "successful" gendering according to the demands of the marriage plot.

In this essay I engage the following questions. How does *Clueless* envision citizenship, and more particularly how does it use the alibi of a critique of "clueless" citizenship to justify and enable a certain gender narrative? How does the film construct Cher's identity through her pursuit of commodities, and how is this representation related to U.S. cultural fantasies of consuming the world? How does the film use the character of Cher to construct the nation—or national/imperial desire—as itself innocent or clueless? In rendering Cher's cluelessness a narrative obstacle to heterosexual romance, what light does the film shed on the power relations implicit in its own "girling" of national discourse?

As these questions imply, in my analysis, *Clueless* is characterized by a degree of ideological and narrative ambiguity that I also find in its heroine, who is neither entirely clueless about her social location nor entirely capable of constructing an alternative to the imperatives of heterosexualization and romantic coupling that largely determine the direction of the film's ending. This reading of Heckerling's film in turn contributes to my larger argument about the ways that conventional narratives of gender ultimately frustrate the capacity of economically privileged First World women to realize their complicity with neo-colonial relations of domination, on the one hand, and to recognize the mutuality of their experience with the manifestly different experience of economically disadvantaged and/or Third World women, on the other. As *Clueless* helps to illustrate, the "proper" gendering of economically privileged First World women will depend, to one degree or another, on their cluelessness about (read: ignorance about as well as "innocence" with regard to) the various interests through which their own privileged identities are established. As the term *clueless* itself suggests, First World women enjoy their privileges from a subject-position that paradoxically denies them status as political and intellectual agents, thereby diminishing their ability to resist conventional scripts of both gender and nation.

In what follows, I develop my argument about *Clueless* by framing it within the context of the issues raised by Heckerling's "Americanization" of Austen's text. In invoking such a term, I do not mean to argue that Cher is simply Emma Woodhouse temporally and geographically transposed from the nineteenth century to the twentieth, and from the English countryside to Southern California. In order for *Clueless*'s representation to "work" in the ways that I am suggesting it does, Heckerling's film must account at the levels of both spectacle and narrative for shifts from a colonial to a neo-colonial order and for the different identity-formations that emerge or recede in the wake of such shifts. Here I am interested in the ways that the film effects a "translation" of Emma, the unwitting heiress of British imperial and colonial enterprises (although she herself has never visited the English seaside), into Cher, a "citizen" of Beverly Hills named after the eternally youthful and ambiguously "ethnic" star of contemporary infomercials, and the beneficiary of a late twentieth-century "global" economic order. My essay thus begins by demonstrating how *Clueless* establishes Cher's identity in and through a tacit discourse of "First World–Third World" economic and social relations. After showing how *Clueless* represents Cher's citizenship in terms of her privileged relation to commodities, as well as both implicitly and explicitly to the labour (and bodies) of Third World women workers, I go on to show how the film forwards the ends of the romance plot by gendering her within the context of her vulnerability to sexualized violence, significantly staged within a symbolically "Third World" locale where Cher cannot hold on to her class privilege. In so doing, I argue, Heckerling's film traces the process through which Cher subtly sheds cluelessness in order to embrace a more acceptable form of domestic virtue, though she initially resists it.

As I suggested in my opening reference to the recent handful of Jane Austen film adaptations, I see *Clueless* as implicated within a larger discourse of U.S. nostalgia for an imagined and romanticized English past. Here *Clueless* might be seen, however, as a potentially liberating departure from the customary translation of "British lit." classics into cinematic "postcards"— realist works that strive authentically to represent the habits, speech, manners and dress of the English landed gentry, the class that served as Austen's primary source of artistic inspiration. Modelled after a string of commercially successful productions by the UK producer-director team Ismail Merchant and James Ivory (including 1986's *A Room with a View*), these "faithful" cinematic translations of Austen's novels circulate within the context of U.S. national fantasies of pre-industrial England as a site of authentic social and cultural tradition.[3] Whereas in films such as *Emma* and *Pride and Prejudice* the consumerist pleasures of the rich are endorsed under the premise of "historical accuracy," in *Clueless* a space is opened up for the interpretation of consumption as a specific social practice, one shaped by factors of gender, race, nation and class. In eschewing the high-minded seriousness and patent nostalgia of these more "faithful" Austen adaptations, in other words, *Clueless* also insinuates its own self-consciously clueless appropriation of a "classic" or high cultural text for a more commercially marketable representation. Perhaps more importantly, in relocating *Emma* to a Southern California location more readily associated in the U.S. cultural imaginary with a "postmodern" lack of historical depth, Heckerling's script plays with ideas of temporality and tradition that are intimately linked to the ideology of Empire, in particular to the notion that imperial power may be duplicated and extended through the establishment of "domestic" traditions in various "foreign" outposts, which may or may not be seen as sustaining their own cultures and traditions.

First World Girls Just Wanna Have Fun

The plot of *Clueless* can be summarized as follows. Cher Horowitz, the most popular girl in her class at Bronson Alcott High School, decides along with her best friend Dionne to devote her considerable energy, imagination and resources to "bettering" the social standing of Tai, the slightly grungy, somewhat *déclassée* new girl at school. Cher herself takes little interest in high school boys, with their gawkiness, social immaturity and goofy ways of dressing, but she has high aspirations for Tai, whom she hopes to set up with Elton, the only boy Cher deems worthy of attention. Not surprisingly, these apparently altruistic intentions backfire when it becomes clear that Elton is merely using Tai to ingratiate himself with Cher. A scene in which Elton tries to force himself sexually on Cher and in which she is subsequently mugged by a stranger establishes her vulnerability and her need for male protection, and yet Cher initially bumbles in this regard by pursuing a romance with the new boy Christian, ignorant of the fact that he is gay.

Eventually, however, Cher comes to realize that she has fallen in love with Josh, the hunky and sensitive older guy who's been living under her father's roof with her all along. On the one hand, this realization is achieved conventionally, as Cher learns to pattern her own desire after the desire displayed by Tai, who has meanwhile recuperated from her disastrous pairing with Elton and redirected her libidinal energies toward Josh. On the other hand, while Cher's attraction to Josh is necessary for the film to achieve closure and to gratify audience expectations, it is not altogether narratively predetermined or determining of the film's meaning. In particular, *Clueless* allows room for some equivocation in its portrayal of the marriage plot by introducing unresolved oedipal ambiguities: to wit, the detail that Josh is Cher's father's ex-stepson (the child of the woman he married after Cher's mother died, and whom he has since divorced). This ambiguity, however minor, carries over into the film's ending, a wedding scene in which Cher predictably catches the bridal bouquet that portends her own imminent marriage to Josh. While the penultimate moments of the film show Cher and Josh passionately kissing, in the final shot Cher turns to address the camera directly, offering a mildly sarcastic "as if"—a phrase through which she perhaps signifies her own mild disbelief at this conventional turn in her "fate." The General Public song "Tenderness" (exemplary of the film's retro-1980s soundtrack) kicks in as the credits roll.

Clueless establishes the contours of its overlapping national, class and gender narratives early on, in a scene that not only ensures Cher's status as a likeable and admirable film heroine, but also organizes its representation of Cher's gender identity through its portrayal of her loyalty to "American" values of inclusion and social equality. In this scene (also one of the film's most humorous), Cher delivers a speech before her high school debating class on the subject of Haitian immigration to the United States. Assigned to argue in favour of Haitian immigration, Cher reveals in both her logic and her delivery how the principle of U.S. altruism toward economically downtrodden or disadvantaged Third World nations is premised on the very assumptions about "correct" femininity and domestic virtue that Cher herself must negotiate if she wants to have a romantic relationship with Josh. That is, by emphasizing Cher's cuteness as she delivers the speech, *Clueless* offers the construction and revision of "feminine" domestic virtue as the rationale for the expansion and revision of American national identity. As she speaks, moreover, we hear the strains of the national anthem, soft at first, as they swell to an increasingly audible crescendo that coincides with her own *rhetorical* crescendo. Given its importance to my argument about *Clueless*'s own construction of national desire, I quote the "Haiti" speech in full:

> "So OK, like, right now for example, the Haitians [pronounced 'Hay-tee-ins'] need to come to America. But some people are all, 'What about the strain on our resources?' Well, it's like when I had this garden party for my father's birthday. I put R.S.V.P. 'cause it was a sit-down dinner. But some people came that, like, did not R.S.V.P. I was totally buggin'! I had to haul ass to the kitchen, redistribute the food, and squish in extra place settings. But by the end of the day it was, like, the more the merrier. And

so, if the government could just get to the kitchen and rearrange some things we could *certainly* party with the Haitians. And in conclusion, may I please remind you that it does not say R.S.V.P. on the Statue of Liberty!"[4]

As is rather obvious, Cher's speech—not to mention Silverstone's wonderful performance of it—is calculated to win her the admiration of the film's audience as well as her own audience of classmates (who respond to the speech with cheers and applause as Cher, ever gracious, curtsies and bows). The speech scene not only serves to establish how gender is produced in and through ideologies of nationhood and national identity, but how narratives of national identity may be framed within the context of (or even serve as the rationale for) ideologies of domestic female virtue. Cher's voicing of a solidly liberal position on Haitian immigration additionally prefigures her compatibility with Josh, who lectures Cher about the environment and who, in contrast to Cher's father, wants to become a lawyer to fulfil his dreams of some day being an advocate for social justice. The only one who is apparently unpersuaded by Cher's speech is MR. Hall, the debate teacher, who gives Cher a grade of C+ (a mark she later contests). Mr. Hall is never given an opportunity to explain his indifference to a performance whose cuteness and charm are so apparent to everyone else (both within and without the world of the film), but one suspects that his frustration derives from Cher's inability to "read" Haiti properly—to understand the plight of would-be Haitian immigrants from a viewpoint informed by the history of U.S.—Haitian relations. As it stands, Cher rationalizes Haitian immigration through an analogy that hints at her proficiency not in history but in husbandry—a proficiency that is confirmed in the scene immediately following this one when Cher's father praises her for looking after him so well.

Yet as the speech hints, here, too, Cher's performance of domestic virtue is inextricable from her role as a consumer of domestic labour, and from her obliviousness to the discrepancy between her parable and the problems that Haitians and Haitian immigrants actually face. As viewers might be led to surmise, in other words, the only way that "real" immigrants attended her father's fiftieth-birthday party were as labourers in the kitchen. Moreover, the garden party scenario merely fosters a simulacrum of parity between the poorest and richest nations in the Western hemisphere without really addressing the sources of such yawning economic disparity; as long as U.S. citizens (those who R.S.V.P.'d) do not object to a redistribution of the abundance of food and space that they already enjoy by virtue of their power, the Haitians (the unanticipated guests who lack the civility to respond to the invitation) can be accommodated at the table.

Here the notion of "sharing" (a pun on Cher's name?) is put forward not only as a form of inclusive, and therefore more ethical, national consumption, but also as the sign of renegotiated social relations between First World and Third World nations. The Haiti speech thus operates on a number of different levels: it ingratiates Cher to the viewing audience, pairing her cluelessness about U.S.–Haitian relations with the audience's affection for her as a liberal advocate of the sort of democratic values associated with national symbols such as the Statue of Liberty; it legitimates gendered domestic virtue as both a principle of international diplomacy and the means by which she can win the approval of her father and then later of Josh; and it establishes altruism (gift-giving) and communitarianism as the logical paradigms of First World–Third World relations, and by analogy of the gendered relations within the "domestic" (that is, the national/public and home/private) spheres.

Cher's Haiti speech enacts a dialectical relationship between cluelessness and innocence that provides the basis for her privileged subjectivity within a neo-colonial world order, as well as the footing for much of the film's comedy. In many ways, too, it is a condensation of *Clueless* itself: both are charming, both are performative, and both manage to keep viewers diverted while also tacitly reinscribing conventional narratives of gender, class and nationality. Both are also *ironic*, in the sense that both invite audience disidentification and distance. After Cher delivers her speech, for example, her debating opponent and social nemesis, Amber, complains that in talking about her father's garden party, Cher hasn't followed the teacher's instructions, which were to talk about Haiti. Amber misses the point, of course; but on another level her grievance models the mistake of reading the scene of Cher's speech too literally, as though she really were an exemplary defender of Haitian liberty and Northern-Southern solidarity. In so far as Amber is Cher's antagonist, that is, we understand her objection to Cher's speech as exemplifying her own (mock?) cluelessness, whereas Amber's refusal/inability to voice the "con" side of the argument (that Haitians should be prohibited from immigrating to the United States) hints at Cher's success at using *her* cluelessness to silence opposition to her speech's liberal narrative.

Cluelessness and Consumer Citizenship

In addition to illustrating the ironic rhetoric of *Clueless*, the Haiti speech correlates to the anticipated trajectory of Cher's transformation from romantically disinclined arranger of others' affairs to the eager subject of her own romance narrative. Like her father's fiftieth birthday party, which turned out to be a success after signs of potential disaster, so *Clueless* must work to avoid the potential "disaster" of an unrealized heterosexual narrative by securing her femininity within a patriarchal and paternalistic system. In order to be made a heroine, that is, Cher must be made to recognize and also surrender to the bounded nature of her own gender identifications.

Given the film's deployment of the Haiti speech as a kind of preamble to its own narrative development, we might ask what kind of gender, class and race "citizenship" the film subsequently imagines for Cher. In pursuing this line of questioning, we find a conflation of national citizenship with highly specific gendered and classed forms of commodity consumption. Whereas in *Emma* the protagonist's innocence is coupled with her enjoyment of material comforts supplied by the British colonial endeavour (as Edward Said has argued in discussions of Austen's work), in *Clueless*, Cher's cluelessness about social relations is coupled with her ability to enjoy a certain gendered consumer "agency" (Said 1994, 89). From its opening shots, *Clueless* quite literally frames Cher's image within an ever-shifting panorama of commodities that lend her world an air of prosperity, convenience and abundance, signifying the presence of wealth that is never actually displayed (in part because the characters buy goods on credit).

The spectacular nature of Cher's identity as a possessor of things suggests a breakdown in the conventional binary distinction between the "private sphere" of the home (where commodities are enjoyed) and the public sites of commodity exchange; Cher's bedroom, the quintessential private sphere of bourgeois girls, is less a private space than an extension (or even a domestic "colony" of) the Galleria, the quintessential Southern California commodity palace, which is significantly also the place where Cher feels most "at home." Just as *Clueless* portrays Cher as seamlessly assimilated into this world of commodities, so commodity consumption is perfectly integrated into Cher's moral universe; when she and Dionne jokingly refer to the affliction they call "buyer's remorse," for example, they mean regret over the purchase of an unwanted item, not regret over the fact of consumption itself. Consumption is not merely an "activity" in which Cher and her girlfriends engage; it is also a sign through which their gendered and classed identities are made and re-made through the mediation of a purchasable relationship to commodities. In *Clueless*, consumption is additionally a primary means of sociability among girls, who alternately "bond" over shared or similar purchases or fan social rivalries through competition over the possession of specific items (for example, a particular party dress).

As a subject who manifests class agency primarily through consumption (in part because her gender and youth preclude any direct access to the means of production), Cher might be said to belong to the "consumer elite"—that recent "class" of national subjects which has emerged, according to Gayatri Spivak, within the context of re-ordered power relations of the global economy of late twentieth-century capitalism.[5] As the phrase implies, "consumer elite" designates an identity-formation that arises in a context in which consumption has become a sign of agency in and of itself. Yet as Arjun Appadurai argues, under such terms consumption is less a manifestation than a chimera of agency: a "fetish" constructed through the discourse of an integrated system (or global economy), which in turn conceals the increasing concentration of power over production (Appadurai 1993, 186). In Appadurai's terms, the consumer elite is thus the "definitive citizen" of a world order in which consumption is not only increasingly divorced from production, but has actually taken the place of production within the social imaginary.

Neither Spivak nor Appadurai situates the emergence of this "new" fetishism of the consumer in terms of a specific discourse of gender or nationality, although Spivak's discussion locates the emergence of a "consumer elite" within the context of Indian decolonization and the social, economic and political re-orderings that characterize the transition from "Empire" to "Nation." In many ways, however, their respective depictions of consumption as a site of contradiction—a space of agency and non-agency alike—correspond to Cher's subject-position as a gendered and classed under-age "citizen" of Beverly Hills. For Cher, consumption signifies ambiguously. It is, on the one hand, an extension of nationalized class privilege that hinges on the "Third World-ization" of production, as well as a form of leisure or "play" that signifies her privileged relation to both gendered domestic labour (that is, shopping isn't a chore) and the global gendering of commodity production. Yet it is also inevitably bound up with Cher's performance of femininity (that is, a properly classed, heterosexual, virginal femininity), and hence associated with the loss of gendered agency (even as such displays of femininity win Cher a degree of approval both at school and at home). Given the trajectory of the romance plot, which requires that Cher begin to question the terms of consumption in order to endear herself to Josh, who is critical of her attachment to clothes and shopping, it is particularly significant that Cher's profligacy as a consumer is paired with her failure accurately to read the social—for example, to realize that Elton likes her and not Tai. This conflation of consumption with cluelessness in turn portends the film's representation of romance as the rationale for the revision of Cher's gendered identity.

Clueless's representation of its protagonist's consumer identity is further complicated—albeit not in ways that are immediately or easily readable—by its coding of Cher as Jewish. Cher's Jewishness is signified both explicitly, through her possession of a recognizably Jewish last name,[6] and more subtly, through references to ubiquitous nose jobs and stereotypical markers of "Jewish" ethnicity (for example, the neurotic family; the characterization of Mel Horowitz as a fast-talking, high-strung attorney), as well as through occasional puns (for example, the fact that it is a character named Christian who is an inappropriate love-object for Cher). Perhaps not incidentally, Jewishness is also part of the discourse of teenage fandom around Silverstone, a "known" Jewish actress whose "all-American" blonde prettiness does not immediately signify as such.[7] Although the film carefully avoids lapsing into anti-Semitic typecasting—for example, coding consumption as a particularly "Jewish" pastime—nevertheless Heckerling's translation of Emma into a Jewish-American "princess" complements the film's re-visioning of national identity in terms of specifically "American" narratives of the upward economic mobility of immigrants. In terms of such nationalized class mythologies, Cher's Jewishness may thus be said to render her quintessentially American, the implication being that her father has risen to a position of authority within WASP society on account of professionally acquired wealth rather than ancestry.[8]

Cher's Jewishness abets the film's narrative of a "multicultural" American nation (already established in the Haiti speech scene), in which racial/ethnic subjects are treated as equals by the white majority, and in which immigrants are capable of ascending the ladder of social and economic success. What this adds up to, in fact, is a portrayal of a Benetton-esque American "diversity" that forwards the film's own nationalist subtext. For example, the film works to dissuade the audience from questioning Cher's social privilege by representing it within the context of harmonious "race relations," as symbolized by her friendships with a pointedly diverse group that includes Dionne, her African-American best friend, and Tai, whose class and ethnic differences (the latter less clear-cut) are coded through her vaguely "New York" accent. Like *Independence Day* (1996), a film that packaged its blatantly nationalist agenda (that is, Americans saving the world from itself) in the guise of a domestic diversity embodied by its black and Jewish male leads (Will Smith and Jeff Goldblum), thereby contributing to the export of "U.S. multiculturalism" itself as a global and imperial commodity, *Clueless* works to convey the impression that Cher's cluelessness with regard to *national* identity is justified because it is shared among a racially and even economically "mixed" group of teenagers. *Clueless*'s innovation, in this regard, is to portray the American public high school—rather than the U.S. Armed Forces—as the site that best illustrates the equality-in-diversity that is a hallmark of the liberal "multicultural" nation-state.

This is not to say, however, that such portrayal of the American nation as welcoming and inclusive, not colonizing or racist, renders the film monolithic in its national discourse or negates the possibility of a critical subtext. For example, in making the comic *excessiveness* of Cher's wealth clear (recall the spectacle of her hyperbolically overstocked and tidy clothes closet), the film encourages young viewers to revel in their *superiority* to her class cluelessness, and thus to establish an ironic distance from her and her friends, who are otherwise shown to have the same menstrual cramps, to suffer the same sexual insecurities, and to blunder incompetently through the same mindless homework assignments. Young audiences of the film are similarly meant to feel pleasure in their recognition of Cher's cluelessness when she offers to donate ski boots and gourmet food items to a charity drive for a homeless shelter, or in their awareness of Cher's ignorance when she complains to Josh that she has trouble understanding Lucy, the Horowitz family's El Salvadoran maid, because Lucy speaks "Mexican."

As this remark about Lucy implies, however, the film's narrative of a "multicultural" and class-transcendent American nation (a narrative that co-exists with its portrayal of distinctions in wealth and status) is repeatedly undermined by references to "Third World" subjects or locales that are not easily assimilable to it. As I have been suggesting, to read *Clueless*'s national narrative we will need to read into some of the film's most "clueless" moments, paying attention to its formulation of relations between the "First" and "Third" worlds. Such relations in turn shed light on the film's construction of Cher as a gendered "First World" subject. For example, Cher's reference to Lucy, an immigrant domestic worker, not only complicates the film's narrative of the United States as a welcoming "domestic" space for all those who seek to establish themselves within its borders, but it is also instrumental in situating Cher as a gendered subject who occupies a position of national, racial and class privilege relative to other gendered subjects within the patriarchal "private sphere." Even as her remark displays her ignorance and a national obtuseness that viewers can laugh at, it also points to the fact that, within the confines of the home, she enjoys a comfort and freedom that are contingent on Lucy's labour. Indeed, the only time domestic work is deemed appropriate for Cher is when she is directly engaged in ministering to her father (for example, his garden party), when such work ceases to signify as domestic labour and instead becomes re-coded as filial duty. In contrast to Lucy's labour, which is naturalized within the domestic sphere, Cher's own service for her father is simultaneously assumed on account of her gender and transformed on account of her social and economic privilege.

It is important to keep in mind, moreover, how such distinctions between women who simultaneously (if unequally) perform domestic work within the patriarchal household are themselves mediated through particular imperial or neo-colonial discourses. What initially appears to be an isolated, "domestic" conflict ("domestic" here maintaining its dual signification as both the feminized, private sphere and the masculinized public sphere of the nation itself) may thus be governed by specific national discourses about "foreigners." Here, for example, Cher's comment about Lucy illustrates her general indifference to national distinctions among Spanish-speaking immigrants and to household "help"; yet it also speaks to her ignorance of the history of U.S. intervention in El Salvador. The point is not merely that we don't expect a character like Cher to know about this history, but that her own raced and classed gender privilege is enabled through this not-knowing. As long as she maintains her cluelessness about the particular histories of El Salvadoran domestic workers in the United States, in other words, Cher can also remain the untroubled beneficiary of Lucy's labour—labour that not coincidentally also affords Cher a privileged mobility within and outside of domestic spaces. In effect, to remain ignorant/innocent of U.S. relations with El Salvador (or for that matter Haiti) means that Cher can remain ignorant/innocent of her own relations with Lucy, and thus of her own position within a gendered economy of national, race and class privilege.

First World–Third World Encounters and the (Re)Construction of Gender

While the conventions of the romance narrative require that Cher be "rewarded" for her compliance with a patriarchal script of gender in her acquisition of a boyfriend, it is significant that the film cannot bring about such narrative closure without the intervention of a scene of gendered violence that is itself inscribed by issues of First World–Third World relations. In particular, the scene in question stages a paradigmatic "encounter" of the gendered First World subject with the violence and disorder of the "street," as Cher, abandoned by Elton on the way home from a party (notably after fending off his unwanted sexual advances), is mugged in a deserted parking lot while making her way home from the distant neighbourhood of Rainbow Heights. The location of the mugging scene is significant because it offers a symbolically "Third World" locale (as the name "Rainbow Heights" implies) as the site in which Cher's class privilege does not "work" to guarantee her safety and agency as a woman, as it does in the "First World" domestic sphere. Although in her immediate response to the mugging Cher continues to insist on her classed invulnerability to gendered violence—she frets loudly at the loss of her cellular phone and the state of her muddied designer dress, for example—at the same time *Clueless* undercuts her comic interpretation of the mugging scene by using it to lay the groundwork for the refashioning of her gender identity and thus for her gradual acquiescence to the romance plot. The scene begins to serve such a legitimizing function with regard to gender when Cher calls Josh, himself in the middle of a date, to ask him to drive out to Rainbow Heights to pick her up. On the one hand, the phone call situates Cher within a gendered economy of power and mobility, in which women are victims and men rescuers, and in which Cher's plea for help constitutes a form of passive consent—if not an active invitation—to romantic courtship. Yet on other hand, the scene also serves a complementary function in engendering masculine desire, providing the first occasion in which Josh sees Cher not as a spoiled Beverly Hills brat, but as a "woman."

The mugging poses the most obvious danger to Cher; yet it is additionally dangerous within the context of *Clueless's* efforts to "domesticate," or otherwise rhetorically tame, the questions the assault raises. By immediately recuperating it as comic, and by using it to initiate the anticipated romance narrative between Cher and Josh, the film avoids having to explicitly contemplate the chastening effects of such violence on Cher's gender identity. In narrative terms, the mugging could itself signify as a moment of crisis, in which Cher might be led to question her own social and ideological alliances, and yet instead it becomes the moment when she recognizes that her interests lie in following a patriarchal script of femininity. In a sense, we might therefore conclude, the scene represents two distinct, if related, kinds of violence: a real violence whose effects are disavowed, and a symbolic, or rhetorical violence that is necessary to the film's expected narrative closure.

The film's disciplining of gender through the romance plot becomes particularly clear in its representation of the effects of her newfound interest in Josh on her previous enthusiasm for shopping. Whereas at the beginning of *Clueless* Cher's identity is defined almost entirely through her role as a consumer (of goods, labour and other people's romantic pleasure), gradually she learns to re-conceptualize her desires, realizing that fulfilment lies not merely or only in the possession of material goods but in the possession of a boyfriend. This shift in Cher's relation to consumption is ironic, if only because Cher is accustomed to finding in shopping—an activity which, significantly, she is more likely to associate with leisure and feminized sociability than with domestic labour—a form of surrogate agency. As she reasons, even when she has a particularly 'bad' day at home or at school, spaces where she is expected to submit to paternal/patriarchal authority in a fashion becoming her gender (that is, to be a "good girl"), she can always make herself feel better by going shopping. At the mall, Cher submits only to the authority of her own desires; whereas home is a space of generational and gendered conflict, the mall is contrastingly a space of perfect equivalence between want and its fulfilment.[9]

In so far as shopping is a form of gendered and classed agency for Cher, it becomes all the more ironic that her habits of consumption are represented as inconsistent with the expression of erotic desire for Josh, who, brimming with paternalistic college affectation (he reads Nietzsche, eschews popular culture and at one point dons a black beret), deems her interest in items such as clothes, makeup and exercise videos frivolous. At his suggestion, Cher even takes it upon herself to engage in charitable activities, such as helping to organize a food drive; she also makes a point of dressing down in his presence and of wearing make-up less conspicuously. However, these apparently more ethical forms of consumption that Josh stands for are ultimately revealed to be a different form of domestic virtue to which Cher must accede if she wants to have a romantic relationship with him. The film wants viewers to applaud Cher's transformation by contrasting her behaviour in the mall, where her habits of conspicuous consumption make visible her cluelessness to her class privilege, with her behaviour around Josh, where she is noticeably more self-conscious and self-critical.

Heckerling underscores these changes in Cher's attitude and appearance with a more sparing use of voiceover in the scenes that feature Josh and Cher, thereby signifying that Cher sheds superficiality and gains in interiority as she becomes closer to Josh. (Here again, however, the film is somewhat ambivalent, since while their romantic attachment is presented as a happy confluence of romance and social convenience—after all, they not only share the same house but the same class status—the incestuous overtones of their attachment enforce a sense that Josh and Cher are potentially mismatched.)

"Girl Power" and U.S. Film

As the film's resolution makes clear, Cher's cluelessness serves conflicting ideological functions. On the one hand, it is inextricably linked to her agency as a gendered and classed First World subject. Being clueless means that Cher is spared the burden of critical self-consciousness that falls to subjects who cannot peremptorily assume that others will greet their presence with warmth and appreciation, or who take for granted a certain freedom of self-expression and/or movement. It also invests her with an aura of gendered innocence that she can draw upon in negotiations with more powerful and/or authoritative figures, from her father to her debate teacher to the man who mugs her. On the other hand, to the degree that it signifies ironically, her cluelessness opens up a space for audience critique of Cher's class and race privilege. In this sense cluelessness offers a means for "clued in" viewers to realize a critique of the national prerogatives that Cher's social and economic entitlement assumes—but only to a degree, since it never actually threatens the terms of stable audience identification with Cher as a likeable protagonist. Finally, and in so far as it is construed as an impediment to the development of a successful heterosexual romance narrative, Cher's cluelessness represents that quality that she must shed in order to become a more conventional cinematic heroine. For Josh to like her, in other words, she must demonstrate through example (rather than mere suggestion) that her cluelessness is merely an aspect of a performance of femininity that she uses to ward off potential romantic suitors.

My attempt to map the ideological function of cluelessness in Heckerling's film finally suggests that cluelessness may be a metaphor for ideology itself—specifically, that 'system of ideas' around issues of gender and class that Cher must shed in order to be rewarded with Josh's (and the audience's) love by the end of the film (Gramsci 1971, 377). Yet even if "cluelessness" constitutes the terrain upon which Cher acquires subjectivity and consciousness, nevertheless, the fact that the film pairs her relinquishing of cluelessness with her embrace of gendered domestic virtue remains deeply problematic, suggesting that the "price" of her insight is submission to the heterosexual romance narrative. Here, too, cluelessness becomes a rhetorical strategy of the film itself, which requires that the audience similarly assent to the revision of Cher's gendered identity, even if we do not welcome the film's insistence on romantic coupling as a narrative climax, in so far as this revision is conflated with her growth in self-consciousness. Just as, through her attraction to Josh, Cher learns to construct her femininity in conformity with his interests and desires; so, too, the audience is led to order its desire in conformity with the romance plot and with the attendant "gendering" of the cinematic heroine, who wins our approval and admiration for having gained in "humanity."

Here *Clueless*'s own status as a cultural commodity becomes particularly salient. In the United States, where it had its biggest audience, *Clueless* was an unanticipated hit, grossing $57 million at the box office and spawning a weekly television series featuring members of the movie cast. Subsequently *Clueless*, a film that was originally based on a pilot for a television show, became a moderately successful Fox television series featuring many of the members of the film cast, with the exception of Silverstone, the film's greatest asset. (Here it is notable that the TV show locates Cher in a "pre-Josh" period, allowing for the formulation of plots centring on Cher, her friends, and their various "clueless" adventures, rather than the determining "master-plot" of heterosexual romance.) In turn, the commercial success of the film—and, to a lesser degree, its TV spin-off—has been widely credited with sparking a trend in the marketing of films specifically for teenage girls, who are perceived by industry executives as an "emerging" and highly profitable audience.

Yet while *Clueless*'s commercial viability and the marketing trends it has encouraged might attest to the "consumer power" of U.S. teenage girls (and could conceivably be a harbinger of such power), they also raise questions concerning the cinematic construction (or reproduction) of national, race and gender identities, both 'domestically' and abroad. In a recent *New York Times* article, for example, Joe Roth, the chairman of Walt Disney Studios, reasoned that film executives are eager to target teenage girls because they may be counted on to generate increased profits for multinational corporations: "They're easier to market to, compared to the older audience, because their tastes are very specific," he is quoted as saying. "They come to a movie over and over again if they like it. They don't work; they don't have families to raise. They're available consumers with money" (Weinraub 1998, B4). Roth's notion of teenage girls as an audience of "available consumers" who "don't work" is telling, not only for its emphasis on girls' perceived docility and therefore their commercial exploitability, but for its conflation of "girlhood" itself with leisure and commodity consumption. Moreover, in so far as his vision of what girls "want" is predictably market-driven, it is difficult to read his allusions to "girl power" (à la English pop group the Spice Girls) as anything but cynical. According to Roth, girls are being rewarded for their loyalty and dependability as consumers with their "own" films; and yet if *Clueless* is what they want, films like *Titanic* are what they are (and dependably will be) given.

I have hastened to add this account of *Clueless*'s ongoing influence within the U.S. film industry in order to outline potential intersections between the discourse of marketing and the discourse of gender, as well as to suggest connections between the apparent "spending power" of "First World" girls and the representation of gendered agency in Heckerling's film. In *Clueless*, as I have argued, Cher is made to realize the bounded nature of her own gender identifications, which are themselves structured in and through the film's narrative of First World–Third World relations. Hence notions of classed and gendered domestic virtue may be recuperated as the rationale for the expansion of national identities, as the winningly patriotic conclusion of Cher's Haiti speech demonstrates. They also serve as the ideological machinery driving Cher's transfer of libidinal energy away from consumption and instead toward heterosexual coupling, such that she does not need to be "convinced" to like Josh, but eventually comes to recognize romance as the object of her "own" desire. Given that (at least by the *New York Times* account) *Clueless* and Cher are paradigmatic, respectively, of the kind of commercially visible movies and "empowered female teen characters" that Hollywood sees girl audiences as "wanting," then the highly touted consumer "agency" of U.S. girls may be no less problematically tethered to the embrace of conventional gender and class narratives cloaked in the rhetoric of the charming, the cute, or the clueless.

Notes

For their helpful suggestions and comments, I would like to thank Ann Cvetkovich, Andrea Levine, Brigid Nuta, You-me Park, Rajeswari Sunder Rajan, and Patricia White.

1. Although the conditions of cultural production and authorship of novels and films are quite different, for the sake of argument I will take Heckerling to be the "author" of *Clueless* throughout this essay. In the film credits, Heckerling is cited as director, screenwriter and executive producer.

2. See Fuchs. Like her literary precursor Emma Woodhouse, Cher Horowitz may be said to live "in the world with very little to distress or vex her" (*Emma*, 5).

3. In this respect, they build upon the previous successes of films such as Merchant-Ivory's *A Room With a View* (1986).

4. My source for this quote is "Movie quotes for Clueless (1995)," which can be found at: http://us.imdb.com/cache/title-more/quotes+19091.

5. Spivak discusses the effect of such shifts in "Woman in difference," an essay that focuses on the representation of subaltern women in the fiction of Mahasweta Devi. In particular, she argues that nationalist discourses of development and progress, specifically those that emerge in the context of post-independence India, conceal the ongoing oppression and domination of subaltern women, a gendered identity produced under the sign of "Empire" and "Nation" alike. The relatively unchanged status of subaltern women—which can be inferred, in part, from Devi's fiction—belies the postcolonial narrative of national "progress" measured in terms of democratization, secularization and capitalist development (1993, 80). Indeed, as Spivak concludes, signs of national "progress" can produce radically differential results for subjects who occupy different social locations within the national imaginary. Hence even if such measurements could assess the impact of decolonization and independence on the lives of poor, socially despised Indian women, the effects of the transition from "Empire" to "Nation" could not be properly understood in abstract, universal terms, because "Empire" and "Nation" are both constitutive of the identities that also "inhabit" them.

6. In "High school confidential," an interview with Heckerling, *Rolling Stone* (1995) cites the name of Silverstone's character as "Cher Hamilton," a divergence which is perhaps attributable to discrepancies in the press material, but which is nevertheless interesting as a potential "Anglicization" of Cher's Eastern European Jewish surname.

7. For example, Silverstone's "Jewish" identity is frequently noted on websites devoted to her, and Silverstone periodically is identified as/identifies herself as Jewish in interviews with the entertainment press.

8. The film does contain one mildly disparaging reference to "Persians," or to the Persian Jews who constitute a small but visible minority of Jewish immigrants in Beverly Hills. *Clueless*'s ambivalence about Cher's Jewishness mirrors the coding of much "American" comic narrative as "Jewish" humour, as in the television show *Seinfeld*.

9. This conflation of domesticity and consumption contrasts with the separation of the public, entrepreneurial sphere (the site of commodity production and purchase) and the private, domestic sphere in *Emma*. For Cher, commodity culture constitutes an alternative form of domesticity, domesticity embodied in the mall. In constructing the mall as an extension of the domestic, *Clueless* references the mall's place within late twentieth-century U.S. culture as a surrogate public sphere—or, more precisely, a fetish of the public (complete with an architecture that conventionally includes fountains, benches, tree-lined pedestrian "avenues" and quaint storefronts—that orders everyday social life even as the "real" public sphere is increasingly controlled by private interests. The mall's link to the street—the old

and perhaps obsolete public sphere—is made explicit, for example, in a scene in which Tai is attacked in the Galleria by a group of rowdy boys who threaten to throw her over a railing.

References

Appadurai, A. 1993. "Disjuncture and Difference in the Global Cultural Economy." In *The Phantom Public Sphere*. Ed. B. Robbins. Minneapolis: University of Minnesota Press.

Boose, L. 1993. "Techno-muscularity and the Boy Eternal: From the Quagmire to the Gulf." In *Cultures of United States Imperialism*. Ed. A. Kaplan and D.E. Pease. Durham, N.C.: Duke University Press.

Clueless. 1995. Dir. Amy Heckerling.

Fuchs, C. *Clueless*. http://www.inform.umd.edu:8080/EdRes/Topic/Womens Studies/ Film Reviews/clueless-fuchs.

Gramsci, A. 1971. *Selections from the Prison Notebooks*. Ed. and trans. Q. Hoare and G.N. Smith. New York: International Publishers.

R.C. 1995. "High School Confidential." *Rolling Stone* 716, September 9, 1995, 53.

Said, E. 1994. *Culture and Imperialism*. New York: Vintage.

Spivak, G.C. 1993. *Outside in the Teaching Machine*. New York: Routledge.

Weinraub, B. 1998. 'Who's lining up at the box office? Lots and lots of girls,' *New York Times*, February 23, 1998, B1, B4.

Emma

England, Peace and Patriotism

BRIAN SOUTHAM

◆　◆　◆

Such is the Patriot's boast, where'er we roam;
His first, best country, ever is at home.
　　　—Oliver Goldsmith, *The Traveller or A Prospect of Society*
　　　　　(1765) reprinted at the head of the *Naval Chronicle*,
　　　　　　　　vol. 28, July–December 1812

How I bless my stars I am of that dear little island, under a
government like ours. When I see other countries and other
people, I am not only proud of being an Englishman, but feel a
sort of superiority, which is in no other manner to be accounted
for than its being common to all Englishmen, and is inherent in
them.
　　　—Captain William Hoste (*Amphion*, 32) in the Adriatic,
　　　　　writing home to his father, 24 September 1809

B EFORE ACCEPTING the Poet Laureateship in September 1813,
Southey asked if the official duty of producing Odes for Royal birthdays
and New Years might be modified. Could he not be permitted, instead, to
write on any great national occasion or event, just as the spirit moved him?
His promoter, John Wilson Croker, the Secretary of the Admiralty, replied
that although it was not for us "to make terms with the Prince Regent,"[1] he
could pass on a discreet enquiry to that effect. However, as he pointed out,
Southey should have no difficulty in composing his first Ode, for the New
Year of 1814: "You can never have a better subject than the present state
of the war affords you."[2] Since mid-1812, the balance of the land war in
Europe had swung in favour of the Allies, and as recently as October 1813,
with the Battle of the Nations at Leipzig—a decisive engagement which

drove the French back across the Rhine—the final phase of the war had opened. With victory in sight, Southey could launch his inaugural Ode on a triumphant note: England's leading part in the war, the defeat of France (now taken for granted), and what stirred him most deeply, an end to Napoleon's blood-stained tyranny, a subject which he had touched upon in the *Life of Nelson*, with an indignant outburst, a truly "purple" passage, at the Emperor's "enormities,"

> those crimes which have incarnadined his soul with a deeper dye than that of the purple for which he committed them;—those acts of perfidy, midnight murder, usurpation, and remorseless tyranny, which have consigned his name to universal execration, now and for ever.[3]

With the Laureateship as his authority and the Ode as his platform, Southey could give vent to his feelings. "Vengeance" called for nothing less than Napoleon's "Death" and France stood "Disgraced . . . to all succeeding times." For the politicians, this poetic rant was a triumphalism too far. Croker called Southey to order, reminding him that the Ode was an official performance and that diplomacy was called for. The Laureate needed to keep his eye on the settlement of the post-war world and France's read-mission to the concert of Europe. With France in the future a "friendly power," asked John Rickman,[4] "[C]an you stay in office this Carmen re-maining on record?"[5] Reluctantly, Southey acted on these warnings. At some cost to his feelings, the most vengeful sections, what he called the "maledictory stanzas,"[6] were removed and incorporated into a new and unacknowledged poem, the "Ode Written during the Negociations with Buonaparte," published anonymously in *The Courier* for 3 February and, with some slight changes, in *The Times* for 21 April 1814.

For Southey, his Laureate Ode was now "spoilt,"[7] no longer, as he told Rickman, a "Carmen Triumphale," but an emasculated "Carmen Castra-tum."[8] The truncated version is tactful; the closing lines speak of "France restored"; and Southey consigned his fulminating to the notes, where he reminded his readers of the unspeakable "cruelties," "atrocities" and "abominations" perpetrated by French troops on their retreat from Por-tugal. Ignoring Allied sensibilities, he also left unrestrained his exultant celebration of England's heroic stand, at times a solitary stand, throughout the length of the Long War:

> O England! O my glorious native land!
> For thou in evil days didst stand

Against leagued Europe all in arms
array'd,
Single and undismay'd,
Thy hope in Heaven and in thine own
right hand.
Now are thy virtuous efforts overpaid,
Thy generous counsels now their
guerdon find, . . .
Glory to God! Deliverance for
Mankind!

The anticipated "Deliverance" was soon to come. On New Year's Day, 1814, the Ode was published and by 21 January, when Jane Austen began *Emma*, the Allied armies had entered mainland France—Blücher across the Rhine and Wellington through the Pyrenees.

By the end of March the Allies were at the gates of Paris and on 6 April Napoleon abdicated. Two days later, the news reached Chawton. Up at the Great House, Fanny Knight recorded the "glorious news of Buonaparte vanquished and dethroned,"[9] an event celebrated a month later by illuminations at Alton and a public supper for the parish poor. Soon, with Napoleon exiled to Elba, the Army and Navy began to wind down. Francis returned from the Baltic; Charles found his duties lightened on the *Namur* and expected to settle down with his family on shore; and the country prepared to welcome the Allied leaders for the Victory celebrations in June, an occasion that Jane Austen greeted with mock impatience, wishing them "all away."[10] In September, half-way through *Emma*, she was advising a novel-writing niece that "3 or 4 Families in a Country village is the very thing to work on," "such a spot as is the delight of my life."[11] Six months later, at the end of March 1815, her own matchless portrait of village England was complete.

STRICTLY SPEAKING, *Emma* falls outside the compass of this book.[12] A land-locked story, it has no naval content whatsoever. Idyllic and pastoral, its mood of high comedy and good humour is as far from the shadows of war as could be. Coming as it does between *Mansfield Park* and *Persuasion*, *Emma* can be regarded as an interlude, a playful interruption to the naval sequence, a gentle teasing of the sailor brothers with a heroine who has never glimpsed the sea and whose father declares it to be "rarely of use to any body" (*Emma*, 101). Its "use," when this does come up, has nothing to do with Britain's naval strength but belongs to a little side-comedy involving the competing claims of "South End" and Cromer as "sea-bathing places" (*E*, 106)—something

Charles would have enjoyed, since he took his family to Southend in the Summer of 1813. When a "ship" enters the story, it is not one of Britain's "wooden walls" but the answer to a charade clue, "the monarch of the seas!" (*E*, 73).

Nonetheless, despite these apparent disqualifications, *Emma* calls for some discussion here. It is the only novel in which Jane Austen examines the ideas of Englishness and patriotism, values which (we are left to assume) are implicit to the motivation of William Price and Captain Wentworth. For while we hear much in *Mansfield Park* and *Persuasion* about the professional ambitions of these sailors, their appetite for glory and wealth, their zeal and sense of duty, their patriotic sentiments remain unspoken. In *Emma*, however, "patriotism" (*E*, 200) is held up for our inspection and the traditional enmity of England and France is played out in the antipathy between George Knightley, a gentlemanly John Bull, and the Frenchified Frank Churchill. By Jane Austen's time, these national stereotypes were well-established and easily evoked. The tradition of the Frenchified Englishman went back over a hundred years, its origins in Restoration drama; and John Bull, an early eighteenth-century creation, figured prominently in the entertaining wartime commentary provided in popular songs and broadsides and the caricatures of Isaac Cruikshank, Rowlandson and Gillray and a host of minor political cartoonists. These were familiar images, close to hand: John Bull, the archetypal Englishman of bull-dog breed, four-square and solid, cudgel at the ready, a ferocious guardian of English virtues and values and rampantly Francophobic; the *quasi* French-Monsieur Englishman artful, devious, glib and deceitful, a foppish, rootless creature of frivolity and fashion.[13]

Among Jane Austen's contemporaries, the novelist who comes closest to representing these national types in the social sphere is Maria Edgeworth, whose writing she knew and admired. During 1814, while at work on *Emma*, she read *Patronage*, Edgeworth's latest novel, with its Frenchwoman of "vivacity, ease, polish, *tact*, and *esprit de société* ranged against "the solidity of understanding, amiable qualities, domestic tastes, and virtues of an Englishwoman." Or, as Mary Crawford puts it succinctly in *Mansfield Park*, to win her brother in marriage, when "English abilities" have failed, the "address of a French-woman" (*Mansfield Park*, 42) is called for.

Edgeworth draws a clear line between "French manners" and "English morals":

French ease, gayety, and politeness; English sincerity, confidence, and safety [the security that comes from acting wisely].—No *simagrée* [affection, pretence], no *espionage*, no intrigue political or gallant.[14]

The use of French loan-words[15] was enough in itself to suggest that artifice was afoot and Jane Austen herself exploits this device towards the end of *Mansfield Park*, where the odour of sexual scandal hangs in the air. Mary Crawford dismisses her brother's escapade with Maria Bertram as nothing more than "a moment's *etourderie*" (*MP*, 437) (thoughtlessness) and in a newspaper report it becomes "a matrimonial *fracas*" (*MP*, 440).

Patronage also has a contrasting pair of brothers, nicknamed "*French* Clay" ("an Englishman aping a Frenchman") and "*English* Clay" ("a cold, reserved, proud, dull looking man . . . Everything about him is English"),[16] broadly corresponding to the contrast Jane Austen draws between Churchill and Knightley. This is not to suggest any direct influence. By the time Jane Austen came to *Patronage*, *Emma* was already half-written and would anyway have been shaping in her mind since the middle of 1813, when she finished work on *Mansfield Park*. The similarity in theme and characterisation belongs to the long-established tradition of French and English types; and that both Edgeworth and Jane Austen chose to take up the subject of Anglo-French differences at this particular moment is no coincidence. It arises from the historical situation. In prospect was an end to the Long War and the emergence of a peace-time society, circumstances calling for a new understanding of national traditions and identity.

Similarities between Edgeworth and Austen also arise from a common fund of vocabulary and phrasing for this subject. Towards the end of *Emma*, when enlightenment dawns, Emma sees the course of deception which Churchill and Jane Fairfax have practised on Highbury as a "system of secresy and concealment" (*E*, 398), "a system of hypocrisy and deceit,— espionage and treachery," (*E*, 399), summoning up Edgeworth's picture of French "intrigue political or gallant" and with a direct echo in "espionage," a word recently arrived in English and still regarded as heavily French. Through these associations of language, Jane Austen attaches "nationalities" to Knightley and Churchill, a process which begins in chapter 18, the final chapter of volume one. Knightley lectures Emma on Churchill's dereliction, his failure to visit Mr. Weston on the occasion of his second marriage, a "duty" "which a man can always do if he chuses . . . not by manoeuvring and finessing, but by vigour and resolution" (*E*, 146).

According to the *OED*, "manoeuvring" came into English in the 1780s as a term for the tactical disposition and movement of troops and ships. It was only a short step from warfare on land and sea to the battlefield of society and Jane Austen was soon using the word—in *Lady Susan* (*c.* 1793–94) and in her letters and novels—to describe scenes and situations where women scheme and manipulate for advantage, usually in money or marriage. In

1809, *Manoeuvring* gained particular prominence as the title of one of Edgeworth's *Tales of Fashionable Life*. This is the story of the tricks and devices of Mrs. Beaumont, a fortune-hunting, marriage-making mother, its essence echoed in Mary Crawford's view of marriage as "a manoeuvring business" (*E*, 46), a cynicism fostered by her experience of Admiral Crawford's household. However, in Knightley's attack on Churchill, "manoeuvring" stands in a moral vein, as an activity inimical to "duty," to "vigour and resolution," a meaning exactly caught in one of Nelson's letters, where he criticises a Danish commander for quitting his ship in the heat of battle, leaving his men to struggle on: "*Here* was no manoeuvring: *it was* downright fighting, and it was his duty to have shown firmness. . . ."[17]

The Frenchness of Churchill's unmanly behaviour is also signalled by his "finessing," a *finesse* (in Johnson's *Dictionary* treated as a French word) being a trick or stratagem; and Knightley uses the word again towards the end of the novel, representing Churchill as self-deceived, trapped in a web of double-dealing: "[H]is own mind full of intrigue, that he should suspect it in others.—Mystery; Finesse—how they pervert understanding!" (*E*, 446).

The process of linguistic labelling is carried a stage further when Knightley sizes up Churchill's "smooth, plausible manners" with definitions which are explicitly nationalistic:

> our amiable young man can be amiable only in French, not in English. He may be very "aimable," have very good manners, and be very agreeable; but he can have no English delicacy towards the feelings of other people: nothing really amiable about him.
>
> (*E*, 149)

The contrast here is between French veneer, the art of pleasing, the "l'aimable" which Lord Chesterfield so impressed upon his son as a means of social ingratiation, leading to social advancement, and the solid worth of English "really amiable," by Knightley's definition—a meaning lost to us today—a quality of thoughtfulness and consideration for others.[18]

With Churchill's arrival, in volume two, the national contrast is taken further. Somewhat in the mould of Henry Crawford, Churchill is a skilled practitioner of "l'aimable," a man of "gallant" gestures and acts of "gallantry." This is not the "gallantry" of war, with its "gallant" heroes, a language of citation with which the Austens were familiar in the *London Gazette* and the *Naval Chronicle*. Rather, this is the terminology of the dilettante art of courtesies and courtliness, the counters of deception in Churchill's "systems" of "secrecy and concealment," his "Disingenuousness and double-dealing," as Knightley calls it, his "gallantry and trick" (*E*, 348), all this alien to the depths of Surrey. It takes an English word to penetrate the facade. Emma realises that permitting Churchill the freedom "to be gallant" towards herself—this is the French word, accented on the second syllable—"must have had such an appearance as no English word but flirtation could very well describe" (*E*, 368). Whereas Knightley, like his brother, is a man of few words and "nothing of ceremony" (*E*, 57). Their "true English style," the "style" of Stanley greeting Livingstone sixty years later, is not outward display but containment and reserve.[19] They greet one-another laconically with " 'How d'ye do, George?' and 'John, how are you?' burying under a calmness that seemed all but indifference the real attachment which would have led either of them, if requisite, to do every thing for the good of the other" (*E*, 99–100). Knightley's proposal is delivered in a similar manner: "[I]n plain, unaffected, gentleman-like English" (*E*, 448). "Not a gallant man," as Emma observes, but "a very humane one,"[20] and Knightley's loan of his carriage to Miss Bates and Jane Fairfax is, in the same vein, "a case of humanity" and "un-ostentatious kindness" (*E*, 223).

On one remarkable occasion, Jane Austen raises the comedy of the "gallant" Churchill and the ungallant Knightley to a level beyond comedy, transforming Knightley's gesture of "unfinished gallantry" into an expression of love, one of the rare instances where Jane Austen's comic vision joins comedy and tenderness:

> He took her hand;—whether she had not herself made the first motion, she could not say—she might, perhaps, have rather offered it—but he took her hand, pressed it, and certainly was on the point of carrying it to his lips—when, from some fancy or other, he suddenly let it go.—Why he should feel such a scruple, why he should change his mind when it was all but done, she could not perceive.—He would have judged better, she thought, if he had not stopped.—The intention, however, was indubitable; and whether it was that his manners had in general so little gallantry, or however else it happened, but she thought nothing became him more.—
>
> (*E*, 386)

(Jane Austen invites the reader to supply the explanation for Knightley's "unfinished gallantry." Presumably, the thought strikes him that the kissing of hands comes too close to Churchill's repertoire of the "aimable.")

By the end of the story, Knightley's reading of Churchill is confirmed. The secret engagement to Jane Fairfax does indeed call for skilful "manoeuvring and finessing," a ready show of agreeableness towards the citizens of Highbury, and an indifference towards other people's feelings, even, at times, towards Jane Fairfax and Emma. Yet we may wonder that, in chapter 18, on the evidence of Churchill's letter alone, Knightley can show such gusto in attacking someone he has never met; that a report of Churchill's visit to Weymouth—a staid and highly respectable resort, and for that reason favoured by George III over many years for the holidays of the Royal Family—should make him, in Knightley's words, a habitué of one of "the idlest haunts in the kingdom" (*E*, 146).[21] The clue lies in the calculated placing of this scene at the close of volume one, a month ahead of Churchill's arrival. Knightley's scathing remarks are aimed at a creature of his own imagining, a construct (as Emma detects) of his prejudice, itself an entertaining mix of phobias, Francophobia and Frankophobia—a punning that Jane Austen would not object to and which, in its literary mode, *Emma* encourages, as a novel of riddles, conundrums and word-play.[22]

A DEEPER SEARCHING of language is conducted on "patriotism." The word occurs in volume two, chapter six (in modern editions chapter 24), the scene in which Churchill continues to bamboozle Emma, pretending that his stay in Highbury is to honour his father while his real purpose is the pursuit of Jane Fairfax, a deceit in which Churchill uses Emma as his stalking horse. To this end, he asks Emma to give him a guided tour. As they move from place to place—from his father's former house, to the cottage of his wet-nurse, and on to the Crown Inn—Emma brings the conversation round to Jane Fairfax: had he seen "her often at Weymouth?" (*E*, 199). Churchill is caught off guard and plays for time. "At that moment they were approaching Ford's" (already known to us as "the principal woollen-draper, linen-draper, and haberdasher's shop united; the shop first in size and fashion in the place") (*E*, 178), and he takes the opportunity to duck Emma's question, steering the conversation far from Weymouth:

> "Ha! this must be the very shop that every body attends every day of their lives, as my father informs me. He comes to Highbury himself, he says, six days out of the seven, and has always business at Ford's. If it be not inconvenient to you, pray let us go in, that I may prove myself to belong to the place, to be a true citizen of Highbury. I must buy something at Ford's. It will be taking out my freedom.—I dare say they sell gloves."
>
> "Oh! yes, gloves and every thing. I do admire your patriotism. You will be adored in Highbury. You were very popular before you came, because you were Mr. Weston's son—but lay out half-a-guinea at Ford's, and your popularity will stand upon your own virtues."
>
> They went in; and while the sleek, well-tied parcels of "Men's Beavers" and "York Tan" were bringing down and displaying on the counter, he

said—"But I beg your pardon, Miss Woodhouse, you were speaking to me, you were saying something at the very moment of this burst of my *amor patriae*. Do not let me lose it. I assure you the utmost stretch of public fame would not make me amends for the loss of any happiness in private life."

(*E*, 199–200)

For a minute or two, Churchill's diversion works. Emma leaves her question about Jane Fairfax and falls in with his bantering tone. Amused and flattered by his inventive chatter, she imagines that they are playing the same burlesquing game and throws in "patriotism" as her contribution to the joke. But Jane Austen's readers would have seen the joke as double-edged. Everyone remembered Johnson's notorious dismissal of "Patriotism" as "the last refuge of a scoundrel." As Boswell goes on to explain, in the *Life of Johnson* (1791),[23] "[H]e did not mean a real and generous love of our country, but that pretended patriotism which so many, in all ages and countries, have made a cloak for self-interest."[24] (Johnson is said to have had the politician John Wilkes in mind.) This is the very "cloak" in which, with Emma's encouragement, Churchill wraps himself now, posing as an ardent Highburyite. Jane Austen's readers would also remember *The Task* (1785), a greatly admired and much quoted poem, in which Cowper reflected on the benefits of rural life. As to public affairs in the 1780s, he found the "age of virtuous politics is past,"

> Patriots are grown too shrewd to be sincere,
> And we too wise to trust them . . .[25]

a verdict that readers of *Emma* could comfortably endorse, seeing before them a "patriot" Churchill.

Just as they occur in this passage, "patriotism" and "*amor patriae*" (the love of one's country) are found together in the titles of books, pamphlets, poems and sermons, particularly during the period of the Long War when the Volunteers were to be enthused or national sentiments appealed to. But the terms were not wholly synonymous. "Patriotism" carried a strong whiff of political expediency. All the factions, alliances and shades of Whig, Tory and Radical opinion wrapped themselves in the "patriot" banner, from "belligerents," the war-mongers, at one extreme to "peacemongers" at the other. It is a word for which sailors could express a healthy contempt, as we see in the Journal of Captain Francis Beaufort, 1805:

> As for patriotism—ha! ha! that is a thing pretty nearly forgotten in
> this country, indeed the word itself would be equally so like any other

unmeaning symbol or hieroglyphic were it not for a few members of
Parliament who make constant use of it (the word, I mean) and for the
pamphleteers who like long words to fill their columns.[26]

"*Amor patriae*," coming from the classical world, conveyed a purer air.
One tradition stems from Ovid. Exiled from Rome to the shores of the
Black Sea, the poet wrote of his "amor patriae ratione valentior" (a love of
my country stronger than reason itself).[27] This was Ovid's impassioned
response to a formal *consolatio* from his friend Rufinus, who argued that he
should resign himself and make the best of his situation. Cowper alludes to
this tradition in describing an exile in modern times:

> Methinks, I see thee straying on the beach,
> And asking of the surge that bathes thy foot
> If ever it has wash'd our distant shore.
> I see thee weep, and thine are honest tears,
> A patriot's for his country . . .[28]

In Canto Sixth of *The Lay of the Last Minstrel* (1805) Scott continued the Ovidian
line, elaborating it into a poetical anathema, a ringing curse of high drama
and sounding rhetoric:

> Breathes there the man, with soul so dead,
> Who never to himself hath said,
>   This is my own, my native land!
> Whose heart hath ne'er within him burn'd,
> As home his footsteps he hath turn'd,
>   From wandering on a foreign strand!
> If such there breathe, go, mark him well;
> For him no Minstrel raptures swell;
> High though his titles, proud his name,
> Boundless his wealth as wish can claim;
> Despite those titles, power, and pelf,
> The wretch, concentred all in self,
> Living, shall forfeit fair renown,
> And, doubly dying, shall go down
> To the vile dust, from whence he sprung,
> Unwept, unhonour'd, and unsung.

Richard Lovell Edgeworth used this passage to illustrate "The love of our country" in the chapter "On Military and Naval Education" in his well-known *Essays on Professional Education.*[29]

The Lay was very popular, by 1814 in its twelfth edition, and so well known that Edgeworth's novelist daughter Maria could float fourteen of these melodious lines, almost verbatim into the mind of Caroline Percy, one of the heroines of *Patronage*, as her unspoken riposte to some offensively unpatriotic comments from "*French* Clay," in which he declares his indifference "whether England be called England or France . . . what is country—or, as people term it, their native land?"[30]

If we see the Ovidian *amor patriae* as a nostalgic, sentimental or romantic tradition, a very different heritage, political in character, stems from book 6 of the *Aeneid*. Here, Virgil parades the early heroes of Rome. Among them is L. Junius Brutus, one of the founders of the Roman Republic. His sons plotted to restore the last King, the tyrant Tarquin the Proud, and were brought before Brutus, charged with treason. Placing country before family, Brutus sentenced them to death. Virgil's final comment (voiced through Anchises) makes the point of the story: "[V]incit amor patriae laudumque immensa cupido" (the love of country and the boundless passion for renown will prevail).[31] This was regarded as one of the most telling episodes in the early Republic. Replete with human drama, it carried a powerful moral for modern times. It was held up as a shining example of civic probity, the triumph of public good over private interest and was a set-piece for schoolboy verse-exercises and for memorising and declamation. Jane Austen would have heard the passage many times, repeated by her brothers and by her father's pupils at Steventon Rectory. Even youngsters at sea were reading Virgil under the tutelage of educated Chaplains. In the *Impetueux* (74), blockading Brest in 1804, Coleridge's young nephew Bernard was reading his two hundred lines of Virgil a day to the ship's Chaplain.[32]

Like any educated man, Churchill knows his Virgil too.[33] Taking his lead from Emma's joke about "patriotism," he can feel confident of not offending her in pushing the joke further, with a "burst" of Virgilian "*amor patriae*" which parodies the moral, turning it inside out.[34] As a customer at Ford's, he can "prove" himself "to be a true citizen of Highbury" and take out his "freedom" (his legal qualification to enjoy the ancient rights of citizenship). On the other hand, he assures Emma, he is not a second Brutus: "[T]he utmost stretch of public fame would not make amends for the loss of any happiness in private life" (*E*, 200). In this roundabout way, Churchill tells Emma he is now ready (having had time to prepare an answer) to turn aside from the business of patriotic shopping and attend to her original question about his contact with Jane Fairfax at Weymouth. What follows is yet more masterly evasiveness and obfuscation as Emma is led further into his "system of hypocrisy and deceit" and the comedy of deception deepens.

IN IDENTIFYING the particular quality of Knightley's patriotism, our best guide is Cobbett's *Rural Rides*, a collection of the reports he made in the 1820s from journeys undertaken to enquire into the state of the countryside.[35] He observed the signs of economic and social decline and the plight of the farming communities from county to county. Cobbett associated the rising levels of agricultural poverty and discontent with the arrival over the last twenty or thirty years of a new breed of land-owner, the war-profiteers (as he saw them) who were now displacing the traditional squirearchy, what he described as

> a resident *native* gentry, attached to the soil, known to every farmer and labourer from their childhood, frequently mixing with them in those pursuits where all artificial distinctions are lost, practising hospitality without ceremony, from habit and not on calculation. . . .

This group he compared with the new class of *arriviste* and absentee land-owners:

> [A] gentry, only now-and-then residing at all, having no relish for country-delights, foreign in their manners, distant and haughty in their behaviour, looking to the soil only for its rents, viewing it as a mere object of speculation, unacquainted with its cultivators, despising them and their pursuits, and relying, for influence, not upon the good will of the vicinage, but upon the dread of their power. The war and paper-system [bank notes and bonds] has brought in nabobs, negro-drivers, generals, admirals, governors, commissaries, contractors, pensioners, sinecurists, commissioners, loan-jobbers, lottery-dealers, bankers, stock-jobbers; not to mention the long and *black list* in gowns and three-tailed wigs. You can see but few good houses not in possession of one or the other of these. These, with the parsons, are now the magistrates.[36]

It may seem odd that Cobbett should include Generals and Admirals on his black list. But he saw "the labouring classes" as carrying the burden, paying "the whole of the expenses of the Knights of Waterloo, and of the other heroes of the war," these gallant and high-ranking veterans enjoying their pensions, pay, lump sums and annuities, with "wives and children . . . to be pensioned, after the death of the heroes themselves"—a memorable instance being the lavish distribution of grants, annuities, and pensions to the Nelson family in 1806, with the enormous lump sum of £90,000 going to Nelson's elder brother to purchase an estate worthy of his new Earldom.[37]

Cobbett would have hailed Knightley as a paragon, the living embodiment of his "resident *native* gentry" and in Donwell Abbey, set in its estate, he would have identified a precious remnant, one of those "few" remaining "good houses." Knightley is close to his tenants, for the parish of Highbury lies within the Donwell property. He is permanently "resident," a fixture of the neighbourhood: in Marilyn Butler's words, "[S]een in the novel much more continuously than he is heard":

> In the middle distance he is everywhere—conferring with Mr. Elton about parish affairs, or with Robert Martin about farming; detected sending apples to Miss Bates, or asking for her errands when he rides to Kingston. Highbury gatherings are not complete without him; unlike Emma, he is always present when the Coles or Eltons entertain.[38]

A visit to London on business brings him hurrying back to "his farm, and his sheep, and his library, and all the parish to manage" (*E*, 225). Running "the home-farm at Donwell" (*E*, 100), his everyday concerns are those of Cobbett's ideal, a proprietor "attached to the soil." His horses are for use on the farm, rarely to draw a carriage. He is ready to lecture Harriet Smith on "modes of agriculture," (*E*, 361), to discuss with Robert Martin "shows of cattle" and "new drills" (*E*, 473) and to speak "as a farmer" to his brother, reporting to John in fine detail "what every field was to bear next year . . . the plan of a drain, the change of a fence, the felling of a tree, and the destination of every acre for wheat, turnips or spring corn" (*E*, 100). Jane Austen's readers would recognise this as the language of agricultural improvement, of scientific farming, a professionalism regarded as fashionable and public-spirited under the royal patronage of "Farmer" George and officially sponsored by the Board of Agriculture.[39] To encourage self-sufficiency in the country's war-time food supplies, the Board commissioned a series of Agricultural Reports surveying farming practice county-by-county. The Report on Surrey, first published in 1809, with a revised edition in 1813, picks out land-owners like Knightley for special praise: "[S]everal of the most considerable and respectable landed proprietors," those who "reside generally on their estates" and "introduce and patronise improvements have tended much to advance the agriculture of Surrey."[40] The tenant at Abbey-Mill Farm, Robert Martin, is an educated yeoman-farmer who shares Knightley's progressive views and, pointedly, Jane Austen makes him a reader of the Agricultural Reports (*E*, 29).[41]

The Surrey Report also remarked on the attractions of the country, its healthy "climate" and "the general beauty of its scenery." It was these recommendations, together with its proximity to London, which made Surrey such a desirable location "for the settlement" of "commercial men" who had "made their fortunes." The process was familiar. In the face of a "great demand for landed property of small extent," the few large estates were being "broken down."[42] Just as Cobbett and others observed, "the resident *native* gentry" surrendered to the power of money; in Repton's bitter comment, "the ancient hereditary gentlemen" joined in the "eager pursuit of gain."[43] Only sixteen miles from London (Jane Austen gives us this precise distance), in other hands Donwell would be an estate under threat. But Knightley is loyal to his heritage, intends that his patrimony should be passed on intact. Sensitive to the interests of the villagers, with their long-established common rights, he chooses not even to re-route a path running across "the home meadows . . . if it were to be the means of inconvenience to the Highbury people" (*E*, 106), a public-spiritedness which marks him out at the very time when land-owners were most heavily engaged in promoting acts of enclosure and blocking ancient rights-of-way.[44] Tall paling fences were raised, "not to confine the deer but to exclude mankind," Repton observed.[45] Ferocious notice boards became a feature of the country scene: "Spring guns and steel traps set here." Travellers became trespassers. But not in Knightley's little corner of Surrey. Here, the "rage for improvements" (to borrow the invective of *Rural Rides*) is contained and the old ways of paternalism and liberality prevail.[46] How high a value Jane Austen placed on these qualities we can judge from *Pride and Prejudice*, where the housekeeper's praise of Darcy at Pemberley—"[T]he best landlord, and the best master . . . that ever lived . . . affable to the poor," a man to whom "his tenants" give a "good name"—warms Elizabeth's heart towards him (*PP*, 249). There is, however, an important difference. In *Pride and Prejudice*, Jane Austen does no more than name the qualities: in *Emma*, we glimpse the detail of what it actually means to be a landowner attached to his heritage and concerned with the welfare of his neighbourhood.

Jane Austen continues this process in the description of Donwell Abbey and its grounds. Long in the family, it is the product of generations of care. Its farming may be up-to-date. But neither the craze for landscape "improvement" nor the pursuit of money has been allowed to ruin the estate. Retaining the formal style of the late seventeenth and early eighteenth century, it boasts an unspoilt "abundance of timber in rows and avenues which neither fashion nor extravagance had rooted up" (*E*, 358). We are reminded of Rushworth's ambitions in *Mansfield Park*. Attracted by Repton's style of landscaping, he plans to improve "the prospect" at Sotherton, opening up its views by removing the "avenue" (*MP*, 55), a scheme that horrifies Fanny Price, stirring her to invoke the famous lines from Cowper: "Ye fallen avenues, once more I mourn your fate unmerited" (*MP*, 56).[47] But no such modernisation has disturbed the grounds of Donwell; they boast "all the old neglect of prospect." And the Abbey itself, ancient and unchanged, remains in "its suitable, becoming, characteristic situation, low and sheltered" (*E*, 358).

"Characteristic"/"character" is a key term for practitioners of the picturesque, whether travellers, amateur artists or landscape gardeners. According to William Gilpin, the leading authority, the "characteristic" "situation" for an abbey, "intended for meditation," is to be "hid in the sequestered vale," just as Donwell is.[48] Unlike General Tilney's Abbey at Northanger, lavishly modernised and equipped with the very latest in domestic technology, Knightley's Donwell is, in the manner of ancient buildings, unshowy and lived-in,

> rambling and irregular, with many comfortable and one or two handsome rooms.—It was just what it ought to be, and it looked what is was— and Emma felt an increasing respect for it, as the residence of a family of such true gentility, untainted in blood and understanding.
>
> (*E*, 358)

Owner and building alike, both are true to themselves and transparently and self-evidently "right." As Jonathan Bate comments:

> A place that was once consecrated to the spiritual good life, to the vertical relationship between humankind and God, it is now consecrated to the social good life: it has become an emblem of productive and harmonious rural being. Instead of being drawn upward to the heavens, the eye looks out horizontally to the well-ordered environment.[49]

Emma's impressions are reinforced by the wider "view" across the valley, towards the curve of the river and Abbey-Mill Farm, "favourably placed and sheltered,"

> with all its appendages of prosperity and beauty, its rich pastures, spreading flocks, orchard in blossom, and light column of smoke ascending.
>
> (*E*, 360)

No hint of social distress or disorder here, the scene is harmonious and satisfying, a consort of man and nature, a balance of "prosperity" and "beauty," a scene typically, and, in the voice of Jane Austen, emphatically "English," a "view" to be contemplated and reflected upon, providing food for thought,

> a sweet view—sweet to the eye and the mind. English verdure, English culture, English comfort, seen under a sun bright, without being oppressive.
>
> (*E*, 360)

The "culture" in question is neither abstract nor fashionable; patriotically weighted, it is the cultivation of *agriculture*, the land-use and practical improvement so much encouraged during the French wars; and "comfort" comprehends such workaday features as good soil, a ready water-supply and fish-ponds ("the old Abbey fish-ponds" remain) for the kitchens, shelter from the wind and weather (*E*, 361); in short, as Repton explains, "comfort" is for those, like the Knightleys past and present, "willing to sacrifice the beauty of prospect for the more solid and permanent advantages of habitable convenience."[50] Accordingly, while "fashion" dictates that the fruit and kitchen-gardens be put at a distance from the house, at Donwell they remain comfortably adjacent and the "pleasure grounds" are relegated to a further remove (*E*, 360).

There is an aesthetic dimension too; not Repton's "beauty of prospect" but Gilpin's contention—here reaffirmed by Jane Austen—that England was just as worthy of painting as Italy. Occasionally, Gilpin would see aspects of Europe in English views. "The whole scene makes a good Alpine picture,"[51] he said, looking towards Box Hill (seven miles from Highbury). But his picturesque tours enumerate the qualities of scene which are distinctively English, the homeland's atmospheric skies and shadowed landscapes much to be preferred by the water-colourist to the harsh Italian light. Hence Jane Austen's sun "bright, without being oppressive." Within the Donwell demesne, Abbey-Mill Farm possesses a vernacular charm, its evocative "column of smoke ascending"—signifying rural peace, prosperity and contentment—found in countless countryside drawings and paintings of the Constable school. As Gilpin pointed out, unlike "the vast tracts on the continent," "England . . . is a country only on a small scale" and "more suited to human vision."[52] So while fashionable chatter was of European landscapes and landscapists—Salvator Rosa for "wildness," Claude for "softness," Poussin for "majesty"—the English painter's "love of locality" was, in the words of Edward Dayes (an aesthetic "Tourist" in the line of Gilpin), to be applauded as an expression of "amor patriae,"[53] an affectionate appreciation of one's native land for which Jane Austen's "sweet view" is the descriptive and ideological counterpart.

The view to be cherished is the view at home, familiar and well-loved. Jane Austen's patriotic intent is undisguised. Who could remain unaffected by this "English" scene? Frank Churchill, for one. Within a few pages, he declares himself "sick of England"; "[W]ould leave it tomorrow, if I could," he confides to Emma, promising her, indifferently, his souvenirs of a European visit: his sketches of "Swisserland" "to look at—or my tour to read—or my poem" (E, 364—65). These were the fashionable trophies, the treasured mementoes, glimpsing the sublime in Alpine vistas, in the wonder of glaciers and the grandeur of mountain peaks and passes, these foreign sights preferred in their "novelty" to the comfortable and undramatic presence of the "English" scene.[54]

But the promise of these gifts leaves Emma unmoved. They were now common currency. By the end of 1814, it was reported: "Already have myriads of Englishmen spread themselves on the continent of Europe."[55] Every traveller's album held amateur sketches and amateur poems; as for European tours, there were more than enough, an inundation, a complaint echoed by the author of Alpine Sketches (1814) at the sight of "Booksellers' windows . . . already crowded with Wanderings, Trips, Tours, Visits, Sketches, and Guides."[56]

Among the earliest readers of Emma Mrs. Cage was someone after Jane's heart, "delighted" with all the characters, she picked out Miss Bates as "incomparable" and found herself transported, "[A]t Highbury all day, & I can't help feeling I have just got into a new set of acquaintance" (Minor Works, 439). But above all, there was the enthusiasm of her sailor brothers, both of whom put Emma at the top of their list. Francis, his judicious views given pride of place at the head of the "Opinions" Jane gathered from her family and friends, "liked it extremely, observing that though there might be more Wit in P. & P.—& an higher Morality in M. P.—yet altogether, on account of its peculiar air of Nature throughout, he preferred it to either" (MW, 436).[57] While Francis was able to enjoy Emma with his family in their cottage at Alton, Charles was in the Mediterranean slowly making his way home, following the loss of the Phoenix. He was in low spirits, caught up (as his diary records) in "sad & melancholy reflections," dreaming "of my lost & ever lamented Fanny and of our poor little ones!"[58] He yearned for England. His copy of Emma (he wrote to Jane) "arrived in time to a moment. I am delighted with her, more so I think than even with my favourite Pride

& *Prejudice*, reading it "three times" during the passage home (*MW*, 439). "Three times" out of respect and affection for his sister's gift, no doubt. But "three times" also for its evocation of village England in all its locality and parochialism, the flavour of its characters and community, things which must have meant so much to a sailor on the high seas. Did Jane Austen have this in mind herself? On learning that Charles, "Poor dear Fellow!," had received "not a Present!" on his birthday in June 1815, she joked about sending him "all the twelve copies" of *Emma* "which were to have been dispersed among my near Connections—beginning with the P.R. & ending with Countess Morley."[59] If any gift could bring comfort to her brother in his remote situation, still grieving the death of his beloved wife, and carry the spirit of the English scene and English life, it was this. Highbury, to borrow the words of Herman Melville, "is not down on any map; true places never are."[60]

Afterword

[A] sweet view—sweet to the eye and the mind. English verdure, English culture, English comfort, seen under a sun bright, without being oppressive.

Emma, 360

Here, Jane Austen insists upon the Englishness of the "view," its qualities observed in "the mind" as well as by "the eye," under an illuminating sun which is "bright" but not "oppressive." This, as Jonathan Bate reminds us, is the "temperate climate" of a "liberal society" and a further chapter on *Emma* would treat the political significance of inherited estates, and the eighteenth- and nineteenth-century conventions of discourse in prose and poetry relating features of the landscape and property to the moral and political state of the nation. Such geopolitical ideas were sharpened at the time of the French Revolution which threw into relief values of rootedness, tradition, ancient rights, patronage, hierarchy, etc., identified as being quintessentially English and epitomised in Donwell, both the Abbey itself and its estate.[61] What the French had to say about *Emma*'s display of English ways and values could make a chapter on its own. Enough to say that the novel's national flavour, if not its nationalism, was registered immediately in the very title of the first translation, published in Paris as early as 1816: *La Nouvelle Emma, ou les Caractères anglais du siècle* (*Nouvelle* to distinguish it from an existing French *Emma* popular for twenty years and more). The emphasis of the title is to advertise the novel as a parade of characters, emphatically English characters, and of the post-Napoleonic present day.

Notes

1. Quoted in Jack Simmons, *Southey* (London: Collins, 1945), 140.

2. Ibid., 143.

3. Robert Southey, *The Life of Nelson* (1813) (London: Dent, 1906), 108.

4. Like Croker, Rickman bridged the worlds of literature and politics. A familiar figure in the Southey-Coleridge-Wordsworth circle, he was Clerk to the Speaker of the House of Commons.

5. *The Life and Correspondence of Robert Southey*, ed. Charles Cuthbert Southey, 6 vols. (London: 1849–50), IV, 52.

6. Ibid., IV, 53.

7. Ibid., IV, 54.

8. *New Letters of Robert Southey*, ed. Kenneth Curry, 2 vols. (New York: Columbia University Press, 1965), II, 92.

9. Diary entry 8 April 1814 (quoted in *Claire Tomalin, Jane Austen: A Life* (London: Viking, 1997), 242.

10. Letter to Cassandra, 23 June 1814, *Jane Austen's Letters*, 264.

11. Letter to Anna Austen, 9 September 1814, *Jane Austen's Letters*, 275.

12. i.e., *Jane Austen and the Navy* (2000). I have not removed this reference since the general remarks made about *Emma* in this and the following paragraph take some of their point from the context of this essay that originally stood as a chapter in a book whose focus was upon the British Navy, and which came between chapters on Austen's naval novels, *Mansfield Park* and *Persuasion*.

13. See Stella Cottrell, "The Devil on Two Sticks: Franco-Phobia in 1803," in *Patriotism: The Making and Unmaking of British National Identity*, ed. Raphael Samuel, 3 vols. (London: Routledge, 1989); Ward Hellstrom, "Francophobia in *Emma*," *Studies in English Literature*, 5 (1965), 606–17; Jeannine Surel, "John Bull" in *Patriotism*, ed. Raphael Samuel (1989); Thomas Wright, *Caricature History of the Georges*, rev. ed. (London, 1867).

14. Maria Edgeworth, *Patronage* (1814), ed. Eva Figes (London: Pandora, 1986), 159.

15. By the time of *Emma*, firm and authoritative lines of resistance against the French intrusion had been laid down by George Campbell and Hugh Blair, formulators of the so-called New Rhetoric. The defence of the English language is clearly established in a work which became the standard text-book, Campbell's *Philosophy of Rhetoric* (1776). Here, the reader is warned against a "tribe of barbarism": "an inundation of foreign words" which leaves "our language" in great danger of "being overwhelmed," words "which are obtruded on it merely through a licentious

affectation of novelty" (i. 413). Amongst Campbell's examples is *"aimable* for *amiable,"* words which Austen brings under critical scrutiny in *Emma.* Campbell also cites "eclaircissement" (which Austen uses in *Lady Susan*): such words "transplanted into another language . . . look rather like strays. . . . They are very much in the condition of exiles, who, having been driven from their families, relations, and friends, are compelled to take refuge in a country where there is not a single person with whom they can claim a connexion, either by blood or by alliance" (i. 414–15).

16. Alfred Percy's unflattering description to his sister Caroline, *Patronage,* 301–2.

17. Letter of 22 April 1801, Nicholas Harris Nicolas, *Dispatches and Letters of Vice-Admiral Lord Viscount Nelson,* 7 vols. (London, 1844–1846), IV, 345.

18. I have not come across any discussion of these particular French and English cognates contemporary with Jane Austen. But doubtless such discussions did go on, since it was part of the categorising spirit of the age to examine and define synonyms and close synonyms, a verbal interest captured by Jane Austen in the titles of *Sense and Sensibility, Pride and Prejudice* and *Persuasion,* where the novels provide a dramatisation of these heavily nuanced terms. Going by Hazlitt's remarks in *Tate's Magazine,* July 1839, on "the loftier English sense" of "amiable," the difference in moral weight between "amiable" and *"aimable"* had long been a matter of comment. Roger Gard offers an example of "amiable" from Maria Edgeworth's *Ormond* (1817) (Gard, 1992, 242).

19. This "style" had various manifestations. John Wilson Croker, the Secretary to the Admiralty, used it in Parliament. Defending the Ministry's handling of the 1812 War with America, he explained that "the British Government send orders to their naval officers, not couched in doubtful terms, but in the plain good old English style, that as the American government had assumed a menacing attitude, they should put in force their standing orders to sink, burn, and destroy their enemy's ships" (*Hansard,* 18 February 1813, col. 1045).

20. Readers of Southey's *Nelson* would remember this word from the final chapter, where it is pronounced as one of the hero's greatest attributes, an aspect of his selfless patriotism: "All men know that his heart was as humane as it was fearless; that there was not in his nature the slightest alloy of selfishness or cupidity; but with perfect and entire devotion, he served his country with all his heart, and with all his soul, and with all his strength; and, therefore, they loved him as truly and fervently as he loved England" (244–45). On the morning of Trafalgar, his prayer was that "humanity after victory" should be "the predominant feature in the British fleet!" (251).

21. When Cassandra visited Weymouth in 1804, hoping to catch sight of the Royal Family, she could report neither idleness nor the dissipation of Brighton;

nothing worse than that there was "no Ice" in the town (Jane's letter of 14 September 1804, *Jane Austen: Letters*, 92).

22. Well discussed in Fiona Stafford's Introduction to the Penguin Classics edition of *Emma* (London: Penguin, 1996).

23. Jane Austen writes to Cassandra of the purchase of the *Life* and "Cowper's works" (probably the 6th edition of the poems, 1797, or the new edition, 1798). (Letter of 25 November 1798, *Letters*, 22). Moreover, we know from Henry Austen that his sister's "favourite moral writers were Johnson in prose, and Cowper in verse." "Biographical Notice," (*Northanger Abbey* and *Persuasion*, 7).

24. Entry for 7 April 1775, *Boswell's Life of Johnson*, ed. G. B. Hill and L. F. Powell, 6 vols. (Oxford: Clarendon Press, 1934–64), II, 348

25. *The Task* (1785), Book V, 495–6.

26. Alfred Friendly, *Beaufort of the Admiralty: The Life of Sir Francis Beaufort* (London: Hutchinson, 1977), 139.

27. *Epistulae ex Ponto*, i. 3. 29.

28. *The Task*, Book I, 654–8.

29. Richard Lovell Edgeworth, *Essays on Professional Education* (1808), 2nd ed. (London, 1812), 141.

30. Edgeworth, *Patronage*, III, 128.

31. *Aeneid*, VI, 823.

32. Bernard John Seymour, Lord Coleridge, *The Story of Devonshire House* (London: privately printed, 1904).

33. Brutus's story was common knowledge amongst the educated. Chapter XII of *Patriotism; or The Love of our Country: An Essay . . . Dedicated to the Volunteers of the United Kingdom* by William Friend (1804), entitled "The trial of a son for treason—Patriotism of a father," treats the story as being so familiar as to require no names.

34. In *Waverley* (1814), Scott was similarly prepared to place *amor patriae* in a half-ironic context, putting the Latin tag in the mouth of the Baron of Bradwardine, an honorable Scots patriot with a pedantic taste for legal jargon and classical quotation (iii. 24, 335).

35. The first edition of *Rural Rides* (1830) collected Cobbett's contributions to the *Political Register*, 1822–26; the second edition, 1853, added further tours.

36. Entry for 21 November, 1821, William Cobbett, *Rural Rides*, ed. J. P. Cobbett (1853) (London: Dent, 1912), 38.

37. 8 August 1823, ibid., 209.

38. Marilyn Butler, *Jane Austen and the War of Ideas* (Oxford: Clarendon Press, 1975), 272.

39. Established in August 1793, the Board was set up to encourage scientific farming, e.g., stockbreeding, crop-rotation and manuring, machinery for seed-drilling, drainage systems, etc.

40. William Stevenson, *General View of the Agriculture of the County of Surrey* (1809), rev. ed. (London, 1813).

41. See B. C. Southam, "Robert Martin and the Agricultural Reports," *Jane Austen Society Report* (1971), 9–11.

42. Stevenson, *General View of Agriculture*, 73–74.

43. Humphrey Repton, *Fragments on the Theory and Practice of Landscape Gardening* (London, 1816), 192.

44. Parliamentary enclosures came in two bursts: in the 1760s and '70s and during the war, this second phase peaking in 1812–14.

45. Repton, 191.

46. *Cobbett*, ed. George Woodcock (Harmondsworth: Penguin, 1967), 122, 139, etc.

47. *The Task*, Book I, 338–9.

48. William Gilpin, *Observations on the River Wye* (London, 1782).

49. Jonathan Bate, "Culture and Environment from Austen to Hardy," *New Literary History*, 30, no. 3. (1999), 545. Jonathan Bate provides a valuable discussion of landscape and culture in Jane Austen in *The Song of the Earth* (London: Picador, 2000), see especially 5–13, 130–1.

50. Humphrey Repton, *An Enquiry into Changes of Taste in Landscape Gardening* (London, 1806).

51. William Gilpin, *Observations on the Western Parts of England* (1798), 2nd. ed. (London, 1808), 27.

52. Ibid., 37.

53. Edward Dayes, *A Pictorial Tour Through the Principal Parts of Yorkshire and Derbyshire* (London, 1805), 2, 268.

54. Henry Coxe, *The Traveller's Guide to Switzerland* (London, 1816), iii: "*novelty* is presented at every step."

55. *Crosby's Gentlemen's Merchants' and Tradesmen's complete Pocket-Book and Journal for the Year 1815* (London, 1815), "On the Peace," 3.

56. [George Wilson Bridges], *A Member of the University of Oxford, Alpine Sketches, Comprised in a Short Tour . . . Switzerland in 1814* (London, 1814), v.

57. "Opinions of *Emma*," reprinted in this casebook, 39.

58. National Maritime Museum, Greenwich, MS AUS/106; diary entries for 28 April and 8 May 1816.

59. Letter to Cassandra, 26 November, 1815, *Jane Austen's Letters*, 302.

60. Melville's words for the island of Kokovoko, Queequeg's home, at the opening to chapter 12 of *Moby Dick*.

61. For recent scholarly discussion see particularly, Nigel Everett, *The Tory View of Landscape* (New Haven, Conn.: Yale University Press, 1994); Timothy Fulford, *Landscape, Liberty and Authority: Poetry, Criticism and Politics from Thomson to Wordsowrth*

(Cambridge: Cambridge University Press, 1996); Jonathan Bate, *The Song of the Earth*; Elizabeth K. Helmsinger, *Rural Scenes and National Representation: Britain, 1815–1850* (Princeton, N.J.: Princeton University Press, 1997); John Dixon Hunt, *Gardens and the Picturesque* (Cambridge, Mass.: M. I. T. Press, 1992); Tom Williamson and Liz Bellamy, *Property and Landscape: A Social History of Land Ownership and the English Countryside* (London: George Philip, 1987).

Jane Austen, *Emma*, and
the Impact of Form

FRANCES FERGUSON

❖   ❖   ❖

O NE OF THE CRITICISMS LEVELED at formalist criticism is that it
claims to be a universal method but that its practice belies those claims.
Skeptical commentators on the New Criticism have regularly conceded its
effectiveness with a variety of poetic texts and have granted that a Cleanth
Brooks might have had a few useful things to say about the poetry of well-
wrought urns and other similarly small and obviously formed objects, but
they have at the same time suggested that formalism was out of its depths
when it tried to deal with prose. The looseness, bagginess, and monstrosity
of the novel, they have said, were more than formalism could swallow.[1]

   This dissatisfaction with formalist criticism's purchase on the novel is
especially striking because many Russian formalists—including Shklovsky,
Propp, and Bakhtin—took the novel and the tale as their special projects.
How are we to understand the charge that they somehow failed to deal
with the novel when their criticism occupied itself with the novel and
fictional narratives more often than not? One explanation is that some
Russian formalists, Shklovsky in particular, treated language as if its highest
form were poetry, understood as an intense figurativeness rather than an
overarching formal structure. When Shklovsky identified poetry and prose
as the twin poles of literary language, poetry could be said to appear in

novels whenever one released the surprise lurking in language. "Defamiliarization" meant that the novel could be infused with such poetic moments and, indeed, that the very success of a novel at achieving such "estrangement" seemed to militate against a consciousness of the novel as a long prose narrative.[2] Shklovskian formalism's ability to uncover the poetic in the novel came to appear as a denigration of the prosaic and quotidian in the novel. By contrast, Propp's account of narrative, based on the anonymous prose of the folktale, stressed the relationship between a whole narrative action and its parts, so that issues of sequence and variation loomed large. Propp's formalism explicitly argued that the anonymity of the folktale's authorship—the sense that anyone and everyone in a community had had a role in the tale's development and preservation—applied to the agents of the tales themselves: agency became such a capacious and formally empty notion that one no longer needed human actors or characters to achieve it; animals and pots and kettles could carry the narrative action as well as a human could.[3] Action, in other words, displaced character, and any sense of characterological depth looked misplaced in an analysis in which both animals and inanimate objects might play active roles.

This essay argues that what formalist criticism has missed in the novel is character and, indeed, that the criticism developed in response to Foucault's work has been formalist not only in its way of identifying discourses but also in its efforts to dispatch character to the shadows. In his classic Foucauldian study *The Novel and the Police* and even in his earlier *Narrative and Its Discontents*, for example, D. A. Miller argues that the novel's self-reflexive operations that give readers the sense of entering a character's consciousness are discursive structures rather than the products of individual consciousness.[4] Discursive regimes, that is, become the pots and kettles of Proppian analysis, the actors that make it clear that activity in no way requires actual persons. Insofar as self-consciousness is identified with policing, the project of inventorying and distribution that Adam Smith describes as a basic function of civil society, self-consciousness does not provide an independent standpoint from which to judge one's society but is instead one of that society's most flexible and effective tools.

As a critique of the techniques of self-reflection that have been formalized in the social sciences, Foucauldian criticism found a new set of grounds on which to eliminate character. It seized on that peculiar novelistic formal invention—*style indirect libre*, also known as "free indirect style" or represented speech and thought—in such a way as to stunt the force of its identifiability as a form. Since I believe that free indirect style is the novel's one and only formal contribution to literature, this essay attempts to explain precisely what that contribution is and what its consequences are. The difficulties may seem to begin with the term itself, which appears to be associated with the unanalyzable notion of style rather than with the more substantial notion of representable form. Style exploits the allusive capacities of the novel or any other verbal medium and its ability to place itself in various genealogical relations with other novels, plays, and poems; style involves all of the things about a novel that prompt literary interpretation and that sometimes approach the palpability of form. With any analysis of a novel from a stylistic point of view, a critic may claim that certain chapters count as distinct and recognizable units (as in Mark Schorer's account of *Emma*), but in the process the critic always assumes that the recognition of the units is very much part of the interpretive work and must be argued for as a critical insight rather than taken as a formal given, as the recognition of the octave and sestet of a sonnet would be.[5]

In calling attention to the question of literary form, I do not mean to suggest that formal devices are formal insofar as they are always being recognized. Obviously, people read sonnets before they know that there are characteristic ways of dividing them up, and their inattention to the octave and sestet does not count as latent knowledge. Before they are conscious of the value of such formal divisions, their impressions of turns and groupings in the sonnet are exactly on a par with the perceived groupings of chapters in a novel; a critic always argues for them as conceptual rather than formal divisions. But the statement that a sonnet contains an octave and a sestet is a formal claim to exactly the same degree as it takes itself to be unimpeachable and past all debate. Even if you failed to notice that the sonnet that Romeo and Juliet speak between them was a sonnet the first time you read Shakespeare's play, you would be able to recognize it as such from the moment that someone pointed it out to you. While you might also want to argue that the conceptual work of the sonnet echoed its formal procedures, much as the sound might echo the sense, you would not need to rely on either a conceptual or an acoustic backup to prove that the sonnet remained a sonnet. It could be said to be formally achieved, in that it would not disappear simply because you were not attending to it. It could regularly be found, pointed out, or returned to, and the sense of its availability would not rest on agreements about its meaning.

TO SUGGEST THAT formalism works in a sonnet the way free indirect style works in novelistic prose is merely to argue, in the first place, that free indirect style is just as formal as any formal feature of poetry and, in the second, that criticism has habitually missed this fact in such a way as to represent it in conceptual rather than formal terms, as if it were a stylistic matter. Indeed, ideological or discursive criticism has consistently treated free indirect style as an example of what I have called the stylistic as opposed to the formal. Such criticism claims that free indirect style is yet another aspect of the deeply conceptual link between individuals and discursive regimes: since certain ideas or ways of proceeding are widely available to members of a general population, the ideas themselves come to have such a strong existence that they effectively eliminate the particularity of their individual agents or operators. Ideological criticism, that is, arises from the classic social-scientific assumption that one can learn something about individual persons' situations by continually comparing them with an aggregative account, inasmuch as the individual and the aggregate are essentially smaller and larger versions of one another. While this body of criticism emphasizes that persons are necessary to operate the tissue of aggregative thought, it also implies the equality, or at least the equivalence, of persons by insisting on the radical interchangeability of all members of a class. The brilliance of ideological criticism, particularly in its supple Foucauldian version, is that it has an answer to the question of the relationship between the social system and the individual. Whereas apparent deviations from social convention might once have looked like a challenge to the society that produced them, Foucault made it clear how unusual it was for persons to challenge their society radically, because the society—conceived as an implicit system—spoke and so made it all but inevitable that anyone would offer a fairly recognizable response. If power came from everywhere, the system of power would ultimately reveal our places in it to us. Individual persons might be rebellious or exceptional or noncompliant in the moment, but these moments would themselves come to look exceptional or more apparent than real, instances not of rebellion but of conventional deviation.

Casey Finch and Peter Bowen, in their fine essay " 'The Tittle-Tattle of Highbury': Gossip and Free Indirect Style in *Emma*," provide an excellent example of the critical stance I want to identify. In their view, "the development in Austen's hands of free indirect style marks a crucial moment in the history of novelistic technique in which narrative authority is seemingly elided, ostensibly giving way to what Flaubert called a transparent style in which the author is 'everywhere felt, but never seen.' "[6] The "very force of free indirect style is the force of gossip because both "function as forms par excellence of surveillance, and both serve ultimately to locate the subject—characterological or political—within a seemingly benign but ultimately coercive narrative of social matrix" (Finch and Bowen, 3–4). Unlike Patricia Meyer Spacks, who stresses the way in which the authority of gossip is minimized by its being gendered female and Jan B. Gordon, who sees gossip as a challenge to the " 'recuperative, paternal authority' that the novel is concerned to uphold," Finch and Bowen point to the ambivalent acknowledgment of gossip as, on the one hand, the "loose" and trivial talk of women and as, on the other, "a serious and privileged form of knowledge (FB, 3).[7] Thus they characterize Austen's use of free indirect style as making each character's interiority "at once perfectly private and absolutely open to public scrutiny" and emphasize the secrecy that attaches to "the source of community concern—for we can never know precisely who speaks in the free indirect style" (FB, 5).

For Finch and Bowen, the difficulty of connecting the narrative authority of gossip and of free indirect style with a specific individual is identical with its force. They therefore conclude that "almost total authority—a near epistemological hegemony—is staged and enacted because its agency is either elided altogether or spread so thinly that it cannot ever be named as such. Ultimately, the irresistible force of public opinion expresses itself by anonymity, by an authority that is every where apparent but whose source is nowhere to be found" (FB, 15). The kinds of questions that Austen criticism once registered in terms of irony or the unreliability of the narrator disappear from their account, and rightly so, since it is difficult to speak of either irony or unreliability that cannot locate itself against an endorsed or at least a stated or reliable position. For them, the collective voice of communal gossip achieves its force by taking over the internal vocal cords of individuals without making them entirely available as individuals, so that Mrs. Weston's approving thoughts about a match between Emma and Mr. Knightley strike them as a good example of how "free indirect style functions specifically to disguise the ideological imperatives of the novel as the autonomous ideation of one of its characters" (FB, 14). As Mel Brooks might say, all the characters are speaking, but Mrs. Weston "has the mouth."

The Finch-Bowen approach, in line with Foucauldian criticism generally, can identify a social collective, but only in such a way as to make all the individuals who are part of it look as if they ought to be relatively interchangeable. Even though they point out not only that gossip "constitutes a community by separating who is and who is not crucial to whatever economic (and marital) exchanges are at stake within the novel's representations" but that its "second fundamental mechanism concerns the establishment of a 'naturally' enforced hierarchy" (FB, 7), the scare quotes around the word "naturally" are designed to make it appear as if the hierarchical gestures of the novel were themselves illusory. Characters in the novel might appear to perform the assessments of value that, as John Barrell has suggested, the eighteenth century introduces into general discourse,[8] but their terms are the social system's unconscious imperatives.

But what does the social system think or feel or say? If, as John Rawls proposes, governments attempt to produce a voice of public reason by instituting procedures to represent the social structure as a subject and to give it a language to speak, his project is an interesting one because of his consciousness of the difficulty of saying exactly when a community speaks.[9] The problem with representing the general will, not just for Rousseau and Kant but for a host of other political thinkers, is that it is extremely difficult to determine—not because it is impossible to take the pulse of popular opinion but because it is too easy. As the professionals who comment on and consult with politicians regularly remind us, George Bush was seventeen percentage points behind Dukakis but won the presidential election in 1988, and he had a 91 percent approval rating during the Gulf War but lost the presidential election in 1992. The moral is not that public opinion is fickle but that changeability means virtually nothing when one attempts to describe public psychology, because what public psychology lacks is precisely the connective tissue that enables individual psychology to count as psychology: the memory and the anticipation that make it possible for one to tell the difference between one's own thoughts and someone else's and that make one feel bound to one's own thoughts and feelings as one is not to other people's thoughts and feelings. What public psychology lacks is the ability to be self-conscious, which is not so much the ability to be accurate about one's own statements and assessments (in the way that Finch and Bowen, for instance, suggest in talking about how individual epistemologies line up with the technology of truth) as the ability to see oneself as an interconnected whole. What keeps public psychology from being a psychology is that, in never being able to see itself as a whole, it never recognizes its changeability as significant. A person may feel the need to explain a point of view and the changes in it; public opinion never does.

The peculiarity of the Foucauldian analysis is that it imagines that the social system is already constituted as a self-sustaining and self-renewing whole, when in fact that wholeness needs regularly to be supplied, either by the kinds of strongly articulated bureaucratic structures that someone like Bentham engineered or by the kind of attention that Rawls pays to introducing the rhythms and reviews of procedural justice into his account of government. It is therefore particularly surprising to hear that any structure that can scarcely recognize itself as a structure is said to be capable of lending fully formed identities to individuals, that it has assignments to give them, words to put in their mouths, and so forth. But if I am arguing that social structures have the appearance of durability and authority only because the demands on their persistence are so minimal, I do not mean that consciousness is merely an individual project. Nor does Austen. The brilliance of her deployment of free indirect style is that it recognizes what we might want to think of as a communal contribution to individuals.

The notion of a communal contribution helps explain a persistent problem in the criticism of *Emma*: that Emma Woodhouse is the heroine even when she produces a series of misjudgments and statements that are rude or at least insensitive. A communal contribution enables us to recognize Emma as good even when she is not. Its voicing in free indirect style taps into the approach of the social sciences that allows us (and direct marketing firms) to see that someday we may well do what many people roughly like us would do. In other words, the sense of a communal contribution makes quantification operate as a strong narrative principle in the novel. Whereas the bildungsroman, in traditional descriptions, emphasizes education as an individual matter (in which one is proved right or wrong by the world), Austen uses a community to foreshadow an individual's actions—to say of Emma, from the very outset, that she will have come out right by the end. In that, the community is simply a version of Freud's much maligned statement that "ontogeny recapitulates phylogeny," which is not so much a claim that each individual progresses through every stage of human evolution as an assertion that the individual can be seen as an individual only through a chorus. It assimilates the narrative present of an individual to the future perfect tense.

The sheer force of communal numbers projects a future from what would otherwise be the simple relation of a series of statements in the present tense. This narrative approach shares a deep affinity with the basic procedures of the social sciences, which project a time line and a series of prophecies for individuals less from their own histories than from an analysis of the group. Derrida's deconstructive analysis may have taught us to question the transfer of the communal or aggregative analysis to the individual, but Austen's fiction anticipates this difficulty in the form of a conundrum: individuals can be described as having temporal extension and a traceable history only from the standpoint of the constant comparison of their current situations to a projected communal stance, but individuals would cease to be individuals (would become indistinguishable from one another) if they ever actually coincided with the communal stance.

This problem dictates the importance of the marriage plot in Austen and enables us to see that her treatment of it is, finally, formal to an extraordinary new degree. This claim may seem counterintuitive, if one thinks of the enormous significance attached to marriage plots in a host of eighteenth-century novels from *Pamela* to *Evelina* and beyond. Yet one can begin to see the extent of Austen's innovation by comparing *Emma* with the eighteenth-century novels thus plotted, in which the marriage serves chiefly to round off the action. Indeed, these novels reflect the vestigial influence of the drama in that they seem to be plotted backward from their endings: the death or deaths for the final scene of a tragedy, the wedding or weddings for the conclusion of a comedy. This large-scale narrative unit, in which the beginning and the ending define the forms of narrative unity that someone like Propp analyzes, can accommodate a great deal of to-and-fro within its framework. (In *Pamela* or *Clarissa* an almost infinite number of reprises and complications can take place without affecting the basic movement of the narrative, just as the tales that Propp describes are open to various complexifying gestures without sustaining any impact to their basic structure.) Yet while *Emma* echoes and relies on this unifying marriage-plot structure, Austen adds a new feature to it: ever attentive to the formation of public language, an amalgam of the thoughts and judgments of many people, she also recognizes the pressure that this formation exerts on individuality.

The eighteenth century had frequently been intrigued with the problem that the emotions posed for communicability, since being able to hear others talk about their emotions and empathize with them was patently different from actually feeling those emotions. Hume had been struck by the difficulty of finding any help for depression in his friends' comfort. Burke had claimed that in principle we could experience other people's emotions if we bothered to put our bodies in the same postures that they adopted, but he was conscious of how rarely we did so. For Hume, individual emotions—certainly those of depression—marked the emotions' inertness in the face of public language. For Burke, individual emotions could speak a completely transmissible language, but individuals rarely exercised the option of acting out other people's bodily movements enough for this communication to take place. (The complications of trying to experience the emotions of several interlocutors at once are immediately apparent.) For Austen, by contrast, the emotions are not so much to be experienced as deduced.

Insofar as free indirect style involves a representation of thought rather than an expression of it, it sharply distinguishes itself from either direct or indirect discourse. In English it does not possess its own distinctive verb forms as it does in French, where it appears in the exclusively written form of récit. English free indirect style may share its verbs with expressive statements, but even so it has clearly identifiable differences from them. We can illustrate this point by translating a statement from direct discourse to indirect discourse and then to free indirect style. Thus the sentence "Susan said, 'God is coming in anger' " in direct discourse becomes "Susan said that God was coming in anger" in indirect discourse. The two are more or less equivalent statements about the state of affairs that a speaker is reporting. But both formulations are, I think, accurately recast in free indirect style if we describe Susan speaking or thinking, break off, and produce the sentence "God is coming, and is she pissed" (with the last three words in free indirect discourse).

The emphasis on a representation that implies what must be thought is strong enough to justify a critic like Ann Banfield in describing free indirect style as producing "unspeakable sentences."[10] Obviously, we do speak in this way a considerable amount of the time—when we tell stories, however much or little they may be based in reality. We speak in this unspeakable mode whenever we proceed as though we could speak from within another person's consciousness. It marks the advent of fictionality in the most ordinary exchanges of daily life. But while free indirect style is not an exclusively literary phenomenon, it is regularly associated with the novel. It is, like the capitalism of the Middle Ages or the class system before Marx, something that one can recognize as a practice even before it has a name. Indeed, many people have wanted to claim a special affinity between the novel and free indirect style and to suggest that it most fully came into a name with the novel. The importance of this connection becomes clear when one looks at the differences between the drama and the epistolary novel, and between the epistolary novel and what we think of as the novel proper. In the theater's basic format of characters representing themselves through their speech and actions, we readily see a basic limitation. It is not that characters are required by the genre to say what they think in the presence of the characters they are both speaking to and interacting with, that they must dare to have views of other characters in their presence—though one of the pleasures of drama is that it depicts characters delivering insults and parodic responses under the cloak of effective invisibility. Simply put, the limitation of theater is that it consists of almost nothing but direct quotation, so that drama must continually create an unfolding plot that motivates individual characters to present their views, to have thoughts that rise to the level of the expressible.

The epistolary novel as Richardson practices it may seem to move in the opposite direction from drama by insisting on the importance of its characters' closeting themselves and not having a reliable audience (since their letters may or may not be read). Yet in one crucial respect it coincides with the imperatives of drama, expanding and exaggerating the requirement that characters represent themselves and the details of daily life in their own persons, and only through their words. The implausibility of such massively examined life has long occupied commentators. Critics from Fielding through Michael McKeon have argued that one could not—indeed, should not—believe that anyone could manage both to live and to conduct such constant self-representation as Pamela does.[11] They charge that the epistolary novel presents its characters with lives that are too extensively self-representing to be true. Moreover, they say, such representations of one's own experience constitute a falsification of it. Fielding suggests in *Shamela* (1741) that conscious self-representation is unimaginable without a will to deceive others, and he aligns the representation of experience with an essentially Machiavellian consciousness of others and the impact one might hope to have on them. McKeon describes the possibility of extreme skepticism that arises when these self-representations seem to know no limit and when one begins to wonder if there are not more letters out there somewhere to alter the record.

The epistolary novel of Richardson and Rousseau, which began in repudiation of the theater's commitment to the spectacular, was quickly faced with an inability to authenticate itself. I do not mean to identify simply the problem of covert authorship implicit in Richardson's pose as editor of the letters of a Pamela or a Clarissa. Indeed that problem can be said to have been laid to rest in Rousseau's preface to *La nouvelle Héloïse*: "Although I carry nothing but the title of editor here, I have worked hard on this book, and I don't disguise it. Have I made the whole thing up, and is the entire correspondence a fiction? People of the world, what difference does it make to you? It's certainly a fiction for you."[12] With that statement, the tables were turned. In saying that the epistolary novel was "certainly a fiction" for worldly readers, Rousseau raised two points at once. First, he made an explicitly realist claim: even the most truthful statements that other people make to us must be fictional to us, insofar as they are reports on their own experience rather than on ours. Rousseau would not be led astray by the effort to bolster the epistolary novel's claim to have stumbled on the letters that it merely packaged for distribution but would stand up and identify himself without disguise. The second aspect of his remark—its emphasis on audience—was more problematic for the novel. For as Rousseau went on to say that "this book wasn't at all made to circulate in the world" and that "the style will repel people of taste" (Rousseau, 5), the epistolary novel came to look less like a fiction than like a denunciation of everyone who found it unreal. It was not merely that the protagonists of epistolary novels like those of Richardson and Rousseau should reside in the country and appear almost as hermits who had sacrificed experience for the representation of experience. It was also that the readers of epistolary novels were asked to occupy the representations of such solitaries. As the "man of letters" who engages in an imaginary dialogue with the "editor" puts it, it is worthwhile, before publishing such a volume, to "remember that the public isn't made up of hermits" (R, 18). Moreover, the publishing world is organized such that the only path by which a solitary's novel can be delivered to its proper audience of solitaries is *through* the public world that it challenges and offends.

The epistolary novelist may divide himself into the "man of letters" and the "editor" for the sake of a dialogue with himself; he may produce letters on behalf of characters who are aware of the persons they direct their correspondence to; but the epistolary novel tries, ultimately, to present those characters as individuals rather than as persons in society. When, as at the end of *Pamela* or *Clarissa* or *La nouvelle Hélaïse*, the novels fill with testimonials to their heroines, the characters who make them are identified less as representatives of the public than as refugees from it, saved by the force of the example of the novels' heroines.

This brief history (which is simultaneously historical and conjectural, in that it tries to locate both a chronological progression and a logic for it) puts us in a position to see the force of free indirect style more clearly. The theater consists of nothing but direct quotation so as to insist on speakability; the epistolary novel regularly confines itself to indirect quotation in the most expansive self-representation imaginable and makes one's individual moral position look like a debating point; but the novel of free indirect style has characters and society speaking the same language. Free indirect style carries with it the implicit claim that characters have what Dorrit Cohn has called "transparent minds," highly legible to their narrator even when they are not directly speaking or acting.[13]

In the mode that Cohn calls "psycho-narration," the narrator is a mind reader, credited with "superior knowledge of the character's inner life and his superior ability to present it and assess it" (Cohn, 29). Yet this very mode threatens the narrator's own individuality: the freestanding and audible narrator of a Fielding becomes an endangered species. For Wayne C. Booth, markedly dissonant psycho-narration that attempts to recuperate that independent narrator becomes an absolute requirement for the ideal novel, the novel of moral guidance whose characters are sorted into good and bad, better and worse.

In the way that Booth or A. Walton Litz reads *Emma*, free indirect style operates as something of a plot against its central character, a thorough record of her errors seen from without, as errors.[14] Taking that record seriously, Booth must first find Emma highly blameworthy and then demonstrate how she is redeemed by the affectionate interest that the other characters have in her. But the standard that Booth establishes for Emma is infinitely higher than any that most of us could meet. At a stretch, we can accuse her of (1) snobbishness toward Robert Martin, the yeoman farmer who is in love with Harriet Smith, and the Coles, the newly prosperous business family in the neighborhood; (2) misplaced disparagement of Robert and excessive optimism about Mr. Elton as prospective spouses for Harriet; (3) a moment of heedless cruelty toward Miss Bates, when she insists that Miss Bates limit herself to three contributions in an improvised parlor game committed to collecting dull observations or clever ones; and (4) a moment of ungenerous speculation to Frank Churchill that the piano given anonymously to Jane Fairfax might have come from Mr. Dixon and thus might be a gift from the man whom Jane's close friend has recently married.

Booth is able to parlay these minor social infractions into serious lapses of judgment and signs of Emma's willful imaginism, and Litz can criticize her for failing to acknowledge that "freedom is dependent upon a recognition of limitations" (Booth, 149), because they fundamentally misconceive the authorial relationship to character in Austen's use of free indirect style. While they insist that there is a clearly available narrative position from which to judge Emma, I would argue, by contrast, that the novel is hard on Emma to exactly the same extent that it is committed to her. Moreover, it is hard on her *because* of this attachment. In reporting Emma's words and actions but especially in using her memory as the central locus for remorse, the novelist makes Emma's blameworthiness inseparable from her privileged position. Emma has been identified to us at the opening of the novel as "doing just what she liked, highly esteeming Miss Taylor's judgment, but directed chiefly by her own." The novel immediately flags the "real evils" of Emma's situation as "the power of having rather too much her own way, and a disposition to think a little too well of herself" (*Emma*, 5), and critics have followed by remarking that Emma is headstrong and spoiled. Yet it is hard to imagine any character we would take seriously— in fiction or in life—who was not "directed chiefly" by her own judgment and who did not suffer from the "real evils" of "having rather too much her own way" and of thinking "a little too well of herself." When Emma and Knightley disagree about the wisdom of Emma's having strongly suggested to Harriet that she should reject Robert's proposal, it is Knightley rather than Emma who is described, by that composite voice that both is and is not Emma's alone, as "absolutely satisfied with" himself and "so entirely convinced that [his] opinions were right and [his] adversary's wrong" (*E*, 67). Neither in his case nor in hers is it a fault to think that the opinions one holds are the right ones, because that is what it means to hold an opinion.

Austen's free indirect style does not, however, simply align itself most closely with Emma and make her memory the one that will be the basis for acknowledging the mistakes that she has made. It also helps operate as a version of the problem that Emma—or any other person or character—must face, namely, that the most nearly indisputable representation of a general will or social character appears in the narrator's free indirect style. Just as our sense of Emma's preeminence in the novel develops from the fact that her mistaken assessments and predictions are taken as seriously as only the person who committed them could take them, so the novel credits Emma and other characters with a sociological knowledge that can be learned only experimentally.

THIS SOCIOLOGICAL KNOWLEDGE of gossip and free indirect style can be developed by trial and error, moreover, precisely because it does not have a consistent enough logic to be predictable. The novel provides exact information about the ages of its eligible young persons: Emma is almost twenty-one (*E*, 5); Knightley is thirty-seven or -eight (*E*, 9); Elton is twenty-six or -seven (*E*, 14); Harriet is seventeen (*E*, 22); Robert is twenty-four (*E*, 30); Frank is twenty-three (*E*, 96); Jane is, at twenty-one, described as "exactly Emma's age" by those who would like them to become friends (*E*, 104). Yet it provides it so scrupulously that one recognizes that there is no fixed age at which a man or a woman expects to marry and no fixed similarity or degree of difference in ages between the partners in marriages. Further, although the novel identifies its characters according to their social circumstances, it does not make the socioeconomic data amount to a real sorting device. Robert is a yeoman farmer; Harriet is the natural daughter of an unnamed somebody (later identified as a tradesman) who has the means with which to send her to a modest boarding school; the Woodhouse family is "first in consequence" in Highbury (*E*, 7); and Knightley is similarly well established at Donwell Abbey in the next parish (*E*, 20). But if the eventual marriages of these couples seems to have been predicted by the happy fit between the partners' individual social circumstances, think of some of the novel's other couples. The Miss Taylor who has just married the widower Mr. Weston at the opening of the book has held "the nominal office of governess" (*E*, 5) in the Woodhouse family, as if to justify Emma's sense that Harriet might well end up as Elton's wife, and Frank and Jane are likewise an economically mismatched pair. Emma and Knightley make a marriage that preserves the economic status quo and even looks as if it could have been arranged just as easily as it could have been entered into exclusively by its principals (particularly given the parallel marriage of her sister and his brother). Yet it is clear that even the traditional understanding of matches is unrecognizable when so many other marriages do not follow the same pattern of identifying partners of equivalent status. There are, then, good reasons that Emma is not as clear-sighted a matchmaker—either for others or for herself—as she might be. Although her mistakes are preserved and foregrounded for us, others are frequently wrong as well. If Emma exaggerates her own success in matching Miss Taylor with Weston and proceeds to try to achieve similar success in marrying Harriet to Elton or to Frank, the Westons make their own miscalculation in trying to pair Emma with Frank.

It may seem as if we were talking about universal mystification when it comes to marriage, so that making a mistake about who ought to marry whom and even about whom or whether one ought to marry oneself is so nearly inevitable that the wisest course is to avoid prediction altogether. But complete indifference to other people's marriages—represented so amply in Mr. Woodhouse's sense that marriages, in producing change, are distressing and best not thought of—is neither common nor highly valued in the novel. Marriages and the courtships that lead to them have become a popular public recreation. If Lord Hardwick's Act of the 1750s decreed that marriages be agreed to in public and that wedding ceremonies themselves be a matter of public concern (so as to thwart what legal language called "abduction of heiress"), the social world of *Emma* has so far absorbed its function as a witness that it constantly promotes marriage. Indeed, the pleasure that the community takes in marriages is so intense that a marriage can effectively wipe an individual's slate clean: in Highbury a "young person, who either marries or dies, is sure of being kindly spoken of" (*E*, 181). Just as Wordsworth essentially says that death makes all of its subjects look good to the living, so Austen suggests that marriage performs the job of transformation and transvaluation.[15]

Marriage counts so much as a breaking of the bank that the first time Emma is recorded as contemplating marriage comes when Mrs. Weston realizes that "all their wishes of giving Emma" the distinction of beginning the ball cannot prevail, that Mrs. Elton "must be asked to begin the ball;

that she would expect it" (*E*, 325). "Emma must submit to stand second to Mrs. Elton, though she had always considered the ball as peculiarly for her. It was almost enough to make her think of marrying" (*E*, 325). Marriage might look as though it revolved around public distinction, as it surely does for Augusta Hawkins Elton, with her references to her *caro sposo* that begin to seem especially pretentious when she calls Elton her *cara sposa* (or, in the Chapman edition, her *caro sposo*) (*E*, 302).[16]

Marriage is less a state or a contract than a distinction, so that characters like the Eltons marry largely to be able to display marriage. Indeed, marriage serves the purposes of conspicuous consumption so effectively for both Eltons that they are never happier than when goading one another to have Elton try to humiliate Harriet by refusing to recognize her as a suitable dancing partner. In this little scene, which Knightley puts an end to by dancing with Harriet himself, it is easy to see the Eltons as people over-reaching themselves and pretending to a status they do not have. Yet they are almost as accurate about their standing in the world as it is possible to be. After all, both George and John Knightley, in warning Emma against her design of pairing Elton with Harriet, have pointed to Elton's consciousness of his value in the world; after all, Mrs. Weston and everyone else automatically if belatedly realizes that Mrs. Elton's being a new bride gives her precedence over every other guest.

With the Eltons one can see the emergence of the concept of a social rule. The Eltons' accurate sense of their standing in the social hierarchy and of the rules of the social game enables them to succeed *against* others' wishes—without, that is, continually being liked or endorsed by them. Mrs. Elton can stand first in the dancing despite the fact that Emma, Mr. and Mrs. Weston, and Frank have thought of it as Emma's ball; Mrs. Elton can wrest an invitation to Donwell Abbey from Knightley in the face of his distinct lack of enthusiasm for her; and Mrs. Elton can find Jane a place as governess even though such a favor is not at all what Jane wanted (*E*, 380). While she looks always in the wrong, Mrs. Elton is identified as never mistaken, both in the sense of never acknowledging herself as mistaken and in the sense of being right about the rules, as if she had consulted Amy Vanderbilt or Martha Stewart for the proper way to stage a picnic. If the novel insists on a relationship between correctness and amiability, free indirect style might involve a representation of a social game that one must learn to read correctly (as Booth and Litz argue). Yet it is a peculiar thing for the successful application of the rules to be associated with a character (Mrs. Elton) or characters (Mr. and Mrs. Elton) singled out for the op-probrium of everyone who is more or less of their generation. Moreover

the Eltons seem to embody exactly the position that Emma always recommends: one that converts the apparently haughty reserve of a Jane into
public expression and goes along with Emma's denunciation of Frank and
Jane for having "come among us with professions of openness and simplicity" and having "completely duped" those who fancied themselves "all
on an equal footing of truth and honor," as Emma so memorably puts it
(E, 275).

The depth of Emma's indignation is striking, because her principal objection to Frank and Jane's secret engagement is that the two of them have
been able to piece together conversations that each has had with other
people: they "may have been carrying around, comparing and sitting in
judgment on words that were never meant for both to hear" (E, 399). This
may seem only Emma's self-defense: to say that "they must take the consequence, if they have heard each other spoken of in a way not perfectly
agreeable" (E, 399) is to mask her criticism of them and to substitute it for
the plausible embarrassment of her speculating about a possibly scandalous
relationship between Jane and Mr. Dixon to the one person in the world
who is most likely to be offended by criticism of Jane. Yet this is not Emma's
concern. To hear her talk, one would think that Frank and Jane's relationship amounted to collusion, to devising in advance and bringing out
some extra combination in the game of charades, which figures so prominently in the novel.

Charades is, after all, introduced early on as an instance of what it
means for there to be a game of translation that depends on combination.
A four-line description of grief yields "woe," a four-line description of
someone who has an experience of grief yields "man," and the overall
solution is "woman." Emma and Harriet are represented as particular fans
of charades and are, in what Austen calls "this age of literature" (E, 44),
making a collection of them early in the novel. In categorizing charades as
copybook schlock rather than the kind of book that Knightley thinks
Emma should read, Austen is being more than high-minded. Charades fail
to be great literature by exactly the degree to which they operate as tests for
their readers. Emma enjoys them because they enable her to "get" them—
and to get them faster and more accurately than anyone else in her party,
especially Harriet. When Elton produces his charade—the one in which
the verses yield the words "court" and "ship" to make up the word
"courtship"—part of the reason Emma does not understand his meaning is
that she is absorbed in relating to the game as if it were, at least for her,
only a test of her skill. Her commitment is not simply to displaying her

own cleverness at unpacking coded messages but to imagining that she has no special advantages in doing so.

In that, Emma treats charades and alphabets (an avatar of what we now, at least in the United States, call Scrabble) as if they conformed to Jean-François Lyotard's alignment of récit with the circulation of stories in a community in which a person may be listener or teller and *anyone* can participate. The importance of the anonymous story lies in the way it produces a social equality that assists social cohesion.[17] In Emma's view, games should function in just such an impersonal way; a point underscored when we learn that Harriet and Emma have been anthologizing examples. Originality is no more the point than beginning from a preferred position.

But now a question emerges about free indirect style, which I have described as employing the verb forms of récit in French. These forms suggest that a statement might be offered by anyone in a society. I have suggested two things in some tension with this: Austen's Emma is foregrounded by her remorse and games like charades, in principle equally open to all participants, afford Emma a chance to demonstrate her own quickness and insight—her superiority. Her greatest delusion is her assumption of a stable standpoint for evaluation—exactly the view that her harshest critics ironically recapitulate. Booth and Litz argue that Austen gives us a bildungsroman because the central character learns to understand her own situation more accurately. Countless readings stress the clarity of the victory through which Emma is awarded Knightley, the husband who counts as the finest trophy in the marriage competition. Their position, moreover, would seem to be justified by Austen's representing Harriet as having made progress because she too has fallen in love with someone "so superior to Mr. Elton" (*E*, 341), Knightley, and to be strengthened by the suggestion that love is merely an assessment of the relative merits of the characters in the social game.

Were this view the whole story, D. H. Lawrence's estimate of Austen as a nasty old maid committed to "knowing in apartness" would be entirely justified, as would his suggestion that she creates a world of "personality" that identifies characters in terms of their interests and evaluations.[18] She would be, that is, wholly committed to writing out a utilitarian calculus in the form of a novelistic plot. The marriage game would itself be the perfection of free indirect style and its notion of a récit in that anyone could assume any position. It would not simply be that Emma and Knightley wanted to marry one another; every man would want to marry

Emma, and every woman Knightley. The novel comes perilously close to this outcome. Elton and Knightley have both wanted to marry Emma; Frank has recognized that it would be plausible for people to think that *he* would; in his own little charade Mr. Weston has spelled out the two syllables of Emma's name to say that they add up to "perfection." Harriet's infatuation with Knightley repeats this pattern in only slightly less emphatic terms. In a Girardian light, desire is always triangulated, simply because Austen's novel looks as though individual choice and larger societal choices—what "everyone" thinks—were being aligned.

Were the marriage plot to identify Emma as the universally acknowledged winner, marriage would simply be one game among others that created a rank order for the characters—that would, this time, privilege Emma in its new version of free indirect style not for being more often mistaken than other characters but for being more often right. Moreover, the line "I shall never marry," which is uttered both by Emma and by Harriet, and the line "Knightley must not marry," uttered only by Emma, would occupy prominent places in the novel as mistaken assessments that dramatized the appeal of what look like winning lines.

The marriage plot, enacted through free indirect style as an externalized game, is the one in which Emma does not so much enlist her author as demonstrate what an author might do as a composite voice of author and character. While she "entertains no doubt of her being in love" with Frank, Emma herself diagnoses and solves a kind of puzzle in saying of her feelings on his departure, "I do not find myself making any use of the word *sacrifice*" (*E*, 264). As she disappointedly but energetically banters with Frank later, she sounds like someone completing a crossword puzzle: she and her author say that "no English word but flirtation could very well describe" and then give the full sentence that might be reported: "Mr. Frank Churchill and Miss Woodhouse flirted together excessively" (*E*, 368). This same deductive model is the one through which Emma infers that Harriet, having just fainted during her encounter with importunate gypsies and having been rescued by Frank, must now be in love with him: "Could a linguist, could a grammarian, could even a mathematician have seen what she did, have witnessed their appearance together, and heard their history of it, without feeling that circumstances had been at work to make them peculiarly interesting to each other?" (*E*, 335).

The trick of the novel is both to suggest why any and all observers would think what they did and to insist that they all would be wrong. Yet just when it might seem important to dispute the claims of this socialized and externalized inference and to defend private experience against it, we have the example of Frank and Jane to contend with. For they do not simply have a secret, their engagement; they also have a secret that they preserve in the kind of private correspondence that the epistolary novel so regularly features and that they adapt to the public world of parlor games with a certain clumsiness. While Emma makes errors, Frank practically trademarks the word "blunder" as he goes from using it in the game of alphabets to apologize for his previous indiscretion to accusing first the post office and then himself of having "blundered." That blunder was the failure to forward his letter of clarification to Jane, so that it remained in his drawer and so compounded his earlier blunder. In two different ways, the epistolary mode of direct testimony and shared secrets comes to look precarious. First, like the coded writing that Caesar is credited with inventing to communicate with his allies, it occupies a peculiarly strained relationship with the surrounding public language in imagining itself more effectively secret than it is (so that one can mistakenly assume that one can say out loud what one intends only for one other person's ears). Second, if its testimony looks as though it represented the voice of experience in protest against an external account, it has a real technological vulnerability: it stakes everything on being able to get this testimony through, past desk drawers and postal services.

But if it now seems as if Austen's whole point in *Emma* were to render romantic communication—whether as direct testimony about one's own feelings or as a deductive statement about what one should feel so vulnerable as to make marriages look like a near impossibility, the most surprising turn of the novel is to unite the two chief pairs of lovers in a common view. The "blunder" that Frank made, and that he meant to apologize for by labeling it a blunder, was to spell out the name Dixon in the game of alphabets and to show it, first to Emma and then to Jane, in an ambivalent reference to Emma's earlier speculation that Mr. Dixon had been the one who had sent the mysterious piano to Jane. Jane's response, of course, was to invoke the rules of the game, "saying only, 'I did not know that proper names were allowed'" (*E*, 349).

It might seem as if the rules of alphabets were a detail so minor as to be irrelevant to any significant issues in the novel. Yet Jane's invocation of the rule has broader applicability than might at first appear. For in its conclusion the novel pivots on what we might think of as the exclusion of the proper name—for a small number of cases. While the marriage plot of the novel has been seen to trace out the process by which a woman exchanges one surname (her father's) for another (her husband's), Austen's *Emma* marks engagement and marriage as a refinement of the first name. Emma, on agreeing to marry Knightley, announces to him that she cannot call him by his name—"George"—or rather; promises to call him by his proper first name "once," "in the building in which N. takes M. for better, for worse" (*E*, 463).

This moment conspicuously repeats one in *Pamela*, when Pamela tells Mr. B—that she will still call him "Master" even after their marriage. It has therefore looked to Nancy Armstrong like a moment in which Austen becomes uncomfortable with a woman's authority, and it has led her to agree with McKeon that gender produces a problem of upward mobility for the novel, so that women can be raised in class by marriage but must always display their subordination in gender.[19] Yet Emma's gesture of avoiding Knightley's first name is not linked to the status hierarchy of *Pamela*, or else it would not find such a ready companion piece in Frank's way of talking about Jane. In the letter in which he tells Emma "the whole story" of his engagement to Jane, he objects to Mrs. Elton's officiousness and "imagined superiority" toward Jane because it has been part and parcel of the "needless repetition" of Jane's name. "You will observe," he writes, "that I have not yet indulged myself in calling her by that name, even to you" (*E*, 441–442).

Free indirect style, like any external or logical representation, does not provide the basis for any individual and individualized point of view for author or character. Austen emphasizes this aspect of the device of represented speech and thought by depicting games as situations in which the players share not only a consciousness of accepting the same rules but also the same assumptions about the preferred outcomes. In suggesting that marriage might be the ultimate social game as seen from without, Austen puts considerable pressure on the marriage plot, since it would seem more likely for the marriage game to issue in everyone's marrying everyone else than in marriage between two persons. Marriage would be not merely bigamous but genuinely communal, because the most desirable partners would look the most desirable not just to one person but to all. Austen's contribution to the marriage plot is to have worked out this understanding with almost fanatical zeal and to have suggested that Emma and everyone else in the novel might eventually arrive at the same evaluations, might produce the absurd outcome of universal marriage. In the face of this problem, the marriages of the novel insist on taking names that have been in the public sphere—for instance, the Emma so widely spoken of as to appear in the title of the novel—and retiring them, as if marriage depicted an intimacy so intense as to create the effect of distance by dispensing with the forms of address that might be used in public, by just anyone.

Notes

1. Catherine Gallagher's "Formalism and Time," *Modern Language Quarterly* 61 (2000): 221–251, strongly argues along these lines in asking for a more diverse and more flexible sense of what our critical paradigms ought to be.

2. See particularly Victor Shklovsky, "The Resurrection of the Word," in *Russian Formalism* (New York: Barnes and Noble, 1973), 41–47.

3. Vladimir Propp, *Morphology of the Folktale*, ed. Louis A. Wagner, trans. Laurence Scott, 2d ed. (Austin: University of Texas Press, 1968), esp. 43–50.

4. Miller, *The Novel and the Police* (Berkeley: University of California Press, 1988); and Miller, *Narrative and Its Discontents: Problems of Closure in the Traditional Novel* (Princeton, N.J.: Princeton University Press, 1981).

5. Schorer, "The Humiliation of Emma Woodhouse," in *Emma: A Casebook*, ed. David Lodge (London: Aurora, 1970), 170–87. Making this claim for the unique importance of free indirect style means treating the chapter less as the novel's defining formal unit than as a divisional marker. Even though the chapter becomes a widely used novelistic unit, it is closer, in my view, to the comma and the period and other formal markers of the units of thought than it is to a formal feature that can detach itself from such markers of thought.

6. Finch and Bowen, " 'The Tittle-Tattle of Highbury': Gossip and Free Indirect Style in *Emma*," *Representations* 31 (Summer 1990): 1–18.

7. Spacks, *Gossip* (New York: Knopf, 1985); Gordon, "A-filiative Families and Subversive Reproduction: Gossip in Jane Austen," *Genre* 21 (1988): 5–46.

8. Barrell, *The Political Theory of Painting from Reynolds to Hazlitt: "The Body of the Public"* (New Haven, Conn.: Yale University Press, 1986), 1–68, esp. 8–10.

9. This position is so very nearly omnipresent in Rawls's work that it makes little sense to identify a specific essay. See Rawls, *A Theory of Justice*, 2d ed. (Cambridge, Mass.: Belknap Press of Harvard University Press, 1999); and Rawls, *Political Liberalism* (New York: Columbia University Press, 1993).

10. Banfield stresses this notion by titling her study of represented speech and thought. *Unspeakable Sentences: Narration and Representation in the Language of Fiction* (Boston: Routledge and Kegan Paul, 1982).

11. McKeon, *The Origins of the English Novel, 1600–1740* (Baltimore, Md.: Johns Hopkins University Press, 1987), esp. 47–64.

12. Jean-Jacques Rousseau, *Julie; ou la nouvelle Héloïse*, ed. Bernard Gagnebin and Marcel Raymond (Paris: Pléiade, 1969), 5.

13. Cohn, *Transparent Minds: Narrative Modes for Presenting Consciousness in Fiction* (Princeton, N.J.: Princeton University Press, 1978).

14. Booth, *The Rhetoric of Fiction* (Chicago: University of Chicago Press, 1961), 243–66, reprinted in this casebook; Litz, *Jane Austen: A Study of Her Artistic Development* (New York: Oxford University Press, 1965), 132–49.

15. "Essay upon Epitaphs," in *The Prose Works of William Wordsworth*, ed. W. J. B. Owen and Jane Worthington Smyser, 3 vols. (Oxford: Clarendon Press, 1974), 2:56–57.

16. In the first edition of *Emma* (1816), Mrs. Elton uses 'caro sposo,' 'cara sposo' and 'cara sposa' at different points in the text. Chapman standardised these and printed 'caro sposo' throughout.

17. Lyotard, *The Postmodern Condition: A Report on Knowledge*, trans. Geoff Bennington and Brian Massumi (Minneapolis: University of Minnesota Press, 1984), 20–21.

18. "A Propos of 'Lady Chatterley's Lover,'" in *Lady Chatterley's Lover*, ed. Michael Squires, *The Cambridge Edition of the Letters and Works of D. H. Lawrence* (Cambridge: Cambridge University Press, 1993), 333.

19. Armstrong, *Desire and Domestic Fiction: A Political History of the Novel* (New York: Oxford University Press, 1987), 151–53; McKeon, 378–81.

Further Reading

Letters

Le Faye, Deirdre (ed.). 1995. *Jane Austen's Letters*. 3rd ed. Oxford: Oxford University Press.

Biography

Austen, Caroline. 1952. *My Aunt Jane: A Memoir*. Alton: The Jane Austen Society.
Austen-Leigh, James. 1870. *A Memoir of Jane Austen*. Ed. Kathryn Sutherland. Oxford: Oxford University Press, 2002.
Honan, Park. 1987. *Jane Austen*. London: St Martin's Press.
Tomalin, Claire. 1997. *Jane Austen*. Rev. ed. London: Penguin, 2000.
Tucker, George Holbert. 1983. *A Goodly Heritage: A History of Jane Austen's Family* (Manchester: Carcanet.)

Bibliography

Chapman, R. W. 1953. *Jane Austen: A Critical Bibliography*. Oxford: Clarendon Press.
Gilson, David. 1982. *A Bibliography of Jane Austen*. Oxford: Clarendon Press.

Jane Austen Society. *Reports, 1940–*.

Roth, Barry. 1996. *An Annotated Bibliography of Jane Austen Studies, 1984–1994*. Athens: Ohio University Press.

————. 1985. *An Annotated Bibliography of Jane Austen Studies, 1973–1983*. Charlottesville: University Press of Virginia.

————, and Joel Weinsheimer. 1973. *An Annotated Bibliography of Jane Austen Studies, 1952–1972*. Charlottesville: University Press of Virginia.

Stafford, Fiona. 1998. "Jane Austen." In *Literature of the Romantic Period: A Bibliographical Guide*. Ed. Michael O'Neill. Oxford: Oxford University Press. 246–68.

Criticism

Armstrong, Nancy. 1987. *Desire and Domestic Fiction: A Political History of the Novel*. New York and London: Oxford University Press.

Babb, Howard. 1962. *Jane Austen's Novels: The Fabric of Dialogue*. Columbus: Ohio State University Press.

Batey, Mavis. 1996. *Jane Austen and the English Landscape*. London: Barn Elms.

Bayley, John. 1967. "Emma and her Critics." *Jane Austen Society Report for the Year 1967*. 16–29.

Booth, Wayne C. 1961. *The Rhetoric of Fiction*. Chicago: University of Chicago Press.

Butler, Marilyn. 1975. *Jane Austen and the War of Ideas*. Oxford: Clarendon Press.

Byrne, Paula. 2002. *Jane Austen and the Theatre*. London: Hambledon.

Chapman, R. W. 1948. *Jane Austen: Facts and Problems*. Oxford: Clarendon Press.

Collins, Irene. 1994. *Jane Austen and the Clergy*. London: Hambledon.

Copeland Edward, and Juliet McMaster (eds.). 1997. *The Cambridge Companion to Jane Austen*. Cambridge: Cambridge University Press.

De Rose, Peter, and S. W. McGuire. 1982. *A Concordance to the Works of Jane Austen*. 3 vols. New York: Garland.

Duckworth, Alistair. 1971. *The Improvement of the Estate: A Study of Jane Austen's Novels*. Rev. ed. London: Athlone, 1994.

Dussinger, John. 1990. *In the Pride of the Moment: Encounters in Jane Austen's World*. Columbus: Ohio University Press.

Everett, Nigel. 1994. *The Tory View of the Landscape*. New Haven and London: Yale University Press.

Finch, C., and P. Bowen. 1990. " 'The Tittle-tattle of Highbury': Gossip and the Free Indirect Style of *Emma*." *Representations* 31:1–18.

Galperin, William. 2002. *The Historical Austen*. Philadelphia: University of Pennsylvania.

————, ed. 2000. *Re-reading Box Hill: The Practice of Reading the Practices of Everyday Life*. Romantic Circles Praxis Series, April 2000, http://www.rc.umd.edu/praxis/boxhill.

Gilbert, Sandra, and Susan Gubar. 1979. *The Madwoman in the Attic: The Woman Writer and the Nineteenth-Century Literary Imagination.* New Haven and London: Yale University Press.

Grey, J. David, A. Walton Litz, and Brian Southam eds. 1986. *The Jane Austen Handbook.* London: Athlone Press.

Harding, D. W. 1998. *Regulated Hatred and Other Essays on Jane Austen.* Ed. Monica Lawlor. London: Athlone Press.

Harris, Jocelyn. 1989. *Jane Austen's Art of Memory.* Cambridge: Cambridge University Press.

Harvey, W. J. 1967. "The Plot of *Emma.*" *Essays in Criticism,* xvii:48–63.

Heydt-Stevenson, Jillian. 2005 *Austen's Unbecoming Conjunctions: Subversive Laughter, Embodied History.* Basingstoke: Macmillan.

Holly, Grant. 1989. "Emmagrammatology." *Studies in Eighteenth-Century Culture* 19:39–51.

Johnson, Claudia L. 1988. *Jane Austen: Women, Politics, and the Novel.* Chicago and London: Chicago University Press.

————. 1995. *Equivocal Beings: Politics, Gender, and Sentimentality in the 1790s —Wollstonecraft, Radcliffe, Burney, Austen.* Chicago and London: Chicago University Press.

Jones, Vivien. 1997. *How to Study a Jane Austen Novel.* 2nd ed. Basingstoke: Macmillan.

Kaplan, Deborah. 1992. *Jane Austen Among Women.* Baltimore and London: Johns Hopkins University Press.

Knox-Shaw, Peter. 2004. *Jane Austen and the Enlightenment.* Cambridge: Cambridge University Press.

Lane, Maggie. 1986. *Jane Austen's England.* London: Robert Hale.

————. 1995. *Jane Austen and Food.* London and Rio Grande: Hambledon.

Litz, A. Walton. 1965. *Jane Austen: A Study of Her Artistic Development.* London: Chatto and Windus.

Lodge, David, ed. 1968. *Emma: A Casebook.* Basingstoke: Macmillan.

Loveridge, Mark. 1983. "Francis Hutcheson and Mr. Weston's Conundrum in *Emma.*" *Notes and Queries* 30, no. 3:214–16.

Lynch, Deidre, ed. 2000. *Janeites: Austen's Disciples and Devotees.* Princeton and Oxford: Princeton University Press.

MacDonagh, Oliver. 1991. *Jane Austen: Real and Imagined Worlds.* New Haven: Yale University Press.

McMaster, Juliet, and Bruce Stovel, eds. 1996. *Jane Austen's Business: Her World and Her Profession.* Basingstoke: Macmillan.

Miller, D. A. 1981. *Narrative and Its Discontents.* Princeton: Princeton University Press.

————. 2003. *Jane Austen, or, The secret of Style.* Princeton: Princeton University Press.

Monaghan, David, ed. 1992. *Emma.* New Casebooks. Basingstoke: Macmillan.

Morgan, Susan. 1980. *In the Meantime: Character and Perception in Jane Austen's Fiction.* Chicago: University of Chicago Press.

Mudrick, Marvin. 1952. *Jane Austen: Irony as Defense and Discovery*. Princeton: Princeton University Press.

Page, Norman. 1972. *The Language of Jane Austen*. Oxford: Blackwell.

Phillipps, K. C. 1970. *Jane Austen's English*. London: Andre Deutsch.

Piggott, Patrick. 1979. *The Innocent Diversion: Music in the Life and Writings of Jane Austen*. London: Cleverdon.

Rogers, Pat. 1994. " 'Caro Sposo': Mrs. Elton, Burneys, Thrales, and Novels." *Review of English Studies* 45, no. 177:70–75.

Rosmarin, Adena. 1984. "Misreading *Emma*: The Powers and Perfidies of Interpretive History." *ELH* 51:315–42.

Sales, Roger. 1994. *Jane Austen and Representations of Regency England*. London: Routledge.

Selwyn, David. 1999. *Jane Austen and Leisure*. London: Hambledon.

Shannon, Edgar. 1956. "Emma, Character and Construction." *PMLA* 71:637–50.

Shorer, Mark. 1959. "The Humiliation of Emma Woodhouse." *Literary Review* 2 4:547–63. Reprinted in Lodge, ed., 1968.

Southam, B.C. 1968. *Jane Austen: The Critical Heritage Vol I: 1811–1870* (London: Routledge and Kegan Paul).

———. 1987. *Jane Austen: The Critical Heritage Vol. II: 1870–1940* (London: Routledge and Kegan Paul).

———. 2000. *Jane Austen and the Navy*. London and New York: Hambledon.

Stewart, Maaja. 1993. *Domestic Realities and Imperial Fictions: Jane Austen's Novels in Eighteenth-Century Contexts*. Athens: University of Georgia Press.

Stokes, Myra. 1991. *The Language of Jane Austen*. Basingstoke: Macmillan.

Stovel, Bruce. 1977. "Comic Symmetry in *Emma*." *Dalhousie Review* 57:453–64.

Sulloway, Alison. 1976. "Emma Woodhouse and *A Vindication of the Rights of Woman*." *The Wordsworth Circle* 7:320–32.

Sutherland, John. 1996. "Apple-Blossom in June." In *Is Heathcliff a Murderer?* Oxford: Oxford University Press. 14–19.

———. 1999. "Apple-Blossom in June—Again." In *Who Betrays Elizabeth Bennet?* Oxford: Oxford University Press. 28–33.

Tanner, Tony. 1986. *Jane Austen*. Basingstoke: Macmillan.

Tave, Stuart. 1973. *Some Words of Jane Austen*. Chicago and London: University of Chicago Press.

Tuite, Clara. 2002. *Romantic Austen: Sexual Politics and the Literary Canon*. Cambridge: Cambridge University Press.

Troost, Linda, and Sayre Greenfield, eds. 1998. *Jane Austen in Hollywood*. Kentucky: University of Kentucky Press.

Waldron, Mary. 1999. *Jane Austen and the Fiction of Her Time*. Cambridge: Cambridge University Press.

Wallace, Tara Ghoshal. 1995. *Jane Austen and Narrative Authority*. Basingstoke: Macmillan.

Watson, Nicola. 1994. *Revolution and the Form of the British Novel, 1790–1825*. Oxford: Clarendon Press.

Watt, Ian, ed. 1963. *Jane Austen: A Collection of Critical Essays*. Englewood Cliffs, N.J.: Prentice Hall.

Wiltshire, John. 1992. *Jane Austen and the Body*. Cambridge: Cambridge University Press.

———. 2001. *Recreating Jane Austen*. Cambridge: Cambridge University Press.

Web Sites

http://www.pemberley.com/The Republic of Pemberley

http://www.jasna.org/The Jane Austen Society of North America